HEGEL'S
Philosophy of Mind

HEGEL'S
Philosophy of Mind

BEING PART THREE OF THE
*ENCYCLOPAEDIA OF
THE PHILOSOPHICAL SCIENCES* (1830)
TRANSLATED BY
WILLIAM WALLACE

TOGETHER WITH THE *ZUSÄTZE*
IN BOUMANN'S TEXT (1845)
TRANSLATED BY
A. V. MILLER

WITH FOREWORD BY
J. N. FINDLAY, F.B.A.

CLARENDON PRESS · OXFORD

*This book has been printed digitally and produced in a standard specification
in order to ensure its continuing availability*

OXFORD
UNIVERSITY PRESS

Great Clarendon Street, Oxford OX2 6DP

Oxford University Press is a department of the University of Oxford.
It furthers the University's objective of excellence in research, scholarship,
and education by publishing worldwide in

Oxford New York

Auckland Bangkok Buenos Aires Cape Town Chennai
Dar es Salaam Delhi Hong Kong Istanbul Karachi Kolkata
Kuala Lumpur Madrid Melbourne Mexico City Mumbai Nairobi
São Paulo Shanghai Taipei Tokyo Toronto

Oxford is a registered trade mark of Oxford University Press
in the UK and in certain other countries

Published in the United States
by Oxford University Press Inc., New York

© Oxford University Press 1971

ISBN 0-19-875014-5

FOREWORD

THE present translation of Hegel's *Philosophie des Geistes* is made up of Wallace's translation of §§ 377–577 of the *Encyclopaedia of the Philosophical Sciences*, first published by the Clarendon Press in 1894 as *Hegel's Philosophy of Mind*, together with a translation of the *Zusätze* which Ludwig Boumann, the editor of this portion of Hegel's work for the Collected Edition—the volume was published in 1845—added to the first section of the work, the treatment of Mind (or Spirit) Subjective. No *Zusätze* were added by the editor to the sections on Objective Mind and Absolute Mind: Hegel's lecture-manuscripts and students' note-material for Objective Mind were all added to the *Philosophy of Right*, and have been translated by T. M. Knox in the Clarendon Press translation of this work, while the corresponding material for Absolute Spirit appears in the published (and translated) Lectures on Aesthetics, Philosophy of Religion, and History of Philosophy. Wallace translated the *Zusätze* to the Encyclopaedia *Logic*, but omitted to translate the *Zusätze* to the *Philosophy of Mind*, which has accordingly never made an impression on Anglo-Saxon philosophy comparable to that made by Hegel's Logic (in its two versions, both translated) or the *Phenomenology of Mind* (translated by J. B. Baillie). There can, however, be no doubt that the material assembled in the *Zusätze* to the *Philosophy of Mind* is of absolutely prime importance for the understanding of Hegel's thought, and that it shows that thought venturing into regions not at all charted in his other writings. To read the paragraphs of the *Philosophy of Mind* together with the *Zusätze* is to see many of Hegel's opinions in a surprisingly fresh, 'modern' light.

The reservations which apply to all the editorial material in Hegel's work of course apply also in this case. There has been much conflation, much tearing from context, a considerable amount of 'scrambling', which the *Hegel-Archiv* will now, for the profit of remote generations, have to unscramble. A few words on the materials and methods used by Ludwig Boumann in assembling the *Zusätze* to the *Philosophy of Mind* will here be in place. He based himself, in the first place, on two manuscripts which Hegel used for his lectures at Heidelberg in 1817 and at Berlin in the year 1820: the latter was much more fully and uniformly elaborated than the former. Both, however, consisted of mere thematic indications and at times of single words: they were not in any sense continuous compositions. Five bodies of notes were also consulted: two were written out by students for Hegel's own use, and actually used for his lectures in 1828 and 1830, and were enriched by many marginal notes. The notes of Major v. Griesheim (1825), Dr. Mullach (1828), and of Boumann himself were also utilized. As to the method used in compiling the *Zusätze*, the following will be illuminating: 'I worked on the view that it was my absolute duty to bring the more or less raw material of the planned lectures into the artistic form rightly demanded of a scientific work. Without such a reworking, there would, in the present case, have been a repugnant lack of harmony between the work to be illuminated and the additions made for this purpose. Hard work was needed to achieve such a harmony. Hegel lectured with great freedom, and what he said had all the enchanting freshness of a new thought-world created at the moment, but such more or less total improvisation unfortunately led to unwitting repetitions, vaguenesses, divagations, and sudden jumps. These defects had to be carefully avoided in my revision. But the necessary changes remained within the authentic, indubitable sense of Hegel. I believe that I have been true to this sense since I have not left out from the *Zusätze* what constituted the *soul* of Hegel's lectures: the dialectical movement to which Hegel thought that one should for the most part give a freer and, in part, a more profound rein in one's lectures than in the printed text; in the case of the latter, extreme compression often gave an impression of externality and of mere asseveration' (*Foreword* of 1845 edition). Who shall say that more of Hegel has not survived in Herr Boumann's reconstruction, based on a living memory of a living performance, than in what will ultimately be served up to us, in all its dismembered repetitiousness, by the *Hegel-Archiv*? Mean-

while the present generation, threatened with a widespread
collapse of its culture, its morals, and its capacity for systematic
insights of any kind, must make do with materials which, whatever
their defects, at every point show the undoubted imprint of
surpassing, saving, philosophical genius. Such at least is how they
appear to the present writer who has long agitated for the completion of Wallace's translations of the *Encyclopaedia*, both by a
complete translation of the *Philosophy of Nature*, and of the hitherto
untranslated *Zusätze* to the *Philosophy of Mind*.

The translation of the *Zusätze* to the present work is the work
of Mr. A. V. Miller, a dedicated Hegelian, who was also responsible for the translation of the *Philosophy of Nature*, and for a
translation of Hegel's *Wissenschaft der Logik*, his so-called *Larger*
(non-Encyclopaedia) *Logic*. Wallace's translation of the *Philosophy
of Mind* paragraphs has not been tampered with, except at some
insignificant points, and 'Mind', instead of 'Spirit', has been
used to translate *Geist* so as to agree with Wallace's translation.
Wallace's renderings have also been followed in other cases. His
translation of the paragraphs is not faultless, but it seemed better
to let it stand, with all its expressive life and its historical interest
to many, than to attempt piecemeal revision. The best of all possible translations, like the best of all possible worlds, is plainly
a self-contradictory concept, and it is proper to be satisfied with
what is in some ways truly good. Wallace's five *Introductory Essays*
have been omitted from the present version: they connected
Hegel's Philosophy of Mind with the contemporary system of
Herbert Spencer and with the philosophy and psychology of the
latter half of the nineteenth century. As this is, in large degree,
quite unfamiliar to the contemporary reader, the introductory
value of these *Essays* has totally vanished. They would themselves
require an introduction, so strange is the thought-scene that they
presuppose. Those who are interested in them can still find them
in the older editions.

The notion of *Geist* (Mind or Spirit) is of course central in
Hegel. It is the lineal descendant of the Kantian Transcendental
Unity of Self-consciousness and of the Absolute Ego of Fichte
and Schelling. It also claims a collateral source in the Aristotelian
νοῦς which, in knowing the form of an object, thereby knows itself,

and which, in its highest phases, may be described as a pure
thinking upon thinking. The Greek influence upon Hegel's thought
is all-important from the beginning of the Jena period, but the
roots of that thought remain Kantian and Fichtean. Kant had
made plain that we require to mind *objects*, unities which proceed
according to rule and which can be reidentified on many occasions,
in order to have that unity in our conscious minding which makes
us enduring conscious selves, and which enables us to be conscious
of ourselves as conscious. In the conscious constitution of objects,
athwart the flux of time, we have the necessary foundation for the
constitution of a consciousness of consciousness, a point remade
latterly and hammered home by Husserl. Our subjective life may
and must be in many ways arbitrary and inconsequent, but
object- and rule-oriented it must also be if it is to have unity at all,
if it is not to evaporate into a truly impossible flux. The unity
which informs, and which we recognize in our conscious life, is
accordingly inherently rational, whatever spice of the irrational it
may also harbour: it essentially operates with patterns that set *limits*
to random variety. It was not, therefore, a new doctrine that Hegel
was proclaiming when he saw a connection between our subjective
being and the presence of categorial principles and intersubjective
norms in our thought and action, and when he described the
conscious Ego as the Universal in Action. Pattern, principle, connection, definiteness of position and range: these are not only the
bases of all that can be identified objectively or discoursed about
intersubjectively; they also underlie the possibility of our being
conscious and self-conscious at all. All this may not have been so
pellucidly put in the diction of classical German idealism as in
certain contemporary treatments, it may even have done scant
justice to what is characteristically subjective about the subjective,
but the lesson remains the same, and it is this lesson that
is crystallized in Hegel's concept of *Geist*. To be a conscious,
thinking subject is to recognize limiting, organizing universals
in things or to impose them on things: remove the limitation
and the organization and one liquidates conscious subjectivity.
It is therefore not a paradox, but a deep truism, when Hegel
says that we most profoundly find ourselves in the world
when we most profoundly lose ourselves in the fixed pattern of

things, and that the transformation effected by thought upon things is also the disengagement of what those things intrinsically are.

There is, however, a profound difference between the position of *Geist* in the thought of Hegel and the position of the transcendental self in the thought of Kant, a difference which may be ascribed to the whole development, the continuous dialectic, which occurred between the two thinkers. Kant in his pre-critical position began by connecting the way things appear with conditions essentially subjective, while still permitting our thought to rove beyond such appearances to 'things-in-themselves': this position inevitably simplified to one in which this last mysterious touch of transcendence vanished, and nothing could be thought by the subject which could not also appear to it, and be subject to the limits of such appearance. The thing-in-itself, deprived of all function, then suffered excision or transformation in later idealism, for which all objectivity, whether given or thought, became no more than a thing posited or constituted by the thinking subject as part of the comprehensive act in and through which it posits or constitutes itself. The productive imagination, that obscure faculty hidden in the depths of the soul, now became the universal artificer, a more mysterious artificer, we may say, than the straightforward makers of earlier cosmogonies. The excision of the thing-in-itself, or its relegation to the realm of the purely ideal, sufficed, however, to change the balance of the whole picture. *Without contrast*, the world of phenomena became the true realm of being, the objective, natural world set over the realm of our subjective approaches, and as much constitutive of the latter as the latter was constitutive of the former. We reach Schelling's neo-Spinozism, where Nature and the Ego are but two sides of an ultimate 'Indifference', neither having any assured prerogative over the other, while the thought-determinations which, on one hand, appear in our thinking, also appear in a 'petrified', encased form in unthinking Nature. The extraordinary wheel of German idealism has thus whirled from realism to a representative semi-realism, thence on to a constructive subjectivism, and thence on to a nice balance where it hardly matters whether one thinks of the world as the construct of the thinking self or the thinking self as the crowning construct of the world. It is at this point that Hegel and his concept of *Geist* enter the sequence, and where there is, on the one hand, a determined dropping of, and a determined refusal to return to, what may be called the *constructivism* of the earlier idealists, together with a determined retention of the view that subjectivity, mind, consciousness has in some sense an explanatory *prerogative* over the realms of Nature and objectivity, that it in some sense overreaches and outflanks them, and a consequent refusal to barter such an explanatory prerogative for a nothing-saying Spinozistic 'Indifference'.

Hegel here calls upon the Aristotelian notion of final causality rather than any form of productive efficiency: conscious subjectivity engineers, and thus explains, its opposition, the world of Nature and of finite, existent consciousness, only in the sense of being its *final cause*, that for the sake of which the opposition exists and assumes its infinitely varied forms. And this has the further result that both conscious subjectivity and its opposition have their roots in an eternal, disembodied Purpose, a pure Idea, in which the various categorial patterns of unspirituality and imperfect spirituality are given as leading up to the categorial pattern of Spirit as universal End, as the Absolute Idea underlying all possible being and the world. The role of the productive imagination now devolves upon a new cosmic faculty: the sensuously concrete world of phenomenal Nature and the world of finite subjectivity become the externalization, the *Entaüsserung*, the release into particularity of the eternal Idea. And Hegel can say in one of the *Zusätze* translated by Miller (§ 448): 'But things are in truth themselves spatial and temporal; this double form of asunderness is not one-sidely given to them by our intuition, but has been originally imparted to them by the intrinsically infinite mind, by the creative eternal Idea.' Many will argue that such a creation by the eternal Idea only represents a new mythology which replaces the old, unsatisfactory mythology of the productive imagination: our understanding of things by ends can, however, be separated from mythical integuments, and is arguably the only type of explanation that can ultimately exorcize all surds, that can, in a deep sense, not to be connected with scientific prediction or detailed logical deduction, leave nothing unexplained. And the sense in which Spirit is the end of the world, including its own opposition, is deeply bound up with its own self-consciousness: it does away with its opposition, not in simply making it not to be, but in re-cognizing itself in it, in seeing it as having no other meaning or function but to call forth itself, to make conscious spirituality possible. It is, in short, in coming to see itself as the end of every-thing, that it effectively and fully *is* the end of everything: its victory over all opposition would not be consummated if it did not see itself as victorious, and its ultimate victory, though led up to and buttressed by countless triumphs of detail, has therefore something ineliminably self-constitutive about it. This is why the Absolute Idea is defined by Hegel as the eternal *vision* of itself in the Other, and why Absolute Spirit is no more than a concrete carrying out, in actual aesthetic, religious, and philosophical experience, of the mode of vision thus described. One is at one's goal when one ceases to imagine that it still lies further ahead. This is not the place to consider all the difficulties of a re-entrant concept like Hegel's notion of the Absolute Idea and Absolute Spirit, nor to allay fears that its undisguised self-reference may involve a regress of some malign or empty type. It is arguable that such a concept, though difficult, can be developed without con-flict or vacuity, and that, as so elaborated, it gives us a rounded and wholly satisfactory grasp never achieved in any other way. The distinct positions and functions recognized in ordinary explanation are not done away with, only it is now one and the same totally explanatory content that occupies them all.

The change of *Geist*, further, from being the centre of the world *for us*, to being the ultimate point of union, the transcendental goal, of all factors and phases in the development of the world and of thought, necessitates precisely that *double* treatment of sub-jectivity which distinguishes the absolutism of Hegel from the transcendentalism of his predecessors. Kant, Fichte, and Schelling could attempt *one* deduction of the categories and the forms of being from a study of the interior structures of subjectivity. Hegel, on the other hand, must show how subjectivity, at first finding itself and its own demands in a seemingly alien world, at length, by a final shift of vision, sees those patterns and demands as the governing patterns, the presiding essentialities of the world, and so in a sense abolishes itself and its own subjective posturings, but must then also show, by a second shift of vision, how subjectivity re-emerges out of the essentialities of logic and the phases of objective Nature, and proceeds to understand and manipulate and see itself as the end of the latter, and so in a sense abrogates all mere objectivity. The former treatment is, of course, that of the *Phenomenology of Spirit*, as the latter is that of our present *Philosophy of Mind (Spirit)*, and the former is taken up and repeated in the structure of the latter. It is, however, in terms of the latter that the former must be interpreted, and not, as the fashion now often is, vice versa. What we have said involves, of course, all the crucial issues of Hegel-interpretation, regarding which we shall offer no further argument. What we have said will make plain what those issues are, whether or not our treatment seems accept-able. What is, however, *not* a matter of argument is the largely naturalistic, teleological character of the *Encyclopaedia* treatment of Mind or Spirit: conscious life is shown emerging from and transforming the natural order, because it is in some sense the logical destiny of the natural order to be thus transformed. The whole development may, by a convinced transcendentalist, be put back into subjective brackets, but in the *Philosophy of Mind* this is not done at all: we are in the sunny outer world, not in the Germanic *Urwald* of our conscious activities. That Hegel's view permits fundamental controversy at so many points is, of course, a sign of its extraordinary truth and vitality. It will, however, be our task, for the rest of this *Foreword*, to dwell on a few of the details of the *Philosophy of Spirit* rather than its over-all interpretation.

The general division of the *Philosophy of Mind* is into Subjective, Objective, and Absolute Mind, the two former being concerned with Spirit in its finitude, as a definite phenomenon or 'shape' in the articulated life of the Absolute, the last being concerned with Spirit in its infinitude, as what has become self-consciously, or for itself, what it has always been unconsciously or in itself, the eternal, vibrant unity which through, and only through, an almost endless series of fissions, oppositions, and restorations, can achieve a true fusion or identification of itself with itself. In Subjective Spirit we have the unitive 'sense' of the world, dispersed and

scattered over the mechanical, physical, and organic parts of
Nature, and dumbly sunk into the materiality of natural being,
gathering itself together in centres of subjectivity, which develop
from being passive experiential mirrors of organic-environmental
interplay, into remote symbolic registers and free projectors of
states and changes in the objective world. In Objective Spirit
we have the same unitive 'sense' flowing over into the natural world,
and creating that legally, conscientiously, and institutionally
patterned social world, whose roots lie in the deep self-recognition
of conscious subjectivity across and through the variety of its
individual embodiments. In Absolute Spirit, finally, we have the
unitive sense of the world articulately set forth, by and for conscious subjects in general, whether in the sensuous immediacy of
art, the emotional picture-thought of religion, or the purely
notional discourse of philosophy. In all this we have not so much
an anthropology developing into an immanental theology, as a
logical development, continuous with that of the Logic proper and
the Philosophy of Nature, in which the idea of a self-differentiating, self-explanatory whole evolves from stinted, truncated, and
abstracted forms to forms which are more truly inclusive and self-
sustaining.

Subjective Spirit begins with Anthropology, the nature-
immersed phases of subjectivity, and on this topic Hegel has so
much to say of a purely naturalistic cast as to assort ill with the
common notions of his philosophy. There is, first of all, an immense stress on the environment, from whose diffused readiness
for psychical centrality the individual soul is carved out: Hegel
even talks in terms of regional souls, though he makes plain
that it is only in individual persons that such souls become fully
actual. There is, further, an immense emphasis on race. Lack of
experience of the changes wrought by emigration or large-scale
industrialization, and other economic or social changes, leads Hegel
to believe in such things as an unchangeable Arabian spirit conditioned to monotheism by the desert, in an English soul whose
environment favours intellectual intuition, in a negro soul compel-
led by African geography to remain permanently apathetic and
naïve, etc., etc. These views seem to us prejudices, but they are the
sort of empirically grounded prejudices from which scientific

anthropology or sociology, rather than philosophy, will afterwards develop. There is, further, immense stress on such things
as the alternations of sleeping and waking, the stages of growth,
maturity, and senescence, and the physiological functions both of
the external sense-organs and of the viscera and musculature used
in emotional expression. In so far as there are any interior aspects
to psychic life at this stage, these take the form of 'feelings', states
devoid of explicit subject-object structure, which none the less in
some manner obscurely condense the whole surrounding 'life-
world' of the conscious person, together with his own reactions
to its contents. At this level, psychic life involves possibilities of
interpenetration which vanish at higher, consciously structured
levels. The mesmerist and his subject, the mother and her unborn
child, deeply sympathetic friends and relatives, all experience a
psychic seepage from the experiences of others which are quite
intelligible on a Hegelian philosophy of spirit, however incredible
they may seem to the naïve materialistic naturalism of the everyday
understanding. The phenomena of extra-sensory perception also
accord well with the basic premisses of Hegelianism, though Hegel
warns us against attributing any extraordinary significance to
them: the whole self-transcendence involved in ordinary knowledge testifies to a profound unity behind dispersed surface-
differences of which extra-sensory knowledge is only a more
spectacular example. Spirit is the truth that matter has no truth,
and this is confirmed in *every* case in which the outsideness and
pure irrelevance of bodies to one another is set aside, and not
merely in the abnormal, surprising cases. Hegel shows the same
questing, cautiously empirical attitude to the extra-sensory and the
mesmeric that he has previously shown to the electrical and the
chemical: they are attested by observation, and astonish only
the understanding. The life of feeling is further characterized by
a possible domination of more or less detached feelings, cut off
from the organized mass which forms our usual sense of the world,
and here we have the possibility of dreams, fantasy, and ultimately
of insanity. Insanity is no more than a big arrest in the thorough-
going integration characteristic of developed psychic life: it also
has its roots in the 'absolute negativity' of the spirit, in virtue
of which a man can identify himself, and in a deep sense *truly*

identify himself, with anything under the sun. The habitual side of conscious life is then dealt with as a useful declension from the actuality of consciousness into unconscious semi-materiality, thereby setting feeling free for more important uses. In all this Hegel emphasizes the deep involvement of our feelings with our bodies, and much of his treatment savours of modern phenomenology rather than of an antique seventeenth-century dualism.

From Anthropology, the study of Soul disengaging itself from the bonds of natural existence, Hegel turns to Phenomenology, the study of Consciousness as such, the state in which the natural world of being comes to stand over against the percipient person, which then learns to see a reflection of itself in the latter. Hegel here draws upon the splendid introductory sections of the *Phenomenology of Spirit*, whose material he logically tightens and purges of brilliant irrelevances. We see the mind, unaware of its deep identity with the Absolute Idea which also underlies natural objects, and which has engendered the latter to arouse, tease, and ultimately promote self-acquaintance in the mind, gradually discovering the mould of its own intelligence in the mysterious things which confront it, and then seeing the mould of this intelligence extending itself to a whole society of conscious persons who recognize and are recognized by one another. We begin with the sensuous consciousness in which the object 'has no other thought-determination than, first, that of simply being, and, secondly, that of being an independent Other over against me, something reflected into itself, an individual confronting me as an individual, an immediate' (*Zus.*, § 418). From this we progress to the perceptual consciousness in which the monolith of sense-encounter dissolves into a swarm of properties and relationships, circling about an obscure point of identity, properties, and relationships endowed with a universality and distinctness of type that accords well with the splintering capacities of the understanding, but only ill with the supposed out-thereness and integrity of the thing. This develops further into the rudimentary scientific vision of forces and laws and unseen generic natures lying beneath the shifting surface of phenomena, a stage which Hegel curiously *intercalates* between the perceptual awareness of the thing-world around us and the introjective awareness of a world of persons, though it is surely arguable that the givenness of a world of persons is much more primitive than that of a world of explanatory scientific objects: persons are in fact required for the practice and criticism of scientific knowledge. However this may be, the argument progresses, as in the *Phenomenology of Spirit*, from the scientific understanding of natural things to the consciousness of self, and this is at first given in the form of a self identified with specific wants or urges (*Begierden*), which it feels confident of realizing in and through the natural things around it. Such appetitive consciousness, certain of a hidden yieldingness or deep I-conformity in objective nature, then goes on to look for the greater I-conformity which objective yieldingness only prefigures, the I-conformity of a selfhood recognized by the self in others, and recognized as recognized by those others in itself. This universal recognitiveness must, however, undergo a long development in which there is first a profound gulf between magisterial, dominant self-consciousnesses, on the one hand, and servile, subjected ones, on the other, and Hegel believes that the discipline of self-conscious servitude is in fact necessary to the subsequent mutual recognition of the free by the free. What is important in this stage of the Philosophy of Mind is that the inner life of the subject, its life of reflection, judgement, memory, deliberation, etc., which will be elaborated in the next section, presupposes the prior capacity to see oneself as a free man among other free men. A man who envisages himself as a slave, an inferior, cannot judge, decide, imagine, agree, nor even have the dreams of reason, or rather, the fact that he succeeds in having them, shows that he is no longer envisaging himself as a mere slave. The possession of an ordered inner life is the prerogative of a free individual, recognized as such by an ordered society.

The Psychology which follows upon this Anthropology and Phenomenology is not one of the most carefully worked-out parts of Hegel's philosophy: it is odd that, with his central concern for subjectivity, he should be so much more skilled in discussing the objective arrangements which lead up to it, or the objective arrangements in which it expresses itself, than the concentrated inner arrangements of subjectivity itself. This is perhaps an inevitable consequence of his view of conscious subjectivity, that, qua finite, it 'is immediately a contradiction, an untruth, and at the same time the process of ridding itself of this untruth' (*Zus.*, § 441). He has no other account to give of the theoretical side of experience than that it is 'the activity by which the seemingly *alien* object receives, instead of the shape of something given, isolated and contingent, the form of something inwardized, subjective, universal, necessary and rational', whereas practical mind has to do only with 'aims which do not appertain to the *particular* subject but exist in their own right (*Zus.*, § 443). Like Kant, Hegel shows a defective interest in the features of arbitrariness, inconsequence, and personal blending which are as necessary to the constitution of human experience, in its essential two-sidedness, as are its rule-governed and intersubjective features.

In the analysis of Theoretical Mind, Hegel begins with *Anschauung* or Intuition, which represents an intellectualized form of perception: the object, given immediately, is none the less placed 'out there' at a more or less definite point in a cosmic space and time, which Hegel is careful to divest of the mere subjectivity given to it by Kantian accounts. From *Anschauung* one goes on to the *Vorstellung* or pictorial idea: the object still stands before us, but detachedly, without a fixed place in the order of space and time. It may be an object vaguely recollected or irresponsibly imagined: it is interesting to note that though Hegal has something to say of the 'productive imagination', he makes absolutely no reference to Kant's use of the term. This has simply dropped out of his philosophy since the early essay on *Glauben und Wissen*. The role of language is sketched in a long paragraph (§ 459), which, considering the wisdom Hegel often attributes to ordinary language, is noteworthy mainly for its chattiness: one would have welcomed an account of the way words mediate our whole vision of the world, but we have to be content with the doctrine of a substitutionary identification which liberates us from the immediacies of the spatio-temporal environment. A less inadequate treatment occurs in the treatment of Memory (*Gedächtnis*), where etymology links our topic with the topic of thought. 'The name', Hegel says in § 462, 'is thus the thing so far as it exists and counts in the ideational realm. Given the name *lion* we need neither the actual vision of the animal, nor its image even: the name alone, if we *understand* it, is the unimaged simple representation. We think in names.' Or again, in § 463, 'Intelligence is the universal, the plain truth of its particular externalizations, and its achieved ownership of them cancels the distinction of meaning and name. The highest inwardizing of representation is its highest externalization, in which it explicitly is the mere *being*, the universal space of names as such, i.e. of senseless words.' Or again, in § 464, 'What exists as a name needs another, the *meaning* of the representing intelligence, in order to be the thing, the true objectivity. Intelligence, as mechanical memory, is at once that external objectivity and its *meaning*.' These apparent concessions to a meaning-as-use doctrine must, however, be read in the full context of Hegel's dialectical treatment. But he is in truth as little interested in thought as a subjective phenomenon, perhaps as inadequately acquainted with it, as that other great dweller on words, Wittgenstein.

In the treatment of volition which follows there are practically no contributions to the phenomenology of choice. We are already well on our way to the morally and socially concerned subject, involved in practically changing the intersubjective realm of reality, and moving quite beyond the vain intensities of mere inwardness. The latent rationality of the heart and the will requires the universalizing touch of the thinking intelligence: man is always implicitly a reasonable animal, whether he feels or wills or thinks. 'A sensible man—a strong character—can find something in agreement with what he wills, without breaking out into feelings of joy—and can conversely undergo misfortune without yielding to a feeling of pain' (*Zus.*, § 472). Interests, impulses (*Triebe*) now emerge out of the mere desires of the heart with their individual leanings towards individual objects: thinking volition sets general ends before us which, while still binding us to the particular and contingent, at least free us from its detailed immediacies. The passions emerge, the great commitments to more or less specific ends for which the person lives, passions in which Hegel sees both a restrictedly operating rationality and the necessary foundation for a truly free rationality. Among these passions, impulses, and interests the subject exercises choice, and in so doing comes to set up the abstractly general end of personal happiness: the reason-saturated, higher-order character of which end, and its total distinction from first-order, impulsive ends, is as clear to Hegel as it was to Butler, and as it was quite obscure to Kant and many other austere moralists. By a change which removes the last vestige of particularity, happiness then yields place to those higher-order ends which transcend the distinction of persons, and which dominate moral and political life. We have passed from Subjective to Objective Mind or Spirit.

It is not necessary or desirable for us here to comment on the paragraphs dealing with Law, Conscience and Social Ethics, the State and History, which, unaccompanied by further *Zusätze* from Herr Boumann, make up the content of the *Encyclopaedia* treatment of Mind Objective. Sir Malcolm Knox's translation of the *Philosophy of Right* will furnish all that is required in this direction. Nor need we say anything about the brief treatment of Art, Religion, and Philosophy which occurs in the condensed paragraphs of the section on Absolute Mind. Hegel's splendid lectures on Aesthetics, the Philosophy of Religion, and the History of Philosophy have all been translated and will no doubt be more adequately retranslated in the future and the content of his views on these, the highest reaches of the human spirit, have been, and will no doubt continue to be, widely commented upon. We have said enough to justify the reissue of Wallace's translation of the *Philosophy of Mind* paragraphs together with Miller's translation of Herr Boumann's *Zusätze*. When the *Logic* has also been reissued with a number of improvements, the Oxford *Encyclopaedia*-translation will remain the valuable source of Hegelianism for the English-speaking world that it has been for some generations in the past.

J. N. FINDLAY

Yale University
7 May 1969

CONTENTS

CONTENTS

INTRODUCTION

§ 377

The knowledge of Mind is the highest and hardest, just because it is the most 'concrete' of sciences. The significance of that 'absolute' commandment, *Know thyself*—whether we look at it in itself or under the historical circumstances of its first utterance—is not to promote mere self-knowledge in respect of the *particular* capacities, character, propensities, and foibles of the single self. The knowledge it commands means that of man's genuine reality —of what is essentially and ultimately true and real—of mind as the true and essential being. Equally little is it the purport of mental philosophy to teach what is called *knowledge of men*—the knowledge whose aim is to detect the *peculiarities*, passions, and foibles of other men, and lay bare what are called the recesses of the human heart. Information of this kind is, for one thing, meaningless, unless on the assumption that we know the *universal* —man as man, and, that always must be, as mind. And for another, being only engaged with casual, insignificant, and *untrue* aspects of mental life, it fails to reach the underlying essence of them all— the mind itself.

Zusatz. The difficulty of the philosophical cognition of mind consists in the fact that in this we are no longer dealing with the comparatively abstract, simple logical Idea, but with the most concrete, most developed form achieved by the Idea in its self-actualization. Even finite or subjective mind, not only absolute mind, must be grasped as an actualization of the Idea. The treatment of mind is only truly philosophical when it cognizes the Notion of mind in its living development and actualization, which simply means, when it comprehends mind as a type of the absolute Idea. But it belongs to the nature of mind to cognize its Notion. Consequently, the summons to the Greeks of the Delphic Apollo, *Know thyself*, does not have the meaning of a law externally imposed on the human mind by an alien power; on the contrary, the god who impels to self-knowledge is none other than the absolute law of mind itself. Mind is, therefore, in its every act only apprehending itself, and the aim of all genuine science is just this, that mind shall recognize itself in everything in heaven and on earth. An out-and-out Other simply does not exist for mind. Even the oriental does not wholly lose himself in the object of his worship; but the Greeks were the first to grasp expressly as mind what they opposed to themselves as the Divine, although even they did not attain, either in philosophy or in religion, to a knowledge of the absolute infinitude of mind; therefore with the Greeks the relation of the human mind to the Divine is still not one of absolute freedom. It was Christianity, by its doctrine of the Incarnation and of the presence of the Holy Spirit in the community of believers, that first gave to human consciousness a perfectly free relationship to the infinite and thereby made possible the comprehensive knowledge of mind in its absolute infinitude.

Henceforth, such a knowledge alone merits the name of a philosophical treatment. Self-knowledge in the usual trivial meaning of an inquiry into the foibles and faults of the single self has interest and importance only for the individual, not for philosophy; but even in relation to the individual, the more the focus of interest is shifted from the general intellectual and moral nature of man, and the more the inquiry, disregarding duties and the genuine content of the will, degenerates into a self-complacent absorption of the individual in the idiosyncrasies so dear to him, the less is the value of that self-knowledge. The same is true of the so-called knowledge of *human nature* which likewise is directed to the peculiarities of individual minds. This knowledge is, of course, useful and necessary in the conduct of life, especially in bad political conditions where right and morality have given place to the self-will, whims and caprice of individuals, in the field of intrigues where characters do not rely on the nature of the matter in hand but hold their own by cunningly exploiting the peculiarities of others and seeking by this means to attain their arbitrary ends. For philosophy, however, this knowledge of human nature is devoid of interest in so far as it is incapable of rising above the consideration of contingent particularities to the understanding of the characters of great men, by which alone the true nature of man in its serene purity is brought to view. But this knowledge of human nature can even be harmful for philosophy if, as happens in the so-called pragmatic treatment of history, through failure to appreciate the substantial character of world-historical individuals and to see that great deeds can only be carried out by great characters, the supposedly clever attempt is made to trace back the greatest events in history to the accidental idiosyncrasies of those heroes, to their presumed petty aims, propensities, and passions. In such a procedure history, which is ruled by divine Providence, is reduced to a play of meaningless activity and contingent happenings.

§ 378

Pneumatology, or, as it was also called, Rational Psychology, has been already alluded to in the Introduction to the Logic as an *abstract* and generalizing metaphysic of the subject. *Empirical* (or inductive) psychology, on the other hand, deals with the 'concrete' mind: and, after the revival of the sciences, when observation and experience had been made the distinctive methods for the study of concrete reality, such psychology was worked on the same lines as other sciences. In this way it came about that the metaphysical theory was kept outside the inductive science, and so prevented from getting any concrete embodiment or detail: whilst at the same time the inductive science clung to the conventional common-sense metaphysic, with its analysis into forces, various activities, etc., and rejected any attempt at a 'speculative' treatment.

The books of Aristotle on the Soul, along with his discussions on its special aspects and states, are for this reason still by far the most admirable, perhaps even the sole, work of philosophical value on this topic. The main aim of a philosophy of mind can only be to reintroduce unity of idea and principle into the theory of mind, and so reinterpret the lesson of those Aristotelian books.

Zusatz. Genuinely speculative philosophy, which excludes the mode of treatment discussed in the previous Paragraph which is directed to the unessential, isolated, empirical phenomena of mind, also excludes the precisely opposite mode of so-called Rational Psychology or Pneumatology, which is concerned only with abstractly universal determinations, with the supposedly unmanifested essence, the 'in-itself' of mind. For speculative philosophy may not take its subject-matter from picture-thinking as a *datum*, nor may it determine such given material merely by categories of the abstractive intellect (*Verstand*) as the said psychology did when it posed the question whether mind or soul is simple and immaterial, whether it is substance. In these questions mind was treated as a thing; for these categories were regarded, in the general manner of the abstractive intellect, as inert, fixed; as such, they are incapable of expressing the nature of mind. Mind is not an inert being but, on the contrary, absolutely restless being, pure activity, the negating or ideality of every fixed category of the abstractive intellect; not abstractly simple but, in its simplicity, at the same time a distinguishing of itself from itself; not an essence that is already finished and complete before its manifestation, keeping itself aloof behind its host of appearances, but an essence which is truly actual only through the specific forms of its necessary self-manifestation; and it is not, as that psychology supposed, a soul-thing only externally connected with the body, but is inwardly bound to the latter by the unity of the Notion.

In the middle, between observation which is directed to the contingent particularity of mind and pneumatology which concerns itself only with the unmanifested essence, stands empirical psychology which has as its starting-point the observation and description of the particular faculties of mind. But neither does this lead to the veritable union of the individual and the universal, to the knowledge of the concretely universal nature or Notion of mind, and therefore it, too, has no claim to the name of genuinely speculative philosophy. It is not only mind as such which empirical psychology takes as a *datum* from picture-thinking, but also the special faculties into which it analyses mind without deriving these particularities from the Notion of mind and so demonstrating that in mind there are necessarily just these faculties and no others.

With this defect of the form there is necessarily linked the despiritualization of the content. When in the two modes of treatment already described, empirical psychology takes the individual on the one hand, and the universal on the other, each as a fixed, independent category, it also holds the particular forms into which it analyses mind to be fixed in their limitation; so that mind is converted into a mere aggregate of independent forces, each of which stands only in reciprocal relation with the others, hence is only externally connected with them. For though this psychology also demands that the various spiritual forces shall be harmoniously integrated—a favourite and oft-recurring catch-phrase on this topic, but one which is just as indefinite as 'perfection' used to be—this gives expression to a unity of mind which only *ought* to be, not to the original unity, and still less does it recognize as necessary and rational the particularization to which the Notion of mind, its intrinsic unity, progresses. This harmonious integration remains, therefore, a vacuous idea which expresses itself in high-sounding but empty phrases but remains ineffective in face of the spiritual forces presupposed as independent.

§ 379

Even our own sense of the mind's *living* unity naturally protests against any attempt to break it up into different faculties, forces, or, what comes to the same thing, activities, conceived as independent of each other. But the craving for a *comprehension* of the unity is still further stimulated, as we soon come across distinctions between mental freedom and mental determinism, antitheses between free *psychic* agency and the corporeity that lies external to it, whilst we equally note the intimate interdependence of the one upon the other. In modern times especially the phenomena of *animal magnetism* have given, even in experience, a lively and visible confirmation of the underlying unity of soul, and of the power of its 'ideality'. Before these facts, the rigid distinctions of practical common sense are struck with confusion; and the necessity of a 'speculative' examination with a view to the removal of difficulties is more directly forced upon the student.

Zusatz. All those finite interpretations of mind depicted in the two previous Paragraphs have been ousted, partly by the vast transformation undergone by philosophy in recent years, and partly, from the empirical side itself, by the phenomena of animal magnetism which are a stumbling-block to finite thought. As regards the former, philosophy has risen above the finite mode of treatment based on merely reflective thought which, since Wolf, had become universal, and also above Fichte's so-called 'facts of consciousness', to a comprehension of mind as the self-knowing, actual Idea, to the Notion of living mind which, in a necessary manner, immanently differentiates itself and returns out of its differences into unity with itself. But in doing so, it has not only overcome the abstractions prevalent in those finite interpretations of mind, the merely individual, merely particular, and merely universal, reducing them to moments of the Notion which is their truth; but also, instead of externally describing a material already to hand, it has vindicated as the only scientific method the rigorous form of the necessary self-development of the content. In contrast to the empirical sciences, where the material as given by experience is taken up from outside and is ordered and brought into context in accordance with an already established general rule, speculative thinking has to demonstrate each of its objects and the explication of them, in their absolute necessity. This is effected by deriving each particular Notion from the self-originating and self-actualizing universal Notion, or the logical Idea. Philosophy must therefore comprehend mind as a necessary development of the eternal Idea and must let the science of mind, as constituted by its particular parts, unfold itself entirely from its Notion. Just as in the living organism generally, everything is already contained, in an ideal manner, in the germ and is brought forth by the germ itself, not by an alien power, so too must all the particular forms of living mind grow out of its Notion as from their germ. In so doing, our thinking, which is actuated by the Notion, remains for the object, which likewise is actuated by the Notion, absolutely immanent; we merely look on, as it were, at the object's own development, not altering it by importing into it our own subjective ideas and fancies. The Notion does not require any external stimulus for its actualization; it embraces the contradiction of simplicity and difference, and therefore its own restless nature impels it to actualize itself, to unfold into actuality the difference which, in the Notion itself, is present only in an ideal manner, that is to say, in the contradictory form of differencelessness, and by this removal of its simplicity as of a defect, a one-sidedness, to make itself actually that whole, of which to begin with it contained only the possibility.

But the Notion is no less independent of our caprice in the conclusion of its development than it is in the beginning and in the course of it. In a merely ratiocinative mode of treatment the conclusion, to be sure, appears more or less arbitrary; in philosophical science, on the contrary, the Notion itself sets a limit to its self-developmentby giving itself an actuality that is perfectly adequate to it. Already in the living being we see this self-limitation of the Notion. The germ of the plant, this sensuously present Notion, closes its development with an actuality like itself, with the production of the seed. The same is true of mind; its development, too, has achieved its goal when the Notion of mind has completely actualized itself or, what is the same thing, when mind has attained to complete consciousness of its Notion. But this contraction of beginning and end into one, this coming of the Notion to its own self in its actualization, appears in mind in a yet more complete form than in the merely living being; for whereas in the latter, the seed produced is not identical with the seed from which it came, in self-knowing mind the product is one and the same as that which produces it.

Only when we contemplate mind in this process of the self-actualization of its Notion, do we know it in its truth (for truth means precisely agreement of the Notion with its actuality). In its immediacy, mind is not yet true, has not yet made its Notion objective to it, has not yet transformed what confronts it in immediate guise, into something which it has posited, has not yet transformed its actuality into one which is adequate to its Notion. The entire development of mind is nothing else but the raising of itself to its truth, and the so-called psychic forces have no other meaning than to be the stages of this ascent. By this self-differentiation, this self-transformation, and the bringing back of its differences to the unity of its Notion, mind as a true being is also a living, organic, systematic being; and only by knowing this its nature is the science of mind likewise true, living, organic, systematic: predicates bestowable neither on rational nor empirical psychology, for the former makes mind into a dead essence divorced from its actualization, while the latter kills the living mind by tearing it asunder into a manifold of independent forces which neither derive from the Notion nor are held together by it.

We have already remarked that animal magnetism has played a part in ousting the untrue, finite interpretation of mind from the standpoint of the merely abstractive intellect. This has been brought about by those marvellous phenomena especially in connection with the treatment of mind on its natural side. Though the other kinds of conditions and natural determinations of mind and also its conscious activities can be grasped, at least externally, by the abstractive intellect which is able to grasp the external connection of cause and effect obtaining alike in the intellect and in finite things, the so-called natural course of things: yet, on the other hand, intellect shows itself incapable of belief in the phenomena of animal magnetism, because in these the bondage of mind to place and time—which in the opinion of the abstractive intellect is absolutely fixed—and to the finite category of causality, loses its meaning, and the elevation of mind over the externality of spatial and temporal relationships, which to intellect remains an incredible miracle, is manifest in sensuous existence itself. Now although it would be very foolish to see in the phenomena of animal magnetism an elevation of mind above even Reason with its ability to comprehend, and to expect from this state a higher knowledge of the eternal than that imparted by philosophy, and although the fact is that the magnetic state must be declared pathological and a degradation of mind below the level even of ordinary consciousness in so far as in that state mind surrenders its thinking as an activity creative of specific distinctions, as an activity contradistinguished from Nature: yet, on the other hand, in the visible liberation of mind in those magnetic phenomena from the limitations of space and time and from all finite associations, there is something akin to philosophy, something which, as brute fact, defies the scepticism of the abstractive intellect and so necessitates the advance from ordinary psychology to the comprehension afforded by speculative philosophy for which alone animal magnetism is not an incomprehensible miracle.

§ 380

The 'concrete' nature of mind involves for the observer the peculiar difficulty that the several grades and special types which develop its intelligible unity in detail are not left standing as so many separate existences confronting its more advanced aspects. It is otherwise in external nature. There, matter and movement, for example, have a manifestation all their own—it is the solar system; and similarly the *differentiae* of sense-perception have a sort of earlier existence in the properties of *bodies*, and still more independently in the four elements. The species and grades of mental evolution, on the contrary, lose their separate existence and become factors, states, and features in the higher grades of development. As a consequence of this, a lower and more abstract aspect of mind betrays the presence in it, even to experience, of a higher grade. Under the guise of sensation, for example, we may find the very highest mental life as its modification or its embodiment. And so sensation, which is but a mere form and vehicle, may to the superficial glance seem to be the proper seat and, as it were, the source of those moral and religious principles with which it is charged; and the moral and religious principles thus modified may seem to call for treatment as species of sensation. But at the same time, when lower grades of mental life are under examination, it becomes necessary, if we desire to point to actual cases of them in experience, to direct attention to more advanced grades for which they are mere forms. In this way subjects will be treated of by anticipation which properly belong to later stages of development (e.g. in dealing with natural awaking from sleep we speak by anticipation of consciousness, or in dealing with mental derangement we must speak of intellect).

What Mind (or Spirit) is

§ 381

From our point of view mind has for its *presupposition* Nature, of which it is the truth, and for that reason its *absolute prius*. In this its truth Nature is vanished, and mind has resulted as the 'Idea' entered on possession of itself. Here the subject and object of the Idea are one—either is the intelligent unity, the notion. This identity is *absolute negativity*—for whereas in Nature the intelligent unity has its objectivity perfect but externalized, this self-externalization has been nullified and the unity in that way been made one and the same with itself. Thus at the same time it *is* this identity only so far as it is a return out of nature.

Zusatz. We have already stated, in the *Zusatz* to § 379, that the Notion of mind is the self-knowing, actual Idea. Philosophy has to demonstrate the necessity of this Notion, as of all its other Notions, which means that philosophy must cognize it as the result of the development of the universal Notion or of the logical Idea. But in this development, mind is preceded not only by the logical Idea but also by external Nature. For the cognition already contained in the simple *logical* Idea is only the Notion of cognition thought *by us*, not cognition existing on its own account, not actual mind but merely its possibility. Actual mind which, in the science of mind, is alone our subject-matter, has external Nature for its proximate, and the logical Idea for its first, presupposition. The Philosophy of Nature, and indirectly Logic, must have, therefore, as its final outcome the proof of the necessity of the Notion of mind. The science of mind, on its part, has to authenticate this Notion by its development and actualization. Accordingly, what we say here assertorically about mind at the beginning of our treatment of it, can only be scientifically proved by philosophy in its entirety. All we can do at the outset is to elucidate the Notion of mind for ordinary thinking.

In order to establish what this Notion is, we must indicate the determinateness by which the Idea has being as mind. But every determinateness is a determinateness only counter to another determinateness; to that of mind in general is opposed, in the first instance, that of Nature; the former can, therefore, only be grasped simultaneously with the latter. We must designate as the distinctive determinateness of the Notion of mind, *ideality*, that is, the reduction of the Idea's otherness to a *moment*, the process of returning—and the accomplished return—into itself of the Idea from its Other; whereas the distinctive feature of the logical Idea is immediate, simple being-within-self, but for Nature it is the self-externality of the Idea. A more detailed development of what was said in passing in the *Zusatz* to § 379 about the logical Idea, would involve too wide a digression here; more necessary at this point is an elucidation of what has been assigned as characteristic of external Nature, for it is to the latter, as we have already remarked, that mind is proximately related.

External Nature, too, like mind, is rational, divine, a representation of the Idea. But in Nature, the Idea appears in the element of asunderness, is external not only to mind but also to itself, precisely because it is external to that actual, self-existent inwardness which constitutes the essential nature of mind. This Notion of Nature which was already enunciated by the Greeks and quite familiar to them, is in complete agreement with our ordinary idea of Nature. We know that natural things are spatial and temporal, that in Nature one thing exists alongside another, that one thing follows another, in brief, that in Nature all things are mutually external, *ad infinitum*; further, that matter, this universal basis of every existent form in Nature, not merely offers resistance to *us*, exists apart from our mind, but holds itself asunder against its own self, divides itself into concrete points, into material atoms, of which it is composed. The differences into which the Notion of Nature unfolds itself are more or less mutually independent existences; true, through their original unity they stand in mutual connection, so that none can be comprehended without the others; but this connection is in a greater or less degree external to them. We rightly say, therefore, that not freedom but necessity reigns in Nature; for this latter in its strictest meaning is precisely the merely internal, and for that reason also merely external, connection of mutually independent existences. Thus, for example, light and the [four] elements appear as mutually independent; similarly the planets, though attracted by the sun and despite this relation to their centre, appear to be independent of it and of one another, this contradiction being represented by the motion of the planet round the sun.

In the living being, of course, a higher necessity is dominant than in the inorganic sphere. Even in the plant, we see a centre which has overflowed into the periphery, a concentration of the differences, a self-development from within outwards, a unity which differentiates itself and from its differentiation produces itself in the bud, something, therefore, to which we attribute an urge (*Trieb*); but this unity remains incomplete because the plant's process of articulating itself is a coming-forth-from-

self of the vegetable subject, each part is the whole plant, a repetition of
it, and consequently the organs are not held in complete subjection to the
unity of the subject.

An even more complete triumph over externality is exhibited in the
animal organism; in this not only does each member generate the other,
is its cause and effect, its means and end, so that it is at the same time itself
and its Other, but the whole is so pervaded by its unity that nothing in it
appears as independent, every determinateness is at once ideal, the
animal remaining in every determinateness the same one universal, so
that in the animal body the complete untruth of asunderness is revealed.
Through this being-with-itself in the determinateness, through this
immediate reflectedness-into-self in and out of its externality, the animal
is self-existent subjectivity and has feeling; feeling is just this omnipresence of the unity of the animal in all its members which immediately
communicate every impression to the one whole which, in the animal,
is an incipient being-for-self. It follows from this subjective inwardness,
that the animal is self-determined, from within outwards, not merely
from outside, that is to say, it has an urge and instinct. The subjectivity
of the animal contains a contradiction and the urge to preserve itself by
resolving this contradiction; this self-preservation is the privilege of the
living being and, in a still higher degree, of mind. The sentient being is
determinate, has a content, and thus a difference within itself; this difference is in the first place still wholly ideal, simple, resolved in the unity
of feeling; the resolved difference subsisting in the unity is a contradiction which is resolved by the difference positing itself *as* difference.
The animal is, therefore, forced out of its simple self-relation into opposition to external Nature. By this opposition the animal falls into a fresh
contradiction, for the difference is now posited in a mode which contradicts
the unity of the Notion; accordingly it, too, must be resolved like the
undifferentiated unity in the first instance. This resolution of the difference is effected by the animal consuming what is destined for it in
external Nature and preserving itself by what it consumes. Thus by the
annihilation of the Other confronting the animal, the original, simple
self-relation and the contradiction contained in it is posited afresh. What
is needed for a veritable resolution of this contradiction is that the Other
with which the animal enters into relation, itself be similar to the latter.
This occurs in the sexual relation; here, each sex feels in the other not
an alien externality but its own self, or the genus common to both. The
sexual relation is, therefore, the highest point of animate Nature; on this
level, Nature is freed in the fullest measure from external necessity,
since the distinct existences in their mutual relationship are no longer
external to each other but have the feeling of their unity. Yet the animal
soul is still not free; for it is always manifest as a *one* determined as feeling
or excitation, as tied to one determinateness; it is only in the form of
individuality that the genus is *for* the animal; the latter merely feels the
genus, but does not know it; in the animal, the soul is not yet *for* the soul,

the universal as such is not *for* the universal. By the removal of the particularity of the sexes which occurs in the genus-process, the animal does not attain to a production of the genus; what is produced by this process is again only a single individual. And thus Nature, even at the highest point of its elevation over finitude, always falls back into it again and in this way exhibits a perpetual cycle. Death, too, which necessarily results from the contradiction between the individual and the genus, since it is not the affirmative supersession of individuality but only the empty, destructive negation of it, even appearing in the form of immediate individuality, likewise does not bring forth the universality that is in and for itself, or the individuality that is in and for itself universal, the subjectivity that has itself for object. Therefore, even in the most perfect form to which Nature raises itself, in animal life, the Notion does not attain to an actuality resembling its soul-like nature, to complete victory over the externality and finitude of its existence. This is first achieved in mind which, just by winning this victory, *distinguishes itself* from Nature, so that this distinguishing is not merely the act of an *external* reflection about the nature of mind.

This triumph over externality which belongs to the Notion of mind, is what we have called the ideality of mind. Every activity of mind is nothing but a distinct mode of reducing what is external to the inwardness which mind itself is, and it is only by this reduction, by this idealization or assimilation, of what is external that it becomes and is mind.

If we consider mind more closely, we find that its primary and simplest determination is the 'I'. The 'I' is something perfectly simple, universal. When we say 'I', we mean, to be sure, an individual; but since everyone is 'I', when we say 'I', we only say something quite universal. The universality of the 'I' enables it to abstract from everything, even from its life. But mind is not merely this abstractly simple being equivalent to light, which was how it was considered when the simplicity of the soul in contrast to the composite nature of the body was under discussion; on the contrary, mind in spite of its simplicity is distinguished within itself; for the 'I' sets itself over against itself, makes itself its own object and returns from this difference, which is, of course, only abstract, not yet concrete, into unity with itself. This being-with-itself of the 'I' in its difference from itself is the 'I's infinitude or ideality. But this ideality is first authenticated in the relation of the 'I' to the infinitely manifold material confronting it. This material, in being seized by the 'I', is at the same time poisoned and transfigured by the latter's universality; it loses its isolated, independent existence and receives a spiritual one. So far, therefore, is mind from being forced out of its simplicity, its being-with-itself, by the endless multiplicity of its images and ideas, into a spatial asunderness, that, on the contrary, its simple self, in undimmed clarity, pervades this multiplicity through and through and does not let it reach an independent existence.

But mind is not satisfied, as *finite* mind, with transposing things by its own ideational activity into its own interior space and thus stripping them of their externality in a manner which is still external; on the contrary, as *religious* consciousness, it pierces through the seemingly absolute independence of things to the one, infinite power of God operative in them and holding all together; and as *philosophical* thinking, it consummates this idealization of things by discerning the specific mode in which the eternal Idea forming their common principle is represented in them. By this cognition, the idealistic nature of mind which is already operative in finite mind, attains its completed, concretest shape, and becomes the actual Idea which perfectly apprehends itself and hence becomes absolute mind. Already in finite mind, ideality has the meaning of a movement returning into its beginning, by which mind, moving onward from its undifferentiated stage, its first position, to an Other, to the negation of that position, and by means of the negation of this negation returning to itself, demonstrates itself to be absolute negativity, infinite self-affirmation; and we have to consider finite mind, conformably to this its nature, first, in its immediate unity with Nature, then in its opposition to it, and lastly, in a unity which contains that opposition as overcome and is mediated by it. Grasped in this manner, finite mind is known as totality, as Idea, and moreover as the Idea which is for itself, which returns to itself out of that opposition and is actual. But in finite mind there is only the beginning of this return which is consummated only in absolute mind; for only in this does the Idea apprehend itself in a form which is neither merely the one-sided form of Notion or subjectivity, nor merely the equally one-sided form of objectivity or actuality, but is the perfect unity of these its distinct moments, that is, in its absolute truth.

What we have said above about the nature of mind is something which philosophy alone can and does demonstrate; it does not need to be confirmed by our ordinary consciousness. But in so far as our non-philosophical thinking, on its part, needs an understandable account of the developed Notion of mind or spirit, it may be reminded that Christian theology, too, conceives of God, that is, of Truth, as spirit and contemplates this, not as something quiescent, something abiding in empty identicalness but as something which necessarily enters into the process of distinguishing itself from itself, of positing its Other, and which comes to itself only through this Other, and by positively overcoming it—not by abandoning it. Theology, as we know, expresses this process in picture-thinking by saying that God the Father (this simple universal or being-within-self), putting aside his solitariness creates Nature (the being that is external to itself, outside of itself), begets a Son (his other 'I'), but in the power of his love beholds in this Other himself, recognizes his likeness therein and in it returns to unity with himself; but this unity is no longer abstract and immediate, but a concrete unity mediated by the moment of difference; it is the Holy Spirit which proceeds from the Father and the Son, reaching its perfect actuality and truth in the community of Christians; and it is as this that God must be known if he is to be grasped in his absolute truth, as the actual Idea in and for itself, and not merely in the form of the pure Notion, of abstract being-within-self, or in the equally untrue form of a detached actuality not corresponding to the universality of his Notion, but in the full agreement of his Notion and his actuality.

So much for the distinctive determinatenesses of external Nature and Mind as such. The explicated difference at the same time provides an indication of the relation in which Nature and mind stand to each other. Since this relation is often misunderstood, this is the appropriate place in which to elucidate it. We have said that mind negates the externality of Nature, assimilates Nature to itself and thereby idealizes it. In finite mind which places Nature outside of it, this idealization has a one-sided shape; here the activity of our willing, as of our thinking, is confronted by an external material which is indifferent to the alteration which we impose on it and suffers quite passively the idealization which thus falls to its lot.

But a different relationship obtains with the mind or spirit that makes world-history. In this case, there no longer stands, on the one side, an activity external to the object, and on the other side, a merely passive object: but the spiritual activity is directed to an object which is active in itself, an object which has spontaneously worked itself up into the result to be brought about by that activity, so that in the activity and in the object, one and the same content is present. Thus, for example, the people and the time which were moulded by the activity of Alexander and Caesar as *their* object, on their own part, qualified themselves for the deeds to be performed by these individuals; it is no less true that the time created these men as that it was created by them; they were as much the instruments of the mind or spirit of their time and their people, as conversely, their people served these heroes as an instrument for the accomplishment of their deeds.

Similar to the relationship just delineated is the manner in which the philosophizing mind relates itself to external Nature. That is to say, philosophical thinking knows that Nature is idealized not merely by us, that Nature's asunderness is not an absolutely insuperable barrier for Nature itself, for its Notion; but that the eternal Idea immanent in Nature or, what is the same thing, the essence of mind itself at work within Nature brings about the idealization, the triumph over the asunderness, because this form of mind's existence conflicts with the inwardness of its essence. Therefore philosophy has, as it were, only to watch how Nature itself overcomes its externality, how it takes back what is self-external into the centre of the Idea, or causes this centre to show forth in the external, how it liberates the Notion concealed in Nature from the covering of externality and thereby overcomes external necessity. This transition from necessity to freedom is not a simple transition but a progression through many stages, whose exposition constitutes the Philosophy of Nature. At the highest stage of this triumph over asunderness, in feeling, the essence of mind which is held captive in Nature attains to an incipient being-for-self and begins to be free. By this being-for-self which is itself still burdened with the form of individuality and externality, consequently also with unfreedom, Nature is driven onwards beyond itself to mind as such, that is, to mind which, by thinking, is in the form of universality, of self-existent, actually free mind.

But it is already evident from our preceding exposition that the procession of mind or spirit from Nature must not be understood as if Nature were the absolutely immediate and the *prius*, and the original positing agent, mind, on the contrary, were only something posited by Nature; rather is it Nature which is posited by mind, and the latter is the absolute *prius*. Mind which exists in and for itself is not the mere result of Nature, but is in truth its own result; it brings forth itself from the presuppositions which it makes for itself, from the logical Idea and external Nature, and is as much the truth of the one as of the other, i.e. is the true form of the mind which is only internal, and of the mind which is only external, to itself. The illusory appearance which makes mind seem to be mediated by an Other is removed by mind itself, since this has, so to speak, the sovereign ingratitude of ridding itself of, of mediatizing, that by which it appears to be mediated, of reducing it to something dependent solely on mind and in this way making itself completely self-subsistent.

From what has been said, it already follows that the transition from Nature to mind is not a transition to an out-and-out Other, but is only a coming-to-itself of mind out of its self-externality in Nature. But equally, the differentia of Nature and mind is not abolished by this transition, for mind does not proceed in a natural manner from Nature. When it was said in § 222 that the death of the merely immediate, individual form of life is the procession of mind or spirit, this procession is not 'according to the flesh' but spiritual, is not to be understood as a natural procession but as a development of the Notion: for in the Notion, the one-sidedness of the genus which fails properly to actualize itself, proving itself in death to be rather the negative power opposed to that actuality, and also the opposite one-sidedness of the animal existence which is tied to individuality, these are both overcome in the individuality which is in and for itself universal or, what is the same thing, in the universal which exists for itself in a universal mode, which universal is mind.

Nature as such in its inwardizing of itself does not attain to this being-for-self, to the consciousness of itself; the animal, the most perfect form of this inwardization, represents only the non-spiritual dialectic of transition from one single sensation filling its whole soul to another single sensation which equally exclusively dominates it; it is man who first raises himself above the singleness of sensation to the universality of thought, to self-knowledge, to the grasp of his subjectivity, of his 'I' in a word, it is only man who is thinking mind and by this, and by this alone, is essentially distinguished from Nature. What belongs to Nature as such lies at the back of mind; it is true that mind has within itself the entire filling of Nature, but in mind the determinations of Nature exist in a radically different manner from their existence in external Nature.

§ 382

For this reason the essential, but formally essential, feature of mind is Liberty: i.e. it is the notion's absolute negativity or self-identity. Considered as this formal aspect, it *may* withdraw itself from everything external and from its own externality, its very existence; it can thus submit to infinite *pain*, the negation of its individual immediacy: in other words, it can keep itself affirmative in this negativity and possess its own identity. All this is possible so long as it is considered in its abstract self-contained universality.

Zusatz. The substance of mind is freedom, i.e. the absence of dependence on an Other, the relating of self to self. Mind is the actualized Notion which is for itself and has itself for object. Its truth and its freedom alike consist in this unity of Notion and objectivity present in it. The truth, as Christ said, makes spirit free; freedom makes it true. But the freedom of mind or spirit is not merely an absence of dependence on an Other won outside of the Other, but won in it; it attains actuality not by fleeing from the Other but by overcoming it. Mind can step out of its abstract, self-existent universality, out of its simple self-relation, can posit within itself a determinate, actual difference, something other than the simple 'I', and hence a negative; and this relation to the Other is, for mind, not merely possible but necessary, because it is through the Other and by the triumph over it, that mind comes to authenticate itself and to be in fact what it ought to be according to its Notion, namely, the ideality of the external, the Idea which returns to itself out of its otherness; or, expressed more abstractly, the self-differentiating universal which in its difference is at home with itself and for itself. The Other, the negative, contradiction, disunity, therefore also belongs to the nature of mind. In this disunity lies the possibility of *pain*. Pain has therefore not reached mind from the outside as is supposed when it is asked in what manner pain entered into the world. Nor does evil, the negative of absolutely self-existent infinite mind, any more than pain, reach mind from the outside; on the contrary, evil is nothing else than mind which puts its separate individuality before all else. Therefore, even in this its extreme disunity, in this violent detachment of itself from the root of its intrinsically ethical nature, in this complete self-contradiction, mind yet remains identical with itself and therefore free. What belongs to external Nature is destroyed by contradiction; if, for example, gold were given a different specific gravity from what it has, it would cease to be gold. But mind has power to preserve itself in contradiction, and, therefore, in pain; power over evil, as well as over misfortune. Ordinary logic is, therefore, in error in supposing that mind completely excludes contradiction from itself. On the contrary, all consciousness contains a unity and a dividedness, hence a contradiction. Thus, for example, the idea of 'house' is completely contradictory to my 'I' and yet the latter endures it. But mind endures contradiction because it knows that it contains no determination that it has not posited itself, and consequently that it cannot in turn get rid of. This power over every content present in it forms the basis of the freedom of mind. But in its immediacy, mind is free only implicitly, in principle or potentially, not yet in actuality; actual freedom does not therefore belong to mind in its immediacy but has to be brought into being by mind's own activity. It is thus as the creator of its freedom that we have to consider mind in philosophy. The entire development of the Notion of mind represents only mind's freeing of itself from all its existential forms which do not accord with its Notion: a liberation which is brought about by the transformation of these forms into an actuality perfectly adequate to the Notion of mind.

§ 383

This universality is also its determinate sphere of being. Having a being of its own, the universal is self-particularizing, whilst it still remains self-identical. Hence the special mode of mental being is *'manifestation'*. The spirit is not some one mode or meaning which finds utterance or externality only in a form distinct from itself: it does not manifest or reveal *something*, but its very mode and meaning is this revelation. And thus in its mere possibility mind is at the same moment an infinite, 'absolute', *actuality*.

Zusatz. Earlier on, we placed the differentia of mind in *ideality*, in the abolition of the otherness of the Idea. If, now, in § 383 above, 'manifestation' is assigned as the determinateness of mind, this is not a new, not a second, determination of mind, but only a development of the determination discussed earlier. For by getting rid of its otherness, the logical Idea, or mind which is only in itself, becomes for itself, in other words, becomes manifest to itself. Mind which is for itself, or mind as such—in distinction from mind which does not know itself and is manifest only to us, which is poured out into the asunderness of Nature and only ideally present therein—is, therefore, that which manifests itself not merely to an Other but to itself; or, what amounts to the same thing, is that which accomplishes its manifestation in its own element, not in an alien material. This determination belongs to mind as such; it holds true therefore of mind not only in so far as this relates itself simply to itself and is an 'I' having itself for object, but also in so far as mind steps out of its abstract, self-existent universality, posits within itself a specific distinction, something other than itself; for mind does not lose itself in this Other, but, on the contrary, preserves and actualizes itself therein, impresses it with mind's own inner nature, converts the Other into an existence corresponding to it, and therefore by this triumph over the Other, over the specific, actual difference, attains to concrete being-for-self, becomes definitely manifest to itself. In the Other, therefore, mind manifests only itself, its own nature; but this consists in self-manifestation. The manifestation of itself to itself is therefore itself the content of mind and not, as it were, only a form externally added to the content; consequently mind, by its manifestation, does not manifest a content different from its form, but manifests its form which expresses the entire content of mind, namely, its self-manifestation. In mind, therefore, form and content are identical with each other. Admittedly, manifestation is usually thought of as an empty form to which must still be added a content from elsewhere; and by content is understood a being-within-self which remains within itself, and by form, on the other hand, the external mode of the relation of the content to something else. But in speculative logic it is demonstrated that, in truth, the content is not merely something which is and remains within itself, but something which spontaneously enters into relation with something else; just as, conversely, in truth, the form must be grasped not merely as something dependent on and external to the content, but rather as that which makes the content into a content, into a being-within-self, into something distinct from something else. The true content contains, therefore, form within itself, and the true form is its own content. But we have to know mind as this true content and as this true form.

In order to elucidate for ordinary thinking this unity of form and content present in mind, the unity of manifestation and what is manifested, we can refer to the teaching of the Christian religion. Christianity says: God has revealed himself through Christ, his only-begotten Son. Ordinary thinking straightway interprets this statement to mean that Christ is only the organ of this revelation, as if what is revealed in this manner were something other than the source of the revelation. But, in truth, this statement properly means that God has revealed that his nature consists in having a Son, i.e. in making a distinction within himself, making himself finite, but in his difference remaining in communion with himself, beholding and revealing himself in the Son, and that by this unity with the Son, by this being-for-himself in the Other, he is absolute mind or spirit; so that the Son is not the mere organ of the revelation but is himself the content of the revelation.

Just as mind represents the unity of form and content, so too is it the unity of possibility and actuality. We understand by the possible as such, that which is still inward, that which has not yet come to utterance, to manifestation. But now we have seen that mind as such only is, in so far as it manifests itself to itself. Actuality, which consists just in mind's manifestation, belongs therefore to its Notion. In finite mind the Notion of mind does not, of course, reach its absolute actualization; but absolute mind is the absolute unity of actuality and the Notion or possibility of mind.

§ 384

Revelation, taken to mean the revelation of the *abstract* Idea, is an unmediated transition to Nature which *comes* to be. As mind is free, its manifestation is to *set forth* Nature as *its* world; but because it is reflection, it, in thus setting forth its world, at the same time *presupposes* the world as a nature independently existing. In the intellectual sphere to reveal is thus to create a world as its being—a being in which the mind procures the *affirmation* and *truth* of its freedom.

The Absolute is Mind (Spirit)—this is the supreme definition of the Absolute. To find this definition and to grasp its meaning and burden was, we may say, the ultimate purpose of all education and all philosophy: it was the point to which turned the impulse of all religion and science: and it is this impulse that must explain the history of the world. The word 'Mind' (Spirit)—and some glimpse of its meaning—was found at an early period: and the spirituality of God is the lesson of Christianity. It remains for philosophy in its own element of intelligible unity to get hold of what was thus given as a mental image, and what implicitly is the ultimate reality; and that problem is not genuinely, and by rational methods, solved so long as liberty and intelligible unity is not the theme and the soul of philosophy.

Zusatz. Self-manifestation is a determination belonging to mind as such; but it has three distinct forms. The first mode in which mind, as [only] in itself or as the logical Idea, manifests itself, consists in the direct release (*Umschlagen*) of the Idea into the immediacy of external and particularized existence. This release is the coming-to-be of Nature. Nature, too, is a posited existence; but its positedness has the form of immediacy, of a being outside of the Idea. This form contradicts the inwardness of the self-positing Idea which brings forth itself from its presuppositions. The Idea, or mind implicit, slumbering in Nature, overcomes, therefore, the externality, separateness, and immediacy, creates for itself an existence conformable to its inwardness and universality and thereby becomes mind which is reflected into itself and is for itself, self-conscious and awakened mind or mind as such.

This gives the second form of mind's manifestation. On this level, mind which is no longer poured out into the asunderness of Nature but exists for itself and is manifest to itself, opposes itself to unconscious Nature which just as much conceals mind as manifests it. Mind converts Nature into an object confronting it, reflects on it, takes back the externality of Nature into its own inwardness, idealizes Nature and thus in its object becomes for itself. But this first being-for-self of mind is itself still immediate, abstract, not absolute; the self-externality of mind is not absolutely overcome by it. The awakening mind does not yet discern here its unity with the mind concealed and implicit in Nature, to which it stands, therefore, in an external relation, does not appear as all in all, but only as one side of the relation; it is true that in its relation to the Other it is also reflected into itself and so is self-consciousness, but yet it lets this unity of consciousness and self-consciousness still exist as a unity that remains so external, empty and superficial that in it self-consciousness and consciousness still fall asunder; and mind, despite its self-communion is at the same time in communion not with itself but with an Other, and its unity with the mind implicitly present and active in the Other does not as yet become *for* mind. Here, mind posits Nature as a reflectedness-into-self, as *its* world, strips Nature of its form of otherness and converts the Other confronting it into something it has itself posited; but, at the same time, this Other still remains independent of mind, something immediately given, not posited but only presupposed by mind, as something, therefore, the positing of which is antecedent to reflective thought. Hence from this standpoint the positedness of Nature by mind is not yet absolute but is effected only in the reflective consciousness; Nature is, therefore, not yet comprehended as existing only through infinite mind, as its creation. Here, consequently, mind still has in Nature a limitation and just by this limitation is finite mind.

Now this limitation is removed by absolute knowledge, which is the third and supreme manifestation of mind. On this level there vanishes, on the one hand, the dualism of a self-subsistent Nature or of mind poured out into asunderness, and, on the other hand, the merely incipient self-awareness of mind which, however, does not yet comprehend its unity with the former. Absolute mind knows that it posits being itself, that it is itself the creator of its Other, of Nature and finite mind, so that this Other loses all semblance of independence in face of mind, ceases altogether to be a limitation for mind and appears only as a means whereby mind attains to absolute being-for-self, to the absolute unity of what it is in itself and what it is for itself, of its Notion and its actuality.

The highest definition of the Absolute is that it is not merely mind in general but that it is mind which is absolutely manifest to itself, self-conscious, infinitely creative mind, which we have just characterized as the third form of its manifestation. Just as in philosophy we progress from the imperfect forms of mind's manifestation delineated above to the highest form of its manifestation, so, too, world-history exhibits a series of conceptions of the Eternal, the last of which first shows forth the Notion of absolute mind. The oriental religions, and the Hebrew, too, stop short at the still abstract concept of God and of spirit (as is done even by the Enlightenment which wants to know only of God the Father); for God the Father, by himself, is the God who is shut up within himself, the abstract god, therefore not yet the spiritual, not yet the true God. In the Greek religion God did, indeed, begin to be manifest in a definite manner. The representation of the Greek gods had beauty for its law, Nature raised to the level of mind. The Beautiful does not remain something abstractly ideal, but in its ideality is at once perfectly determinate, individualized. The Greek gods are, however, at first only representations for sensuous intuition or for picture-thinking, they are not yet grasped in thought. But the medium of sense can only exhibit the totality of mind as an asunderness, as a circle of independent, mental or spiritual shapes; the unity embracing all these shapes remains, therefore, a wholly indeterminate, alien power over against the gods. It is in the Christian religion that the immanently differentiated *one* nature of God, the totality of the divine mind in the form of unity, has first been manifested. This content, presented in the guise of picture-thinking, has to be raised by philosophy into the form of the Notion or of absolute knowledge which, as we have said, is the highest manifestation of that content.

Subdivision

§ 385

The development of Mind (Spirit) is in three stages:

(1) In the form of self-relation: within it it has the *ideal* totality of the Idea—i.e. it has before it all that its notion contains: its being is to be self-contained and free. This is *Mind Subjective.*

(2) In the form of *reality*: realized, i.e. in a *world* produced and to be produced by it: in this world freedom presents itself under the shape of necessity. This is *Mind Objective.*

(3) In that unity of mind as objectivity and of mind as ideality and concept, which essentially and actually is and for ever produces itself, mind in its absolute truth. This is *Mind Absolute.*

Zusatz. Mind is always Idea; but to begin with it is only the Notion of the Idea, or the Idea in its indeterminateness, in the most abstract mode of reality, in other words, in the mode of being. In the beginning we have only the quite universal, undeveloped determination of mind, not yet mind in its particular aspect; this we obtain only when we pass from one thing to something else: for the particular contains a One and an Other; but it is just at the beginning that we have not yet made this transition. The reality of mind is, therefore, to begin with still a quite universal, not particularized reality: the development of this reality will be completed only by the entire Philosophy of Mind. The still quite abstract, immediate reality is, however, the natural, the unspiritual. This is the reason why the child is still in the grip of natural life, has only natural impulses, is not actually but only potentially or notionally a rational being. Accordingly, we must characterize the first reality of mind as the most inappropriate for mind, simply because it is still an abstract, immediate reality in the natural sphere; but the true reality must be defined as the totality of the developed moments of the Notion which remains the soul, the unity of these moments. In this development of its reality, the Notion's progress is prescribed by necessity, for the form of immediacy, of indeterminateness, which its reality has at first is in contradiction with it; that which in mind appears to be immediately present is not truly immediate, but is intrinsically something posited, mediated. Mind is impelled by this contradiction to rid itself of its own presupposition in the guise of immediacy, of otherness. It is by doing this that it first comes to itself, first emerges *as* mind. Consequently, we cannot begin with mind as such, but must start from its most inappropriate reality. Mind, it is true, is already mind at the outset, but it does not yet know that it is. It is not mind itself that, at the outset, has already grasped its Notion: it is only we who contemplate it who know its Notion. That mind comes to a knowledge of what it is, this constitutes its realization. Mind is essentially only what it knows itself to be. At first, it is only potentially mind; its becoming-for-itself makes it an actuality. But it becomes for itself only by particularizing, determining itself, making itself into its own presupposition, into the Other of itself, first relating itself to this Other as to its immediacy, but making itself free of this Other *qua* Other. As long as mind stands related to itself as to an Other, it is only *subjective* mind, originating in Nature and at first itself natural mind. But the entire activity of subjective mind is directed to grasping itself as its own self, proving itself to be the ideality of its immediate reality. When it has attained to a being-for-self, then it is no longer merely subjective, but *objective* mind. Whereas subjective mind on account of its connection with an Other is still unfree or, what is the same thing, is free only in principle, in objective mind there comes into existence freedom, mind's knowledge of itself as free. Mind that is objective is a person, and as such has a reality of its freedom in property; for in property, the thing is posited as what it is, namely, something lacking a subsistence of its own, something which essentially has the significance of being only the reality of the free will of a person, and for that reason, of being for any other person inviolable. Here we see a subjective mind that knows itself to be free, and, at the same time, an external reality of this freedom; here, therefore, mind attains to a being-for-self, the objectivity of mind receives its due. Thus mind has emerged from the form of mere subjectivity. But the full realization of that freedom which in property is still incomplete, still [only] formal, the consummation of the realization of the Notion of objective mind, is achieved only in the State, in which mind develops its freedom into a world posited by mind itself, into the ethical world. Yet mind must pass beyond this level too. The defect of this objectivity of mind consists in its being only posited. Mind must again freely let go the world, what mind has posited must at the same time be grasped as having an immediate being. This happens on the third level of mind, the standpoint of absolute mind, i.e. of art, religion, and philosophy.

§ 386

The two first parts of the doctrine of Mind embrace the finite mind. Mind is the infinite Idea, and finitude here means the disproportion between the concept and the reality—but with the qualification that it is a shadow cast by the mind's own light—a show or illusion which the mind implicitly imposes as a barrier to itself, in order, by its removal, actually to realize and become conscious of freedom as *its* very being, i.e. to be fully *manifested*. The several steps of this activity, on each of which, with their semblance of being, it is the function of the finite mind to linger, and through which it has to pass, are steps in its liberation. In the full truth of that liberation is given the identification of the three stages—finding a world presupposed before us, generating a world as our own creation, and gaining freedom from it and in it. To the infinite form of this truth the show purifies itself till it becomes a consciousness of it.

A rigid application of the category of finitude by the abstract logician is chiefly seen in dealing with Mind and reason: it is held not a mere matter of strict logic, but treated also as a moral and religious concern, to adhere to the point of view of finitude, and the wish to go further is reckoned a mark of audacity, if not of insanity, of thought. Whereas in fact such a *modesty* of thought, as treats the finite as something altogether fixed and *absolute*, is the worst of virtues; and to stick to a post which has no sound ground in itself is the most unsound sort of theory. The category of finitude was at a much earlier period elucidated and explained at its place in the Logic: an elucidation which, as in logic for the more specific though still simple thought-forms of finitude, so in the rest of philosophy for the concrete forms, has merely to show that the finite *is not*, i.e. is not the truth, but merely a transition and an emergence to something higher. This finitude of the spheres so far examined is the dialectic that makes a thing have its cessation by another and in another: but Spirit, the intelligent unity and the *implicit* Eternal, is itself just the consummation of that internal act by which nullity is nullified and vanity is made vain. And so, the modesty alluded to is a retention of this vanity—the finite—in opposition to the true: it is itself therefore vanity. In the course of the mind's development we shall see this vanity appear as *wickedness* at that turning-point at which mind has reached its extreme immersion in its subjectivity and its most central contradiction.

Zusatz. Subjective and objective mind are still finite. But it is necessary to know what we mean by the finitude of mind. This is usually thought of as an absolute limitation, as a fixed quality, the removal of which would result in mind ceasing to be mind; just as the essence of natural things is tied to a specific quality, as, for example, gold cannot be separated from its specific gravity, this or that animal cannot be without claws, incisors, etc. But in truth, the finitude of mind must be regarded not as a fixed determination, but must be recognized as a mere moment; for as we have already said, mind is essentially the Idea in the form of ideality, in other words, in the form of the negatedness of the finite. In mind, therefore, the finite has only the significance of a being which is not simply affirmative but has been reduced to a moment. Accordingly, the peculiar quality of mind is rather to be the true infinite, that is, the infinite which does not one-sidedly stand over against the finite but contains the finite within itself as a moment. It is, therefore, meaningless to say: There are finite minds. Mind *qua* mind *is* not finite, it *has* finitude within itself, but only as a finitude which is to be, and has been, reduced to a moment. The genuine definition of finitude here—this is not the place for a detailed discussion of it—must be that the finite is a reality that is not adequate to its Notion. Thus the sun is a finite entity, for it cannot be thought without other entities, since the reality of its Notion comprises not merely the sun itself but the entire solar system. Indeed, the whole solar system is a finite entity, because every heavenly body in it exhibits an illusory independence of the others; consequently this collective reality does not as yet correspond to its Notion, does not as yet represent the same ideality which the nature of the Notion is. It is only the reality of mind that is itself ideality, and it is therefore only in mind that we find absolute unity of Notion and reality, and hence true infinitude. The very fact that we know a limitation is evidence that we are beyond it, evidence of our freedom from limitation. Natural objects are finite simply because their limitation does not exist for the objects themselves, but only for us who compare them with one another. We make ourselves finite by receiving an Other into our consciousness; but in the very fact of our knowing this Other we have transcended this limitation. Only he who does not know is limited, for he does not know his limitation; whereas he who knows the limitation knows it, not as a limitation of his knowing, but as something known, as something belonging to his knowledge; only the unknown would be a limitation of knowledge, whereas the known limitation, on the contrary, is not; therefore to know one's limitation means to know of one's unlimitedness. But when we pronounce mind to be unlimited, truly infinite, this does not mean that mind is free from any limitation whatsoever; on the contrary, we must recognize that mind must determine itself and so make itself finite, limit itself. But the abstractive intellect (*Verstand*) is wrong in treating this finitude as something inflexible, in holding the difference between the limitation and infinitude to be absolutely fixed, and accordingly maintaining that mind is *either* limited *or* unlimited. Finitude, truly comprehended, is as we have said, contained in infinitude, limitation in the unlimited. Mind is, therefore, *as well* infinite *as* finite, and *neither* merely the one *nor* merely the other; in making itself finite it remains infinite, for it reduces the finitude within it to a mere moment; nothing in it is fixed, simply affirmatively present but, on the contrary, everything is only an ideal moment, only an appearance. So must God, because he is mind or spirit, determine himself, posit finitude in himself (else he would be only a dead, empty abstraction); but since the reality he gives himself by his self-determining is perfectly conformable to him, God is not thereby made finite. Therefore, limitation *is* not in God and in mind: it is only posited by mind in order to be reduced to a moment. Only momentarily can mind seem to be fixed in a finite content; by its ideality it is raised above it and it knows that the limitation is not a permanent one. It therefore transcends it, frees itself from it; and this liberation is not, as the abstractive intellect supposes, something never completed, a liberation only striven for endlessly; on the contrary, mind wrests itself out of this progress to infinity, frees itself absolutely from the limitation, from its Other, and so attains to absolute being-for-self, makes itself truly infinite.

SECTION ONE ← MIND SUBJECTIVE

§ 387

Mind, on the ideal stage of its development, is mind as *cognitive*. Cognition, however, being taken here not as a merely logical category of the Idea (§ 223), but in the sense appropriate to the *concrete* mind.

Subjective mind is:

(A) Immediate or implicit: a soul—the Spirit in *Nature*—the object treated by *Anthropology*.

(B) Mediate or explicit: still as identical reflection into itself and into other things: mind in correlation or particularization: consciousness—the object treated by the *Phenomenology of Mind*.

(C) Mind defining itself in itself, as an independent subject— the object treated by *Psychology*.

In the *Soul* is the *awaking* of *Consciousness*: Consciousness sets itself up as Reason, awaking at one bound to the sense of its rationality: and this Reason by its activity emancipates itself to objectivity and the consciousness of its intelligent unity.

For an intelligible unity or principle of comprehension each modification it presents is an advance of *development*: and so in mind every character under which it appears is a stage in a process of specification and development, a step forward towards its goal, in order to make itself into, and to realize in itself, what it implicitly is. Each step, again, is itself such a process, and its product is that what the mind was implicitly at the beginning (and so for the observer) it is *for itself*—for the special form, viz. which the mind has in that step. The ordinary method of psychology is to narrate what the mind or soul is, what happens to it, what it does. The soul is presupposed as a ready-made agent, which displays such features as its acts and utterances, from which we can learn what it is, what sort of faculties and powers it possesses—all without being aware that the act and utterance of what the soul is really invests it with that character in our conception and makes it reach a higher stage of being than it explicitly had before.

We must, however, distinguish and keep apart from the progress here to be studied what we call education and instruction. The sphere of education is the individuals only: and its aim is to bring the universal mind to exist in them. But in the philosophic theory of mind, mind is studied as self-instruction and self-education in very essence; and its acts and utterances are stages in the process which brings it forward to itself, links it in unity with itself, and so makes it actual mind.

Zusatz. In § 385 we distinguished the three main forms of Mind: subjective, objective, and absolute Mind, and also pointed out the necessity of the progress from the first to the second and from this to the third. We called the first form of mind we have to consider *subjective* mind, because here mind is still in its undeveloped Notion, has not as yet made its Notion an object for itself. But in this its subjectivity mind is at the same time objective, has an immediate reality by overcoming which it first becomes for itself, attains to a grasp of its Notion, of its subjectivity. We could therefore just as well say that mind is, to begin with, objective and has to become subjective, as conversely, that it is first subjective and has to make itself objective. Consequently, we must not regard the difference between subjective and objective mind as fixed. Even at the beginning, we have to grasp mind not as mere Notion, as something merely subjective, but as Idea, as a unity of subjectivity and objectivity, and any progress from this beginning is a movement away from and beyond the first, simple subjectivity of mind, a progress in the development of its reality or objectivity. This development brings forth a succession of shapes; these, it is true, must be specified empirically, but in the philosophical treatment cannot remain externally juxtaposed, but must be known as the corresponding expression of a necessary series of specific Notions, and they are of interest to philosophy only in so far as they express such a series of Notions. However, at first, we can only assert what the different forms of subjective mind are; their necessity will emerge only from the specific development of subjective mind.

The three main forms of subjective mind are: (1) Soul, (2) Consciousness, and (3) Mind as such. As soul, mind has the form of abstract universality, as consciousness, that of particularization, and as explicitly for itself, that of individuality. This is how subjective mind in its development represents the development of the Notion. The reason why, in the above Paragraph, the names Anthropology, Phenomenology, and Psychology have been given to the parts of the science corresponding to these three forms of subjective mind, will become evident from a more detailed, provisional statement of the contents of the science of subjective mind.

We must begin our treatment with immediate mind; but this is natural mind, *soul*. To suppose that we begin with the mere Notion of mind would be a mistake; for as we have already said, mind is always Idea, therefore realized Notion. But at the beginning, the Notion of mind cannot as yet have the mediated reality which it receives in abstract thought; true, at the beginning, its reality, too, must already be an abstract one, only thus does it correspond to the ideality of mind; but it is necessarily a reality that is still unmediated, not yet posited, consequently a simply affirmative reality given by Nature and external to mind. We must start, therefore, from mind which is still in the grip of Nature and connected with its corporeity, mind which is not as yet in communion with itself, not yet free. This—if we may so express it—basis of man is the subject-matter of Anthropology. In this part of the science of subjective mind, the thought Notion of mind is only in us who think it, not as yet in the object itself; the object of our treatment here is formed by the, at first, merely immediate Notion of mind, mind which has not as yet grasped its Notion and is still external to itself.

The first stage in Anthropology is the qualitatively determined soul which is tied to its natural forms (racial differences, for example, belong here). Out of this immediate oneness with its natural aspect, soul enters into opposition and conflict with it (this embraces the states of insanity and somnambulism). The outcome of this conflict is the triumph of the soul over its corporeity, the process of reducing, and the accomplished reduction of, this corporeity to a sign, to the representation of the soul. The ideality of the soul thus becomes apparent in its corporeity and this reality of mind is posited as ideal but in a still corporeal mode.

In Phenomenology, the soul, by the negation of its corporeity, raises itself to purely ideal self-identity, becomes *consciousness*, becomes 'I', is for itself over against its Other. But this first being-for-self of mind is still conditioned by the Other from which it proceeds. The 'I' is still perfectly empty, a quite abstract subjectivity which posits the whole content of immediate mind outside of it and relates itself to it as to a world already in existence. Thus what was at first only *our* object, does indeed become an object for mind itself, but the 'I' does not as yet know that what confronts it is natural mind itself. Therefore, the 'I', in spite of its being-for-self, is at the same time still not for itself, for it is only in relation to an Other, to something given. The freedom of the 'I' is consequently only an abstract, conditioned, relative freedom. True, mind here is no longer immersed in Nature but reflected into itself and in a relation to Nature, but it only *appears*, stands only in a relation to actuality, is not yet *actual* mind. Therefore, we call the part of the science in which this form of mind is treated, Phenomenology. But now the 'I', in reflecting itself out of its relation-to-other into itself, becomes *self*-consciousness. In this form, the 'I' at first knows itself only as the empty, unfulfilled 'I', and all concrete content as something other than it. Here the activity of the 'I' consists in filling the void of its abstract subjectivity, in building objectivity into itself but, on the other hand, in making subjectivity objective. In this way, self-consciousness overcomes the one-sidedness of its subjectivity, breaks away from its particularity, from its opposition to objectivity, and attains to the universality which embraces both sides and represents within itself the immanent unity of itself with consciousness; for the content of mind here becomes an objective content as in consciousness, and at the same time, as in self-consciousness, a subjective content. This universal self-consciousness is, in itself or for us, Reason; but it is only in the third part of the science of subjective mind that Reason becomes objective to itself.

This third part, Psychology, treats of mind as such, mind which, in the object, is only *self*-related, is occupied only with its own determinations, mind which grasps its own Notion. Thus mind comes to its truth; for the unity of subjectivity and objectivity which, in mere soul, is still immediate, still abstract, is now, after the resolution of the opposition arising in consciousness between these determinations, restored as a mediated unity; and the Idea of mind, leaving behind it its contradictory form of simple Notion and the equally contradictory separation of its moments, attains, therefore, to a mediated unity and accordingly to true actuality. In this shape, mind is Reason which is explicitly for itself. Mind and Reason stand in a similar relation to each other as body and its heaviness, as will and freedom. Reason forms the substantial nature of mind; it is only another expression for Truth or the Idea which constitutes the essence of mind; but it is only mind as such that knows that its nature is Reason and Truth. Mind which embraces both sides, subjectivity and objectivity, now posits itself first in the form of subjectivity: as such it is Intelligence; secondly, in the form of objectivity: as such it is Will. Intelligence, which is itself at first without content, sets aside its form of subjectivity which does not conform to the Notion of mind, by applying to the objective content confronting it which is still burdened with the form of an isolated *datum*, the absolute standard of Reason, clothes this content with rationality, informs it with the Idea, transforms it into a concrete universal, and thus receives it into itself. Intelligence thereby reaches the stage where what it knows is no abstraction but the objective Notion, and where, on the other hand, the object loses its character of 'givenness' and acquires the shape of a content belonging to mind itself. But intelligence, in becoming aware that it is itself the source of its content, becomes practical mind which sets only itself for its goal, becomes *will* which, unlike intelligence, does not begin with an isolated object externally given, but with something it knows to be its own. Then, reflecting itself into itself out of this content of impulses, tendencies, it relates the content to a universal; and lastly, it raises itself to the willing of the universal in and for itself, of freedom, of its Notion. Having reached this goal, mind has just as much returned to its beginning, to self-unity, as it has progressed to absolute, truly immanently determined self-unity, to a unity in which the determinations are determinations not of Nature but of the Notion.

A. ANTHROPOLOGY

THE SOUL

§ 388

Spirit (Mind) *came into* being as the truth of Nature. But not merely is it, as such a result, to be held the true and real first of what went before: this becoming or transition bears in the sphere of the notion the special meaning of *'free judgement'*. Mind, thus come into being, means therefore that Nature in its own self realizes its untruth and sets itself aside: it means that Mind presupposes itself no longer as the universality which in corporal individuality is always self-externalized, but as a universality which in its concretion and totality is one and simple. At such a stage it is not yet mind, but *soul*.

§ 389

The soul is no separate immaterial entity. Wherever there is Nature, the soul is its universal immaterialism, its simple 'ideal' life. Soul is the *substance* or 'absolute' basis of all the particularizing and individualizing of mind: it is in the soul that mind finds the material on which its character is wrought, and the soul remains the pervading, identical ideality of it all. But as it is still conceived thus abstractly, the soul is only the *sleep* of mind—the passive νοῦς of Aristotle, which is potentially all things.

The question of the immateriality of the soul has no interest, except where, on the one hand, matter is regarded as something *true*, and mind conceived as a *thing*, on the other. But in modern times even the physicists have found matters grow thinner in their hands: they have come upon *imponderable* matters, like heat, light, etc., to which they might perhaps add space and time. These 'imponderables', which have lost the property (peculiar to matter) of gravity and, in a sense, even the capacity of offering resistance, have still, however, a sensible existence and outness of part to part; whereas the *'vital' matter*, which may also be found enumerated among them, not merely lacks gravity, but even every other aspect of existence which might lead us to treat it as material.

The fact is that in the Idea of Life the self-externalism of nature is *implicitly* at an end: subjectivity is the very substance and conception of life—with this proviso, however, that its existence or objectivity is still at the same time forfeited to the sway of self-externalism. It is otherwise with Mind. There, in the intelligible unity which exists as freedom, as absolute negativity, and not as the immediate or natural individual, the object or the reality of the intelligible unity is the unity itself; and so the self-externalism, which is the fundamental feature of matter, has been completely dissipated and transmuted into universality, or the subjective ideality of the conceptual unity. Mind is the existent truth of matter—the truth that matter itself has no truth.

A cognate question is that of the *community of soul and body*. This community (interdependence) was assumed as a *fact*, and the only problem was how to *comprehend* it. The usual answer, perhaps, was to call it an *incomprehensible* mystery; and, indeed, if we take them to be absolutely antithetical and absolutely independent, they are as impenetrable to each other as one piece of matter to another, each being supposed to be found only in the pores of the other, i.e. where the other is not: whence Epicurus, when attributing to the gods a residence in the pores, was consistent in not imposing on them any connection with the world. A somewhat different answer has been given by all philosophers since this relation came to be expressly discussed. Descartes, Malebranche, Spinoza, and Leibniz have all indicated God as this *nexus*. They meant that the finitude of soul and matter were only ideal and unreal distinctions; and, so holding, these philosophers took God, not, as so often is done, merely as another word for the incomprehensible, but rather as the sole true identity of finite mind and matter. But either this identity, as in the case of Spinoza, is too abstract, or, as in the case of Leibniz, though his Monad of monads brings things into being, it does so only by an act of judgement or choice. Hence, with Leibniz, the result is a distinction between soul and the corporeal (or material), and the identity is only like the *copula* of a judgement, and does not rise or develop into system, into the absolute syllogism.

Zusatz. In the introduction to the Philosophy of Mind, we pointed out that Nature itself rids itself of its externality and separateness, of its materiality, as an untruth which is inadequate to its immanent Notion, and that by thus acquiring immateriality it passes over into mind. That is why in the above Paragraph, immediate mind, soul, was defined as immaterial not merely on its own account, but as the universal immateriality of Nature, and also as substance, as unity of thought and being. This unity constitutes the fundamental intuition even in oriental religions. Light, which in the Persian religion was contemplated as the Absolute, signified just as much a spiritual as a natural being. Spinoza grasped this unity more specifically as the absolute foundation of everything. Even though mind may withdraw into itself, may place itself at the extreme point of its subjectivity, yet it is *implicitly* in that unity. But it cannot stop there; it can only attain to absolute being-for-self, to a perfectly adequate form, by developing in an immanent manner the moment of difference, which in substance is still simple, into an actual difference, and by bringing this back into a unity; only by doing this does it rise above the state of sleep which belongs to it as soul. For in soul, the difference is still shrouded in the form of undifferentiatedness and therefore of unconsciousness. The defect of Spinozism consists, therefore, just in this, that in it substance does not progress to its immanent development, the manifold is added to substance only in an external manner. The same unity of thought and being is contained in the νοῦς of Anaxagoras; but this νοῦς fails even more than Spinoza's substance to achieve its own immanent development. Pantheism fails altogether to organize and systematize its content. Where it appears in the form of picture-thinking, it is a reeling life, a bacchanalian intuitive vision, which does not let the individual shapes of the universe show forth in their organized forms but perpetually submerges them in the universal again and indulges in the sublime and the monstrous. This intuition, however, forms a natural starting-point for every sound intelligence. In youth especially, we feel a kinship and sympathy with the whole of Nature through a life which ensouls ourselves and everything around us and so we have a feeling of the world-soul, of the unity of mind and Nature, of the immateriality of the latter.

But when we leave *feeling* behind us and go on to *reflection*, the opposition of soul and matter, of my subjective 'I' and its bodily nature, becomes for us a fixed opposition, and the reciprocal relation of body and soul becomes an interaction of independent entities. The usual physiological and psychological treatment does not know how to overcome the fixity of this opposition. In that treatment, the 'I' as absolutely simple and unitary, this abyss of all general ideas and representations, and Matter as the Many, the Composite, confront each other as sheer opposites, and the answer to the question: How is this Many united with that abstract One, is naturally declared to be impossible.

The immateriality of one side of this opposition, namely, of the soul, is readily conceded; but the other, the material, side remains for us at the standpoint of merely reflective thought as something fixed, as something which we allow to be no less valid than the immateriality of the soul; so we ascribe to what is material the same being as to the immaterial and hold both to be equally substantial and absolute. This mode of treatment also prevailed in former metaphysics. This metaphysics, however, though firmly holding the opposition between the material and the immaterial to be insuperable, yet, on the other hand, unwittingly resolved it again by making the soul a *thing*, consequently, something which, though quite abstract, was for all that sensuously determined. This it did by its inquiry into the seat of the soul: thereby placing this in space; similarly by its inquiry into the origin and decease of the soul: thereby placing it in time; and thirdly, by inquiring into the properties of the soul, for soul was thereby treated as something quiescent, stable, as the focal point of these determinations. Even Leibniz treated soul as a *thing* in making it, like all else, into a monad; the monad is equally quiescent as is a *thing*, and the entire difference between soul and a material thing, according to Leibniz, consists only in soul being a somewhat more distinct, more developed, monad than the rest of matter; a conception whereby matter is doubtless exalted, but soul is degraded to, rather than distinguished from, a material thing.

Speculative logic lifts us above the whole of this merely reflective mode of treatment simply by showing that all those categories applied to the soul like Thing, Simplicity, Indivisibility, One, are untrue and switch round into their opposites. But the Philosophy of Mind continues this proof of the untruth of the categories of the abstractive intellect (*Verstand*) by demonstrating how mind, by its ideality, annuls every fixed category in it.

Now as regards the other side of the opposition in question, namely, *matter*, we have already remarked that externality, separateness, multiplicity, are regarded as its fixed determination, and the unity of this multiplicity is therefore declared to be only a superficial bond, a composition, and accordingly everything material to be divisible. We must, of course, admit that whereas with mind, the concrete unity is the essential feature and the multiplicity is an illusory show, with matter the opposite is true; ancient metaphysics already had a glimpse of this truth when it raised the question of the priority of the One or the Many with mind. But the presupposition that the externality and multiplicity of matter is, for Nature, an insuperable obstacle, is something which, from our standpoint, that of speculative philosophy, we have here long since put behind us as quite false. The Philosophy of Nature teaches us how Nature rids itself of its externality by stages: how matter already refutes the independence of the separate individual, of the Many, by *gravity*, and how this refutation begun by gravity, and still more by simple, indivisible Light, is completed by animal life, by the sentient creature, since this manifests to us the omnipresence of the one soul at every point of its corporeity, and therewith the accomplished triumph over asunderness. Since, then, everything material is overcome by the action of mind implicit in Nature, this triumph being consummated in the substance of soul, the latter emerges as the ideality of *everything* material, as *all* immateriality, so that everything called matter, no matter how much it conveys to ordinary thinking the illusory appearance of independence, is known to have no independence relatively to mind.

The opposition of soul and body must, of course, be made. Just as the indeterminate universal soul determines and individualizes itself, just as mind thereby becomes consciousness—and it needs must progress to this —so does mind place itself at the standpoint of opposition between itself and its Other, so does its Other appear to it as a reality, as external to mind and to itself, as something material. From this standpoint, the question as to the possibility of the community of soul and body is quite natural. If soul and body are absolutely opposed to one another as is maintained by the abstractive intellectual consciousness, then there is no possibility of any community between them. This community was, how-ever, recognized by ancient metaphysics as an undeniable fact. There-fore, the question arose as to how the contradiction, to wit, that entities which are absolutely independent and for themselves, are yet in unity with one another, could be solved. The question as thus posed was un-answerable. But it is just this form of the question that must be recognized as inadmissible; for in truth the immaterial is not related to the material as a particular is to a particular, but as the true universal which overarches and embraces particularity is related to the particular; the particular material thing in its isolation has no truth, no independence in face of the immaterial. Consequently, the standpoint which separates them is not to be regarded as final, as absolutely true. On the contrary, the separation of the material and the immaterial can be explained only on the basis of the original unity of both. Therefore, in the philosophies of Descartes, Malebranche, and Spinoza, a return was made to such unity of thought and being, of spirit and matter, and this unity was placed in God. Malebranche said: 'We see everything in God.' He treated God as the mediation, as the positive medium, between what thinks and what is non-thinking, and, moreover, as the immanent, pervasive Being in which both sides are reduced to moments, consequently, not as a *tertium quid* over against two extremes which themselves possessed actuality; for in that case the question would recur as to how that *tertium quid* came together with these two extremes. But in placing the unity of the material and the immaterial in God, who is to be grasped essentially as spirit, these philosophers wished to make it known that this unity must not be taken as something neutral in which two extremes of equal significance and independence are united, since the material has absolutely no meaning beyond that of being a negative over against spirit and over against itself, or must be described—in the words of Plato and other ancient philoso-phers—as 'the Other of itself', whereas the nature of spirit is to be recognized as the positive, as the speculative, because the material, which lacks independence in face of spirit, is freely pervaded by the latter which overarches this its Other, does not account it as something truly real but reduces it to an ideal moment and to something mediated.

Opposed to this speculative interpretation of the opposition between mind and matter is materialism which represents Thought as resulting from Matter, derives the simplicity of Thought from what is manifold. The explanations given in materialistic writings of the various relationships and combinations which are supposed to produce a result such as Thought, are unsatisfactory in the extreme. Such explanations entirely overlook the fact that, just as the cause is sublated in the effect and the means in the realized end, so, too, that from which Thought is supposed to result is itself deprived of its independence in Thought; also that mind as such is not produced by an Other, but spontaneously raises itself from a merely implicit being to an explicit existence, from its Notion to actuality, and that by which Thought was supposed to be posited is itself converted by Thought into a posited being. All the same, we must recognize in materialism the enthusiastic effort to transcend the dualism which postulates two different worlds as equally substantial and true, to nullify this tearing asunder of what is originally One.

§ 390

The Soul is at first—

(a) In its immediate natural mode—the natural soul, which only *is*.

(b) Secondly, it is a soul which *feels*, as individualized, enters into correlation with its immediate being, and, in the modes of that being, retains an abstract independence.

(c) Thirdly, its immediate being—or corporeity—is moulded into it, and with that corporeity it exists as *actual* soul.

Zusatz. The first part of Anthropology indicated in this Paragraph which embraces the merely immediate natural soul, in its turn splits up into three sections. In the first section we have at first to deal with the still quite universal, immediate substance of mind, with the simple pulsation, the mere inward stirring, of soul. In this rudimentary life of mind there is as yet no posited difference either between individuality and universality or between soul and the natural world. This simple life has its explication in Nature and mind; itself as such merely *is*, has as yet no determinate existence, no particularized being, no actuality. But just as in Logic, being must pass over into determinate being, so soul too necessarily progresses from its indeterminateness to determinateness. This determinateness has, in the first instance, as already remarked, a natural form. But the natural mode of soul is, as totality, to be grasped as a type (*Abbild*) of the Notion. The first stage here consists therefore of the quite

universal, qualitative determinations of soul. To this belong the racial
differences both physical and mental of humanity and also the differences
of national mentality.

These sundered specifications or differences are then taken back into
the unity of soul or, what is the same thing, are carried further to the
point where they become individual souls: this forms the transition to the
second section. Just as light bursts asunder into an infinite host of stars, so
too does the universal natural soul sunder itself into an infinite host of
individual souls; only with this difference, that whereas light appears to
have an existence independently of the stars, the universal natural soul
attains actuality solely in individual souls. Now the separated universal
qualities considered in the first section, in being taken back, as we have
said, into the unity of the individual human soul, acquire in place of
the form of externality the shape of natural *alterations* of the individual
subject who retains his identity throughout. These alterations, alike mental
and physical, are manifested in the successive *ages* of man. Here the
difference ceases to be an external one. But it is in the sexual relation that
the difference becomes the actual specification, the real opposition, of
the individual to itself. From this point onwards, the soul enters into
opposition to its natural qualities, to its universal being which, by this
very act, is reduced to the status of the soul's Other, to a mere aspect, to
a transitory state, namely, the *sleeping* state. Thus originates *natural
waking*, the opening out of the soul. But here in Anthropology we have
not as yet to consider the content of waking consciousness but waking
only in so far as it is a natural state.

Out of this relationship of opposition, or of real specification, soul
now returns, in the third section, to unity with itself; and it does this by
taking from its Other its fixed static character, resolving it into its ideality.
Soul has thus progressed from merely universal and only implicit individuality to explicit, actual individuality; and in doing just this it has
progressed to *feeling*. In the first instance, we have to deal only with the
form of feeling. *What* soul feels will not be specified until we come to
the second part of Anthropology. The transition to this part is formed by
the extension of internal feeling to the soul that has a dim awareness [of
its concrete natural life].

(*a*) THE PHYSICAL SOUL[1]

§ 391

The soul universal, described, it may be, as an *anima mundi*, a
world-soul, must not be fixed on that account as a single subject;
it is rather the universal *substance* which has its actual truth only

[1] Natürliche Seele.

in individuals and single subjects. Thus, when it presents itself
as a single soul, it is a single soul which *is* merely: its only modes
are modes of natural life. These have, so to speak, behind its
ideality a free existence: i.e. they are natural objects for consciousness, but objects to which the soul as such does not behave
as to something external. These features rather are *physical
qualities* of which it finds itself possessed.

Zusatz. The soul, when contrasted with the macrocosm of Nature as a
whole, can be described as the microcosm into which the former is
compressed, thereby removing its asunderness. Accordingly the same
determinations which in outer Nature appear as freely existent spheres,
as a series of independent shapes, are here in the soul deposed to mere
qualities. The soul stands midway between Nature which lies behind her,
on the one hand, and the world of ethical freedom which extricates itself
from natural mind, on the other hand. Just as the simple determinations
of soul-life have their disrupted counterpart in the universal life of Nature,
so that which in the individual man has the form of subjectivity, of a
particular impulse, and is only unconsciously and immediately present
in him, unfolds in the State into a system of distinct spheres of freedom,
into a world created by self-conscious human Reason.

(α) *Physical Qualities*[1]

§ 392

(1) While still a 'substance' (i.e. a physical soul) the mind takes
part in the general planetary life, feels the difference of climates,
the changes of the seasons, and the periods of the day, etc. This
life of nature for the main shows itself only in occasional strain
or disturbance of mental tone.

In recent times a good deal has been said of the cosmical,
sidereal, and telluric life of man. In such a sympathy with nature
the animals essentially live: their specific characters and their
particular phases of growth depend, in many cases completely,
and always more or less, upon it. In the case of man these points
of dependence lose importance, just in proportion to his civilization, and the more his whole frame of soul is based upon a sub-
structure of mental freedom. The history of the world is not

---

[1] Natürliche Qualitäten.

bound up with revolutions in the solar system, any more than the destinies of individuals with the positions of the planets.

The difference of climate has a more solid and vigorous influence. But the response to the changes of the seasons and hours of the day is found only in faint changes of mood, which come expressly to the fore only in morbid states (including insanity) and at periods when the self-conscious life suffers depression.

In nations less intellectually emancipated, which therefore live more in harmony with nature, we find amid their superstitions and aberrations of imbecility *a few* real cases of such sympathy, and on that foundation what seems to be marvellous prophetic vision of coming conditions and of events arising therefrom. But as mental freedom gets a deeper hold, even these few and slight susceptibilities, based upon participation in the common life of nature, disappear. Animals and plants, on the contrary, remain for ever subject to such influences.

Zusatz. It is clear from § 391 and its *Zusatz* that the universal life of Nature is also the life of the soul, that the latter lives in sympathy with that universal life. But it would be a complete mistake to make this participation of the soul in the life of the whole universe into the highest object of the science of mind. For the activity of mind essentially consists just in raising itself above this entanglement in merely natural life, in grasping itself in its self-dependence, subduing the world to its thinking and creating it from the Notion. Therefore in mind, the universal life of Nature is only a quite subordinate moment, the cosmic and telluric powers are dominated by mind in which they can produce only unimportant moods.

Now the universal life of Nature is first, the life of the Solar System generally, and secondly, the life of the Earth, in which the former life receives a more individual form.

As regards the connection of the soul with the Solar System, we may note that astrology links the destinies of humanity and of individuals with the configurations and positions of the planets; (lately, the world in general has been considered as a mirror of mind in the sense that the latter could be explained from the world). The content of astrology is to be rejected as superstition; but science is under the obligation to assign the specific ground for this rejection. This ground must not be simply that the planets are [only] bodies and remote from us, but more specifically that the planetary life of the Solar System is only a life of *motion*, in other words, is a life in which the determining factor is constituted by space and time (for space and time are the moments of motion). The laws of planetary motion are determined solely by the Notion of space and of time; it is, therefore, in the planets that absolutely free motion has its actuality. But even in what is physically individual this abstract motion is a completely subordinate factor; the individual as such makes its own space and time; its alteration is determined by its concrete nature. The animal body attains to even greater self-dependence than the merely physical [inorganic] individual; the course of its development is quite independent of the motions of the planets and the period of its life is not measured by them; its health and the course run by its disease do not depend on the planets; periodic fevers, for example, have their own specific measure, the determinant is not time as time, but the animal organism. But for mind, the abstract determinations of space and time, the mechanics of free motion, have absolutely no significance and no power; the determinations of self-conscious mind are infinitely more sub-stantial, more concrete, than the abstract determinations of juxtaposition and succession. Mind, as embodied, is indeed in a definite place and in a definite time; but for all that it is exalted over them. Of course, the life of man is conditioned by a specific measure of distance, that of the Earth from the Sun; he could not live at either a greater or less distance from the Sun; but the influence of the position of the Earth on mankind does not go beyond that.

The strictly terrestrial phenomena, too—the annual revolution of the Earth round the Sun, the daily axial rotation of the Earth, the inclination of the Earth's axis to the ecliptic—all these determinations belonging to the Earth's individuality, though not without influence on mankind, have no significance on mind as such. The Church itself has therefore rightly rejected as superstitious and unethical the belief in a power exercised over the human spirit by these terrestrial and cosmic relationships. Man should regard himself as free from such relationships of Nature; but in that superstition he thinks of himself as a creature of Nature. Accordingly, too, the efforts of those who would connect the evolutionary epochs of the Earth with the epochs of human history must be pronounced invalid, those who have tried to discover the origins of religions and their symbols in the sphere of astronomy and of natural phenomena and so have hit on the quite baseless idea that with the shifting forward of the equinox from the Bull to the Ram, Apis worship had necessarily to be followed by Chris-tianity, by the worship of the Lamb.

But as regards the actual influence of terrestrial phenomena on man, here we can only mention the main factors, since the details belong to the natural history of man and the Earth. In the seasons and the diurnal periods, the motion of the Earth acquires a physical significance. These alternations do, of course, affect man; the merely natural mind, the soul, lives in sympathy with the mood of the season and of the time of day. But whereas plants are completely bound to the alternation of the seasons and even animals are unconsciously dominated by it, being instinctively impelled to mate and some to migration: in the human soul this alternation does not produce any stimulus to which man would be involuntarily subjected. Winter disposes to withdrawal into onself, to collecting one's thoughts, to family life, to the worship of the *penates*. In summer, on the other hand, we feel more inclined to travel, feel drawn into the open air, and the ordinary folk are moved to go on pilgrimages. Yet there is nothing merely instinctive about either this more intimate family life or these pilgrimages and journeyings. The Christian feasts are linked with the changing seasons; the birth of Christ is celebrated at Christmas when the Sun seems to go forth again; the resurrection of Christ is placed at the beginning of spring, in the period of Nature's awakening. But this association of the religious with the natural, too, is not instinctively but consciously made.

As regards the phases of the Moon, these have only a limited influence even on the physical nature of man. Such an influence has been observed on lunatics; but in these, it is not free mind that prevails but the dominion of Nature. Also the times of day, of course, bring with them a characteristic disposition of the soul. We are attuned to different moods in the morning and evening. In the morning we are more seriously disposed, mind is still more in identity with itself and Nature. The day belongs to opposition, to work. In the evening, reflection and fancy predominate. At midnight, mind retires into itself from the distractions of the day, is alone with itself and inclined to contemplation. Most people die after midnight; human nature is unable to start another day. There is also a certain connection between the times of day and the public life of nations. The ancients, who were more drawn to Nature than we are, held their public assemblies in the morning; in England, on the contrary, in keeping with the introverted character of the English, parliamentary proceedings are started in the evening and sometimes continued far into the night. But these moods produced with the times of the day are modified by climate; in hot countries, for example, one feels at midday more disposed to rest than to activity. With respect to the influence of meteorological changes it can be remarked that sensitivity to these phenomena is distinctly noticeable in plants and animals. Thus animals have presentiments of thunder-storms and earthquakes, i.e. they feel atmospheric changes which are not yet perceptible to us. Human beings, too, feel in wounds changes in the weather not yet indicated by the barometer; the weak spot formed by the wound admits of a greater sensitivity to the dominion of Nature. What thus affects the organism has also a significance for weak minds and is felt as an effect. Indeed whole nations, the Greeks and Romans, made their decisions dependent on natural phenomena which to them seemed to hang together with meterological changes. As we know, they consulted on affairs of State, not only the priests but also the entrails and eating habits of animals. On the day of the battle of Plataea, for example, when the freedom of Greece, perhaps of the whole of Europe, the repulse of oriental despotism, was at stake, Pausanias anxiously spent the whole morning trying to get favourable signs from sacrificed animals. This seems directly to conflict with the nature of the Greek spirit in art, religion, and science, but it can be quite well explained from the standpoint of the Greek spirit. It is characteristic of modern man to make his own decisions and in all cases to follow the course dictated by a prudent consideration of all the circumstances; private persons as well as princes form their own decisions; with us the subjective will cuts across all the grounds recommended by a considered view of the matter and forms the decision to act. The ancients, on the other hand, who had not yet attained to this might of subjectivity, to this strength of self-certainty, let their affairs be decided by an oracle, by external phenomena, in which they sought confirmation and verification of their plans and intentions. Now as regards the case of battle in particular, the important factor is not merely the ethical disposition but also to be in good spirits, to feel physically strong. But with the ancients, this latter was of even more importance than it is with the moderns with whom the main thing is the discipline of the army and the talent of the commander, whereas with the ancients, who lived more in unity with Nature, the most decisive factor in battle was the bravery of individuals whose courage always had its source in their physical nature. Now stoutness of heart is connected with other physical dispositions, e.g. with geographical, atmospheric, seasonal, and climatic conditions. But the sympathetic moods of the ensouled creature are more visibly apparent in animals than in human beings, since the former live in a closer unity with Nature. It was for this reason that the Greek commander only went into battle when he believed he had found in the animals healthy dispositions which seemed to permit the inference of healthy dispositions in his men. So it was that Xenophon who carried out his famous retreat with such skill, sacrificed daily and made his military dispositions in accordance with the result of the sacrifice. But the ancients carried this search for a connection between the natural and the mental or spiritual too far. Their superstition made them see more in the animals' entrails than there is to be seen in them. In doing so, the 'I' surrendered its self-dependence, subjected itself to external circumstances and determinations and treated these as determinations of mind.

§ 393

(2) According to the concrete differences of the terrestrial globe, the general planetary life of the nature-governed mind specializes itself and breaks up into the several nature-governed minds which, on the whole, give expression to the nature of the geographical continents and constitute the diversities of *race*.

The contrast between the earth's poles, the land towards the north pole being more aggregated and preponderant over sea, whereas in the southern hemisphere it runs out in sharp points, widely distant from each other, introduces into the differences of continents a further modification which Treviranus (*Biology*, Part II) has exhibited in the case of the flora and fauna.

Zusatz. With respect to the diversity of races of mankind it must be remembered first of all that the purely historical question, whether all these races sprang from a single pair of human beings or from several, is of no concern whatever to us in philosophy. Importance was attached to this question because it was believed that by assuming descent from several couples, the mental or spiritual superiority of one race over another could be explained, indeed, it was hoped to prove that human beings are by nature so differently endowed with mental or spiritual capacities that some can be dominated like animals. But descent affords no ground for granting or denying freedom and dominion to human beings. Man is implicitly rational; herein lies the possibility of equal justice for all men and the futility of a rigid distinction between races which have rights and those which have none. The difference between the races of mankind is still a natural difference, that is, a difference which, in the first instance, concerns the natural soul. As such, the difference is connected with the geographical differences of those parts of the world where human beings are gathered together in masses. These different parts are what we call continents. In these organic divisions of the Earth's individuality there is an element of necessity, the detailed exposition of which belongs to geography

The basic division of the Earth is into the Old and the New World. In the first instance, this distinction relates to the earlier or later knowledge of the continents in world history. Here, this distinction is for us a matter of indifference. What we are concerned with is the determinateness which constitutes the distinctive character of the continents. In this respect, it must be said that America has a younger appearance than the Old World and in its historical development is inferior to the latter. America exhibits only the general difference of north and south with a quite narrow middle between the two extremes. The indigenous races of this continent are dying out; the Old World is refashioning itself in the New. The Old World is distinguished from America by the fact that it is sundered into specific differences, into three continents, of which one, Africa, taken as a whole, appears as a land mass belonging to a compact unity, as a lofty mountain range shutting off the coast; the second, Asia, presents the antithesis of highlands and great valleys irrigated by broad rivers; while the third, Europe, reveals the unity of the undifferentiated unity of Africa and the unmediated antithesis of Asia, since in it mountain and valley are not juxtaposed as two great halves of the continent as in Asia, but everywhere penetrate each other. These three continents which are circumjacent to the Mediterranean are not separated but linked together by it. North Africa up to the boundary of the sandy desert already by its character belongs to Europe; the inhabitants of this part of Africa are not strictly Africans, that is, negroes, but are akin to Europeans. Similarly the whole of Western Asia is European in character; the Asiatic race proper, the Mongols, inhabit the Far East.

After having thus attempted to show that the differences between the continents are not contingent but necessary, we shall now characterize the racial diversities of humanity in their physical and mental or spiritual bearings which go together with these differences. As regards physical characteristics, physiology distinguishes the Caucasian, Ethiopian, and Mongolian races, with which must also be reckoned the races of Malay and America which, however, form an aggregate of infinitely various particularities rather than a sharply distinct race. Now the physical difference between all these races is shown mainly in the formation of the skull and the face. The formation of the skull is defined by a horizontal and a vertical line, the former running from the outer ear-ducts to the root of the nose, the latter from the frontal bone to the upper jaw-bone. It is by the angle formed by these two lines that the head of the animal is distinguished from the human head; in animals this angle is extremely acute. Another important factor, noted by Blumenbach, concerns the greater or less prominence of the cheek-bones. The arching and width of the forehead is also a determining factor.

Now in the Caucasian race this angle is almost or entirely a right-angle. This applies particularly to the Italian, Georgian, and Circassian physiognomy. In this race the skull is spherical on top, the forehead gently arched, the cheek-bones pushed back, the front teeth in both jaws perpendicular, the skin white with red cheeks and the hair long and soft.

The characteristic of the Mongol race is revealed in the prominence of the cheek-bones, in the eyes which are not round but narrow-slit, in the compressed nose, in the yellow colour of the skin and in the short stiff black hair.

Negroes have narrower skulls than Mongols and Caucasians, their foreheads are arched but bulging, their jaw-bones are prominent and the teeth slope, their lower jaw juts well out, their skin is more or less black, their hair is woolly and black.

The Malayan and American Indian races are less sharply distinguished in their physical formation than the races just described; the skin of the Malays is brown and that of the American Indian copper-coloured.

The mental and spiritual characteristics of these races are as follows.

Negroes are to be regarded as a race of children who remain immersed in their state of uninterested *naïveté*. They are sold, and let themselves be sold, without any reflection on the rights or wrongs of the matter. The Higher which they feel they do not hold fast to, it is only a fugitive thought. This Higher they transfer to the first stone they come across, thus making it their fetish and they throw this fetish away if it fails to help them. Good-natured and harmless when at peace, they can become suddenly enraged and then commit the most frightful cruelties. They cannot be denied a capacity for education; not only have they, here and there, adopted

Christianity with the greatest gratitude and spoken movingly of the freedom they have acquired through Christianity after a long spiritual servitude, but in Haiti they have even formed a State on Christian principles. But they do not show an inherent striving for culture. In their native country the most shocking despotism prevails. There they do not attain to the feeling of human personality, their mentality is quite dormant, remaining sunk within itself and making no progress, and thus corresponding to the compact, differenceless mass of the African continent.

The Mongols, on the other hand, rise above this childish *naïveté*; they reveal as their characteristic feature a restless mobility which comes to no fixed result and impels them to spread like monstrous locust swarms over other countries and then to sink back again into the thoughtless indifference and dull inertia which preceded this outburst. Similarly, the Mongols display in themselves an acute contrast between the sublime and monstrous, on the one hand, and the most trivial, pettiest pedantry, on the other. Their religion already contains the conception of a universal which they venerate as God. But they cannot as yet endure this God as invisible; he is present in human shape, or at least announces himself through some human being or other. This occurs with the Tibetans, where often a child is chosen to be the present, visible god, and when such a god dies, the monks seek another one among the people; but all this succession of gods enjoys the profoundest veneration. The essential feature of this religion reaches as far as India where the Hindus likewise regard a human being, the Brahmin, as god, and the withdrawal of the human spirit into its indeterminate universality is held to be divine, to be the immediate identity with God. In the Asiatic race, therefore, mind is already beginning to awake, to separate itself from the life of Nature. But this separation is not yet clear-cut, not yet absolute. Mind does not as yet grasp itself in its absolute freedom, does not as yet know itself as the concrete universal which is for itself, has not as yet made its Notion into an object for itself in the form of thought. For this reason it still exists as an immediate individual, a form which contradicts the nature of mind. God does indeed become objective, but not in the form of absolutely free thought, but in that of an immediately existent finite mind or spirit. With this is connected the worship of the dead, for in these the life of Nature has perished; the remembrance of them holds fast only to the universal manifested in them and rises, therefore, above the individuality of the manifestation. But the universal is always, on the one hand, held fast only as a quite abstract universal, and on the other hand, is perceived only in an out-and-out contingent, immediate existence. The Hindus, for example, contemplate the universal God as present in the whole of Nature, in rivers and mountains just as in men. Asia represents, therefore, both in a physical and a spiritual reference the moment of opposition, but of unmediated opposition, the mediationless collapse of the opposed determinations. Here, on the one hand, mind separates itself from Nature, and on the other hand, falls back again into the life of Nature, since it attains actuality not within itself but only in the natural sphere. In this identity of mind with Nature true freedom is impossible. Here man cannot as yet attain to consciousness of his personality and in his individuality has neither value nor rights, neither with the Hindus nor the Chinese; the latter have no compunction in exposing or simply destroying their infants.

It is in the Caucasian race that mind first attains to absolute unity with itself. Here for the first time mind enters into complete opposition to the life of Nature, apprehends itself in its absolute self-dependence, wrests itself free from the fluctuation between one extreme and the other, achieves *self*-determination, *self*-development, and in doing so creates world-history. The Mongols, as we have already mentioned, are characterized by an impetuosity which impels them outwards beyond their borders, but it dies away as quickly as it came, acts not constructively but only destructively, and produces no advance in world-history. This advance is first brought about by the Caucasian race.

In this, however, we have to distinguish two sides, the Western Asiatics and the Europeans; this distinction now coincides with that of Mohammedans and Christians.

In Mohammedanism the limited principle of the Jews is expanded into universality and thereby overcome. Here, God is no longer, as with the Asiatics, contemplated as existent in immediately sensuous mode but is apprehended as the one infinite sublime Power beyond all the multiplicity of the world. Mohammedanism is, therefore, in the strictest sense of the word, the religion of sublimity. The character of the western Asiatics, especially the Arabs, is completely in accord with this religion. This race, in its aspiration to the One God, is indifferent to everything finite, to all misery, and gives generously of its life and its wealth; even today its courage and liberality earns our recognition. But the western Asiatic mind which clings to the abstract One does not get as far as the determination, the particularization, of the universal and consequently does not attain to a concrete formation. Here, it is true, this mind destroys the caste system and all its works which prevail in India, and every Mohammedan is free; despotism in the strict meaning of the word does not exist among them. Political life, however, does not yet achieve the form of a rationally organized whole, of a differentiation into special governmental powers. And as regards individuals these, on the one hand, certainly hold themselves sublimely aloof from subjective, finite aims but again, on the other hand, they also hurl themselves with unbridled instincts into the pursuit of such aims which, with them, lack all trace of the universal because here the universal has so far not attained to an immanent self-differentiation. So it is that here, along with the noblest sentiments, there exists the greatest vindictiveness and guile.

Europeans, on the contrary, have for their principle and character the concrete universal, self-determining Thought. The Christian God is not merely the differenceless One, but the triune God who contains difference within himself, who has become man and who reveals himself. In this religious conception the opposition of universal and particular, of Thought and Being, is present in its most developed form and yet has also been brought back again to unity. Here, then, the particular is not left so quiescent in its immediacy as in Mohammedanism; on the contrary, it is determined by thought, just as, conversely, the universal here develops itself to particularization. The principle of the European mind is, therefore, self-conscious Reason which is confident that for it there can be no insuperable barrier and which therefore takes an interest in everything in order to become present to itself therein. The European mind opposes the world to itself, makes itself free of it, but in turn annuls this opposition, takes its Other, the manifold, back into itself, into its unitary nature. In Europe, therefore, there prevails this infinite thirst for knowledge which is alien to other races. The European is interested in the world, he wants to know it, to make this Other confronting him his own, to bring to view the genus, law, universal, thought, the inner rationality, in the particular forms of the world. As in the theoretical, so too in the practical sphere, the European mind strives to make manifest the unity between itself and the outer world. It subdues the outer world to its ends with an energy which has ensured for it the mastery of the world. The individual here, in his particular actions proceeds from fixed general principles; and in Europe the State, by its rational institutions, exhibits more or less the development and realization of freedom unimpeded by the caprice of a despot.

But finally, with regard to the original inhabitants of America, we have to remark that they are a vanishing, feeble race. It is true that in some parts of America at the time of its discovery, a pretty considerable civilization was to be found; this, however, was not comparable with European culture and disappeared with the original inhabitants. In addition, the dullest savages dwell there, e.g. the Pecherais and Eskimos. The Caribs of earlier times are almost completely extinct. When brought into contact with brandy and guns, these savages become extinct. In South America, it is the Creoles who have made themselves independent of Spain; the native Indians were incapable of doing so. In Paraguay, they were just like small children and were even treated as such by the Jesuits. The natives of America are, therefore, clearly not in a position to maintain themselves in face of the Europeans. The latter will begin a new culture over there on the soil they have conquered from the natives.

§ 394

This diversity descends into specialities, that may be termed *local* minds—shown in the outward modes of life and occupation, bodily structure and disposition, but still more in the inner tendency and capacity of the intellectual and moral character of the several peoples.

Back to the very beginnings of national history we see the several nations each possessing a persistent type of its own.

Zusatz. The racial differences depicted in the *Zusatz* to § 393 are the essential ones, the differences of the universal mind in Nature as determined by the Notion. But the mind in Nature does not stop at this general differentiation of itself; the natural mode of mind does not have the power of asserting itself as the pure copy of the determinations of the Notion; it goes on to a further specification of these general differences and lapses into the plurality of local or national minds. The detailed characteristics of these minds belong partly to the natural history of man and partly to the philosophy of world-history. The former science depicts the disposition of national character as affected by natural conditions, physical formation, mode of life, occupation, and also the particular interests to which the intelligence and the will of nations are directed. The philosophy of history, on the other hand, has for its subject-matter the world-historical significance of races, that is to say, if we take world-history in the most comprehensive sense of the word, the highest development to which the original disposition of the national character attains, the most spiritual form to which the natural mind indwelling the nations raises itself. Here in philosophical anthropology we cannot go into the details of this; they are included in the subject-matter of the two sciences just mentioned. We have here to consider national character only in so far as it contains the germ from which the history of nations develops.

As the outset it can be remarked that national differences are just as fixed as the racial diversity of mankind; that the Arabs, for example, still everywhere exhibit the same characteristics as are related of them in the remotest times. The unchangeableness of climate, of the whole character of the country in which a nation has its permanent abode, contributes to the unchangeableness of the national character. A desert, proximity to the sea or remoteness from it, all these circumstances can have an influence on the national character. Specially important in this connection is the contact with the sea. In the interior of Africa proper, surrounded by high mountains in the coastal regions and in this way cut off from this free element of the sea, the mind of the African remains shut up within itself, feels no urge to be free and endures without resistance universal slavery. Proximity to the sea cannot, however, of itself alone make mind or spirit free. This is proved by the natives of India who have slavishly submitted to a law existing among them from the earliest times which forbids them to cross the sea which Nature has opened to them. In this despotic separation of them from this wide, free element, from this natural existence of universality, they show no sign of being able to free themselves from the freedom-destroying ossification of the class divisions

of the caste system which would be intolerable to a nation navigating the
oceans of its own free will.

But now as regards the specific difference of the various national minds,
in the African race this is insignificant in the highest degree; even in the
Asiatic race proper it is much less apparent than in Europeans, in whom
mind or spirit first emerges from its abstract universality to display the
wealth of its particular forms. For this reason, we propose to speak here
only of the immanently varied character of the European peoples, and of
them, only those which are distinguished from one another mainly
by their role in world-history, namely, the Greeks, the Romans, and
the Germanic races. Nor shall we characterize them in their mutual
relationships, a task we must leave to the philosophy of history. On
the other hand, we can indicate here the differences within the Greek
nation and among those Christian peoples of Europe which are more or
less permeated by Germanic elements, which have made themselves
prominent.

As regards the Greeks, the specially outstanding peoples among them
in the period of their full world-historical development—the Lacedemonians, the Thebans, and the Athenians—are distinguished from one
another as follows. With the Lacedemonians, the compact undifferentiated life in the ethical substance predominates: with them, therefore,
property and the family relationship do not receive their due. With the
Thebans, on the other hand, the opposite principle makes its appearance;
with them the subjective element of the heart and feelings, so far as the
Greeks can be credited with this at all, preponderates. The finest lyrical
poet of the Greeks, Pindar, was a Theban. The friendship-league of
youths bound to each other in life and in death, which developed among
the Thebans, also affords evidence of this withdrawal into the inwardness
of feeling which prevailed among this people. The Athenians, however,
represent the unity of these opposites; in them, mind or spirit has emerged
from the Theban subjectivity without losing itself in the Spartan objectivity of ethical life. With the Athenians the rights of the State and of
the individual found as perfect a union as was possible at all at the level
of the Greek spirit. But just as Athens, through this mediation of the
Spartan and Theban spirit forms the unity of northern and southern
Greece, so also we see in that State the union of the eastern and western
Greeks, in so far as Plato in Athens defined the Absolute as the Idea
in which both the Absolute of the natural element in the Ionic philosophy,
and the wholly abstract thought which formed the principle of the Italic
philosophy, are reduced to moments. With these intimations regarding
the character of the principal nations of Greece we must be content
here; to develop further what has been intimated would involve encroach-
ing on the sphere of world-history and particularly on the history of
philosophy too.

An even greater diversity of national character is to be seen in the
Christian nations of Europe. The fundamental category in the nature of

these peoples is a preponderant inwardness, a self-possessed subjectivity. This is modified mainly according to the southern or northern situation of the countries inhabited by them. In the south, the individuality naïvely reveals itself in its isolatedness. This is especially true of the Italians; with them the individual character does not wish to be other than what it is; universal aims do not disturb its *naïveté*. Such a character is more appropriate to the feminine nature than to the masculine. The Italian individuality has, therefore, flowered into its finest beauty in the feminine individuality; not infrequently Italian women and maidens have died instantaneously from grief over an unhappy love affair; so much had their whole nature entered into the individual relationship that when this was broken they died. Connected with this *naïveté* of the individuality is the strong propensity to gesticulation of the Italians; their spirit spills over without reserve into its bodily nature. The charm of their behaviour has the same foundation. The same predominance of the individual element also shows itself in the political life of the Italians. Even before the Roman domination as well as after its disappearance, we see Italy disintegrated into a collection of small States. In the Middle Ages we see there the many separate communities everywhere so torn by factions that half of the citizens of such States always lived in exile. The general interest of the State could not prevail over the predominant party spirit. The individuals who put themselves forward as the sole representatives of the commonweal, themselves pursued their own ends by preference, and they sometimes did this in the most tyrannical and cruel manner. Neither in these autocracies nor in the republics torn by party conflicts was it possible to fashion political rights into a solid rational structure. Only Roman civil law was studied and opposed, as an ineffectual barrier, to the tyranny alike of individuals and of the many.

    With the Spaniards, too, we find the predominance of individuality; but this does not have the Italian *naïveté* but is already associated more with reflection. The individual content which is here given its due is already clothed with the form of universality. That is why honour especially is the driving principle with Spaniards. Here the individual demands recognition, not in his immediate individuality, but on account of the agreement of his actions and conduct with certain fixed principles which, according to the national mentality, must be law for every man of honour. But since the Spaniard is guided in all his behaviour by these principles which transcend the whims of the individual and have not yet been shaken by the sophistry of the abstractive intellect, he is more steadfast, more persevering than the Italian who obeys rather the impulse of the moment and lives more in feeling than in fixed ideas. This difference between the two peoples is specially prominent in connection with religion. The Italian does not let religious scruples noticeably interfere with his cheerful enjoyment of life. The Spaniard, on the other hand, has hitherto adhered with fanatical zeal to the letter of Catholic doctrine and for centuries, through the Inquisition, has persecuted with savage cruelty those suspected of deviating from it. Also politically the two peoples differ in a manner that accords with the character attributed to them. Italian national unity, which Petrarch in his day yearned for, is today still a dream; this land is still split up into an aggregate of States which trouble themselves very little about one another. In Spain, on the contrary, where as we have said, the universal attains to some degree of mastery over the particular, the separate States which formerly existed in that country have already been welded into a single State, though the provinces indeed still seek too great a measure of independence.

Now whereas with the Italians mobility of feeling predominates, and in Spaniards fixity of ideas, the French display both fixity of intellect and a flowing wit. The French have always been reproached with frivolity, also with vanity and the desire to please. But through striving to please, they have brought social education to an extreme of refinement and by virtue of just this have raised themselves in a remarkable way above the crude selfishness of the 'natural' man; for this education consists precisely in not forgetting those with whom we have intercourse, but in paying heed to them and showing ourselves well disposed towards them. Both to the individual and to the public, the French—be they statesmen, artists, or scholars—in all their dealings accord the most respectful attention. Yet it must be admitted that occasionally this deference to the opinion of others degenerates into the effort to please at all costs, even at the expense of truth. It is from this striving, too, that spring the ideals of mere chatterboxes. But what the French regard as the surest means of pleasing everyone is what they call *esprit*. This *esprit* is restricted in superficial natures to associating ideas only remotely connected, but in talented persons like Montesquieu and Voltaire, for example, by bringing together what the intellect has separated, it becomes a brilliant form of the rational; for the essential character of the rational is just to bring together what is separated. But this form of the rational is still not that of comprehensive cognition; the profound, clever thoughts which are to be found in abundance in men like those we have mentioned, are not developed from a single universal thought, from the Notion of the matter in hand, but are thrown out like flashes of lightning. The acuteness of the French intellect is revealed in the clarity and precision of expression, in speech and writings alike. Their language which is governed by the strictest rules, corresponds to the orderliness and conciseness of their thoughts. This has made the French patterns of political and juristic exposition. But in their political dealings, too, one cannot fail to detect the acuteness of their intellect. In the midst of the storm of revolutionary passions, their intellect showed itself in the decisiveness with which they succeeded in creating the new ethical world-order in face of the powerful alliance of the numerous adherents of the old, realizing one after another all the elements of the new political life to be developed, and embodying the characteristics of these elements both in themselves and in their mutual opposition, with the utmost precision. The very fact that these elements were pushed to the extreme of one-sidedness, each one-sided political principle being pursued to its ultimate consequences, has resulted in their being brought by the dialectic of world-historical Reason to a political condition in which all the previous one-sidednesses of the life of the State appear cancelled.

The English might be called the people of intellectual intuition. They recognize the rational less in the form of universality than in that of individuality. That is why their poets rank higher than their philosophers. Originality in the individual is a very prominent feature of the English. But their originality is not naïve and natural, but stems from thought and will. Here the individual in all his relationships aims to be independent of others, his connection with the universal bearing his own peculiar stamp. For this reason, political freedom with the English exists mostly in the shape of privileges, of rights which are traditional, not derived from general ideas. The sending of representatives to Parliament by the individual municipalities and counties is everywhere based on special privileges, not on general principles consistently carried out. Certainly the Englishman is proud of the honour and freedom of his whole nation, but his national pride is founded mainly on the consciousness that in England the individual can retain and exercise his particular rights. Associated with this tenacity of the individual who, though pursuing the universal, in his connection with it clings to his own particularity, is the conspicuous aptitude of the English for trade.

As for the Germans, they usually think of themselves last, either from modesty or because one saves the best till the end. We have the reputation of being profound, though not infrequently obscure, thinkers; we aim at comprehending the innermost nature of things and their necessary connection; therefore, we go extremely systematically to work in science, though in doing so we occasionally lapse into the formalism of an external, arbitrary construction. Our intelligence, more than that of any other nation is, in general, turned inwards. We prefer to live in the inwardness of feeling and thinking. In this interior life, in this hermit-like solitude of spirit, we first busy ourselves before we act with carefully defining the principles on which we propose to act. That is why we are somewhat slow in getting into action, now and again, in cases which demand a quick decision, remaining undecided and with the sincere desire to do the thing really well, often fail to achieve anything at all, The French proverb: 'le meilleur tue le bien', can therefore rightly be applied to the Germans. Before they do anything they must first find valid grounds for doing it. But since grounds can be found for everything, this validation often becomes a mere formalism in which the universal thought of right does not reach its immanent development but remains an abstraction into which the particular is arbitrarily imported from outside. This formalism has also shown itself in the Germans in the circumstance that they have sometimes been content for centuries to preserve certain of their political rights merely by solemn protestations. But whereas in this way the subjects accomplished very little for themselves, on the other hand, they often did only the bare minimum for the government. Living in the inwardness of feeling, the Germans have, indeed, always liked to speak of their loyalty and integrity; often, however, they could not be brought to the proof of this substantial sentiment of theirs; on the contrary, they have not hesitated to employ the general statutory codes against prince and emperor, merely to conceal their unwillingness to do something for the State, without prejudice to their excellent opinion of their loyalty and integrity. But although their political-mindedness, their patriotism, was mostly not very lively, yet from early times they have been animated by an inordinate desire for the honour of an official post and have been of the opinion that office and title make the man, that the importance of persons and the respect due to them, could in almost every case be measured with perfect certainty by the difference of title. This has made the Germans so ridiculous that the only parallel to be found in Europe is the Spaniard's mania for a long string of names.

§ 395

(3) The soul is further de-universalized into the individualized subject. But this subjectivity is here only considered as a differentiation and singling out of the modes which nature gives; we find it as the special temperament, talent, character, physiognomy, or other disposition and idiosyncrasy, of families or single individuals.

Zusatz. As we have seen, mind or spirit in Nature at first falls asunder into the *general* differences of the races of mankind, and reaches in the national minds or spirits a difference which has the form of a *particularization.* The third stage is that mind in Nature goes on to separate itself into *individuals*, and as individual soul opposes itself to itself. But the opposition arising here is not as yet the opposition which belongs to the essence of consciousness. The singularity or individuality of the soul comes into account here in anthropology only as a natural determinateness.

Now first of all we must remark that it is in the individual soul that the sphere of contingency begins, for only the universal is the necessary. Individual souls are distinguished from one another by an infinite number of contingent modifications. But this infinity belongs to the spurious kind of infinite. One should not therefore rate the peculiarities of people too highly. On the contrary, the assertion that the teacher should carefully adjust himself to the individuality of each of his pupils, studying and developing it, must be treated as idle chatter. He has simply no time to do this. The peculiarities of children are tolerated within the family circle; but at school there begins a life subject to general regulations, to a rule which applies to all; it is the place where mind must be brought to lay aside its idiosyncrasies, to know and to desire the universal, to accept the existing general culture. This reshaping of the soul, this alone is what education means. The more educated a man is, the less is there apparent in his behaviour anything peculiar only to him, anything therefore that is merely contingent.

Now the peculiarity of the individual has various aspects. These are distinguished as natural disposition, temperament, and character.

By disposition is understood the natural endowments of a man in contrast to what he has become by his own efforts. These natural endowments include talent and genius. Both words express a definite direction which the individual mind has been given by Nature. Genius, however, is wider in scope than talent; the product of the latter lies only in the sphere of the particular, whereas genius creates a new *genre*. But since talent and genius are, to begin with, merely dispositions, they must be developed— if they are not to be wasted or squandered or to degenerate into a spurious originality—in accordance with universally valid principles. It is only by the development of these dispositions that their existence can be demonstrated, as also their power and range. Prior to such development one can be deceived about the existence of a talent; to busy oneself when young with painting, for example, may seem to betray talent for this art and yet this hobby can fail to accomplish anything. Talent alone is, therefore, not to be esteemed higher than Reason which by its own activity has come to a knowledge of its Notion, as an absolutely free thinking and willing. In philosophy, genius by itself does not carry one very far; it must subject itself to the strict discipline of logical thinking; it is only by this subjection that genius succeeds in philosophy in achieving its perfect freedom. As regards the will, however, one cannot say that there is a genius for virtue; for virtue is something universal, to be required of all men; it is not innate but is to be produced in the individual by his own efforts. Differences in natural dispositions are, therefore, of no importance whatever for ethics; they would come into account only, if we may so express ourselves, in a natural history of mind.

The various kinds of talent and genius are distinguished from one another by the different spheres of mental activity in which they are practised. Difference of temperaments, on the other hand, has no such reference outwards. It is difficult to say what is meant by temperament; the meaning does not relate to the ethical nature of an action, nor to the talent revealed in the action, nor finally to passion, which always has a specific content. It is therefore best to define temperament as the quite general mode and manner in which the individual is active, in which he objectifies himself, maintains himself in the actual world. From this definition it follows that for the free mind, temperament is not so important as was formerly supposed. In a highly developed cultural epoch, the various accidental mannerisms of conduct and action disappear, and with them the diversities of temperament, in just the same way that, in such a period, the shallow characters in comedies of a less culturally developed epoch—the completely frivolous, the ridiculously absent-minded, the sordidly avaricious—become much rarer. The attempts to distinguish between the various temperaments have produced such indefinite results that it is difficult to know how to apply them to individuals, since these exhibit the various temperaments more or less in association with one another. Just as four cardinal virtues were distinguished, so too, as we know, four temperaments were assumed: the choleric, the sanguine, the phlegmatic, and the melancholic. Kant has a great deal to say about them. The main difference between these temperaments is based on whether a person gives himself up to the matter in hand or whether he is more concerned with his own individuality. The former case occurs with the sanguine and phlegmatic temperaments, the latter with the choleric and melancholic. The sanguine person forgets himself in what he is doing, and more specifically in such wise that by virtue of the superficial versatility of his nature, he involves himself in a variety of affairs; the phlegmatic person, on the contrary, steadfastly applies himself to one object. But in choleric and melancholic persons it is, as we have already indicated, the clinging to subjectivity that predominates; however, these two temperaments are in turn distinguished from each other by the fact that in the choleric, versatility predominates, and in the melancholic, apathy; so that in this connection the choleric temperament corresponds to the sanguine and the melancholic to the phlegmatic.

We have already remarked that difference of temperament loses its importance in a period when the mode and manner of conduct, and the behaviour of individuals, is regulated by the general culture. Character, on the other hand, remains something which always distinguishes in-dividuals. Only by his character does a man establish the definite quality of his individuality. Character demands, in the first place, the formal element of energy with which a man, without letting himself be diverted, pursues his aims and interests and in all his actions preserves his harmony with himself. Lacking character, a man remains indefinite or shifts from one direction to the opposite. Every person should therefore be required to show character. A man with character impresses others because they know the kind of man they are dealing with. But besides the formal ele-ment of energy character demands, in the second place, that the will should possess a substantial, universal content. Only by realizing great aims does a man reveal a great character, making him a beacon for others; and his aims must be inwardly justified if his character is to exhibit the absolute unity of the content and the formal activity of the will and thus to possess complete truth. If, on the contrary, the will clings to sheer particularities, to what lacks substantial interest, then it becomes *self-will* or *caprice*. This has only the form, not the content, of character. Through self-will, this parody of character, the individuality of a man is accentuated to a point where it has a disturbing influence on social intercourse.

A still more individual kind of particularity is exhibited by the so-called *idiosyncrasies* which occur both in the physical nature and in the mentality of man. Some people, for example, can scent the presence of cats near them. Others are quite peculiarly affected by certain diseases. King James I of England fainted if he saw a dagger. Mental idiosyncrasies are displayed especially in youth, e.g. in the incredible rapidity of mental arithmetic in particular children. In addition, it is not merely individuals who are distinguished from one another by the forms of mind or spirit in its natural modes discussed above, but families, too, more or less, especially when they have intermarried among themselves and not with outsiders, as has been the case, for example, in Berne and in some German cities.

Now that we have depicted the three forms of the qualitative natural mode of the individual soul—natural disposition, temperament, and character—we have still to indicate the rational necessity why this natural mode has just these three forms and no others, and why these forms have to be considered in the order we have followed. We began with natural disposition, more specifically with talent and genius, because in natural disposition the qualitative natural mode of the individual soul has predominantly the form of something that merely *is*, something immediately fixed and of such a nature that its inner differentiation is related to a difference existing outside of it. In temperament, on the other hand, this natural mode loses such a fixed shape; for whereas either one talent prevails exclusively in the individual, or several exist alongside one another in him quiescently and without passing into one another, each form of temperament can pass into the opposite in one and the same individual, so that no temperament has a fixed being in him. At the same time, the difference of the natural mode in question is reflected into the interior of the individual soul out of the reference to something existing outside of it. But in character, we see the fixity of the natural disposition united with the changeableness of the various temperaments, the predominant reference outwards in the former, united with the reflectedness-into-self of the soul prevailing in the different temperaments. The fixity of character is not so immediate, is not so innate, as the fixity of natural disposition, but has to be developed by the will. Character consists in something more than an even blending of the various temperaments. All the same, it cannot be denied that it has a *natural* foundation, that some people are more naturally disposed to possess a strong character than others. For this reason, we were right in speaking of character here in Anthropology, although it is only in the sphere of free mind or spirit that it is fully unfolded.

(β) *Physical Alterations*

§ 396

Taking the soul as an individual, we find its diversities, as alterations in it, the one permanent subject, and as stages in its development. As they are at once physical and mental diversities, a more concrete definition or description of them would require us to anticipate an acquaintance with the formed and matured mind.

(1) The first of these is the natural lapse of the ages in man's life. He begins with *Childhood*—mind wrapped up in itself. His next step is the fully developed antithesis, the strain and struggle of a universality which is still subjective (as seen in ideals, fancies, hopes, ambitions) against his immediate individuality. And that individuality marks both the world which, as it exists, fails to meet his ideal requirements, and the position of the individual himself, who is still short of independence and not fully equipped for the part he has to play (*Youth*). Thirdly, we see man in his true relation to his environment, recognizing the objective necessity and reasonableness of the world as he finds it—a world no longer incomplete, but able in the work which it collectively achieves to afford the individual a place and a security for his performance. By his share in this collective work he first is really *somebody*, gaining an effective existence and an objective value (*Manhood*). Last of all comes the finishing touch to this unity with objectivity: a unity which, while on its realist side it passes into the *inertia* of deadening habit, on its idealist side gains freedom from the limited interests and entanglements of the outward present (*Old Age*).

Zusatz. The soul, which at first is completely universal, having in the way we have indicated particularized itself and finally determined itself to the stage of individuality, now enters into opposition to its inner universality, to its substance. This contradiction of the immediate individuality and the substantial universality implicitly present in it, establishes the life-process of the individual soul, a process by which the immediate individuality of the soul is made conformable to the universal, actualizing the latter in the former and thus raising the initial, simple unity of the soul with itself to a unity mediated by the opposition, developing the initially abstract universality of the soul to concrete universality. This process of development is education. Even merely animal life in its own way exhibits this process in principle. But, as we have already seen, it does not have the power to actualize within itself the genus in its true form; its immediate, merely affirmative, abstract individuality remains permanently in contradiction with its genus, excludes it no less than includes it. By this incapacity of merely animal life to represent perfectly the genus, it perishes. In the animal, the genus proves itself to be the power in face of which the former must perish. Therefore, in the death of the individual, the genus attains a realization which is no less abstract than the individuality of merely animal life; it just as much excludes that individuality as it remains excluded by it. The genus is truly realized, on the other hand, in mind, in Thought, in this element which is homogeneous with the genus. But in the anthropological sphere this actualization, since it takes place in the natural individual mind, is still present in a natural mode. Consequently it falls into time. Thus arises a series of distinct stages through which the individual as such passes, a sequence of differences which no longer possess the fixity of the immediate differences of universal mind in its natural mode which prevail in the various races of mankind and in the national minds, but manifest in one and the same individual as transient forms which pass into one another.

This sequence of distinct stages is the series of ages in man's life.

It begins with the immediate, still undifferentiated unity of the genus and the individuality, with the abstract origin of the immediate individuality, the birth of the individual, and closes with the in-forming of the genus within the individuality, or of the latter within the former, that is, with the triumph of the genus over the individuality, with the abstract negation of the latter, with death.

What in animal life as such is *genus*, is in the sphere of mind *rationality*; for the genus already possesses the character of inner universality which belongs to the rational being. In this unity of the genus and the rational being lies the reason why the mental phenomena appearing in the passage of the ages of man correspond to the physical alterations of the individual developed in that process. The correspondence of the mental and the physical is here more definite than in racial diversities where we have to do only with the universal fixed differences of mind in Nature and with the equally fixed differences of men, whereas here the specific alterations to be considered are those of the individual soul and its corporeity. But, on the other hand, we must not go the length of seeking in the physiological development of the individual the clearly outlined counterpart of his mental or spiritual unfoldment; for in the latter, the opposition prominent in it and the unity which is to issue from that opposition, have a much higher significance than in the physiological sphere. Mind here reveals its independence of its corporeity in the fact that it can develop itself earlier than this. Children have often a mental development far in advance of their years. This has mainly occurred with outstanding artistic talents, especially with musical geniuses. Such precocity is not infrequently shown too in connection with an easy assimilation of various kinds of information, especially in the mathematical field, and also in connection with a capacity for formal reasoning even on ethical and religious topics. In general, however, it must be admitted that intellect does not come before its time. It is almost solely in the case of artistic talents that their premature appearance is an indication of excellence. On the other hand, the premature development of intelligence generally which has been observed in some children has not, as a rule, been followed by great intellectual distinction in manhood.

Now the process of development of the natural human individual splits up into a series of processes whose difference rests on the different relationship of the individual to the genus and establishes the difference between the child, the adult, and the old. These differences represent the differences of the Notion. Childhood is, therefore, the time of natural harmony, of the peace of the individual with himself and with the world; the beginning which contains no opposition, just as old age is the end which is free from it. The oppositions which may occur in childhood remain devoid of any serious interest. The child lives in innocence, without any lasting pain, in the love it has for its parents and in the feeling of being loved by them. This immediate and therefore non-spiritual, purely natural unity of the individual with its genus and with the world generally, must be superseded; the individual must go forward to the stage where he opposes himself to the universal as that which exists in and for itself, already finished and complete, must go on to apprehend himself in his self-dependence. But this self-dependence, this opposition, at first appears in just as one-sided a shape as does the unity of subjectivity and objectivity in the child. The youth analyses the Idea which is actualized in the world, in the following manner: to himself he attributes the character of the substantial, of the true and the good, which appertain to the nature of the Idea; but the world, on the other hand, he regards as something contingent, accidental. This untrue opposition must not be a stopping-place; instead the youth must rise above it and learn to see that, on the contrary, the world is the substantial element and the individual merely an accident, and that therefore a man can find his essential occupation and satisfaction only in the world which pursues its own course independently in face of him, and that for this reason he must procure for himself the skill necessary to accomplish his work. Reaching this standpoint, the youth has become a *man*. The mature man also considers the ethical world-order as something which in its essential nature is already in existence, which has not waited for him to bring it into being. Thus he is for, not against, the existing order of things, is interested in promoting, not opposing it; he has thus risen above the one-sided subjectivity of youth to the standpoint to an objective intelligence. Old age, on the other hand, is the return to an absence of interest in the world around; the old man has lived himself into his world and just because of this unity with the world in which the opposition has vanished, gives up his active interest in the world.

This general indication of the differences of the different ages of man's life we now propose to characterize in more detail.

Childhood we can differentiate again into three, or if we wish to include in our treatment the unborn child which is identical with its mother, into four stages.

The unborn child has not as yet a proper individuality, not an individuality which could enter into relation with particular objects in a particular manner or could take in an external object at a specific point of its organism. The life of the unborn child resembles that of the plant. Just as the latter does not possess an interrupted intussusception but feeds itself by a continuous flow of nutriment, so, too, does the babe feed itself at first by a continual sucking and does not as yet possess a rhythmic respiration.

When the babe is brought into the world out of this vegetative state in which it exists in the womb, it passes into the animal mode of life. Birth is, therefore, a tremendous leap. By it the child emerges from the state of a life completely devoid of opposition into the state of a separate existence, into the relationship to light and air and into a perpetually unfolding relationship to an individualized objectivity and especially to individualized nourishment. The first way in which the child constitutes itself a self-dependent organism is by *respiration*, the inhalation and exhalation of air at a single point of its body, a process which interrupts the flow of that element. Immediately after the birth of the child, its body already reveals itself as almost fully organized; only single details alter in it. Thus, for example, the so-called *foramen ovale* does not close up until later. The main alteration in the child's body consists of *growth*. In connection with this alteration it is hardly necessary to recall that in animal life generally, in contrast to plant life, growth is not a coming-out-of-self, not a process of being drawn out of and beyond self, not a production of new shapes, but is only a development of the organism producing merely quantitative, formal difference, namely, that of the degree of strength and of dimensions. Just as little do we need here to do what has already been done in the appropriate place in the Philosophy of Nature, namely, to explain at length that the completeness of the bodily structure which is lacking in the plant and is first accomplished in the animal organism, this leading back of all the members to the negative, simple unity of life, is the ground of the origin of self-feeling in the animal, and therefore also in the child. But, on the other hand, we must emphasize here that in man the animal organism reaches its most perfect form. Even the highest animal is unable to exhibit this delicately organized, infinitely plastic body which we already perceive in the newly born child. At first, however, the child is much more dependent and in much more need than the animal. Yet in this, too, the child already manifests its higher nature. It at once makes known its wants in unruly, stormy, and peremptory fashion. Whereas the animal is silent or expresses its pain only by groaning, the child makes known its wants by screaming. By this ideal activity, the child shows that it is straightway imbued with the certainty that it has a right to demand from the outer world the satisfaction of its needs, that the independence of the outer world is non-existent where man is concerned.

Now as regards the mental development of the child in this first stage of its life, it can be said that man never learns more than in this period. Here the child makes itself gradually familiar w·th all the specifications of the world of the senses. The outer world now becomes something actual for it. It progresses from sensation to perception. To begin with, the child has only a sensation of light by which things are manifest to it. This mere sensation misleads the child into reaching out for something distant as if it were near. But through the sense of touch the child orientates itself in regard to distances. In this way it succeeds in measuring with its eyes and simply projects from itself the outer world. In this period, too, the child learns that external things offer resistance.

The transition from childhood to boyhood is marked by the development of the child's behaviour to the outer world; the child, in reaching a feeling of the actuality of the outer world, begins to become an *actual* human being himself and to feel himself as such; but in doing so he passes on to the practical inclination to test himself in this actual world. The child is enabled to make this practical approach to the world by growing teeth, by learning to stand, to walk, and to talk. The first thing to be learnt at this stage is to stand upright. This is peculiar to man and can only be effected by his will; a man stands only so long as he wills to stand. When we no longer will to stand, we collapse. Standing is, therefore, the habit of willing to stand. Man acquires a yet freer relation to the outer world by walking; by this he overcomes the asunderness of space and gives himself his own place. But speech enables man to apprehend things as universal, to attain to the consciousness of his own universality, to express himself as 'I'. This laying hold of his ego-hood is an extremely important point in the mental development of the child; at this point it begins to reflect itself into itself out of its immersion in the outer world. To begin with, this incipient self-dependence expresses itself in the child's learning to play with tangible things. But the most rational thing that children can do with their toys is to break them.

In passing from play to the seriousness of learning, the child becomes a boy. At this stage children begin to be curious, especially for stories; what interests them in these is ideas which do not come to them in an immediate manner. But here the main thing is the awakening feeling in them that as yet they *are* not what they *ought* to be, and the active desire to become like the adults in whose surroundings they are living. It is this desire which gives rise to the imitativeness of children. Whereas the feeling of immediate unity with the parents is the spiritual mother's milk on which children thrive, it is the children's own need to grow up which acts as the stimulus to that growth. This striving after education on the part of children themselves is the immanent factor in all education. But since the boy is still at the stage of immediacy, the higher to which he is to raise himself appears to him, not in the form of universality or of the matter in hand, but in the shape of something given, of an individual, an authority. It is this or that man who forms the ideal which the boy strives to know and to imitate; only in this concrete manner does the child at this stage perceive his own essential nature. What the child is to learn must therefore be given to him on and with authority; he has the feeling that what is thus given to him is superior to him. This feeling must be carefully fostered in education. For this reason we must describe as completely preposterous the pedagogy which bases itself on play, which proposes that children should be made acquainted with serious things in the form of play and demands that the educator should lower himself to the childish level of intelligence of the pupils instead of lifting them up to an appreciation of the seriousness of the matter in hand. This education by playing at lessons can result in the boy throughout his whole life treating everything disdainfully. Such a regrettable result can also be produced by perpetually stimulating children to indulge in argument and disputation, a method recommended by unintelligent pedagogues; this can easily make children impertinent. Children must, of course, be roused to think for themselves; but the worth of the matter in hand should not be put at the mercy of their immature, vain understanding.

With regard to one side of education, namely, discipline, the boy should not be allowed to follow his own inclination; he must obey in order that he may learn to command. Obedience is the beginning of all wisdom; for the will which as yet does not know what is true and objective, does not make this its goal and therefore far from being truly self-dependent and free is still immature; such a will is enabled through obedience inwardly to accept the authority of the rational will coming to it externally and gradually to make this its own. On the other hand, to allow children to do as they please, to be so foolish as to provide them into the bargain with reasons for their whims, is to fall into the worst of all educational practices; such children develop the deplorable habit of fixing their attention on their own inclinations, their own peculiar cleverness, their own selfish interests, and this is the root of all evil. By nature, the child is neither bad nor good, since it starts without any knowledge either of good or of evil. To deem this unknowing innocence an ideal and to yearn to return to it would be silly; it has no value and is short-lived. Self-will and evil soon make their appearance in the child. This self-will, this germ of evil, must be broken and destroyed by discipline.

With regard to the other side of education, namely, instruction, it is to be observed that this rationally begins with the most abstract thing that the child can grasp; and that is the alphabet. This presupposes a power of abstraction to which entire races, for example, even the Chinese, have not attained. Language as such is this airy element, at once sensuous and non-sensuous, and it is by the child's increasing command of language that its intelligence rises more and more above the sensuous, from the individual to the universal, to thought. This growing ability to think is the most useful part of primary education. But the child only gets as far as *picture-thinking*; the world is only for his representational thinking. He learns the qualities of things, becomes acquainted with the facts of the worlds of Nature and mind, develops an interest in things but does not as yet cognize the world in its inner connectedness. This knowledge comes only with manhood, though even in boyhood there is an imperfect understanding of the worlds of Nature and mind. It is, therefore, a mistake to assert that a boy understands as yet nothing whatever of religion and right, that therefore he must not be bothered with these matters, that on no account must ideas be forced on him but, on the contrary, he must be provided with experiences of his own and one must be content to let him be stimulated by what is sensuously present to him. Even the ancients did not allow children to dwell for any length of time on objects of sense. The modern spirit, however, involves a wholly different exaltation above the world of the senses, a much deeper absorption in its own inwardness, than is characteristic of the antique spirit. Therefore, in the present-day world, a boy should be made acquainted with the idea of the supersensuous world at an early age. This is done in a much higher degree in the school than in the family. In the latter, the child is accepted in its immediate individuality, is loved whether its behaviour is good or bad. In school, on the other hand, the immediacy of the child no longer counts; here it is esteemed only according to its worth, according to its achievements, is not merely loved but criticized and guided in accordance with universal principles, moulded by instruction according to fixed rules, in general, subjected to a universal order which forbids many things innocent in themselves because everyone cannot be permitted to do them. The school thus forms the transition from the family into civil society. But to the latter the boy has at first only an undefined relationship; his interest is still divided between learning and playing.

With the onset of puberty the boy becomes a youth, when the life of the genus begins to stir in him and to seek satisfaction. The youth turns, in general, to the substantial universal; his ideal no longer appears to him, as it does to the boy, in the person of a man, but is conceived by him as a universal, independent of such individuality. But in the youth this ideal still has a more or less subjective shape, whether it lives in him as an ideal of love and friendship or as an ideal of a universal state of the world. In this subjectivity of the substantial content of such an ideal there is involved its opposition to the existing world, but also the urge to remove this opposition by realizing the ideal. The content of the ideal imbues the youth with the feeling of power to act; he therefore fancies himself called and qualified to transform the world, or at least to put the world back on the right path from which, so it seems to him, it has strayed. The fact that the substantial universal contained in his ideal, in keeping with its essential nature, has already succeeded in explicating and actualizing itself, this is not perceived by the enthusiastic spirit of the youth. To him the actualization of that universal seems a lapse from it. For this

reason he feels that both his ideal and his own personality are not recognized by the world, and thus the youth, unlike the child, is no longer
at peace with the world. Because of this turning to the ideal, youth
seems to possess a nobler sense and greater altruism than is displayed
by the man who attends to his particular, temporal interests. As against
this, it must be pointed out that the man is no longer wrapped up in his
particular impulses and subjective views and occupied only with his
personal development; on the contrary, he has plunged into the Reason
of the actual world and shown himself to be active on its behalf. The youth
necessarily arrives at this goal; but *his* immediate aim is to train and
discipline himself so that he will be able to realize his ideals. In the attempt
to make these actual he becomes a man.

At first, the transition from his ideal life into civil society can appear to
the youth as a painful transition into the life of the Philistine. The youth,
who hitherto has been occupied only with general objects and has worked
only for himself, now that he is growing into manhood and entering into
practical life, must be active for others and concern himself with details.
Now, much as this belongs to the nature of things, since if something is
to be done it is with details that one must deal, the occupation with
details can at first be very distressing to the man, and the impossibility
of an immediate realization of his ideals can turn him into a hypochon-
driac. This hypochondria, however difficult it may be to discern it in
many cases, is not easily escaped by anyone. The later the age at which it
attacks a man, the more serious are its symptoms. In weak natures it can
persist throughout the entire lifetime. In this diseased frame of mind the
man will not give up his subjectivity, is unable to overcome his repug-
nance to the actual world, and by this very fact finds himself in a state of
relative incapacity which easily becomes an actual incapacity. If, therefore, the man does not want to perish, he must recognize the world as a
self-dependent world which in its essential nature is already complete,
must accept the conditions set for him by the world and wrest from it what
he wants for himself. As a rule, the man believes that this submission is
only forced on him by necessity. But, in truth, this unity with the world
must be recognized, not as a relation imposed by necessity, but as the
rational. The rational, the divine, possesses the absolute power to actualize
itself and has, right from the beginning, fulfilled itself; it is not so impotent that it would have to wait for the beginning of its actualization.
The world is this actualization of divine Reason; it is only on its surface
that the play of contingency prevails. It can claim, therefore, with at least
as much right, indeed with even greater right, than the adolescent to be
esteemed as complete and self-dependent; and therefore the man behaves
quite rationally in abandoning his plan for completely transforming the
world and in striving to realize his personal aims, passions, and interests
only within the framework of the world of which he is a part. Even
so, this leaves him scope for an honourable, far-reaching and creative
activity. For although the world must be recognized as already complete

in its essential nature, yet it is not a dead, absolutely inert world but, like the life-process, a world which perpetually creates itself anew, which while merely preserving itself, at the same time progresses. It is in this conservation and advancement of the world that the man's work consists. Therefore, on the one hand we can say that the man only creates what is already there; yet on the other hand, his activity must also bring about an advance. But the world's progress occurs only on the large scale and only comes to view in a large aggregate of what has been produced. If the man after a labour of fifty years looks back on his past, he will readily recognize the progress made. This knowledge, as also the insight into the rationality of the world, liberates him from mourning over the destruction of his ideals. What is *true* in these ideals is preserved in the practical activity; what the man must purge himself of is only what is untrue, the empty abstractions. The scope and nature of his activity can vary considerably; but the substantial element in all human activities is the same, namely, the interests of right, ethics, and religion. Therefore, men can find satisfaction and honour in all spheres of their practical activity if they accomplish throughout what is rightly required of them in the particular sphere to which they belong either by chance, outer necessity, or free choice. But to this end it is above all else necessary that the education of the adolescent be completed, that he has finished his studies, and secondly, that he resolve to earn his subsistence himself, that he begin to be active on behalf of others. Education alone is not enough to make him a complete, mature man; he becomes such only through his own intelligent concern for his temporal interests; just as nations only attain their majority when they have reached the stage where they are not excluded by a so-called paternal government from attending to their material and spiritual interests.

With his entry now into practical life, the man may well be vexed and morose about the state of the world and lose hope of any improvement in it; but in spite of this he finds his place in the world of objective relationships and becomes habituated to it and to his work. The objects with which he has to concern himself are, it is true, particular and mutable, and in their peculiarity are more or less new. But at the same time, these particulars contain a universal, a rule, something conformable to law; and the longer the man is active in his work, the more does this universal rise into prominence out of the welter of particulars. In this way he gets to be completely at home in his profession and grows thoroughly accustomed to his lot. The substantial element in all those things with which he deals is then quite familiar to him and only the particular, unessential can occasionally present him with something new. The very fact, however, that his activity has become so *conformed* to his work, that his activity no longer meets with any resistance from its objects, this complete facility of execution, brings in its train the *extinction* of its vitality; for with the disappearance of the opposition between subject and object there also disappears the interest of the former in the latter. Thus the habit of mental life, equally with the dulling of the functions of his physical organism, changes the man into an old man.

The old man lives without any definite interest, for he has abandoned the hope of realizing the ideals which he cherished when he was young and the future seems to hold no promise of anything new at all; on the contrary, he believes that he already knows what is universal and substantial in anything he may yet encounter. The mind of the old man is thus turned only towards this universal and to the past to which he owes the knowledge of this universal. But in thus dwelling in the memory of the past and of the substantial element, he loses his memory for details of the present and for arbitrary things, names, for example, in the same measure that, conversely, he firmly retains in his mind the maxims of experience and feels obliged to preach to those younger than himself. But this wisdom, this lifeless, complete coincidence of the subject's activity with its world, leads back to the childhood in which there is no opposition, in the same way that the reduction of his physical functions to a process-less habit leads on to the abstract negation of the living individuality, to death.

The sequence of ages in man's life is thus rounded into a notionally determined totality of alterations which are produced by the process of the genus with the individual.

When describing the racial differences of mankind and the characteristics of the national minds, we had to anticipate a knowledge of concrete mind, for this does not come within the scope of Anthropology: similarly, since concrete mind enters into the above-mentioned process, we must anticipate a knowledge of it in order that we may speak categorically about the sequence of the ages of man and must make use of this knowledge for distinguishing the different stages of that process.

§ 397

(2) Next we find the individual subject to a *real* antithesis, leading it to seek and find *itself* in *another* individual. This—the *sexual relation*—on a physical basis, shows, on its one side, subjectivity remaining in an instinctive and emotional harmony of moral life and love, and not pushing these tendencies to an extreme *universal* phase, in purposes political, scientific, or artistic; and on the other, shows an active half, where the individual is the vehicle of a struggle of universal and objective interests with the given conditions (both of his own existence and of that of the external world), carrying out these universal principles into a unity with the world which is his own work. The sexual tie acquires its moral and spiritual significance and function in the *family*.

§ 398

(3) When the individuality, or self-centralized being, distinguishes itself from its *mere* being, this immediate judgement is the *waking* of the soul, which confronts its self-absorbed natural life, in the first instance, as one natural quality and state confronts another state, viz. *sleep*.—The waking is not merely for the observer, or externally distinct from the sleep: it is itself the *judgement* (primary partition) of the individual soul—which is self-existing only as it relates its self-existence to its mere existence, distinguishing itself from its still undifferentiated universality. The waking state includes generally all self-conscious and rational activity in which the mind realizes its own distinct self.—Sleep is an invigoration of this activity—not as a merely negative rest from it, but as a return back from the world of specialization, from dispersion into phases where it has grown hard and stiff—a return into the general nature of subjectivity, which is the substance of those specialized energies and their absolute master.

The distinction between sleep and waking is one of those *posers*, as they may be called, which are often addressed to philosophy:—Napoleon, for example, on a visit to the University of Pavia, put this question to the class of ideology. The characterization given in the section is abstract; it primarily treats waking merely as a natural fact, containing the mental element *implicite* but not yet as invested with a special being of its own. If we are to speak more concretely of this distinction (in fundamentals it remains the same), we must take the self-existence of the individual soul in its higher aspects as the Ego of consciousness and as intelligent mind. The difficulty raised anent the distinction of the two states properly arises, only when we also take into account the dreams in sleep and describe these dreams, as well as the mental representations in the sober waking consciousness under one and the same title of mental representations. Thus superficially classified as states of mental representation the two coincide, because we have lost sight of the difference; and in the case of any assignable distinction of waking consciousness, we can always return to the trivial remark that all this is nothing more than mental idea. But the concrete theory of the waking soul in its realized being views it as *consciousness* and *intellect*: and the world of intelligent consciousness is something quite different from a picture of mere ideas and images. The latter are in the main only externally conjoined, in an unintelligent way, by the laws of the so-called *Association of Ideas*; though here and there of course logical principles may also be operative. But in the waking state man behaves essentially as a concrete ego, an intelligence: and because of this intelligence his sense-perception stands before him as a concrete totality of features in which each member, each point, takes up its place as at the same time determined through and with all the rest. Thus the facts embodied in his sensation are authenticated, not by his mere subjective representation and distinction of the facts as something external from the person, but by virtue of the concrete interconnection in which each part stands with all parts of this complex. The waking state is the concrete consciousness of this mutual corroboration of each single factor of its content by all the others in the picture as perceived. The consciousness of this interdependence need not be explicit and distinct. Still this general setting to all sensations is implicitly present in the concrete feeling of self.—In order to see the difference between dreaming and waking we need only keep in view the Kantian distinction between subjectivity and objectivity of mental representation (the latter depending upon determination through categories): remembering, as already noted, that what is actually present in mind need not be therefore explicitly realized in consciousness, just as little as the exaltation of the intellectual sense to God need stand before consciousness in the shape of proofs of God's existence, although, as before explained, these proofs only serve to express the net worth and content of that feeling.

Zusatz. By its *waking*, the natural soul of the human individual enters into a relation to its substance which must be regarded as the truth, as the unity of the two relations which occur, on the one hand, in the development which produces the sequence of the *ages of man*, and, on the other hand, in the *sexual-relation*, that is, between the individuality and the substantial universality or genus of man. For whereas in the former process the soul appears as the permanent *one* subject, the differences which appear in it being only alterations, hence only *transient*, not abiding differences, while in the sexual-relation the individual reaches a *fixed* difference, a real opposition to himself, and the relation of the individual to the genus active in him develops into a relation to an individual of the opposite sex: in other words, whereas in the former case the *simple unity*, and in the latter case the *fixed opposition*, predominates, we see in the *waking* soul a self-relation which is not merely simple but, on the contrary, is mediated by opposition; but in this being-for-self of the soul we see the difference as neither so transient as in the sequence of the ages of man nor as so fixed as in the sexual-relation, but as the spontaneous *enduring* alternation in one and the same individual of the states of sleep and waking. The necessity of the dialectical progress from the sexual-relation to the waking of the soul stems, however, more nearly from the fact that since in the sexual-relation each of the individuals, in virtue of their implicit unity, finds in the other its own self, the soul develops from its merely implicit being, from being merely in itself, to being for itself, in other words, from its sleep to its waking. What is distributed in the sexual-relation between two individuals, namely, a subjectivity remaining immediately united with its substance and a subjectivity entering into opposition to this substance, *that*, in the waking soul, is united, and so has lost the fixity of its opposition and preserved that fluidity of the difference whereby it is converted into mere *states*. Sleep is the state in which the soul is immersed in its differenceless unity. Waking, on the other hand, is the state in which the soul has entered into opposition to this simple unity. Here the natural life of mind still persists; for although the first immediacy of the soul is already overcome and is now reduced to a mere state, yet the soul's being-for-self resulting from the negation of that immediacy likewise still appears in the shape of a mere state. The being-for-self, the soul's subjectivity, is not yet included in its intrinsic substantiality; both determinations still appear as mutually exclusive, alternating states. Of course, veritable mental activity, will and intelligence, fall into the waking state; but here we have not as yet to consider the waking state in this concrete significance but only as a state, consequently, as something essentially distinct from will and intelligence. But that the states of sleep and waking are inherent in mind which, in its truth, is to be grasped as pure activity, this stems from the fact that mind is also soul and as *soul*, lowers itself to the status of natural, immediate being, of a passive being. In this shape, mind only *suffers* the process whereby it comes to be for itself. It can, therefore, be said that waking is brought about by the lightning-stroke of subjectivity breaking through the form of mind's immediacy. Free mind can indeed also determine its waking; but here in Anthropology we are contemplating waking only in so far as it is a [passive] happening and, too, a still quite indeterminate happening such that mind simply *finds* a world confronting it; a *finding of itself* which, to begin with, only gets as far as sensation, but still remains quite remote from the concrete determination of intelligence and will. It is just in this fact that the soul on waking merely *finds* itself and the world—this duality, this opposition—that the natural life of mind consists.

The distinguishing of the soul, on waking, from itself and from the world is linked on account of its natural life, with a natural distinction, that of the alternation of day and night. It is natural for man to wake by day and sleep by night; for just as sleep is the state of the soul's undifferentiatedness, so does night obscure the difference of things; and just as waking represents the soul's distinguishing of itself from itself, so does daylight allow the differences of things to appear.

But not only in physical Nature but also in the human organism there is a difference which corresponds to the distinction between the sleeping and the waking of the soul. In the animal organism it is essential to distinguish between the side of its self-absorption and the side of its outward-turned activity. Bichat has called the former the *organic* life, the latter the *animal* life. The organic life he takes to be the reproductive system: digestion, circulation of the blood, transpiration, and breathing. This life continues in sleep and ceases only with death. The animal life, on the other hand, which according to Bichat comprises the system of sensibility and of irritability, nervous and muscular activity, this theoretical and practical outward-turned activity ceases in sleep; this is why the ancients called sleep and death, brothers. The only way in which the animal organism while asleep maintains its connection with the outer world is by breathing, this quite abstract relation to the distinctionless element of air. With the particularized outer world, on the other hand, the healthy organism while asleep no longer maintains any connection. If, therefore, a man while asleep is active outwardly he is ill. This is the case with sleep-walkers. These move about with the utmost safety; some have written letters and sealed them. Yet in sleep-walking the sense of sight is paralysed and the eye is in a cataleptic state.

In what Bichat calls animal life, then, there is an alternation of rest and activity; hence, as in waking, an opposition, while the organic life which does not participate in that alternation, corresponds to the undifferentiatedness of the soul in sleep.

But besides this difference in the organism's activity, we must also note a difference in the structure of the organs of the internal and the outward-turned life, a difference corresponding to that between sleep and waking. The outer organs, eyes and ears, and the extremities, the hands and feet, are symmetrically doubled, and we may remark in passing that this symmetry renders them capable of being a subject-matter for art. The internal organs, on the other hand, are either not doubled at all or else display only an asymmetric doubling. We have only one stomach. The lung, it is true, has two lobes, as the heart has two ventricles; but both heart and lungs already imply the connection of the organism with an opposite, with the outer world. Besides, neither the lobes of the lung nor the cardiac ventricles are as symmetrical as the outer organs.

As regards the mental or spiritual difference between waking and sleep we may also add the following remarks. We have defined sleep as the state in which the soul distinguishes itself neither inwardly nor from the outer world. This definition which has its own necessity is confirmed by experience. For when our soul goes on feeling or imagining only one and the same thing, it becomes sleepy. So can the regular motion of a cradle, a monotonous singing, the murmuring of a brook, induce somnolence in us. The same effect is produced by rambling talk, by disconnected point-less narration. Our mind only feels fully awake when it is presented with something interesting, something both new and meaningful, something with a differentiated and coherent content; for in such an object it finds itself again. The vitality of the waking state requires, therefore, the opposition and the unity of mind with its object. If, on the contrary, mind does not find again in the object the same internally differentiated totality which it is itself, then it withdraws from this object into its distinctionless unity, is bored, and falls asleep. But it is already implied in the foregoing remark that it is not mind *in general*, but more specifically reflective and rational thinking whose interest must be aroused by the object if the waking state is to exist in its complete distinction from sleep and dreaming. We can, while awake, taking the word in its abstract meaning, be very bored; and, conversely, it is possible for us to have a lively interest in something in a dream. But in a dream it is only our picture-thinking, not our conceptual thinking, whose interest is aroused.

But inadequate as is the vague idea of 'being interested in the object' for distinguishing waking from sleep, no less inadequate, too, can appear the determination of *clarity* for that distinction. For in the first place this determination is only a quantitative one; it expresses only the immediacy of intuition and therefore not its true element. The latter we have only when we are convinced that what we perceive is a self-contained rational totality. And secondly, we know quite well that dreaming, far from being distinguished from waking by its inferior clarity, is often clearer than waking, especially in disease and in visionaries.

Lastly, it is also inadequate to fix the distinction by saying vaguely that it is only in the waking state that man *thinks*. For thought *in general* is so much inherent in the nature of man that he is always thinking, even in sleep. In every form of mind, in feeling, intuition, as in picture-thinking, thought remains the basis. In so far, therefore, as thought is this indeterminate basis, it is unaffected by the alternation of sleep and waking; it does not constitute exclusively one of the alternating sides here but, on the contrary, as this wholly universal activity, stands above them both. On the other hand, the position is different as regards thought in so far as this, as a distinct form of mental activity, *stands opposed to* other forms of mind. In this sense, thought ceases in sleep and dreaming. Intellect and Reason, the modes of thought proper, are active only in the waking state. It is in intellect that the abstract determination in which the waking soul distinguishes itself from the natural world, from its distinctionless substance and from the outer world, first attains its in-tensive, concrete significance; for intellect is the infinite being-within-self which has developed itself into totality, and by this very act has freed itself from the singularity of the outer world. But when the 'I' is in its own self free, it also makes objects independent of its subjectivity, contemplates them likewise as totalities and as members of an all-embracing totality. Now in what is external, the totality is present, not as free Idea, but as the connection of necessity. This objective connection is that by which our waking ideas are essentially distinguished from those we have in dreams. If, therefore, when awake I encounter something whose connection with the rest of the outer world I am unable to discover, then I can ask: Am I awake or dreaming? In dreams it is only our picture-thinking which comes into play and its products are not governed by the categories of intellect. But mere picture-thinking wrests things completely out of their concrete context, isolates them. That is why in dreams everything drifts apart, criss-crosses in the wildest disorder, objects lose all necessary, objective, rational connection and are associated only in an entirely superficial, contingent and subjective manner. Thus it happens that what we hear in sleep, we bring into quite a different context from what it has in actuality. One hears, for example, a door slam, believes a shot has been fired, and now imagines in detail a story of robbers. Or while asleep, one feels a pressure on one's chest and puts it down to a nightmare. The reason why such ideas are possible in sleep is that in this state, mind is not explicitly the totality with which, in the waking state, it compares all its sensations, intuitions, and general ideas in order to ascertain from the agreement or non-agreement of the separate sensations, intuitions, and ideas with its explicit totality, the objectivity or non-objectivity of that content. It is true that in day-dreaming a man can give himself up to quite empty, subjective fancies; but if he has not lost his reason, he knows at the same time that these fancies are only fancies because they conflict with his present totality.

Only occasionally does a dream contain something that has a tolerable connection with the real world. Especially is this so with dreams before midnight; in these the fancies can in some measure be fitted in with the real world with which we are concerned in the daytime. At midnight, as thieves well know, we sleep soundest; the soul has then withdrawn into itself away from all interest in the outer world. After midnight, dreams become more fanciful. Occasionally, however, we feel a presentiment of something which in the distraction of our waking life we do not notice. Thus a sluggish or melancholic blood (*schweres Blut*) can evoke in a man the distinct feeling of an illness of which, in his waking state, he had not as yet the slightest inkling. Similarly in a dream the smell of something smouldering can provoke dreams of conflagrations which do not break out until several days later and whose warning signs we have not previously noticed in our waking state.

Finally we must add that waking, as a natural state, as a natural tension between the individual soul and the outer world, has a *limit*, a measure, and that therefore the activity of the waking mind is affected by fatigue and so induces sleep which, on its side, likewise has a limit and must progress to its opposite. This double *transition* is the way in which, in this sphere, the unity of the implicit substantiality of the soul with the self-existent individuality of the latter, makes its appearance.

(γ) *Sensibility*[1]

§ 399

Sleep and waking are, primarily, it is true, not mere alterations, but *alternating* conditions (a progression *in infinitum*). This is their formal and negative relationship: but in it the *affirmative* relationship is also involved. In the self-certified existence of waking soul its mere existence is implicit as an 'ideal' factor: the features which make up its sleeping nature, where they are implicitly as in their substance, are *found* by the waking soul, in its own self, and, be it noted, for itself. The fact that these particulars, though as a mode of mind they are distinguished from the self-identity of our self-centred being, are yet simply contained in its simplicity, is what we call sensibility.

Zusatz. As regards the dialectical progress from the waking soul to sensibility we have to remark as follows. The sleep which follows waking is the *natural* mode of the soul's return from difference to distinctionless unity with itself. In so far as mind remains entangled in the bonds of natural life, this return represents nothing but the empty *repetition* of the beginning—a monotonous cycle. But *in itself*, or in principle, this return at the same time contains a *progress.* For the transition of sleep into waking and of waking into sleep, has *for us* a result which is no less positive than negative; namely, that both the undifferentiated substantial being of the soul in sleep and the still quite abstract, still quite empty, being-for-self of the soul achieved in its waking state, when taken in their separateness, prove themselves to be one-sided, untrue determinations and their concrete *unity* emerges as their truth. In the reiterated alternation of sleep and waking, these determinations are perpetually striving towards their concrete unity without ever reaching it; in this alternation each of the determinations always simply falls from its own one-sidedness into that of the opposite determination. But the unity vainly striven for in that alternation becomes an actuality in the sentient soul. As sentient, the soul is dealing with an immediate, merely given, determination, one which it has not itself produced but which it only finds to hand, given either internally or externally and therefore not dependent on it. But at the same time, this determination is immersed in the soul's universality and is thereby negated in its immediacy and so

[1] Empfindung.

characterized as of ideal nature. Consequently in this Other, the sentient soul returns to itself, and in the immediate, merely given object which it senses, is in communion with itself. Thus the soul's abstract being-for-self in the waking state obtains its first fulfilment through the determinations which are ideally contained in the soul's sleeping nature, in the soul's substantial being. Actualized and self-certain by means of this fulfilment, the soul is authenticated in its being-for-self, in its awakened state; not merely *is* it for itself, it also *posits* itself as such, as subjectivity, as the negativity of its immediate determinations. It is in this manner that the soul has first attained its *true* individuality. This subjective point of the soul now no longer stands separated off and opposed to its immediacy, but asserts itself in the manifold which is virtually contained in that immediacy. The sentient soul places the manifold within itself and removes therefore the opposition between its being-for-self or subjectivity, and its immediacy or substantial, merely implicit, being; not, however, in such a manner that, as in the relapse of the waking state into sleep, its being-for-self makes place for its opposite, that merely implicit being. On the contrary, its being-for-self preserves, develops, and authenticates itself in the alteration, in the Other, and the soul's immediacy is reduced from the form of a state existing *alongside* that being-for-self, to a deter-mination subsisting only *in* that being-for-self, consequently, is reduced to an *illusory* being. With sensation, therefore, the soul has reached the stage where the universal constituting its nature becomes explicitly for it in an immediate determinateness. It is only by this process of becoming explicitly for itself that the soul is sentient. The reason why the inanimate is not sentient is precisely because in it, the universal remains immersed in the determinateness in which it does not become for itself. In coloured water, for example, the distinction between its coloured and uncoloured state is only *for us*. If one and the same water were at the same time ordinary and coloured water, this distinctive determinateness would be for the water itself which therefore, would have sensation; for something has sensation by maintaining itself as a universal in its determinateness.

In the above discussion of the nature of sensation it is already implied that if, in § 398, the waking state might be called a *judgement* (partition) of the individual soul—because this state produces a *parting* of the soul into a soul which is *for itself* and a soul which merely *is*, and at the same time an *immediate* connection of its subjectivity with something else—we can assert the existence in sensation of a *syllogism*, from which we can derive the self-certainty of the waking state achieved by means of sensation. On waking, we find ourselves at first only quite vaguely dis-tinguished from the outer world generally. It is only when we start to have sensations that this distinction becomes definite. In order, therefore, to become fully awake and certain of it, we open our eyes, take hold of ourselves, in short, examine ourselves to find out whether something is, for us, a definite Other, is definitely distinct from us. In this examination we do not relate ourselves directly to the Other, but indirectly. Thus, for example, *touch* is the mediation between myself and the Other, since though it is distinct from these two sides of the opposition, yet at the same time it unites them. Here, therefore, as in sensation generally, the soul by the mediation of something standing between itself and the Other, unites with itself in the content of its sensation, reflects itself out of the Other into itself, separates itself from it and thereby assures itself of its being-for-self. This union of the soul with itself is the progress made by the soul—which in waking had parted itself—by its transition to sensation.

§ 400

Sensibility (feeling) is the form of the dull stirring, the inarticulate breathing, of the spirit through its unconscious and unintelligent individuality, where every definite feature is still 'immediate'— neither specially developed in its content nor set in distinction as objective to subject, but treated as belonging to its most special, its natural peculiarity. The content of sensation is thus limited and transient, belonging as it does to natural, immediate being— to what is therefore qualitative and finite.

Everything is in sensation (feeling): if you will, everything that emerges in conscious intelligence and in reason has its source and origin in sensation; for source and origin just means the first immediate manner in which a thing appears. Let it not be enough to have principles and religion only in the head: they must also be in the heart, in the feeling. What we merely have in the head is in consciousness, in a general way: the facts of it are objective— set over against consciousness, so that as it is put in me (my abstract ego) it can also be kept away and apart from me (from my concrete subjectivity). But if put in the feeling, the fact is a mode of my individuality, however crude that individuality be in such a form: it is thus treated as my *very own*. My own is something inseparate from the actual concrete self: and this immediate unity of the soul with its underlying self in all its definite content is just this inseparability; which, however, yet falls short of the ego of developed consciousness, and still more of the freedom of rational mind-life. It is with a quite different intensity and permanency that the will, the conscience, and the character, are our very own, than can ever be true of feeling and of the group of feelings (the heart): and this we need no philosophy to tell us. No doubt it is correct to say that above everything the *heart* must be good. But feeling and heart is not the form by which anything is legitimated as religious, moral, true, just, etc., and an appeal to heart and feeling either means nothing or means something bad. This should hardly need enforcing. Can any experience be more trite than that feelings and hearts are also bad, evil, godless, mean, etc.? That the heart is the source only of such feelings is stated in the words: 'From the heart proceed evil thoughts, murder, adultery, fornication, blasphemy, etc.' In such times when 'scientific' theology and philosophy make the heart and feeling the criterion of what is good, moral, and religious, it is necessary to remind them of these trite experiences; just as it is nowadays necessary to repeat that thinking is the characteristic property by which man is distinguished from the beasts, and that he has feeling in common with them.

Zusatz. Although the peculiarly human content belonging to free mind assumes the form of sensation (*Empfindung*), yet this form as such is common to the animal as well as the human soul and is, therefore, inadequate to that content. The contradiction between the *mental* content and sensation consists in the fact that the former is in and for itself universal, necessary, and objective; sensation, on the other hand, is an isolated particular, contingent, a one-sided subjectivity. We propose to explain briefly here to what extent the last-named determinations must be predicated of sensation. As we have already remarked, the content of sensation has essentially the form of an immediate, of something merely present, no matter whether it originates in free mind or in the sensible world. The idealization which the things of *external* Nature undergo in being sensed is still quite superficial and far removed from the complete removal of the immediacy of this content. But the mental material which, in itself, is opposed to this merely given content, becomes in the sentient soul an existent in the guise of immediacy. Now since what is unmediated is an isolated particular, everything sensed has the form of an isolated particular. This will readily be admitted of the sensations of the outer world, but it must also be asserted of the sensations of the inner world. The spiritual, rational, lawful, ethical, and religious content in assuming the form of feeling, receives the shape of an object of sense, of a separated existence lacking all connection, and thus acquires a similarity to the content of a sensation coming from the outer world which, though perceived only in its particularity, for example, as individual colours, yet, like the mental content, contains in itself or in principle a universal, for example, colour as such. The more comprehensive, superior nature of the mental or spiritual sphere is therefore manifested not in feeling, but only in comprehensive thinking. But in the particularization of the content in sensation, the *contingency* and one-sided subjective form of that content is also established. The *subjectivity* of feeling must be sought not in the mere fact that in sensation man posits something *in himself*—for in thinking, too, he posits something in himself —but more specifically in the fact that he posits something in his natural, immediate, particular subjectivity, not in his free, spiritual, universal subjectivity. This *natural* subjectivity is not as yet a self-determining one following its own laws and acting according to necessity, but a subjectivity determined from outside, tied to *this* space and *this* time and dependent on contingent circumstances. Therefore, being placed in this subjectivity every content becomes contingent and receives determinations which belong only to this particular subject. For this reason, it is quite inadmissible for anyone to appeal simply to his feelings. He who does so withdraws from the sphere, common to all, of reasoned argument, of thought, of the matter in hand, into his particular subjectivity which, since it is essentially passive, is just as receptive of the worst and most irrational as it is of the reasonable and the good. It is evident from all this that feeling is the worst form of a mental or spiritual content and that it can spoil the best content.

At the same time, it is already implied in the above that the opposition between the feeling subject and the object felt is still foreign to mere feeling. The subjectivity of the sentient soul is one so immediate, so undeveloped, so little self-determining and self-differentiating, that the soul to the extent that it *only* feels, does not as yet seize itself as a subject confronting an object. This difference belongs only to *consciousness* and so does not appear until the soul has attained to the abstract thought of its 'I', of its infinite being-for-self. This difference will therefore not fall to be discussed until we reach Phenomenology. Here in Anthropology we have only to consider the difference given by the *content* of feeling. This we shall do in § 401.

§ 401

What the sentient soul finds within it is, on one hand, the naturally immediate, as 'ideally' in it and made its own. On the other hand and conversely, what originally belongs to the central individuality (which as further deepened and enlarged is the conscious ego and free mind) gets the features of the natural corporeity, and is so felt. In this way we have two spheres of feeling. One, where what at first is a corporeal affection (e.g. of the eye or of any bodily part whatever) is made feeling (sensation) by being driven inward, memorized in the soul's self-centred part. Another, where affections originating in the mind and belonging to it, are in order to be felt, and to be as if found, invested with corporeity. Thus the mode or affection gets a place in the subject: it is felt in the soul. The detailed specification of the former branch of sensibility is seen in the system of the senses. But the other or inwardly originated modes of feeling no less necessarily systematize themselves; and their corporization, as put in the living and concretely developed natural being, works itself out, following the special character of the mental mode, in a special system of bodily organs.

Sensibility in general is the healthy fellowship of the individual mind in the life of its bodily part. The senses form the simple system of corporeity specified. (a) The 'ideal' side of physical things breaks up into two—because in it, as immediate and not yet subjective ideality, distinction appears as mere variety—the senses of definite *light*, (§ 317)—and of *sound*, (§ 300). The 'real' aspect similarly is with its difference double: (b) the senses of smell and taste, (§§ 321, 322); (c) the sense of solid reality, of heavy matter, of heat (§ 303) and shape (§ 310). Around the centre of the sentient individuality these specifications arrange themselves more simply than when they are developed in the natural corporeity.

The system by which the internal sensation comes to give itself specific bodily forms would deserve to be treated in detail in a peculiar science—a *psychical physiology*. Somewhat pointing to such a system is implied in the feeling of the appropriateness or inappropriateness of an immediate sensation to the persistent tone of internal sensibility (the pleasant and unpleasant): as also in the distinct parallelism which underlies the symbolical employment of sensations, e.g. of colours, tones, smells. But the most interesting side of a psychical physiology would lie in studying not the mere sympathy, but more definitely the bodily form adopted by certain mental modifications, especially the passions or emotions. We should have, for example, to explain the line of connection by which anger and courage are felt in the breast, the blood, the 'irritable' system, just as thinking and mental occupation are felt in the head, the centre of the 'sensible' system. We should want a more satisfactory explanation than hitherto of the most familar connections by which tears, and voice in general, with its varieties of language, laughter, sighs, with many other specializations lying in the line of pathognomy and physiognomy, are formed from their mental source. In physiology the viscera and the organs are treated merely as parts subservient to the animal organism; but they form at the same time a physical system for the expression of mental states, and in this way they get quite another interpretation.

Zusatz. The content of sensation either originates in the outer world or belongs to the soul's interior; a sensation is therefore either external or internal. Here we have to consider the latter class of sensations only in so far as they are corporealized; on the side of their inwardness they are proper to the sphere of psychology. The external sensations, on the other hand, are exclusively the subject-matter of Anthropology.

The first thing to be said about the last-named class of sensations is that we receive them through the various senses. The sentient subject is thus determined from outside, that is to say, his corporeity is determined by something external. The various modes of this determining constitute the different external sensations. Each such different mode is a general possibility of being determined, a circle of single sensations. Seeing, for example, contains the indefinite possibility of a multiplicity of visual sensations. The universal nature of the ensouled individual is also displayed in the fact that the individual is not tied to one single thing in the specific modes of sensation but embraces a whole circle of particulars. If, on the contrary, I could see only what was blue, this limitation would be a quality of me. But since, in contrast to natural things, I am the universal that is at home with itself in the determinateness, I can see any colour, or rather the whole range of different colours.

The general modes of sensation are related to the physical and chemical qualities of natural objects, the necessity of which has to be demonstrated in the Philosophy of Nature, and are mediated by the various sense-organs. The fact that in general the sensation of the external world falls asunder into such diverse, mutually indifferent modes of sensation, this lies in the nature of its content, since this is sensuous; but the sensuous is synonymous with the self-external in such a manner that even the internal sensations by their mutual externality acquire a sensuous character.

Now why we have just the familiar *five* senses, no more and no less, with their distinctive forms, the rational necessity of this must, in a philosophical treatment, be demonstrated. This is done when we grasp the senses as representations of the Notion's moments. These moments are, as we know, only *three*. But the five senses reduce quite naturally to three groups of senses. The first is formed by the senses of physical *ideality*, the second by those of *real difference*, and the third comprises the sense of *earthly totality*.

As representing the Notion's moments, each of these three groups must form a totality in itself. But now the first group contains the sense of what is abstractly universal, abstractly ideal, and therefore of what is not truly a totality. Here, therefore, the totality cannot exist as a concrete, but only as a sundered totality, as one which is split up into *two abstract* moments. This is why the first group embraces two senses—*sight* and *hearing*. For sight, the ideal element is in the form of a simple self-relation, and for hearing it exists as a product of the negation of the material element. The second group as the group of di˚ rence, represents the sphere of *process*, of decomposition and dissolution of concrete corporeity. But from the determination of difference, a doubling of the senses of this group at once follows. The second group contains, therefore, the senses of *smell* and *taste*. The former is the sense of the abstract, the latter the sense of the concrete, process. Lastly the third group embraces only one sense, that of *feeling* or *touch*, because touch is the sense of the *concrete* totality.

Let us now consider more closely the individual senses.

Sight is the sense of that physical ideality which we call light. We can say of light that it is, as it were, physicalized space. For light, like space, is indivisible, a serene ideality, ex˚ension absolutely devoid of determination, without any reflection-into-self, and therefore without internality. Light manifests something else and this manifesting constitutes its essential nature; but within itself it is abstract self-identity, the opposite of Nature's asunderness appearing within Nature itself, and therefore immaterial matter. For this reason light does not offer resistance, contains no limitation, expands illimitably in all directions, is absolutely weightless, imponderable. It is only with this ideal element and with its obscuration by the element of darkness, in other words, with colour, that sight has to do. Colour is what is seen, light is the medium of seeing. The really material aspect of corporeity, on the other hand, does not as yet concern us in seeing. Therefore the objects we see can be remote from us. In seeing things we form, as it were, a merely theoretical, not as yet a practical, relationship; for in seeing things we let them continue to exist in peace and relate ourselves only to their ideal side. On account of this independence of sight of corporeity proper, it can be called the noblest sense. On the other hand, sight is a very imperfect sense because by it the object does not present itself to us immediately as a spatial totality, not as *body*, but always only as surface, only according to the two dimensions of width and height, and we only get to see the body in its total shape by looking at it from various points of view and seeing it successively in all its dimensions. The most distant objects originally appear to sight, as we can observe in children, on one and the same surface as those nearest to us, just because sight does not directly see *depth*. Only in noticing that to the depth we have perceived by touch there corresponds something dark, a shadow, do we come to believe that where a shadow becomes visible we see a depth. Connected with this is the fact that we do not directly perceive by sight the measure of the distance of the body but can only infer it from the smaller or greater appearance of objects.

In contrast to sight which is the sense of ideality devoid of any inwardness, hearing is the sense of the pure inwardness of the corporeal. Just as sight is connected with physicalized space, with light, so hearing is connected with physicalized time, with sound. For in sound, corporeity has become posited as time, as the movement, the vibration of the body internally, a trembling, a mechanical shock in which the body, without having to alter its relative position as a whole body, moves only its parts, posits its inner spatiality as temporal, and therefore overcomes its indifferent asunderness, thereby letting its pure inwardness manifest, but immediately restoring itself from the superficial alteration it suffered from the mechanical shock. But the medium through which sound reaches our hearing is not alone the element of air but in still greater measure the concrete corporeity stretching between us and the sonorous object: the earth, for example, for when the ear is held to the ground cannonades can sometimes be heard which could not be heard through the medium of air alone.

The senses of the second group are related to *real* corporeity; but not as yet to real corporeity as a being-for-self and as offering resistance, but only in so far as it is in a state of dissolution, has entered into its *process*. This process is a necessary one. Bodies are, of course, destroyed partly by external, contingent causes; but apart from this contingent destruction bodies perish by their own nature, destroy themselves, but in such a manner that their destruction seems to approach them from outside. This is the action of air which gives rise to the silent, imperceptible process of the spontaneous dissipation of all bodies, the volatilization of all vegetable and animal forms. Now although both smell and taste are connected with spontaneously dissolving corporeity, yet these two senses are distinguished from each other by the fact that smell receives body in the *abstract*, simple, indeterminate process of volatilization or evaporation; taste, on the other hand, is connected with the *real* concrete process of body and with the chemical qualities issuing from that process, namely, sweetness, bitterness, alkalinity, acidity, and saltiness. For taste, a direct contact with the object is indispensable, whereas for smell this is not so. In hearing, such contact is still less necessary and in sight is completely absent.

As already remarked, the third group contains only the one sense of feeling. Since this is located chiefly in the fingers it is also called touch. Touch is the most concrete of all the senses; for its distinctive nature is the connection—not with the abstractly universal or ideal physical element, nor with the self-separating qualities of the corporeal—but with the solid reality of the latter. It is, therefore, really only for touch that there is a self-existent Other, a self-existent individual, over against the sentient subject as another self-existent individual. This is why touch is the sense affected by gravity, that is, by the unity sought by bodies which hold on to their being-for-self and do not enter into the process of dissolution but offer resistance. In general, it is material being-for-self which is for touch. But to the different modes of this being-for-self there belongs not only weight but also the kind of *cohesion*—hardness, softness, rigidity, brittleness, roughness, smoothness. But it is not only perdurable, solid corporeity which is for touch, but also the negativity of this material being-for-self, namely, *heat*. By this, the specific gravity and cohesion of bodies are altered. Hence, this alteration affects what is essential in the nature of body; it can therefore be said that also in being affected by heat, *solid* corporeity is for touch. Lastly, shape with its three dimensions comes within the province of touch; for determinateness in the sphere of mechanics appertains entirely to touch.

Besides the stated *qualitative* differences, the senses have also a *quantitative* determination of sensation, an intensity or weakness of it. Here quantity necessarily appears as *intensive* magnitude because sensation is simple. Thus, for example, the feeling of pressure exerted by a specific mass on the sense of touch exists as an intensity, although this intensity also exists extensively, as a measurable amount of pounds, etc. But the quantitative side of sensation offers no interest for philosophical treatment in so far as this quantitative determination becomes also qualitative and so forms a *measure*, beyond which feeling becomes too intense and therefore painful, and below which it becomes imperceptible.

On the other hand, the connection between the outer sensations and the inwardness of the sentient subject is important for philosophical anthropology. This inwardness is not absolutely indeterminate, undifferentiated. The very fact that the magnitude of the feeling is intensive and must have a certain measure, involves a connection between the sense-impression and the subject as an inherently self-determined being, a certain determinateness of the subject's sensibility, a reaction of the subjectivity to externality, and so the germ or the beginning of internal feeling. Already by this inner determinateness of the subject, man's outer sensibility is distinguished more or less from that of the animal. Some animals can, in certain circumstances, feel something outside of them which for human sensation does not as yet exist. Camels, for example, can even scent wells and streams miles away.

But it is more by its connection with the *mental* or *spiritual* inwardness than by this peculiar measure of sensibility that outer sensation becomes something peculiarly anthropological. Now this connection has manifold sides, though not all of them fall to be considered here. Excluded here from consideration is, for instance, the determination of feeling as pleasant or unpleasant, this comparison, more or less interwoven with reflection, of outer sensation with our inherently self-determined nature whose satisfaction or non-satisfaction by a sensation makes the latter in the first case a pleasant, in the second case an unpleasant, sensation. Just as little can the awakening of instincts by sensations be drawn into the field of our examination here. This awakening belongs to the sphere of practical mind which still lies far ahead. What we have to consider at this stage is simply and solely the *unconscious* relationship between outer sensation and mental or spiritual inwardness. Through this connection there originates in us what we call *mood*; this is a manifestation of mind of which, admittedly, we find an analogue in animals (like pleasant and unpleasant sensations and the awakening of instincts by sensations), but which (like the above-named other mental or spiritual manifestations), at the same time has a peculiarly human character and further, acquires an anthropological significance in our stricter sense of the word, by the fact that it is something not yet known by the subject with full consciousness. Even when we were considering the natural soul which had not yet attained to individuality, we had to speak of its moods which correspond to something external. At that stage, this externality consisted of still quite general circumstances of such an indeterminate universality that one cannot really say that these circumstances are felt. On the other hand, at the stage we have now reached in following out the development of the soul, it is outer sensation itself which provokes the mood. But this effect is produced by outer sensation in so far as an inner meaning is immediately—that means without the intervention of conscious intelligence—associated with it. By this meaning, the outer sensation becomes something *symbolical*. We must observe, however, that what we have here is not yet a symbol in the proper meaning of the word; for in its strict meaning a symbol is an external object distinct from us in which we are conscious of an inner quality, or which we generally connect with such a quality. In a mood provoked by an outer sensation we are not as yet in relation with an external object distinct from us, we are not yet Consciousness. Consequently, as we have said, the symbolical here is not yet manifested in its proper shape.

Now the mental or spiritual sympathies aroused by the symbolical nature of sense-impressions are something with which we are all quite familiar. We receive them from colours, sounds, smells, tastes, and also from tactual impressions. As regards colours, there are grave, gay, fiery, cold, sad, and soothing colours. Specific colours are therefore chosen as signs of our existing mood. Thus for the expression of grief, of inner gloom, of the shrouding of the spirit in darkness, we take the colour of night, of the darkness which is not brightened by light, the colourless *black*. Solemnity and dignity are also symbolized by black, because in it the play of contingency, of manifoldness and mutability, finds no place. The pure, luminous *white*, on the other hand, corresponds to the simplicity and serenity of innocence. The proper colours have, so to speak, a more concrete meaning than black and white. *Purple*, for example, has ranked from time immemorial as the royal colour; for this is the most powerful colour, the most aggressive for the eye; it is the interpenetration of the bright and the dark in the full intensity of their unity and their opposition. *Blue*, on the other hand, as the simple unity of the bright and the dark and tending to the passive dark, is the symbol of gentleness, of femininity, of love and faithfulness; and that is why painters, too, have almost always painted the Queen of Heaven in a blue garment. *Yellow* is not merely the symbol of ordinary gaiety but also of jaundiced envy.

Of course, the choice of colour for clothing can be very much a matter of convention; though at the same time, as we have observed, that choice reveals a rational meaning. There is also something symbolical in the *lustre* and dullness of colour; the former corresponds to the gaiety of people on brilliant occasions; a dull colour, on the other hand, to the simplicity and quietness of the character which disdains ostentation. In white itself there is a difference of lustre and dullness depending on whether it appears, for example, on linen, on cotton, or on silk; and one finds in many races a definite feeling for the symbolical aspect of this difference.

Besides colours, it is especially *sounds* which evoke in us a corresponding mood. This is chiefly true of the human voice; for this is the principal way in which a person shows forth his inner nature; what he is, that he puts into his voice. In a harmonious voice, therefore, we believe we can safely recognize the beauty of soul of the speaker, and in the raucous voice, coarse feelings. In the first case, the sound evokes our sympathy, in the latter case our antipathy. Blind people are particularly sensitive to the symbolical element in the human voice. It is even asserted that they claim to detect a person's physical beauty in the harmony of his voice, that they even pretend to detect a pock-marked person by the slightly nasal way of speaking.

So much for the connection between *outer* sensations and mental or spiritual inwardness. We have already seen in considering this connection that the inwardness of the sentient subject is not absolutely empty, not completely indeterminate, but on the contrary that it is inherently self-determined. This is true even of the animal soul, but incomparably truer of human inwardness. Accordingly, the latter has a content which is for it explicitly *internal*, not external. But before this content can be felt two things are necessary, an external occasion and a corporealization of the inner content, and therefore a transformation or a connection of it which constitutes the opposite of that connection into which the content given by the outer senses is brought by its symbolic nature. Just as the *outer* sensations symbolize themselves, i.e. are connected with the mental or spiritual *inwardness*, so do the *inner* sensations necessarily *outwardize*, corporealize, themselves because they belong to the natural soul and consequently possess an affirmative being, therefore must acquire an immediate existence in which the soul becomes for itself. When we speak of the inner determination of the sentient subject, without reference to its corporealization, we are considering only how this subject is *for us*, but not as yet how it is for itself and at home with itself in its determination, how it feels itself in the latter. It is only by the corporealiza-tion of its inner determinations that the subject is enabled to feel them; for before they can be felt it is necessary that they be posited both as distinct from the subject and as identical with it; but this occurs only by making outward, by the corporealization of, the inner determinations of the sentient subject. The corporealizing of these manifold inner deter-minations presupposes a sphere of corporeity in which this takes place.

This sphere, this restricted sphere, is my body. Its destiny is thus to be a sphere in which both inner and outer determinations of the soul are felt. The vitality of my body consists in this, that its materiality is unable to be for itself, cannot resist me, but is subject to me, is pervaded through and through by my soul for which it is an ideal medium. This ideal nature of my body makes possible and necessary the corporealization of my feelings, and makes the movements of my soul directly into movements of my bodily nature.

Now the inner sensations (feelings) are of two kinds:

First, those which concern my immediate *individuality* as it exists in some particular relationship or condition; here, for example, belong anger, revenge, envy, shame, remorse.

Secondly, those which are connected with an absolute universal, with right, morality, religion, the beautiful, and the true.

Both kinds of inner feelings, as we have already remarked, have this in common, that they are determinations which my immediately individual, my natural mind finds within it. On the one hand, both kinds can approach each other either by the felt content of right, morality, and religion acquiring more and more the form of a particular subjectivity, or, conversely, by the feelings which at first concern the particular subject becoming charged more strongly with the universal content. On the other hand, the difference between the two kinds of inner feelings becomes more and more pronounced the more the feelings of right, morality, and religion are freed from the admixture of the subject's particularity and are thereby raised to pure forms of the universal in and for itself. But in the same measure that the particular element in the inner feelings yields to the universal, so are these feelings spiritualized and the materiality of their expression diminished.

We have already stated above that further details of the content of the inner feelings cannot be included in our exposition here in Anthropology. Just as we accepted the content of the *outer* feelings from the Philosophy of Nature now behind us, where the rational necessity of that content had been demonstrated, so here we must anticipate as far as it is necessary the content of the *inner* feelings which finds its proper place only in the third part of the doctrine of subjective mind. Our subject-matter just now is only the *corporealization* of the inner feelings, and more specifically only the involuntary, not my intentional, corporealization of my feelings by means of *gestures*. This latter kind of corporealization does not belong to this part of our exposition because it presupposes that mind has already become master of its bodily nature, has consciously made it into an expression of its inner feelings, something which has not as yet taken place. Here, as we have said, we have only to consider the immediate transition of inner feeling into the corporeal mode of existence, which corporealization can, it is true, also become visible to others, can shape itself into a *sign* of the inner feeling, but does not necessarily—and in any case without the will of the sentient subject—become such a sign.

Now just as mind employs the organs of its *outward*-turned life, of its animal life, to use Bichat's term, its face, hands, and feet, to exhibit its inner feelings to others by means of gestures: so, on the other hand, it is chiefly the organs of the *inward*-turned life, the so-called 'precious viscera' in which the inner feelings of the sentient subject are corporealized *for himself*, not necessarily for others, in an immediate, involuntary manner.

The main phenomena of this corporealization are already familiar to everyone through language, which contains a good deal bearing on this topic which cannot very well be explained away as an age-old error. In general, it may be said that the inner feelings can be either beneficial or harmful and even ruinous, both to soul and to the whole body. Cheerfulness preserves health, anxiety undermines it. A psychic shock produced by grief and pain and giving itself an existence in the body can, if it occurs suddenly and exceeds a certain limit, lead to death or the loss of reason. Equally dangerous is sudden excessive joy; this, as in the case of overwhelming pain, produces in the mind such a violent contrast between the preceding and present states of the sentient subject, such a disharmony in his inner life, that its corporealization can result in the disruption of the organism, death, or insanity. A man of character, however, is much less exposed than others to such effects, since his mind has made itself much freer of his bodily nature and has acquired a much firmer hold of itself than has the 'natural' man who is poor in imaginative and intellectual resources and so is unable to endure the negativity of a sudden violent attack of pain.

But even if this corporealization does not have a destructively stimulating or depressing effect, yet it attacks more or less directly the *whole* organism, since in this all the organs and systems exist in a living unity. All the same, it is not to be denied that the inner feelings, according to the variety of their content, also have a *special* organ in which they primarily and preferably assume a corporeal form. This connection between a specific feeling and its special mode of corporeal manifestation, cannot be disproved by single cases which do not conform to rule. Such exceptions, chargeable to the impotence of Nature, do not justify ascribing this connection to pure contingency and imagining perhaps that anger could equally well be felt in the belly or the head as in the heart. Even language has sufficient understanding to employ *heart* for courage, *head* for intelligence, and not heart, say, for intelligence. But science is bound to show the necessary connection prevailing between a specific inner feeling and the physiological significance of the organ in which this assumes a corporeal form. We propose here to touch briefly on the most general phenomena which concern this point. It is one of the most undeniable experiences that *grief*, this impotent burying of the soul within itself, finds corporeal expression mainly as an abdominal illness, that is, in the reproductive system, hence in that system which represents the negative return of the animal subject to itself. *Courage* and *anger*, on the other hand, this negative turning-outwards against an alien power, against an injury which enrages us, has its immediate seat in the breast, in the heart, the focal point of irritability, of the negative act of expulsion. In anger the heart throbs, the blood gets hot and mounts to the face, and the muscles get tense. In this emotion, especially in vexation where the anger remains more internal rather than exhausts itself in a fit of rage, it may well happen that the *bile*, which belongs to the reproductive system, overflows even to the point of producing jaundice. But here we must remark that bile is, as it were, the *fiery* matter, by the emission of which the reproductive system, so to say, vents its anger, its irritability, on the food, dissolving and consuming it with the aid of the 'animal *water*' poured out by the pancreas. *Shame*, which is closely akin to anger, likewise corporealizes itself in the circulatory system. In shame, one begins to be a little angry with oneself; for shame contains a reaction to the contradiction between what I appear to be and what I ought and want to be, and is therefore a defence of my inner self against my incongruous appearance. This mental or spiritual turning-outwards is corporealized by the blood being sent to the face, so that the person blushes and in this way alters his appearance. In contrast to shame, *fear*, this shrinking into itself of the soul in face of a seemingly insurmountable negative, expresses itself by the blood receding from the cheeks, by growing pale, and by trembling. If, on the other hand, Nature is perverse enough to create some people who grow pale from shame and blush from fear, science must not let such inconsistencies of Nature prevent it from recognizing the opposite of these irregularities as law. Finally, thinking, too, in so far as it takes time and belongs to the immediate individuality, has a corporeal manifestation, is felt and especially in the head, in the brain, in general in the system of sensibility, of the simple general inwardness of the sentient subject.

In all the corporealizations of the mental or spiritual just considered, only that externalization of the emotions occurs which is necessary for them to be felt or which can serve to indicate the inner sensations. But this externalization is only complete when it becomes an *expulsion*, when it gets rid of the inner sensations.

An example of this corporealization which gets rid of the inner sensation is shown in *laughter*, more so in *weeping*, in sighing and sobbing, in general, in the *voice*, even before this is articulate, before it becomes *language*.

To comprehend the connection between these physiological phenomena and their corresponding emotions is a matter of no little difficulty.

As regards the spiritual side of these phenomena, we know in the case of *laughter* that it is produced by an immediately obvious contradiction, by something turning at once into its opposite, hence by something directly self-destructive, assuming that we ourselves are not involved in this worthless content, are not contemplating it as our own; for if we ourselves felt injured by the destruction of this content, we should *weep*. If, for example, someone with a proud bearing falls over, this can give rise to laughter, because he experiences in his own person the simple dialectic that what happens to him is the opposite of what he intended. The risible element in genuine *comedies* also essentially consists, therefore, in the immediate conversion of an intrinsically worthless end into its opposite; whereas in *tragedy* it is substantial ends which destroy themselves in their mutual conflict. In the case of the dialectic suffered by the object of comedy, the subjectivity of the spectator or listener attains to a serene and untroubled enjoyment of itself, since it is the ideality, the infinite power over any limited content, consequently the pure dialectic by which, in fact, the comical object is destroyed. Herein lies the reason for the gaiety induced in us by the comical. But the *physiological* manifestation of this state of gaiety which specially interests us here, is in harmony with this reason. For in *laughter*, the subjectivity which has attained to the serene enjoyment of itself, this pure self, this spiritual light, corporealizes itself as a lighting-up of the face, and at the same time the spiritual act by which the soul repels the ridiculous from itself finds a physical expression in the forcible intermittent expulsion of the breath. For the rest, though laughter pertains to the natural soul, hence is an anthropological phenomenon, it ranges from the vulgar peals of side-splitting laughter of an empty-headed or uneducated person to the gentle smile of the noble soul, to a smiling through tears, a series of gradations in which it frees itself more and more from its merely natural mode until in smiling it becomes a *gesture*, that is, something originating in the free will. The various modes of laughter indicate, therefore, the cultural level of individuals in a very characteristic manner. A reflective person never, or only rarely, abandons himself to peals of laughter; Pericles, for example, is supposed not to have laughed any more after he had dedicated himself to public affairs. Excessive laughter is rightly held to be evidence of dullness and a foolish mind that is insensitive to all the great, truly substantial interests, treating them as external and alien to itself.

Weeping, as we know, is the opposite of laughter. Just as in the latter, the subject corporealizes its felt harmony with itself at the expense of the comical object, so in weeping, the inner *disharmony* of the sentient subject, the pain produced by a negative, finds expression. Tears are a critical outburst and therefore not merely the expression but also the elimination of the *pain*; accordingly, they have just as beneficial an effect on health in the case of serious emotional disturbances, as pain which does not relieve itself in tears can be harmful to health and life. In tears, *pain*, the feeling of the rending opposition which has disrupted the soul, turns to water, to a neutral, indifferent material; and this neutral material itself into which pain is transformed is expelled by the soul from its corporeity. In this expulsion, as in that corporealization, lies the cause of the therapeutic effect of weeping. But that the *eyes* should be the organ from which the pain that relieves itself in tears forces its way out, this stems from the fact that the eye has a twofold function: on the one hand, it is the organ of sight, and thus of the sensation of external objects; and on the other hand, it is the place where the soul reveals itself in the *simplest* manner, since the eye's expression represents the fleeting, as it were, exhaled, portrait of the soul; and that is why people, in order to know each other, start by looking each other in the eye. Now the negative which a person feels as pain inhibits his activity, reduces him to passivity, clouds the ideality, the *light* of his soul, and to a greater or less degree breaks up the soul's firm unity with itself; accordingly, this state of the soul corporealizes itself by a dimming of the eyes, and still more by inducing a moisture in them which can so inhibit the function of sight, this ideal activity of the eye, that the person can no longer bear to see out of them.

A still more perfect corporealization and also elimination of the internal sensations than takes place in laughing and crying is produced by the *voice*. For in this there occurs not merely the shaping of something external already to hand as in laughing, nor the expulsion of a real material as in crying, but the production of, so to speak, an incorporeal corporeity, that is, a material in which the internality of the subject retains throughout the character of internality, the self-existent ideality of the soul receives a fully correspondent external reality, a reality which immediately vanishes in its arising, since the propagation of sound is just as much the vanishing of it. Therefore, in the voice, sensation obtains an embodiment in which it dies away just as fast as it is uttered. This is the ground of the higher power present in the voice of externalizing what is inwardly felt. That is why the Romans who were well acquainted with this power deliberately allowed women to wail at funerals in order that the pain they felt should be made into something extraneous to them.

Now although the abstract corporeity of the voice can become a sign for others who recognize it as such, here at the stage of the natural soul it is not as yet a sign voluntarily produced, not as yet speech articulated by the energy of intelligence and will, but merely a sound, the immediate product of sensation which, however, though inarticulate, is capable of a variety of modifications. Animals, in giving utterance to their sensations, remain inarticulate, emitting only cries of pain or pleasure; and some animals achieve this ideal utterance of their inwardness only in extreme need. Man, however, does not stop short at this animal mode of expressing himself; he creates *articulate* speech by which his internal sensations are turned into *words*, are expressed in their entire determinateness, are objective to him as subject, and at the same time become external and extraneous to him. Articulate speech is thus the highest mode in which man rids himself of his internal sensations. It is, therefore, with good reason that on the occasion of someone's death funeral hymns are sung and condolences conveyed; and though on occasion these may seem to be, or in fact be, wearisome yet they have this advantage, that the continual talk about the bereavement results in the pain of it being lifted out of the constricted sphere of the emotions into the ideational sphere and so converted into something objective, something standing over against the grieving mourner. But it is the writing of poetry especially that has the power to liberate one from emotional distress. Goethe, for example, more than once regained his spiritual freedom by pouring out his suffering in a poem.

Here, however, in Anthropology we can speak only in anticipation of the expression and the elimination of the internal sensations by articulate speech.

What remains to be mentioned at this stage is the physiological side of voice. Regarding this, we know that the voice, this simple vibration of the animal organism, has its origin in the diaphragm, but also that it is closely connected with the respiratory organs and receives its final shaping in the mouth, which has the dual function of initiating the immediate conversion of food into organic structures in the animal organism and also, in contrast to this inwardizing of the outer, of completing the objectification of subjectivity occurring in the voice.

§ 402

Sensations, just because they are immediate and are found existing, are single and transient aspects of psychic life—alterations in the substantiality of the soul, set in its self-centred life, with which that substance is one. But this self-centred being is not merely a formal factor of sensation: the soul is virtually a reflected totality of sensations—it feels *in itself* the total substantiality which it *virtually* is—it is a soul which feels.

In the usage of ordinary language, sensation and feeling are not clearly distinguished: still we do not speak of the sensation—but of the feeling (sense) of right, of self; sentimentality (sensibility) is connected with sensation: we may therefore say sensation emphasizes rather the side of passivity—the fact that we find ourselves feeling, i.e. the immediacy of mode in feeling—whereas feeling at the same time rather notes the fact that it is *we ourselves* who feel.

Zusatz. With the contents of the preceding Paragraph, we have completed the first part of Anthropology. In that part, we had at first to do with the wholly *qualitatively* determined soul, or with soul in its immediate determinateness. By the immanent progressive development of our subject-matter we have finally arrived at the individual soul which posits its determinateness as an *ideal moment* and in doing so returns to itself and becomes for itself: in other words, the *sentient* or *feeling* individual soul. This brings us to the transition to the second part of Anthropology, a part as difficult as it is interesting and in which the soul opposes itself to its substantiality, stands over against itself, and in its determinate sensations at the same time attains to the consciousness of its totality, but a consciousness which is not as yet objective but only subjective. Now since sensation is tied to the single individual, the soul at this stage ceases to be merely sentient. In this part, because the soul here appears as divided against itself, we shall have to consider it in its *diseased* state. In this sphere, there prevails a conflict between the freedom and unfreedom of the soul; for, on the one hand, soul is still fettered to its substantiality, conditioned by its naturalness, while, on the other hand, it is beginning to separate itself from its substance, from its naturalness, and is thus raising itself to the intermediate stage between its immediate, natural life and objective, free consciousness. In what measure the soul now is involved in this *intermediate stage* we propose to elucidate briefly here.

Mere sensation, as we have just remarked, has to do only with what is *individual* and *contingent*, with what is immediately given and present; and this content appears to the feeling soul as its *own* concrete actuality. On the other hand, when I raise myself to the standpoint of *consciousness*, I enter into a relationship with a world *outside* of me, with an objective totality, with an immanently connected sphere of manifold and complex objects standing over against me. As an objective consciousness I certainly have, in the first instance, an immediate sensation, but at the same time the sensed object is for me a point in the general context of things, something, therefore, which points away from and beyond its sensible individuality and immediate presence. So little is objective consciousness tied to the sensible presence of things that I can also have knowledge of something which is not sensibly present to me as, for example, a distant country familiar to me only through books. But consciousness effects its independence of the material of sensation by raising it from the form of a detached individuality into the form of universality, omitting what is purely contingent and indifferent in it and holding fast what is essential; by this transformation, the sensed object becomes something ideated. This alteration effected by abstract consciousness is something subjective which can go to the length of being arbitrary and unreal, and can produce ideas to which nothing actual corresponds.

Now the soul which *feels* or *glimpses* itself in its totality and universality and which we have now to consider in the second part of Anthropology, occupies the middle place between the ideational consciousness on the one hand, and immediate sensation on the other. To feel the universal seems a contradiction; for sensation as such has, as we know, only what is individual for its content. But this contradiction does not concern what we call the *feeling* soul; for this is neither involved in immediate sensuous feeling and dependent on what is immediately and sensibly present, nor, conversely, is it related to the pure universal which can be grasped only through the mediation of pure thought; the truth is that it possesses a content in which the universal and the individual, the subjective and the objective, have not yet become separated. At this stage, what I feel, I *am*, and what I am, I feel. I am here immediately present in the content, which only subsequently appears as a self-dependent world confronting me when I become an objective *consciousness*. This content is still related to the sentient soul as accidents are to substance; the soul still appears as the subject and centre of every determination of the content, as the power which, in an immediate manner, dominates the world of feeling.

Now the transition to the second part of Anthropology occurs more specifically in the following manner. First of all, we must remark that the distinction of external and internal sensations considered by us in the preceding Paragraph is only *for us*, that is to say, is for the reflective consciousness, but is definitely not for the soul itself. The simple unity of the soul, its serene ideality, does not as yet grasp itself in its distinction from an external world. But though the soul has not as yet any consciousness of this its ideal nature, it is none the less the *ideality* or *negativity* of all the various kinds of sensations, each of which in the soul seems to be for itself and indifferent to the others. Just as the objective world displays itself to our intuition not as something divided into different sides or aspects, but as a concrete divided into distinct objects, each of which is in its turn *for itself* a concrete, a complex of the most diverse determinations, so the soul itself is a totality of infinitely many distinct determinatenesses which in the soul come together in a unity, so that in them the soul remains *implicitly* an infinite *being-for-self*. In this totality or ideality, in the timeless, undifferentiated inwardness of the soul, the sensations which crowd each other out do not, however, vanish absolutely without trace, but remain in the soul as ideal moments, obtain in it their subsistence, at first as a merely *possible* content, which only becomes an *actuality* by becoming *for* the soul or by the soul becoming *for itself* in it. Accordingly, even though the soul does not retain the content of sensation as a *being-for-self*, yet it does bear that content *within it*. This preservation which relates only to an inwardly self-existent content, to an affection of myself, to mere sensation, is still remote from *recollection* in the strict meaning of the word; for this starts from the intuition of an externally posited object which is to be made internal, and here such an object, as we have already remarked, does not as yet exist for the soul.

But the soul has yet another side to its filling than the content which has already *been* in sensation and which we began by discussing. Besides this material we are also, *qua* actual individuality, in ourselves a world of concrete content with an infinite periphery, we have within us a countless host of relationships and connections which are always in us even if they do not enter into our sensation and ideation and which, no matter how much these relationships can alter, even without our knowledge, none the less belong to the concrete content of the human soul; so that the latter, on account of the infinite wealth of its content, may be described as the soul of a *world*, as the *individually* determined *world-soul*. Because the human soul is an *individual* soul determined on all sides and therefore *limited*, it is also related to a universe determined in accordance with its (the soul's) *individual* standpoint. This world confronting the soul is not something external to it. On the contrary, the totality of relations in which the individual human soul finds itself, constitutes its actual living-ness and subjectivity and accordingly has grown together with it just as firmly as, to use a simile, the leaves grow with the tree; the leaves, though distinct from the tree, yet belong to it so essentially that the tree dies if it is repeatedly stripped of them. Naturally, those who through a life rich in activity and experience have developed a more independent human nature, are better able to endure the loss of a part of what constitutes their world than those who have grown up in simple circumstances and are incapable of making efforts to enrich their experience; in the latter class of persons the feeling of being alive is sometimes so firmly bound up with their homeland that they suffer from home-sickness when abroad and are like a plant which can thrive only in a particular soil. All the same, the concrete self-feeling of even the strongest natures requires a certain range of external relationships, an adequate portion, so to speak, of the universe; for without such an individual world the human soul, as we have said, would have no individuality at all, would not attain to a specifically distinct individuality. But the human soul does not merely possess *natural differences*, it *differentiates itself inwardly*, separates its *substantial totality*, its individual world, from itself, sets this over against itself as subject. Its aim in this process is that what soul or mind is *in itself* is to become explicitly *for* mind, that the cosmos *virtually* contained in mind is to enter into mind's *consciousness*. But as we have already remarked, at the level of soul, of mind which is still unfree, there is no *objective* conscious-ness, no knowledge of the world as a world actually *projected out of myself*. The *feeling* soul communes merely with its *interior* states. The opposition between itself and that which is *for* it, remains still shut up within it. Only when the soul has negatively posited the manifold, immediate content of its individual world, converted it into a simple entity, into an abstract universal, hence only when a *pure* universal is *for* the universality of the soul and the soul, just by this process, has developed into the self-existent 'I', the self-objective 'I', into this self-related perfect universal (a development which the soul as such still lacks), only, therefore, after reaching this goal does the soul progress from its subjective feeling to a truly objective consciousness; for it is only the 'I' that is for itself, that is freed, at least in an abstract manner to begin with, from the immediate material [of its content], that also allows the material to exist freely *apart* from the 'I'. What we have therefore to consider prior to the attain-ment of this goal, is the struggle for liberation which the soul has to wage against the immediacy of its substantial content in order to become com-pletely master of itself and adequate to its Notion, or to make itself into what it is *in itself* or in its *Notion*, namely, into that self-related, *simple* subjectivity which exists in the 'I'. The elevation of the soul to this level of development exhibits a sequence of three stages which here can be indicated in anticipation.

In the first stage we see the soul entangled in the dreaming away and dim presaging of its *concrete natural life*. In order to comprehend the miraculous element in this form of the soul which lately has received general attention, we must bear in mind that here the soul is still in immediate, undifferentiated unity with its objectivity.

The second stage is the standpoint of *insanity*, which means the soul divided against itself, on the one hand already master of itself, and on the other hand not yet master of itself, but held fast in an isolated particularity in which it has its actuality.

Lastly, in the third stage, the soul becomes master of its natural individuality, of its bodily nature, reduces this to a subservient means, and projects from itself as an objective world that content of its substantial totality which does *not* belong to its bodily nature. Reaching this goal, the soul appears in the abstract freedom of the 'I' and thus becomes *consciousness*.

But about all these stages we must remark as we have already done in connection with the earlier stages of the soul's development that here, too, activities of mind which can only be considered in their free shape at a later stage must be mentioned in anticipation because they are already at work in the feeling soul.

(*b*) THE FEELING SOUL—(SOUL AS SENTIENCY)[1]

§ 403

The feeling or sentient individual is the simple 'ideality' or subjective side of sensation. What it has to do, therefore, is to raise its substantiality, its merely virtual filling-up, to the character of subjectivity, to take possession of it, to realize its mastery over its own. As sentient, the soul is no longer a mere natural, but an inward, individuality: the individuality which in the merely substantial totality was only formal to it has to be liberated and made independent.

Nowhere so much as in the case of the soul (and still more of the mind) if we are to understand it, must that feature of 'ideality' be kept in view, which represents it as the *negation* of the real, but a negation, where the real is put past, virtually retained, although it does not *exist*. The feature is one with which we are familiar in regard to our mental ideas or to memory. Every individual is an infinite treasury of sensations, ideas, acquired lore, thoughts, etc.; and yet the ego is one and uncompounded, a deep

---

[1] Die fühlende Seele.

featureless characterless mine, in which all this is stored up, without existing. It is only when *I* call to mind *an* idea, that I bring it out of that interior to existence before consciousness. Sometimes, in sickness, ideas and information, supposed to have been forgotten years ago, because for so long they had not been brought into consciousness, once more come to light. They were not in our possession, nor by such reproduction as occurs in sickness do they for the future come into our possession; and yet they were in us and continue to be in us still. Thus a person can never know how much of things he once learned he really has in him, should he have once forgotten them: they belong not to his actuality or subjectivity as such, but only to his implicit self. And under all the superstructure of specialized and instrumental consciousness that may subsequently be added to it, the individuality always remains this single-souled inner life. At the present stage this singleness is, primarily, to be defined as one of feeling—as embracing the corporeal in itself: thus denying the view that this body is something material, with parts outside parts and outside the soul. Just as the number and variety of mental representations is no argument for an extended and real multeity in the ego; so the 'real' outness of parts in the body has no truth for the sentient soul. As sentient, the soul is characterized as immediate, and so as natural and corporeal: but the outness of parts and sensible multiplicity of this corporeal counts for the soul (as it counts for the intelligible unity) not as anything real, and therefore not as a barrier: the soul is this intelligible unity *in existence*—the existent speculative principle. Thus in the body it is one simple, omnipresent unity. As to the representative faculty the body is but *one* representation, and the infinite variety of its material structure and organization is reduced to the *simplicity* of one definite conception: so in the sentient soul, the corporeity, and all that outness of parts to parts which belongs to it, is reduced to *ideality* (the *truth* of the natural multiplicity). The soul is virtually the totality of nature: as an individual soul it is a monad: it is itself the explicitly put totality of its particular world—that world being included in it and filling it up; and to that world it stands but as to itself.

§ 404

As *individual*, the soul is exclusive and always exclusive: any difference there is, it brings within itself. What is differentiated from it is as yet no external object (as in consciousness), but only the aspects of its own sentient totality, etc. In this partition (judgement) of itself it is always subject: its object is its substance, which is at the same time its predicate. This *substance* is still the content of its natural life, but turned into the content of the individual sensation-laden soul; yet as the soul is in that content still particular, the content is its particular world, so far as that is, in an implicit mode, included in the ideality of the subject.

By itself, this stage of mind is the stage of its darkness: its features are not developed to conscious and intelligent content: so far it is formal and only formal. It acquires a peculiar interest in cases where it is as a *form* and appears as a special *state* of mind (§ 380), to which the soul, which has already advanced to consciousness and intelligence, may again sink down. But when a truer phase of mind thus exists in a more subordinate and abstract one, it implies a want of adaptation, which is *disease*. In the present stage we must treat, first, of the abstract psychical modifications by themselves, secondly, as morbid states of mind: the latter being only explicable by means of the former.

(α) *The feeling soul in its immediacy*

§ 405

(αα) Though the sensitive individuality is undoubtedly a monadic individual, it is, because immediate, not yet as *its self*, not a true subject reflected into itself, and is therefore passive. Hence the individuality of its true self is a different subject from it—a subject which may even exist as another individual. By the self-hood of the latter it—a substance, which is only a non-independent predicate—is then set in vibration and controlled without the least resistance on its part. This other subject by which it is so controlled may be called its *genius*.

In the ordinary course of nature this is the condition of the child in its mother's womb:—a condition neither merely bodily nor merely mental, but psychical—a correlation of soul to soul. Here are two individuals, yet in undivided psychic unity: the one as yet no *self*, as yet nothing impenetrable, incapable of resistance: the other is its actuating subject, the *single* self of the two. The mother is the *genius* of the child; for by genius we commonly mean the total mental self-hood, as it has existence of its own, and constitutes the subjective substantiality of some one else who is only externally treated as an individual and has only a nominal independence. The underlying essence of the genius is the sum total of existence, of life, and of character, not as a mere possibility, or capacity, or virtuality, but as efficiency and realized activity, as concrete subjectivity.

If we look only to the spatial and material aspects of the child's existence as an embryo in its special integuments, and as connected with the mother by means of umbilical cord, placenta, etc., all that is presented to the senses and reflection are certain anatomical and physiological facts—externalities and instrumentalities in the sensible and material which are insignificant as regards the main point, the psychical relationship. What ought to be noted as regards this psychical tie are not merely the striking effects communicated to and stamped upon the child by violent emotions, injuries, etc., of the mother, but the whole psychical *judgement* (partition) of the underlying nature, by which the female (like the monocotyledons among vegetables) can suffer disruption in twain, so that the child has not merely got *communicated* to it, but has originally received morbid dispositions as well as other pre-dispositions of shape, temper, character, talent, idiosyncrasies, etc.

Sporadic examples and traces of this *magic* tie appear elsewhere in the range of self-possessed conscious life, say between friends, especially female friends with delicate nerves (a tie which may go so far as to show 'magnetic' phenomena), between husband and wife and between members of the same family.

The total sensitivity has its self here in a separate subjectivity, which, in the case cited of this sentient life in the ordinary course of nature, is visibly present as another and a different individual. But this sensitive totality is meant to elevate its self-hood out of itself to subjectivity in one and the same individual: which is then its indwelling consciousness, self-possessed, intelligent, and reasonable. For such a consciousness the merely sentient life serves as an underlying and only implicitly existent material; and the self-possessed subjectivity is the rational, self-conscious, controlling genius thereof. But this sensitive nucleus includes not merely the purely unconscious, congenital disposition and temperament, but within its enveloping simplicity it acquires and retains also (in habit, as to which see later) all further ties and essential relationships, fortunes, principles—everything in short belonging to the character, and in whose elaboration self-conscious activity has most effectively participated. The sensitivity is thus a soul in which the whole mental life is condensed. The total individual under this concentrated aspect is distinct from the existing and actual play of his consciousness, his secular ideas, developed interests, inclinations, etc. As contrasted with this looser aggregate of means and methods the more intensive form of individuality is termed the genius, whose decision is ultimate whatever may be the show of reasons, intentions, means, of which the more public consciousness is so liberal. This concentrated individuality also reveals itself under the aspect of what is called the heart and soul of feeling. A man is said to be heartless and unfeeling when he looks at things with self-possession and acts according to his permanent purposes, be they great substantial aims or petty and unjust interests: a good-hearted man, on the other hand, means rather one who is at the mercy of his individual sentiment, even when it is of narrow range and is wholly made up of particularities. Of such good nature or goodness of heart it may be said that it is less the genius itself than the *indulgere genio*.

Zusatz. What we described in the *Zusatz* to § 402 as the soul that is entangled in dreaming away and dimly presaging its individual world, this has been called in the heading of the above Paragraph, 'The Feeling Soul in its Immediacy'. We propose to give here a more specific exposition of this developmental form of the human soul than was given in the above Remark. Already in the Remark to § 404 it was said that the stage of dreaming and presaging is also a form to which, as a state of sickness, even mind which has developed into consciousness and intellect can again relapse. Both modes of mind, rational consciousness on the one hand, and the dreaming, presaging soul on the other hand, can now, in the first developmental stage of the feeling soul now under discussion, exist as more or less *mutually interpenetrating*: since the peculiarity of this

stage consists precisely in the fact that here the dull, subjective, or presaging consciousness is not as yet posited in *direct opposition* to the free,
objective, or rational consciousness as it is in the second stage of the
feeling soul, that of *insanity*, but, on the contrary, has only the relation
to it of something merely *different*, as something therefore which can be
mixed with the rational consciousness. Mind at this stage therefore does
not as yet exist as an *internal contradiction*; the two sides which, in insanity,
fall into contradiction with each other here stand in a relationship which
is still unconstrained. This standpoint can be called the *magical* relationship of the feeling soul, for this term connotes a relation of inner to outer
or to something else generally, which dispenses with any mediation; a
magical power is one whose action is not determined by the interconnection, the conditions and mediations of objective relations; but such a
power which produces effects without any mediation is 'the feeling soul
in its immediacy'.

For an understanding of this stage in the soul's development it will
not be superfluous to explain in more detail the notion of magic. *Absolute
magic* would be the magic of *mind as such*. This, too, exercises a magical
influence on objects, acts magically on another mind. But in this relation
immediacy is only a *moment*; mediation by means of thought and intuition,
as well as speech and gesture, forms the other moment in it. The child
is, of course, infected (*inficiert*) in a proponderantly *immediate* manner
by the mind of the adults it sees around it; at the same time, however,
this relation is *mediated* by consciousness and by the incipient independence of the child. Among adults, a superior mind exercises a magical
power over weaker minds; thus, for example, Lear over Kent, who felt
himself irresistibly drawn to the unhappy monarch because the king
seemed to him to have something in his countenance which he, as he puts
it, 'would fain call master'. A similar answer, too, was given by a queen
of France who, when accused of practising sorcery on her husband,
replied that she had used no other magical power against him than that
which Nature bestows on the stronger mind to dominate the weaker.

In the cases just cited, the magic consists in an immediate influence of
one mind on another, and generally in magic or sorcery, even when this is
related to natural objects like the sun and moon, there has always existed
the belief that sorcery produces its effects essentially by the power of the
mind acting directly on its object, a power which is not divine but dia-
bolical; so that the power possessed by the magician is the precise measure
of his subjection to the devil.

But the magic which is devoid of any mediation whatever is that which
the individual mind exercises over its *own* bodily nature, making this a
subservient, unresisting intrument of its will. And also over animals man
exercises a magical power which dispenses with any kind of mediation at
all, for these cannot endure the gaze of man.

Besides the magical modes of mind's activity just cited which *actually*
exist, there has also been *incorrectly* ascribed to humanity a primitive

magical state in which the human mind, without any developed consciousness or any mediation, possessed a knowledge of the laws of external
Nature and of its own true being, and also of the nature of God, in a much
more perfect manner than now. This whole conception is contrary just
as much to the Bible as to Reason; for in the myth of the Fall, the Bible
expressly declares that man acquired knowledge of the Truth only when
that original paradisal unity of man with Nature had been *disrupted*.
The fabled profound knowledge of astronomy and other sciences of
primitive man shrinks to nothing on closer examination. It can, of course,
be said that the *mysteries* contain the remnants of an earlier knowledge;
traces of Reason instinctively at work are found in the earliest and rudest
epochs. But such instinctive products of human Reason, lacking the form
of Thought, must not be taken as proofs of a *primitive scientific* knowledge;
on the contrary, they are of necessity thoroughly *unscientific* in character,
belonging merely to the sphere of feeling and intuition, since science
cannot be the first, but only the final, state of knowledge.

So much for the essential nature of magic as such. But as regards the
precise manner in which it appears in the sphere of Anthropology, we
must here distinguish two different forms of the magical relation of the
soul.

The first of these forms can be designated as the *formal* subjectivity
of life. This subjectivity is formal, because far from possessing what
properly belongs to objective consciousness, it really constitutes only a
moment of objective life. For this reason it is no more something that
ought *not* to be, something *pathological*, than, for example, dentition is;
on the contrary, it is a necessary factor in the healthy human being.
But the formal nature, the undifferentiated simplicity, of this subjectivity, at the same time implies that there can be no question at this
stage even of a *relationship between two independent* personalities, let alone
the *direct opposition* of the subjective consciousness to the objective
consciousness which only comes on the scene in insanity and is completely
ruled out here; such a relationship will only present itself in the second
form of the magical state of the soul.

The first form of this state to be discussed next contains, on its part,
three different states:

1. natural dreaming;
2. the life of the child in the womb; and
3. the behaviour of our conscious life in relation to our secret inner
   life, to our specific spiritual nature, or to what has been called the
   genius of man.

1. *Dreaming*

In treating of the *waking* of the individual soul (§ 398) and more precisely in fixing the specific difference between *sleep* and *waking*, we already
had to speak in anticipation of *natural dreaming*, because this is a moment

of sleep, and from a superficial standpoint can be regarded as proof of the identical nature of sleep and waking; but this superficiality must be countered by bearing firmly in mind the essential difference between these two states and their relation to dreaming. But the proper place to consider the last-named activity of the soul is at the start of its development where it is entangled in the dreaming away and presaging of its concrete natural life (§ 405). Recalling what was said in the Remark and *Zusatz* to § 398 about the thoroughly subjective nature of dreams and their complete lack of rational objectivity, all that we have now to add is that in the dreaming state the human soul is filled not merely with single, isolated feelings but, more than is usually the case in the distractions of the waking soul, attains to a profound, powerful feeling of its *entire individual* nature, of the *total compass* of its past, present, and future; and just because in this state the individual totality of the soul is felt, dreaming must be included in our consideration of the self-feeling soul.

2. *The child in the womb*

Whereas in dreaming, the individual who has attained to a feeling of himself is gripped in a simple, immediate self-relation, and this, his being-for-self, has at least the *form* of subjectivity, the child in the womb, on the other hand, reveals a soul which, in the child, is not as yet actually for itself but is so only in the mother, which cannot as yet support itself but is supported only by the mother's soul; so that here, in place of the simple *self*-relation of the soul existent in dreaming, there exists an equally simple, immediate relation to *another* individual in whom the as yet selfless soul of the foetus finds its Self. There is something marvellous about this relationship for the abstractive intellect which is unable to grasp the unity of distinct terms; for here we see an undivided soul-unity of two individuals living immediately in each other, one of which is an *actual*, independent self-supporting Self, while the other has at least a *formal* being-for-self and is more and more approaching the stage where it will actually possess an independent being of its own. But for speculative thought there is nothing incomprehensible about this undivided soul-unity, for the simple reason that the Self of the child is utterly incapable as yet of resisting the Self of the mother, but is completely open to the immediate influence of the mother's soul. This influence is revealed in those phenomena called birth-marks. Many of the phenomena classed under this head may well have a purely organic cause. But as regards many physiological phenomena there can be no doubt that these derive from the feeling of the mother and that, therefore, they have a psychic origin. There are, for example, reports of children being born with an injured arm because the mother either had actually broken an arm or at least had knocked it so severely that she feared it was broken, or, again, because she had been frightened by the sight of someone else's broken arm. Similar examples are too familiar to require mention here. Such a corporealization of the mother's inner feelings can be explained partly by the weakness of the foetus which offers no resistance, and partly by the fact that in the mother who is enfeebled by pregnancy and no longer has a completely independent vitality of her own but shares it with the child, the feelings acquire an unusual degree of vigour and intensity, overpowering the mother herself. To this power of the mother's feelings, the infant itself is still very much subjected; unpleasant emotions can, as we know, spoil the mother's milk and thus injuriously affect the child she is suckling. On the other hand, in the relationship of parents to their grown-up children a magical element has revealed itself in the fact that children and parents who had long been separated and did not know each other, unconsciously felt a mutual attraction. However, it cannot be said that this feeling is anything universal and necessary; for there are examples of fathers killing their sons in battle and sons their fathers, in circumstances where they would have been able to avoid slaying each other if they had had a presentiment of their natural relationship.

3. *The relationship of the individual to his genius*

The third mode in which the human soul achieves the feeling of its totality is the relation of the individual to his *genius*. By *genius*, we are to understand the particular nature of a man which, in every situation and circumstance, decides his action and destiny. I am in fact a duality: on the one hand, what I know myself to be according to my *outward* life and *general* ideas, and on the other hand, what I am in my *inner* life which is determined in a *particular* manner. This particular nature of my inwardness constitutes my *destiny*; for it is the oracle on whose pronouncement depends every resolve of the individual; it forms the objective element which asserts itself from out of the inwardness of the individual's character. That the circumstances and conditions in which the individual finds himself give just *this* rather than another direction to his destiny—this is the result not simply of them, of their peculiar character, nor simply of the *general* character alone of the individual, but also of his particular character. In the same circumstances, this specific individual behaves differently from a hundred other individuals; certain circumstances can have a magical effect on one individual, while another individual will remain quite unaffected by them. Circumstances are, therefore, blended with the inwardness of individuals in a contingent, particular manner; so that what these become is the outcome partly of circumstances and of generally accepted principles, and partly of their own particular inner character. Of course, the particular nature of the individual provides *grounds*, that is, *universally valid* principles, for what he does and does not do; but in doing so he acts essentially from *feeling*, and therefore always in a *particular* manner. Consequently, even the alert, rational consciousness which acts on universal principles is determined by its genius in such an overpowering manner that the individual appears to have lost his independence, a state which can be compared to the dependence of the foetus on the mother's soul, or to the passive way in which the soul, in dreams, arrives at the representation of its individual world. But on the other hand, the relation of the individual to his genius is distinguished from the two relations of the feeling soul previously considered, by the fact that it is their *unity*, that it brings together into a *unity* the moment of the *simple self-unity* of the soul contained in natural dreaming, and the moment of the *duality* of soul-life existing in the relation of the foetus to the mother: since the genius, on the one hand, is a *self-like other* over against the individual, like the mother's soul in relation to the foetus, and, on the other hand, forms an equally *indivisible unity* with the individual, as does the soul with its dream-world.

§ 406

(ββ) The sensitive life, when it becomes a *form* or *state* of the self-conscious, educated, self-possessed human being is a disease. The individual in such a morbid state stands in direct contact with the concrete contents of his own self, whilst he keeps his self-possessed consciousness of self and of the causal order of things apart as a distinct state of mind. This morbid condition is seen in *magnetic somnambulism* and cognate states.

In this summary encyclopaedic account it is impossible to supply a demonstration of what the paragraph states as the nature of the remarkable condition produced chiefly by animal magnetism —to show, in other words, that it is in harmony with the facts. To that end the phenomena, so complex in their nature and so very different one from another, would have first of all to be brought under their general points of view. The facts, it might seem, first of all call for verification. But such a verification would, it must be added, be superfluous for those on whose account it was called for: for they facilitate the inquiry for themselves by declaring the narratives—infinitely numerous though they be and accredited by the education and character of the witnesses—to be mere deception and imposture. The *a priori* conceptions of these inquirers are so rooted that no testimony can avail against them, and they have even denied what they have seen with their own eyes. In order to believe in this department even what one's own eyes have seen and still more to understand it, the first requisite is not to be in bondage to the hard and fast categories of the practical intellect.

The chief points on which the discussion turns may here be given:

(α) To the *concrete* existence of the individual belongs the aggregate of his fundamental *interests*, both the essential and the particular empirical ties which connect him with other men and the world at large. This totality forms *his* actuality, in the sense that it lies in fact immanent in him; it has already been called his *genius*. This genius is not the free mind which wills and thinks: the form of sensitivity, in which the individual here appears immersed, is, on the contrary, a surrender of his self-possessed intelligent existence. The first conclusion to which these considerations lead, with reference to the contents of consciousness in the somnambulist stage, is that it is only the range of his individually moulded world (of his private interests and narrow relationships) which appear there. Scientific theories and philosophic conceptions or general truths require a different soil—require an intelligence which has risen out of the inarticulate mass of mere sensitivity to free consciousness. It is foolish therefore to expect revelations about the higher ideas from the somnambulist state.

(β) Where a human being's senses and intellect are sound, he is fully and intelligently alive to that reality of his which gives concrete filling to his individuality: but he is awake to it in the form of interconnection between himself and the features of that reality conceived as an external and a separate world, and he is aware that this world is in itself also a complex of interconnections of a practically intelligible kind. In his subjective ideas and plans he has also before him this causally connected scheme of things he calls his world and the series of means which bring his ideas and his purposes into adjustment with the objective existences, which are also means and ends to each other. At the same time, this world which is outside him has its threads in him to such a degree that it is these threads which make him what he really is: he too would become extinct if these externalities were to disappear, unless by the aid of religion, subjective reason, and character, he is in a remarkable degree self-supporting and independent of them. But, then, in the latter case he is less susceptible of the psychical state here spoken of.—As an illustration of that identity with the surroundings may be noted the effect produced by the death of beloved relatives, friends, etc. on those left behind, so that the one dies or pines away with the loss of the other. (Thus Cato, after the downfall of the Roman republic, could live no longer: his inner reality was neither wider nor higher than it.) Compare homesickness, and the like.

(γ) But when all that occupies the waking consciousness, the world outside it and its relationship to that world, is under a veil, and the soul is thus sunk in sleep (in magnetic sleep, in catalepsy, and other diseases, for example, those connected with female development, or at the approach of death, etc.), then that *immanent actuality* of the individual remains the same substantial total as before, but now as a purely sensitive life with an inward vision and an inward consciousness. And because it is the adult, formed, and developed consciousness which is degraded into this state of sensitivity, it retains along with its content a certain nominal self-hood, a formal vision and awareness, which, however, does not go so far as the conscious judgement or discernment by which its contents, when it is healthy and awake, exist for it as an outward objectivity. The individual is thus a monad which is inwardly aware of its actuality—a genius which beholds itself. The characteristic point in such knowledge is that the very same facts (which for the healthy consciousness are an objective practical reality, and to know which, in its sober moods, it needs the intelligent chain of means and conditions in all their real expansion) are now immediately known and perceived in this immanence. This perception is a sort of *clairvoyance*; for it is a consciousness living in the undivided substantiality of the genius, and finding itself in the very heart of the interconnection, and so can dispense with the series of conditions, external one to another, which lead up to the result—conditions which cool reflection has in succession to traverse and in so doing feels the limits of its own external individuality. But such clairvoyance—just because its dim and turbid vision does not present the facts in a rational interconnection—is for that very reason at the mercy of every private contingency of feeling and fancy, etc.—not to mention that foreign *suggestions* (see later) intrude into its vision. It is thus impossible to make out whether what the clairvoyants really see preponderates over what they deceive themselves in.—But it is absurd to treat this visionary state as a sublime mental phase and as a truer state, capable of conveying general truths.[1]

(δ) An essential feature of this sensitivity, with its absence of intelligent and volitional personality, is this, that it is a state of passivity, like that of the child in the womb. The patient in this condition is accordingly made, and continues to be, subject to the power of another person, the magnetizer; so that when the two are thus in psychical *rapport*, the selfless individual, not really a 'person', has for his subjective consciousness the consciousness of the other. This latter self-possessed individual is thus the effective subjective soul of the former, and the genius which may even supply him with a train of ideas. That the somnambulist perceives in himself tastes and smells which are present in the person with whom he stands *en rapport*, and that he is aware of the other inner ideas and present perceptions of the latter as if they were his own, shows the substantial identity which the soul (which even in its concreteness is also truly immaterial) is capable of holding with another. When the substance of both is thus made one, there is only one subjectivity of consciousness: the patient has a sort of individuality, but it is empty, not on the spot, not actual: and this nominal self accordingly derives its whole stock of ideas from the sensations and ideas of the other, in whom it sees, smells, tastes, reads, and hears. It is further to be noted on this point that the somnambulist is thus brought into *rapport* with two genii and a twofold set of ideas, his own and that of the magnetizer. But it is impossible to say precisely which sensations and which visions he, in this nominal perception, receives,

---

[1] Plato had a better idea of the relation of prophecy generally to the state of sober consciousness than many moderns, who supposed that the Platonic language on the subject of enthusiasm authorized their belief in the sublimity of the revelations of somnambulistic vision. Plato says in the *Timaeus* (p. 71), 'The author of our being so ordered our inferior parts that they too might obtain a measure of truth, and in the liver placed their oracle (the power of divination by dreams). And herein is a proof that God has given the art of divination, not to the wisdom, but to the foolishness of man; for no man when in his wits attains prophetic truth and inspiration; but when he receives the inspired word, either his intelligence is enthralled by sleep, or he is demented by some distemper or possession (enthusiasm).' Plato very correctly notes not merely the bodily conditions on which such visionary knowledge depends, and the possibility of the truth of the dreams, but also the inferiority of them to the reasonable frame of mind.

beholds, and brings to knowledge from his own inward self, and which from the suggestions of the person with whom he stands in relation. This uncertainty may be the source of many deceptions, and accounts among other things for the diversity that inevitably shows itself among somnambulists from different countries and under *rapport* with persons of different education, as regards their views on morbid states and the methods of cure, or medicines for them, as well as on scientific and intellectual topics.

(ε) As in this sensitive substantiality there is no contrast to external objectivity, so within itself the subject is so entirely one that all varieties of sensation have disappeared, and hence, when the activity of the sense-organs is asleep, the 'common sense', or 'general feeling' specifies itself to several functions; one sees and hears with the fingers, and especially with the pit of the stomach, etc.

To comprehend a thing means in the language of practical intelligence to be able to trace the series of means intervening between a phenomenon and some other existence on which it depends—to discover what is called the ordinary course of nature, in compliance with the laws and relations of the intellect, for example, causality, reasons, etc. The purely sensitive life, on the contrary, even when it retains that mere nominal consciousness, as in the morbid state alluded to, is just this form of immediacy, without any distinctions between subjective and objective, between intelligent personality and objective world, and without the aforementioned finite ties between them. Hence to understand this intimate conjunction, which, though all-embracing, is without any definite points of attachment, is impossible, so long as we assume independent personalities, independent one of another and of the objective world which is their content—so long as we assume the absolute spatial and material externality of one part of being to another.

Zusatz. In the *Zusatz* to § 405 we said that two different forms of the *magical* relationship must be distinguished and that the first of these forms can be called the *formal* subjectivity of life. Consideration of this first form was concluded in the above-mentioned *Zusatz*. We have therefore now to consider the second form of this magical relationship, namely, the *real* subjectivity of the feeling soul. We call this subjectivity

real because here, in place of the *undivided*, substantial soul-unity which
is the dominant factor in dreaming and also in the foetal state and in the
relation of the individual to his genius, there appears an *actually twofold*
psychical life, *each side* of which is endowed with a peculiar existence of
its own. The first of these two sides is the unmediated relation of the
feeling soul to its individual world and substantial actuality; the second
side, on the other hand, is the mediated connection of the soul with its
objectively interrelated world. When these two sides become separated
and mutually independent, this must be designated an *illness*, since this
separation, in contrast to the modes of formal subjectivity considered in
the *Zusatz* to § 405, does not constitute a moment of the objective life
itself. Just as *physical* illness consists in the fixation of an organ or system
in opposition to the general harmony of the individual life, such obstruc-
tion and isolation sometimes going so far that the particular activity of
a system converts itself into a centre into which the rest of the body's
activity is concentrated, into a parasitical growth: so, too, in the *psychical
life* illness results if the merely *psychical* side of the organism, freeing itself
from the power of the *mental* or *spiritual* consciousness, usurps the latter's
function and mind or spirit, in losing control over the psychical element
belonging to it, no longer retains its self-mastery but itself sinks to the
form of psychical life and in doing so surrenders that relation to the actual
which to the sound mind is essential and objective, that is, the relation
resulting from the reduction to a *moment* of what is posited as external.
That psychical life can become independent of the mind and even usurp
its function, is possible because although it is in itself identical with
mind, it is no less distinct from it. In isolating itself from mind and positing itself as independent, the psychical life gives itself the illusory
appearance of being what mind in truth is, namely, the soul which exists
for itself in the form of *universality*. But mental illness is not merely to be
compared with physical illness, but is more or less *bound up* with it,
because when the psychical life wrests itself free from mind, the corporeity
which is as necessary for the empirical existence of mind as it is for that
of soul, is divided between these two separated sides and accordingly is
divided within itself and therefore sick.

Now the morbid states in which such a separation of psychical life
from mental or spiritual consciousness makes its appearance are very
varied; almost every illness can reach the point of this separation. But
here in the philosophical treatment of our subject-matter we do not have
to pursue this indefinite multiplicity of morbid states but only to determine
the main forms of the *universal* which shapes itself in them. Among the
illnesses in which this universal can be manifested are somnambulism,
catalepsy, the oncoming of puberty in girls, pregnancy, also St. Vitus's
dance, and the moment of approaching death, when this splitting up of
the vital energies leads to an enfeeblement of the healthy, mediated consciousness and to an ever-increasing ascendancy of the psychical life
with its intuitions and presentiments. But especially must we examine

here, too, the state which has been called *animal magnetism*, both in its spontaneous manifestation in an individual and in its production in a particular manner in one individual by another. Spiritual causes, especially religious and political exaltation, can also lead to this dividedness of the psychical life. In the war of the Cevennes, for example, the freely manifested psychical element took the form of a high degree of seership in children, in girls and especially in old people. The most remarkable example of such exaltation is the famous one of Joan of Arc, in whom we see, on the one hand, the patriotic enthusiasm of a quite pure, simple soul and, on the other hand, a kind of magnetic state.

After these preliminary remarks we shall consider the particular main forms in which is manifested a separation of psychical life from objective consciousness. We hardly need to recall here what we have already said about the difference between these two ways in which man relates himself to his world: namely, that as objective consciousness he knows the world as an objectivity *external* to him, as infinitely *manifold*, but in all its parts necessarily interrelated and containing nothing unmediated within it; and he relates himself to it in a corresponding manner, that is, in a manner which is equally manifold, determinate, mediated, and necessary, and is therefore able to enter into relation with a *specific* form of external objectivity only by a *specific* sense organ, for example, is able to see only with the eyes; whereas feeling, or the subjective way of knowing, dispenses wholly, or at least in part, with the mediations and conditions indispensable to an objective knowledge and can, for example, perceive visible things without the aid of the eyes or without the mediation of light.

1. This immediate Knowing is manifest first and foremost in so-called *metal-* and *water-diviners*. These are persons who, fully awake and without using the sense of sight, perceive metal or water existing underneath the ground. The not infrequent appearance of such persons cannot be doubted. Amoretti asserts that he has discovered this peculiar sensitivity in more than four hundred individuals, a proportion of whom enjoyed quite good health. Besides metal and water, the presence of salt can also be felt by some persons without the aid of any intermediary; when salt is present in large quantities it produces malaise and uneasiness in them. In looking for hidden water and metals, and salt too, these individuals also employ a divining-rod. This is a hazel twig shaped like a fork, the two ends being held in the hands and the other end bending down towards the objects just mentioned. Obviously the movement of the wood is not caused by anything in the wood itself but is determined solely by the sensitivity of the person; just as, in the use of the pendulum— although here if several metals are employed there can be a certain reciprocal action between them—human sensitivity is always the main determining factor. For if, for example, a gold ring is held over a glass of water and the edge of the glass is struck by the ring as many times as the clock shows hours, the explanation is to be found solely in the fact that if, for example, eleven o'clock strikes and I know that it is eleven o'clock,

my knowing this is sufficient to stop the pendulum. But sensitivity armed with the divining-rod is supposed not merely to have discovered inanimate natural objects but occasionally also to have helped in tracking down thieves and murderers. Whatever charlatanism there may be in accounts of such happenings, some of the cases mentioned seem worthy of credence, particularly, for example, the case which occurred in the seventeenth century, when a French peasant accused of murder, on being taken into the cellar where the murder had been committed, broke out into a cold sweat and received such an impression of the murderers that he was able to find the road they had taken and where they had stayed. He discovered one of the murderers in a prison in southern France and pursued the other up to the Spanish frontier where he was forced to turn back. Such an individual has a sensitivity as acute as that of the dog which follows the scent of its master over a distance of several miles.

2. The second manifestation to be considered here of a Knowing which is immediate or sensed, has this in common with the first just discussed: in both cases, an object is sensed without the mediation of the *specific* sense-organ with which the object is mainly connected. But at the same time, this second phenomenon is distinguished from the first by the fact that in it there is not such a complete absence of mediation as in the first, since the specific sense concerned is replaced either by the *generalized sense* operating mainly in the pit of the stomach, or by the sense of touch. This form of feeling or sensing is displayed both in catalepsy as such, a state in which the organs are paralysed, and especially in somnambulism, a kind of cataleptic state in which dreaming expresses itself not merely in speech but also in walking about and in other actions, underlying which there is often an accurate awareness of the relations of surrounding objects. As regards the manifestation of this state, it can be induced by a specific disposition to it or by purely external things, for example, by certain articles of food eaten during the evening. In this state, the soul equally remains dependent on external things; for example, the sound of music played near a sleep-walker caused him to recite whole stories. But with regard to the functioning of the senses, it must be noted that true sleep-walkers though they can *hear* and *feel*, do not *see*, for their eyes, whether open or shut, are fixed; that therefore in this state where the subjective and the objective are *not separated*, the sense of sight for which, more than for any other sense, objects appear in the normal state of consciousness at their proper *distance* from me, in this state ceases to function. As we have already remarked, in somnambulism sight is replaced by the sense of touch. This substitution also occurs in persons actually blind, but only to a slight extent and, moreover, in both cases must not be understood as if, by the dulling of one sense, the other sense became more acute in a purely physical manner; the truth is rather that this greater acuteness results merely from the soul attending with undivided energy to the sense of touch. However, this is by no means always a sure guide for the sleep-walker, whose actions generally follow an arbitrary sequence.

Such persons do occasionally write letters in their sleep; but they are often betrayed by their feelings, for example, believing they are mounted on a horse when in fact they are sitting on a roof. But besides the astonishingly increased acuteness of the sense of touch in cataleptic states, the generalized sense, mainly in the pit of the stomach, becomes as we have already remarked, so active that it takes the place of sight, hearing, or even taste. Thus at Lyons, at a time when animal magnetism was still unknown, a French physician treated a patient who could hear and read only in the pit of the stomach and who could read a book held by someone in another room who was put *en rapport* with another person standing by the pit of the patient's stomach by means of a chain of persons arranged by the physician. This seeing at a distance has, however, been variously described by those in whom it occurred. These often say that they see the objects internally; or they assert that it seems to them as if the objects emitted rays. But as regards the just-mentioned substitution of taste by a generalized sense, there are instances of persons tasting food placed on their stomachs.

3. The third manifestation of immediate Knowing is that without the aid of any specific sense-organ and without a general sensitivity becoming active in any particular part of the body, an undefined feeling gives rise to an intimation or a vision of something not sensibly present but distant in space or time, either past or future. Now though it is often difficult to distinguish purely subjective visions of non-existent objects from those visions which have something actual for their content, yet this distinction must be maintained. The first kind of vision does occur in somnambulism, but mostly in a predominantly physical state of illness, for example, in a feverish delirium and even in waking consciousness. An instance of such subjective vision is given by Fr. Nicolai, who, while awake, saw perfectly distinctly other houses in the street than those actually existing, and yet knew that this was an illusion. The predominantly physical basis of this poetic illusion of an otherwise thoroughly prosaic individual was demonstrated when the illusion was dispelled by the application of leeches to the rectum.

But what we have mainly to keep in view in our anthropological exposition is the second kind of visions, those which relate to actually existent objects. In order to understand the miraculous aspect of this class of phenomena it is important to bear in mind the following points of view relative to the soul.

The soul pervades everything, it does not exist merely in a particular individual; for as we have previously said, the soul must be grasped as the truth, as the ideality, of everything material, as the wholly universal being in which all differences are only ideal and which does not one-sidedly stand over against its Other, but overarches it. But the soul is, at the same time, an individual, specifically determined soul; it contains therefore various determinations or specifications which appear, for example, as impulses and tendencies. These determinations, though distinct from one another, are nevertheless on their own mere *generalities*; it is only in me as a *specific* individual that they first acquire a *determinate* content. Thus, for example, love for my parents, relatives, friends, and so on, becomes individualized in me; for I cannot be a friend and so on *in general*, but am necessarily for these *particular* friends a *particular* friend living in a *particular* place at a *particular* time and in a *particular* situation. All the general determinations of the soul individualized in me and experienced by me constitute my actuality, and are therefore not left to my caprice but, on the contrary, are powers controlling my life and just as much belong to my actual being as my head or my breast belong to my organic existence. I *am* this whole circle of determinations: these have grown up with my individuality; each single point in this circle—for example, the fact that I am now sitting here—shows itself to be removed from the caprice of my imagining by the fact that it is set in the totality of my self-feeling as a link in the chain of determinations or, in other words, is embraced by the feeling of totality of my actual existence. But in so far as I am at first only a feeling soul, not as yet a wakened, free self-consciousness, I am aware of this actuality of mine, of this world of mine, in a *purely immediate*, quite *abstractly positive* manner, since, as we have already remarked, at this stage I have not as yet posited the world as separate from me, not as yet posited it as an external existence, and my knowledge of it is therefore not as yet *mediated* by the opposition of subjectivity and objectivity and by the removal of this opposition.

The *content* of this intuitive knowing, we must now determine in more detail.

(1) First, there are states in which the soul becomes aware of a content it had long since forgotten and which, in the waking state, it is no longer able to bring to mind. This phenomenon occurs in various illnesses. The most striking phenomenon of this kind is that a sick person will talk in a language which, though he had studied it when young, he can no longer speak in his normal waking state. It also happens that ordinary people who normally are accustomed to speaking only Low German, in magnetic trance talk in High German without any effort. It is also an undoubted fact that persons in such a state recite with perfect facility something they had read a considerable time before, which they had never committed to memory and which had vanished from their waking consciousness. For instance, someone recited from Young's *Night Thoughts* a long passage which he could no longer remember while awake. Another very remarkable instance is that of a boy who, while quite young, was operated on for a brain injury caused by a fall and gradually lost his memory until he could not remember what he had done an hour earlier; when put into a magnetic trance, however, he regained his memory so completely that he could state the cause of his illness, what instruments were used in the operation, and the people who were present at it.

(2) But what can seem more wonderful than this knowledge of a content already deposited in the *interior* of the soul, is the unmediated

knowing of events which are still *outside* of the feeling subject. For with respect to this second content of the intuitively clairvoyant soul, we know that the existence of anything external is tied to space and time, and our ordinary consciousness is mediated by these two forms of asunderness.

In the first place, as regards what is distant from us in *space*, we can be aware of it in our waking consciousness only on condition that we overcome the distance by a mediation. But this condition does not exist for the clairvoyant soul. Space pertains not to the soul but to outer Nature; and this outer existence, in being apprehended by the soul ceases to be spatial since, transformed by the soul's ideality, it is no longer external either to itself or to us. Consequently, when the free, intellectual consciousness sinks to the form of the merely feeling soul, the subject is no longer tied to space. There have been a great number of instances of this independence of the soul relatively to space. Here we must distinguish two cases. Either the happenings are *absolutely external* to the clairvoyant subject who is aware of them without any kind of mediation; or, on the contrary, they have already begun to receive for the subject the form of inwardness and therefore of something which is *not* extraneous to it, the form of a mediated content through being known in an entirely *objective* manner by *another* subject, between whom and the clairvoyant there exists such complete psychical *rapport* that what is in the objective consciousness of the former also penetrates the soul of the latter. We shall not consider the form of clairvoyance mediated by *another* person until later, when dealing with the magnetic state proper. Here, however, we must concern ourselves with the first-mentioned case, that of a completely unmediated knowledge of spatially remote, external happenings.

Instances of this kind of clairvoyance were commoner in ancient times, when the psychical life was more predominant, than in the modern period in which the independence of the intellectual consciousness has developed to a much greater extent. The old chronicles, which are not to be too hastily charged with error and falsehood, relate many a case coming under this head. Sometimes the clairvoyant has a clear consciousness of the distant object seen in a vision and sometimes only an obscure awareness of it. This fluctuation in the clarity of clairvoyant vision was shown, for example, in the case of a girl who had a brother in Spain but in her waking consciousness did not know this; she saw this brother clairvoyantly in a hospital, at first only indistinctly; she then thought she saw him dead and opened up for autopsy, but subsequently alive again; it was later ascertained that she had seen correctly, in so far as at the time of her vision her brother had actually been in a hospital at Valladolid, but that she was mistaken in thinking she saw him dead, since it was not her brother who had died but another person lying near him at the time. In Spain and Italy, where the life of Nature in man is more general than it is with us, apparitions such as the one just mentioned relating to distant friends and husbands are not infrequent, especially in the case of women and friends.

Secondly, the clairvoyant soul also rises above the condition of *time*, no less than that of space. We have already seen above that the soul in the visionary state can make present to itself again something that the *lapse* of time has completely removed from waking consciousness. A more interesting question, however, for mental representation is whether one is also able to have clear knowledge of something separated from him by *future* time. Our reply to this question must be as follows. First and foremost we can say that, just as picture-thinking errs when it holds the above-mentioned clairvoyant vision of a particular object, which by reason of its *spatial* distance is physically completely out of sight, to be superior to knowledge of the truths of Reason, so also it is the victim of a similar error when it imagines that a perfectly certain and clearly defined knowledge of the *future* would be something very sublime, and that in the absence of such knowledge one must look around for grounds with which to console oneself. On the contrary, it must be said that it would be desperately wearisome to have exact foreknowledge of one's destiny and then to live through it in each and every detail in turn. But a foreknowledge of *this* kind is an impossibility; for what is as yet only in the *future* and therefore merely *implicit* or a *possibility*, this simply cannot be an object of perceptive, intellectual consciousness, since only what *exists*, only what has attained to the *particularity* of something *sensibly present* is perceived. The human mind is, of course, able to rise above the Knowing which is occupied exclusively with sensibly present particulars; but the *absolute* elevation over them only takes place in the philosophical cognition of the Eternal, for the Eternal, unlike the particular of sense, is not affected by the flux of coming-to-be and passing-away and is, therefore, neither in the past nor in the future; on the contrary, it is the absolutely *present*, raised above Time and containing within itself all the differences of Time in their ideality. In magnetic trance, on the other hand, only a *conditioned* elevation above the Knowing of what is immediately present can take place. The foreknowledge revealed in this state always relates only to the *particular* sphere of existence of the clairvoyant, and especially to his individual disposition to disease, and does not possess, as regards form, the necessary interconnection and definite certainty of the objective, intellectual consciousness. The clairvoyant is in a state of *concentration* and contemplates this veiled life of his with all its content in a *concentrated* manner. In the determinateness of this concentrated state, the determinations of space and time are also *veiled*. However, these forms of the external world are not apprehended *qua* space and time by the clairvoyant's soul which is buried in its interior life; *this* is done only by the objective consciousness which sets *its* actual world over against itself. But since the clairvoyant is, *at the same time*, an *ideational* being he must also make *outwardly apparent* these determinations *veiled* in his concentrated life or, what is the same thing, must give this concentrated state an *outer* existence in the forms of space and time, must, in general, display it after the manner of the waking consciousness. It is evident from this in what sense this clairvoyant seeing contains a mediation of time, while, on the other hand, it does not require this mediation and is for that very reason able to see into the future. But the *quantum* of future time involved in the clairvoyant state is not an independent, fixed amount, but is a special mode of the *quality* of the clairvoyantly seen content, something belonging to this quality, just as, for example, the period of three or four days is proper to the specific nature of fever The process of making explicit this quantum of time consists, therefore, in penetrating and developing the intensive aspect of the object thus seen. Now in this development endless deception is possible. The clairvoyant never states an exact time; on the contrary, most of the prophesyings of such persons come to nothing, especially if these visions have for their content happenings dependent on the free will of other persons. That clairvoyants are so often deceived on this point is quite natural; for they see a future event only according to their quite indefinite, contingent feeling which varies according to circumstances, and then they expound it in an equally indefinite and contingent manner. But, on the other hand, the occurrence of very marvellous premonitions and visions of this kind which have actually come to pass can certainly not be denied. For instance, people have been awakened and impelled to leave a room or a house by a premonition that the ceiling or the house was about to collapse, which it subsequently did. Sailors, too, are said sometimes to have an infallible premonition of a coming storm of which the intellectual consciousness has not yet noticed the slightest sign. It is also asserted that many people have predicted the hour of their death. Abundant instances of premonitions of coming events are to be found mainly in the Scottish Highlands, in Holland, and Westphalia. Especially among Highlanders, the faculty of so-called 'second sight' is even now not uncommon. Persons with this gift see themselves double, see themselves in situations and circumstances in which they will find themselves only subsequently. In explanation of this marvellous phenomenon the following may be said. As has been remarked, in Scotland 'second sight' used to be much more common than it is now. It seems, therefore, that for its manifestation a peculiar stage of mental or spiritual development is necesssary, a stage that is equally removed from primitiveness and from an advanced culture, where people do not pursue any *universal* aims but occupy themselves merely with their own *personal* affairs, their concontingent, particular aims, without any deep insight into the nature of the matters to be dealt with and indolently following in the footsteps of their forefathers; hence, lacking any interest in knowing what is universal and necessary, they busy themselves only with contingent, isolated matters. It is just because of this immersion of mind in what is *particular* and *contingent* that people often seem to have the gift of seeing a *particular* event which is still hidden in the future, especially if this is not a matter of indifference to them. However, in these as in similar phenomena, philosophy obviously cannot set out to explain all the particular details which often are not properly authenticated but, on the contrary, extremely doubtful; rather must we restrict ourselves in a philosophical treatment, as we have done above, to bringing into prominence the main points of view of the phenomena in question which are to be borne in mind.

(3) Now whereas in the intuitive knowledge considered under (1), the soul immersed in its interior life only brings back to consciousness a content which it *already possessed*, and in the case of the material discussed under (2), on the contrary, is immersed in the vision of a particular *external* circumstance, in the third form of the soul's clairvoyant knowledge of its *own inner* life, of its psychical and physical state, it returns from this reference to an external object back to itself. This side of clairvoyance occupies a very wide field and can also attain to considerable clarity and precision. But it is only clairvoyants who are medically trained and who consequently possess in their waking consciousness an exact knowledge of the nature of the human organism, who can give any perfectly precise and correct information about their physical state. From those, on the other hand, who are untrained medically one cannot expect any completely accurate anatomical and physiological information; such persons, on the contrary, will have the greatest difficulty in giving a coherent, intelligent account of the concentrated vision which they have of their physical state: they can only translate what they see into the form of *their* waking consciousness, that is, of a consciousness more or less vague and ignorant. But just as clairvoyants vary considerably as regards the immediate knowledge of their bodily state, so also do they differ widely with respect to the intuitive knowledge of their mental or spiritual inwardness as regards both form and content. Clairvoyance is a state in which the substantial nature of the soul is manifested, and therefore in that state noble natures experience a wealth of noble feelings, their true self, their better spiritual side, which often appears to them as a special guardian angel. Base natures, on the other hand, reveal in this state their baseness and give themselves over to it unreservedly. Lastly, individuals of mediocre worth often undergo during clairvoyance a moral conflict with themselves, since in this new life, in this serene inner vision, the more important and nobler element in their character is manifested and this turns destructively on the individual's failings.

(4) In addition to the clairvoyant's knowledge of his *own* mental and physical state, there is a fourth phenomenon, that of clairvoyant knowledge of someone else's psychical and physical state. This occurs particularly in magnetically induced somnambulism when, through the *rapport* effected between the magnetized subject and another person, their two spheres of life have been made, as it were, into one.

(5) Finally, when this *rapport* attains its highest degree of intimacy and intensity, there occurs, fifthly, the phenomenon in which the clairvoyant knows, sees, and feels, not merely *about* someone else but *in* someone else and, without directly turning his attention to the individual, *immediately shares* his feelings, contains the other individual's feelings as

his *own*. There are the most astonishing examples of this phenomenon. A French physician, for instance, treated two women who had a deep affection for each other and who, although a considerable distance apart, both experienced the same illness. Another case of this kind is that of the soldier whose mother had been tied up by thieves; although he was some distance away from her, he had such a vivid direct feeling of her anguish that he felt an irresistible impulse to hasten to her without delay.

The five phenomena discussed above are the main moments of clair-voyant knowledge. The one feature which they all have in common is that they are always related to the *individual* world of the feeling soul. This common feature does not mean, however, that these phenomena are so inseparably connected that they must always all appear in one and the same subject. Secondly, these phenomena can occur both as a result of physical illness and also in the case of otherwise healthy persons, in virtue of a certain particular disposition. In both cases the phenomena are *immediate* natural states and it is only as such that we have so far considered them. But they can also be *deliberately* evoked. When this happens they constitute animal magnetism proper, which we now have to consider.

In the first place, as regards the name 'animal magnetism', its origin is to be found in the fact that Mesmer began by using *magnets* to induce the magnetic state. This name was subsequently retained because in animal magnetism, too, as in *inorganic* magnetism, there occurs an im-mediate reciprocal connection of two existences. Besides this name, the state has sometimes also been called *mesmerism, solarism,* and *tellurism*. However, the first of these three appellations does not in itself characterize the phenomenon, and the two others relate to quite another sphere than that of animal magnetism; the mental or spiritual nature to which the latter makes claim possesses a content quite different from merely *solar* and *telluric* moments, from these quite *abstract* determinations which we have already considered (§ 392) under the heading of the natural soul which has not yet developed to the stage of the individual subject.

It was animal magnetism proper that first directed general attention to magnetic states, for with its aid all the possible forms of this state could be elicited and developed. But the phenomena deliberately produced in this way do not differ from those states already discussed and produced without the aid of animal magnetism proper; the latter only gives *explicit* existence to what is otherwise present as an *immediate* natural state.

1. Now first of all, in order to comprehend the *possibility* of deliber-ately inducing the magnetic state, we need only recall what we have indicated as the fundamental Notion of this entire sphere of the soul. The magnetic state is an *illness*; for *in general* the essence of disease must be held to consist in the isolation of a particular system of the organism from the general physiological life, and in virtue of this *alienation* of the particular system from the general life, the animal exhibits its own finitude, its impotence and dependence on an *alien* power. Now the particular way

in which this *general* Notion of disease is determined in relation to the *magnetic* state is that in this particular illness a rupture occurs between my psychical and my waking being, between my spontaneous natural feeling, and my mediated, intellectual consciousness, a rupture which, since everyone embraces these two sides in himself, is of course a *possibility* in even the healthiest individuals, but does not actually *exist* in everyone, but only in those who have a particular disposition to it, and it becomes an illness only when it develops from its potentiality into actuality. But if my psychical life separates itself from my intellectual consciousness and takes over its function, I forfeit my freedom which is rooted in that consciousness, I lose the ability to protect myself from an alien power, in fact, become subjected to it. Now just as the *spontaneously* produced magnetic state produces dependence on an alien power, so, conversely, an external power, too, can form the starting-point and, laying hold of the *implicit* separation in me of my psychical life and my thinking consciousness, give this rupture an *explicit existence*, so that the magnetic state is *artificially* produced. However, as we have already pointed out, only those individuals who are already specially predisposed to this state easily become and remain epopts; whereas individuals who fall into this state as a result of illness are never perfect epopts. But the alien power which induces magnetic somnambulism in a subject is mainly another individual; there are, however, also medicinal substances, especially henbane, also water or metal, which can exercise this power. Consequently, the subject who is predisposed to magnetic somnambulism is able to put himself in that state by subjecting himself to the influence of such inorganic or vegetable substances.* Of the methods employed to induce the magnetic state, special mention must be made of the *baquet*. This consists of a vessel with iron rods which are touched by the persons to be magnetized, and forms the link between the magnetizer and these persons. Whereas in general, *metals* serve to *intensify* the magnetic state, *glass* and *silk* produce an *isolating* effect. Moreover, the power of the magnetizer acts not only on human beings but also on animals, for example, on dogs, cats, and monkeys; for it is quite generally the psychical life and only the psychical life which can be put into the magnetic state, no matter whether it belongs to a *mind* or not.

2. As regards the particular manner in which the magnetic state is induced, this varies. Usually the magnetizer produces this effect by contact. Just as in galvanism the metals act on each other by direct contact,

* The shamans of the Mongols are already familiar with this method. When they are going to prophesy they induce the magnetic state by means of certain drinks. The same thing is done even now by Indians and for the same purpose. Something similar probably took place with the oracle at Delphi where the priestess, sitting on a tripod over a cave, fell into an ecstasy, often gentle but sometimes very agitated, and in this state emitted more or less articulate sounds which were interpreted by the priests who lived in the intuition of the substantial elements of the life of the Greek people.

so too does the magnetizer act directly on his patient. However, the former as a self-poised individual possessing a will of his own, can only operate *on condition* that he is resolutely determined to communicate his power to the person to be magnetized, in other words, by the act of magnetization to bring, as it were, the two animal spheres confronting each other into a single existence.

More exactly, the magnetizer operates by *stroking* the patient, though this need not involve actual contact and the hand of the magnetizer can be kept about an inch away from the patient's body. The hand is moved from the head towards the pit of the stomach and from there towards the extremities; care must be taken to avoid stroking backwards because this very easily gives rise to cramp. Sometimes the movement of the hands can be successful when made at a greater distance from the body than that mentioned, that is, at a distance of several paces, especially when *rapport* has already been established; in which case the power of the magnetizer in too close a proximity would often be too great and would produce harmful effects. The magnetizer can tell whether he is still effective at a particular distance by feeling a certain warmth in his hand. But stroking at a greater or less distance is not necessary in every case; on the contrary, the magnetic *rapport* can be induced merely by the laying-on of the hand, particularly on the head, on the stomach or the pit of the stomach; often only a pressure of the hand is necessary. That is why the miraculous cures said to have been effected in various epochs by priests and other individuals are correctly ascribed to animal magnetism. Occasionally even a single glance and the command of the magnetizer is sufficient to induce magnetic trance. Indeed, faith and will alone are said sometimes to have produced this effect at a great distance. In this magical relationship, the main point is that one individual acts on another whose will is *weaker* and *less independent*. Therefore, very powerful natures exercise the greatest power over weak ones, a power often so irresistible that the latter can be put into a magnetic trance by the former whether they wish it or not. For this same reason, strong men are especially qualified to magnetize female persons.

3. The third point to be discussed here concerns the *effects* produced by magnetization. In regard to these it may be said that after the numerous experiments which have been made, this subject is now so thoroughly understood that essentially new phenomena are no longer to be expected. If one wishes to study the phenomena of animal magnetism in their *naïveté* it is mainly to the older magnetizers that one must go. In France, men of the noblest sentiments and highest culture have interested themselves in animal magnetism and have studied it with an impartial mind. Among them, Lieut.-General Puységur in particular deserves mention. When the Germans ridicule, as they often do, the faulty theories of the French, it can be asserted, at least as regards animal magnetism, that the naïve metaphysics employed by the French is more satisfactory than the often fanciful explanations and the lame as well as erroneous theorizing of

German savants. A useful, superficial classification of the phenomena of animal magnetism has been given by Kluge. Van Ghert, a reliable man rich in ideas and well read in recent philosophy, has given an account of magnetic cures in the form of a diary. Karl Schelling, brother of the philosopher, has also communicated a part of his magnetic experiments. So much for the relevant literature of animal magnetism and the scope of our knowledge of the subject.

After these preliminaries let us now turn to a brief consideration of the magnetic phenomena themselves. The immediate general *effect* of magnetizing is to plunge the magnetized person into the state where he is wrapped up in his undifferentiated natural life, that is, into sleep. Falling asleep indicates the beginning of the magnetic state. But sleep is not absolutely necessary and magnetic cures can be carried out in its absence. The only necessary condition here is that the feeling soul must become independent, must be separated from the mediated, intellectual consciousness. The second point we have to consider here concerns the physiological side or basis of the magnetic state. What must be said about this is that in this state the function of the *outwardly directed* organs is transferred to the *internal* organs, that the function exercised by the brain in the waking state of the intellectual consciousness is taken over by the reproductive system during magnetic somnambulism, because in this state consciousness is degraded to the simple, undifferentiated naturalness of psychical life; but this simple naturalness, this self-enclosed life, is in contradiction with the sensibility which is directed outwards; whereas the reproductive system which is directed inwards, which is dominant in the simplest animal organisms and which forms animality *as such*, is absolutely inseparable from this self-enclosed psychical life. This then is the reason why, during magnetic somnambulism, the soul's activity descends into the brain of the reproductive system, namely, into the ganglia, these heavily nodulated (*vielfach verknoteten*) nerves in the abdomen. This was the experience of van Helmont after he had rubbed himself with henbane ointment and taken the juice of the plant. According to his description he felt as if his thinking consciousness was going from his head into his abdomen, especially into his stomach, and it seemed to him that with this transference his thinking became more acute and was associated with a particularly pleasant feeling. This concentration of the psychical life in the abdomen is considered by a famous French magnetizer to depend on the fact that during magnetic somnambulism the blood in the region of the pit of the stomach remains very fluid, even when in the other parts it is extremely thick. But the unusual stimulation of the reproductive system occurring in the magnetic state is seen not only in the mental or spiritual form of clairvoyance but also in the more sensuous shape of sexual desire which becomes more or less active, especially in female persons.

After this mainly *physiological* consideration of animal magnetism we have to determine more precisely the nature of this state with respect to the soul. As in the spontaneously occurring magnetic states previously considered, so too, in deliberately induced animal magnetism, the soul immersed in its inwardness contemplates its individual world not *outside*, but *within* itself. This sinking of the soul into its inwardness can, as already remarked, stop short half-way, so to speak; in this case sleep does not occur. But it is also possible that life may be *completely* cut off from its connection with the outside world by sleep. With this rupture, too, there can be a suspension of magnetic phenomena. But the transition from magnetic sleep to clairvoyance is equally possible. Most magnetic persons will find themselves in this clairvoyant state without remembering it afterwards. The existence of clairvoyance in individuals has often been revealed only by chance; it mostly comes to light when the magnetized person is spoken to by the magnetizer; if he had not spoken, the patient would perhaps only have gone on sleeping. Now though the answers of clairvoyants seem to come out of another world, yet these individuals can only have knowledge of what they, *qua* objective consciousness, know. Often, however, they talk of their intellectual consciousness as if it were another person. When clairvoyance develops a more determinate form, the magnetized persons are able to give accounts of their physical condition and their psychical inner state. But their feelings are as vague as the ideas of a blind man who does not know the difference between light and dark, about things outside of him. What the clairvoyant sees, often only becomes clearer to him some days later, but is never so clear that it does not need to be interpreted. Sometimes, however, the magnetized persons completely fail in this task and often, at least, their accounts are so symbolical and bizarre that they in their turn need to be interpreted by the intellectual consciousness of the magnetizer, so that the final outcome of the magnetic clairvoyance mostly consists of a varied mixture of truth and falsehood. Yet, on the other hand, it cannot be denied that clairvoyants sometimes give very distinct accounts of the nature and course of their illness; that they usually know very accurately when their attacks will come on, when and how long they will need magnetic sleep, and how long their treatment will last; and finally, they sometimes discover a connection between a remedy and a disease which is perhaps still unknown to the intellectual consciousness, thus making it easier for the physician to effect an otherwise difficult cure. In this respect clairvoyants can be compared to animals, for these instinctively know which things will cure them. But as regards the further content of artificially induced clairvoyance we need hardly remark that in this, as in natural clairvoyance, the soul is able to read and hear with the pit of the stomach. Here we want to emphasize only two points; first, that what lies outside of the content of the magnetized person's *substantial* life is not contacted in somnambulism, and that consequently clairvoyance does not, for example, extend to foreknowledge of the winning numbers in a lottery, and in general cannot be used for selfish ends. But the position is otherwise when great world-events are concerned. For instance it is recorded that a somnambulist on the eve of Waterloo cried out in great exaltation: 'Tomorrow, he who has caused us so much harm will perish either by lightning or the sword.' The second point to be mentioned here is that since in clairvoyance the soul leads a life *cut off* from its intellectual consciousness, clairvoyants on waking no longer have immediate knowledge of what they have seen in the somnambulistic state, although they can indirectly become aware of it by dreaming about it and then remembering the dream on waking. Also some recollection of what has been seen can be intentionally brought about by the physician ordering the patient in his waking state to make the effort to retain what happens to him in the magnetic sleep.

4. Fourthly, as regards the intimate connection between the magnetized person and the magnetizer and the dependence of the former on the latter, there remains to be added to what was said in the Remark to § 406 under δ about the physical side of this connection, that the clairvoyant can at first hear only the magnetizer—though sometimes he cannot hear or see at all—and he can hear other individuals only when they are *en rapport* with the latter; further, in this exclusive vital relationship between the magnetizer and his subject, if the latter is touched by a third person this can have extremely dangerous consequences and can produce convulsions and catalepsy. But with respect to the psychical relationship between the magnetizer and his subject, we may also mention that clairvoyants, by coming into possession of knowledge belonging to the magnetizer, often acquire the ability to know something that they themselves do not directly inwardly perceive. They can, for example, say what time it is without any direct sense-perception of their own provided that the magnetizer knows the time. A knowledge of this intimate shared life precludes any foolish astonishment at the learning sometimes paraded by clairvoyants; this learning very often belongs not to the clairvoyant but to the person with whom he is *en rapport*. Besides this *knowing* in common, especially when clairvoyance is continued over a lengthy period, the clairvoyant can also form other psychical relationships with the magnetizer in which mannerisms, passions, and character are concerned. Especially can the vanity of clairvoyants be easily aroused if one makes the mistake of letting them think that one attaches great importance to their deliverances. They are then seized with a craze to talk about all and everything, even about things of which they have no clairvoyant knowledge whatever. In this case, clairvoyance is completely useless and, in fact, becomes suspect. This is why magnetizers have often discussed among themselves whether clairvoyance should be developed and preserved when it is spontaneous, and deliberately produced when it is not, or whether, on the contrary, efforts should be made to check it. As already mentioned, clairvoyance manifests itself and is developed as a result of repeated questioning of the magnetized person. Now if the clairvoyant is questioned on all kinds of things, he can easily become distracted and his attention be more or less turned away from himself so that he is less able to describe his illness and

to indicate the remedy to be employed, thus considerably retarding a cure. For this reason the magnetizer must, in his questioning, take the greatest care to avoid arousing the vanity of the somnambulist and distracting him. But above all, he must not let himself become controlled by his patient. This wrong relationship was commoner when magnetizers drew more on their own strength than it has been since they have used the *baquet*. With the use of this instrument, the magnetizer is less involved in the state of the patient. Even so, a great deal depends on the strength of mind, of character and of physique, of the magnetizers. If these give in to the whims of the magnetized person—which happens particularly when the magnetizer is not a physician—if they have not the courage to contradict and stand up to him and the magnetized person gets to feel, on his side, that he is exercising influence on the magnetizer, then like a spoilt child he will give himself up to every whim, get hold of the queerest ideas, and make fun of the unsuspecting magnetizer, thus preventing his own cure. However, it is not merely in this bad sense that the magnetized person can acquire a certain independence; if he normally possesses a good moral character, he will also retain in the magnetic trance a firmness of moral feeling on which any impure intentions of the magnetizer will be shattered. For instance, a magnetized woman declared that she would not obey the order of the magnetizer to undress in front of him.

5. The fifth and last point that we have to touch on in animal magnetism concerns the real aim of magnetic treatment, namely, cure. Undoubtedly many cases of ancient times which were considered miraculous must be regarded as nothing else but the results of animal magnetism. But there is no need to appeal to marvellous tales wrapped in the obscurity of the distant past; for in modern times men of unimpeachable integrity have performed so many cures by magnetic treatment that anyone forming an unbiassed judgement can no longer doubt the curative power of animal magnetism. Consequently, all that we have to do now is to indicate how magnetism effects a cure. For this purpose we may remember that ordinary medical treatment consists in getting rid of the interference with the identity of animal life which causes the disease, in restoring the internal fluidity of the organism. Now in magnetic treatment this end is achieved either by inducing sleep and clairvoyance or by the individual life being simply concentrated within itself, returning into its simple universality. Just as *natural* sleep fortifies the healthy life by withdrawing the entire man from his contact with the outer world in which he spends his scattered energies, into the substantial totality and harmony of life, so too, the state of magnetic trance, because it serves to restore the unity-with-self of the inwardly disrupted organism, forms the basis of the restoration of health. However, it must not be forgotten here that this concentration of the feeling life can, in its own turn, become so one-sided that it firmly establishes itself in opposition to the other aspects of organic life and to consciousness and becomes a disease. It is this possibility which gives

rise to doubts about the deliberate production of this concentration. If this duplication of the personality is carried too far, the process defeats its own end, namely, the cure, since a separation is produced which is greater than that which the magnetic treatment is intended to get rid of. There is a danger in such unwise treatment that severe crises, frightful convulsions, may occur and that the conflict to which these give rise may remain not merely physical but in various ways become a conflict in the consciousness itself of the somnambulist. If, on the other hand, one proceeds with caution, avoiding any excessive concentration in the magnetic state of the feeling life, this concentration forms, as already remarked, the foundation for a restoration of health, and one is in a position to complete the cure by gradually leading the rest of the organism, which though still divided is powerless against its concentrated life, back into this its substantial unity, into its simple harmony with itself, and by so doing to enable it without detriment to its inner unity to involve itself afresh in division and opposition.

(β) *Self-feeling (sense of self)*[1]

§ 407

(αα) The sensitive totality is, in its capacity as individual, essentially the tendency to distinguish itself in itself, and to wake up to the *judgement in itself*, in virtue of which it has *particular* feelings and stands as a *subject* in respect of these aspects of itself. The subject as such gives these feelings a place as *its own* in itself. In these private and personal sensations it is immersed, and at the same time, because of the 'ideality' of the particulars, it combines itself in them with itself as a subjective unit. In this way it is *self-feeling*, and is so at the same time only in the *particular feeling*.

§ 408

(ββ) In consequence of the immediacy, which still marks the self-feeling, i.e. in consequence of the element of corporeality which is still undetached from the mental life, and as the feeling too is itself particular and bound up with a special corporeal form, it follows that although the subject has been brought to acquire intelligent consciousness, it is still susceptible of disease, so far as to remain fast in a *special* phase of its self-feeling, unable to refine

---

[1] Selbstgefühl.

it to 'ideality' and get the better of it. The fully furnished self of intelligent consciousness is a conscious subject, which is consistent in itself according to an order and behaviour which follows from its individual position and its connection with the external world, which is no less a world of law. But when it is engrossed with a single phase of feeling, it fails to assign that phase its proper place and due subordination in the individual system of the world which a conscious subject is. In this way the subject finds itself in contradiction between the totality systematized in its consciousness, and the single phase or fixed idea which is not reduced to its proper place and rank. This is Insanity or mental Derangement.

In considering insanity we must, as in other cases, anticipate the full-grown and intelligent conscious subject, which is at the same time the *natural* self of *self-feeling*. In such a phase the self can be liable to the contradiction between its own free subjectivity and a particularity which, instead of being 'idealized' in the former, remains as a fixed element in self-feeling. Mind as such is free, and therefore not susceptible of this malady. But in older metaphysics mind was treated as a soul, as a thing; and it is only as a thing, i.e. as something natural and existent, that it is liable to insanity— the settled fixture of some finite element in it. Insanity is therefore a psychical disease, i.e. a disease of body and mind alike: the commencement may appear to start from the one more than the other, and so also may the cure.

The self-possessed and healthy subject has an active and present consciousness of the ordered whole of his individual world, into the system of which he subsumes each special content of sensation, idea, desire, inclination, etc., as it arises, so as to insert them in their proper place. He is the *dominant genius* over these particularities. Between this and insanity the difference is like that between waking and dreaming: only that in insanity the dream falls within the waking limits, and so makes part of the actual self-feeling. Error and that sort of thing is a proposition consistently admitted to a place in the objective interconnection of things. In the concrete, however, it is often difficult to say where it begins to become derangement. A violent, but groundless and senseless outburst of hatred, etc., may, in contrast to a presupposed higher self-possession and stability of character, make its victim seem to

be beside himself with frenzy. But the main point in derangement
is the contradiction which a feeling with a fixed corporeal embodiment sets up against the whole mass of adjustments forming the
concrete consciousness. The mind which is in a condition of mere
being, and where such being is not rendered fluid in its consciousness, is diseased. The contents which are set free in this reversion
to mere nature are the self-seeking affections of the heart, such as
vanity, pride, and the rest of the passions—fancies and hopes—
merely personal love and hatred. When the influence of self-
possession and of general principles, moral and theoretical, is
relaxed, and ceases to keep the natural temper under lock and
key, the earthly elements are set free—that evil which is always
latent in the heart, because the heart as immediate is natural and
selfish. It is the evil genius of man which gains the upper hand in
insanity, but in distinction from and contrast to the better and
more intelligent part, which is there also. Hence this state is mental
derangement and distress. The right psychical treatment therefore
keeps in view the truth that insanity is not an abstract *loss* of reason
(neither in the point of intelligence nor of will and its responsibility), but only derangement, only a contradiction in a still
subsisting reason;—just as physical disease is not an abstract, i.e.
mere and total, loss of health (if it were that, it would be death),
but a contradiction in it. This humane treatment, no less benevolent than reasonable (the services of Pinel towards which deserve
the highest acknowledgement), presupposes the patient's rationality, and in that assumption has the sound basis for dealing with
him on this side—just as in the case of bodily disease the physician
bases his treatment on the vitality which as such still contains
health.

Zusatz. What follows may serve to elucidate the above **Paragraph**:
Already in the *Zusatz* to § 402, we interpreted insanity as the second
of the three developmental stages passed through by the feeling soul in
its struggle with the immediacy of its substantial content to raise itself
to the self-related simple subjectivity present in the 'I', whereby it
becomes completely self-possessed and conscious of itself. This interpretation of insanity as a necessarily occurring form or stage in the
development of the soul is naturally not to be understood as if we were
asserting that *every* mind, *every* soul, must go through this stage of
extreme derangement. Such an assertion would be as absurd as to assume

that because in the Philosophy of Right crime is considered as a necessary manifestation of the human will, therefore to commit crime is an inevitable necessity for *every* individual. Crime and insanity are *extremes* which the human mind *in general* has to overcome in the course of its development, but which do not appear as extremes in every individual but only in the form of limitations, errors, follies, and offences not of a criminal nature. This is sufficient to justify our consideration of insanity as an essential stage in the development of the soul.

But as regards the determination of the *Notion* of insanity, we have already indicated in the *Zusatz* to § 405 what it is that distinguishes this state from magnetic somnambulism, the first of the three stages in the development of the feeling soul considered by us, namely, that in insanity the relationship of the psychical element to the objective consciousness is no longer one of mere difference, but of direct opposition, and therefore the two are no longer *mixed*. We will demonstrate here the truth of this statement by a more detailed treatment and thereby also prove the rational necessity of the progress of our exposition from the magnetic states to insanity. The necessity of this progress lies in the fact that the soul is already *in itself* the contradiction of being an *individual*, a *singular*, and yet being at the same time immediately identical with the *universal* natural soul, with its substance. This opposition existing in the soul in the contradictory form of identity, must be made *explicit* as opposition, as contradiction. This first happens in insanity; for it is first in this state that the subjectivity of the soul not merely separates itself from its substance with which in somnambulism it is still immediately identical, but comes into direct opposition to it, into complete contradiction with the objective consciousness, thereby becoming a purely formal, empty, abstract subjectivity, and in this its one-sidedness arrogates to itself the significance of a veritable unity of the subjective and the objective. Therefore, the unity and separation in insanity of the opposed sides just mentioned is still an imperfect one. This unity and this separation only exist in their perfection in the rational, actually objective consciousness. When I have raised myself to rational thinking I am not only *for myself, objective to myself*, and therefore a *subjective* identity of the subjective and objective, but I have also *separated* this identity from myself, set it over against me as an actually *objective* identity. In order to achieve this complete separation, the feeling soul must overcome its *immediacy*, its *naturalness* and *corporeality*, must convert this into an ideal moment, appropriate it to itself, thereby transforming itself into an *objective* unity of the subjective and objective and in doing this not only freeing itself from its Other but at the same time discharging this Other from its immediate identity with the feeling soul. But at the stage we are now considering, the soul has not yet reached this goal. In so far as it is insane, it clings to a *merely subjective* identity of the subjective and objective, rather than to an *objective* unity of these two sides; and only in so far as, with all its folly and derangement, it is still rational and stands therefore on a level *other* than the one now to be considered, does the soul attain to an objective unity of the subjective and objective. In insanity proper, in fact, the two modes of finite mind—the immanently developed, rational consciousness with its objective world, and the world of inner feeling which clings to itself and has its objectivity *within* it—are each developed into a separately existing *totality*, into a separate *personality*. The *objective* consciousness of the insane shows itself in the most diverse ways; they know, for example, that they are in a lunatic asylum; they know their attendants; they also know that the other people there are insane; make fun among themselves of their madness; are employed on all kinds of duties, sometimes even being appointed overseers. But at the same time they are *dreaming while awake* and are *dominated* by a *fixed idea* which they cannot harmonize with their objective consciousness. This waking *dreaming* of theirs is akin to somnambulism; but the two states are also distinct from one another. In somnambulism the two personalities present in the one individual do not make contact with one another, the somnam- bulistic consciousness, on the contrary, being so separated from the waking consciousness that neither side is aware of the other, the dual personalities also manifesting as a duality of states; in insanity proper, on the other hand, the two different personalities are not two different states but are in one and the same state; so that these *negatively* related per- sonalities—the psychical and the intellectual consciousness—have mutual contact and are aware of each other. The insane subject is there- fore in communion with himself in the negative of himself; in other words, his consciousness immediately contains the negative of itself. This negative is not vanquished by the insane person, the duality into which it is split up is not brought back to unity. Consequently, though the insane person is *in himself* or *implicitly* one and the same subject, yet he does not know himself objectively as a self-accordant, inwardly undivided subject, but as a subject disrupted into two different personalities.

The *specific* meaning of this derangement, of this self-communion of mind in the *negative* of itself, requires still further elucidation. In insanity this negative acquires a concreter significance than it has possessed hitherto in our exposition; just as the self-communion of mind must be taken here in a richer, concreter sense than the being-for-self hitherto attained by the soul.

In the first place, therefore, we must distinguish this negative of the soul characteristic of insanity from the other kind of negative. To illus- trate: when we suffer, for example, aches and pains we are also communing with ourselves in a negative, but we need not therefore be mad. This we would be only if we endured the aches and pains without having a rational aim which could only be attained by means of them. For example, a journey to the Holy Sepulchre undertaken for the purpose of fortifying one's soul may be regarded as the act of a lunatic, because such a journey is quite useless for the end in view and is therefore not a necessary means for procuring it. For the same reason, the journeys across whole countries made by Indians crawling on their stomachs can be pronounced the acts of lunatics. The negative endured in insanity is, therefore, one in which only the *feeling*, not the *intellectual* and *rational*, consciousness finds itself again.

But in insanity the *negative* constitutes, as we have just said, a determination which belongs both to the psychical and to the intellectual consciousness in their mutual relation. This relation of these two opposed modes of the *self-communion* of mind likewise requires a more precise characterization to prevent its being confused with the relation in which *mere error* and *folly* stand to the *objective*, rational consciousness.

In order to clarify this point, let us remember that when the soul becomes *consciousness*, following on the separation of what in the natural soul exists in an immediate unity, there arises for it the opposition of a subjective thinking and an outer world; two worlds which, indeed, are *in truth* identical with one another (*ordo rerum atque idearum idem est*, says Spinoza), but which, however, to the merely *reflective* consciousness, to *finite* thinking, appear as *essentially distinct* and *independent* of one another. The soul, as consciousness, thus enters the sphere of finitude and contingency, of self-externality, hence of the isolated particular. What I know at this level, I know *primarily* as a particular, unmediated something, consequently as something contingent and given, something merely found. What I find and feel, I transform into mental representations, at the same time making it into an external object. But I recognize this content, when I bring my understanding and reason to bear on it, as being at the same time not merely isolated and contingent but an element of a great interrelated whole, as infinitely *mediated* with other contents, and by this mediation becoming a *necessary* content. Only when I proceed in this way do I act from a *rational* standpoint, the content with which I am filled receiving in its turn the form of objectivity. This objectivity which is the goal of my theoretical striving also forms the norm of my practical conduct. If, therefore, I want to transfer my aims and interests, i.e. conceptions originating in *me*, from their subjectivity into objectivity, then if I am to be rational, I must conceive of the material, the reality confronting me in which I intend to actualize this content, as it is in truth. But just as I must have a correct conception of the objectivity confronting me if I am to behave rationally, so too must I have a correct conception of *myself*, that is to say, a conception which harmonizes with the *totality* of my actual being, with my infinitely determined individuality as distinct from my substantial being.

Now, of course, I can be mistaken not only about the outer world but also about myself. Unintelligent individuals have empty, subjective ideas, unrealizable desires, which all the same they hope to realize in the future. They confine themselves to quite particular aims and interests, cling to one-sided principles and so come into conflict with the world of actuality. But this narrow-mindedness and this error are still not madness if these persons at the same time know that their subjective idea does not as yet have an objective existence. Error and folly only become madness when the individual believes his merely subjective idea to be objectively present to him and clings to it in face of the actual objectivity which contradicts it. To the madman, his purely subjective world is quite as real as the objective world. In his merely subjective idea, for example in the fancied belief that he is someone who, in fact, he is not, he has the *certainty of himself*, and his *being* clings to this idea. When addressing a madman one must therefore always begin by reminding him of all the facts and circumstances of his situation, of his concrete actual world. Then, if in spite of being made aware of this objective interrelated whole he still sticks to his false idea, there can be no doubt that such a person is insane.

It follows from what has just been said that an idea can be called *insane* if the madman regards an empty abstraction and a mere possibility as something concrete and actual; for, as we have seen, in this idea abstraction is made from the concrete actual world of the madman. If, for example, I take myself to be a king, although I am very far from being one, this idea which is in contradiction with my total actual world and is therefore insane, has no other ground and content whatever than the indeterminate general possibility that since a man, in general, can be a king, I myself, this particular man, am a king.

But the reason why such a fixed idea, irreconcilable with my concrete actual world, *can* arise in me is that I am, in the first instance, a wholly abstract, completely indeterminate 'I' and therefore open to any arbitrary content. In so far as I am such an 'I', I can fill myself with the most nonsensical ideas, for example, I can believe that I am a dog (in fairy-tales men have indeed been turned into dogs), or I can imagine that I am able to fly, because there is enough room to do this and other living creatures are able to fly. But when, on the other hand, I become a *concrete* 'I', acquire *determinate* thoughts of the actual world, when, for example, in the last-mentioned case I think of my *heaviness*, then I see the impossibility of my flying. Man alone has the capacity of grasping himself in this complete *abstraction of the 'I'*. This is why he has, so to speak, the privilege of folly and madness. But this illness only develops in the concrete, self-possessed consciousness in so far as this is degraded to the level of the impotent, passive, abstract 'I' of which we have just spoken. By this degradation, the concrete 'I' loses its absolute power over the entire system of its determinations, deprives itself of the ability to put in its proper place every psychical content, to remain perfectly present to itself in all its mental representations; and by letting itself be imprisoned in a particular, merely subjective idea, is driven out of its mind, is shifted out from the centre of its actual world and, since it also still retains a consciousness of this world, has two centres, one in the remainder of its *rational* consciousness and the other in its *deranged* idea.

In the deranged consciousness, the contradiction between the abstract universality of the immediate, passive 'I' and a particular, isolated idea severed from the total actual world, is unresolved. This consciousness is, therefore, not a true self-communion but a self-communion which remains fixed in the negative of the 'I'. An equally unresolved contradiction prevails here between this particular, isolated idea and the abstract universality of the 'I' on the one hand, and the inwardly harmonious total actual world, on the other. This explains why the proposition: 'What I think is true', which is rightly disputed by a rational intelligence, receives in the mentally deranged a wrong, an irrational meaning and becomes just as false as the counter assertion made by the unintelligence of the abstractive intellect, that the subjective and objective are *absolutely separate*. There is more rationality in even the mere *feeling* of the *healthy* soul than in the said unintelligence or in insanity, since it contains the *actual* unity of the subjective and objective. As we have already said, this unity, however, only receives its perfect form in speculative Reason; for *only* what is thought by *this* is true in regard both to its form and its content—a *perfect* unity of Thought and Being. In insanity, on the contrary, the unity and the difference of the subjective and the objective still have a merely *formal* significance from which the concrete content of the actual world is excluded.

We wish at this stage to repeat in a more condensed and, if possible, more exact form, something which has already been touched on several times in the above Paragraph and Remark, partly on account of the context and partly with the aim of more fully elucidating it. The point is that insanity must be grasped essentially as an illness *at once mental and physical*, and for this reason, that the unity of the subjective and the objective which prevails in insanity is still wholly *immediate* and is not as yet the outcome of infinite mediation; because the 'I' afflicted with insanity, no matter how acute this point of self-feeling may be, is still a natural, immediate, passive 'I', and consequently the moment of *difference* can become fixed as a passive, simply affirmative being; or, to put it still more specifically, because in insanity a particular feeling which conflicts with the objective consciousness of the insane person is *held fast*, is *not* transformed into an *ideality*, this feeling consequently having the form of a *simply affirmative*, hence *corporeal*, being, with the result that a *duality of being* is produced in him which is not overcome by his objective consciousness, a difference which remains purely *affirmative* and which becomes for the insane person a fixed limitation.

Further, as regards the other question which likewise has already been posed in the above Paragraph: How does mind come to be insane? we may supplement the answer there given by remarking that this question already presupposes the fixed, objective consciousness not yet attained by the soul at its present stage of development; and that, at this point, it is rather the converse of this question that should be asked, namely, How does the soul which is shut up in its *inwardness* and is immediately identical with its individual world, emerge from the merely *formal*, empty difference of the subjective and the objective and attain to the *actual* difference of these two sides, and thus to the *truly objective* intellectual and rational consciousness? The answer to this will be given in the last four Paragraphs of the first part of the doctrine of subjective mind.

From what was said at the beginning of this Anthropology about the necessity of starting the philosophical consideration of subjective mind with the natural mind, and from the *Notion of insanity* developed above in all its aspects, it will be sufficiently clear why insanity must be discussed before the healthy, intellectual consciousness, although it has that consciousness for its *presupposition* and is nothing else but the extreme limit of sickness to which the latter can succumb. We had to discuss insanity already in Anthropology because in this state the psychical element, the natural self—abstract, formal subjectivity—gains the mastery over the objective, rational, concrete consciousness, and consideration of the abstract, natural self must precede the exposition of concrete, free mind. But in order that this progress from something abstract to a concrete which contains it as a possibility, may not be regarded as an isolated and therefore doubtful phenomenon, we can remind ourselves that in the Philosophy of Right a similar progress must take place. In this science, too, we begin with something abstract, namely, with the Notion of Will; we then go on to the actualization of the as yet abstract will in an external existent, to the sphere of formal right; from there we go on to the will that is reflected into itself out of external existence, to the sphere of morality; and thirdly and lastly we come to the will that unites within itself these two abstract moments and is therefore the concrete, ethical will. In the ethical sphere itself we again start from an immediate, from the natural, undeveloped shape possessed by the ethical mind in the *family*; then we come to the *splitting up* of the ethical substance in *civil society*; and finally, in the State, attain the unity and truth of those two one-sided forms of the ethical mind. But this course followed by our exposition does not in the least mean that we would make the ethical life *later in time* than right and morality, or would explain the family and civil society to be *antecedent* to the State in the *actual* world. On the contrary, we are well aware that the ethical life is the foundation of right and morality, as also that the family and civil society with their well-ordered distinctions already presuppose the existence of the State. In the *philosophical* development of the ethical sphere, however, we cannot begin with the State, since in this the ethical sphere has unfolded itself into its most concrete form, whereas the beginning is necessarily something abstract. For this reason, the moral sphere, too, must be considered before the ethical sphere, although the former to a certain extent comes to view in the latter only as a sickness. But for the same reason in the sphere of Anthropology, too, we have had to discuss insanity *before* the *concrete*, objective consciousness, since insanity, as we have seen, consists in an *abstraction* rigidly held in opposition to that concrete objective consciousness.

This concludes the remarks we had to make at this point about the Notion of insanity in general.

As regards the various forms of insanity, these are usually classified not so much according to an *inner* characteristic as according to the *manifestations* of this illness; but this is inadequate for the philosophical treatment of the subject. We must recognize that even insanity is a state which is *differentiated within itself* in a *necessary* and therefore rational manner. But a necessary differentiation of this psychical state cannot be derived from the *particular* content of the formal unity of the subjective and the objective present in insanity; for this content is something infinitely manifold and therefore contingent. On the contrary, therefore, it is on the quite general differences of form appearing in insanity that we must fix our attention. To this end, we must refer back to our characterization of insanity as a state in which the mind is shut up within itself, has sunk into itself, whose peculiarity—in contrast to the being-within-self of mind present in somnambulism—consists in its being no longer in *immediate contact* with actuality but in having positively *separated itself* from it.

Now this state in which mind has sunk into itself is, on the one hand, the *general* feature in *all* forms of insanity; on the other hand, when it remains this *indeterminate, vacuous* state, it forms a *particular* kind of insanity. It is with this that we have to begin our consideration of the various forms of insanity.

But if this quite indeterminate being-within-self acquires a definite content, is linked to a merely subjective, particular idea and takes this to be something objective, then we have the second form of insanity.

The third and last main form of this illness appears when that which *confronts* the soul's delusion is also *for* the soul, when the lunatic *compares* his merely subjective idea with his objective consciousness, discovers the sharp difference existing between the two, and thus obtains the unhappy feeling of his self-contradiction. Here we see the soul in the more or less despairing effort to overcome the *discord* which, though already present in the second form of insanity, is there felt only slightly or not at all, and to restore its *concrete self-identity*, the inner *harmony* of the self-conciousness which remains unshakeably fixed in the *one* centre of its actuality.

Let us now consider in more detail these three main forms of insanity.

1. *Idiocy, the distracted mind*, and *the rambling mind*

The first of these three main forms, the quite indeterminate state of self-absorption, appears in the first place as

Idiocy

This takes different forms. There is *natural* idiocy and this is incurable. Particularly what is called *cretinism* comes under this head. This disease is partly sporadic in its occurrence and partly endemic in certain areas, especially in narrow valleys and marshy districts. Cretins are misshapen, deformed persons, often afflicted with goitre; their completely stupid facial expression singles them out and their undeveloped soul can often find expression only in quite inarticulate sounds.

But besides this natural idiocy there is also an idiocy which can be caused either by an undeserved misfortune or by a person's own fault. With regard to the former class, Pinel cites the example of a congenital idiot whose dull-wittedness was believed to be the result of an extremely violent fright experienced by her mother during pregnancy. Idiocy is often a consequence of frenzy, in which case there is very little hope of cure; epilepsy, too, often terminates in idiocy. But this state is no less frequently brought on by excesses. We may also add that idiocy occasionally manifests as catalepsy, as a complete paralysis of both physical and mental activity. Idiocy occurs, too, not only as a permanent, but also as a transitory, state. For instance an Englishman fell into a state of indifference to everything, first to politics and then to his own affairs and to his family. He would sit quietly, looking straight in front of him and for years did not utter a word, and he appeared to be so dull-witted that it was doubtful whether he knew his wife and children or not. He was cured when someone else, dressed exactly like him sat opposite him and imitated him in everything he did. This threw the patient into a violent frenzy which forced him to attend to things outside of him and drove him permanently out of his state of self-absorption.

The distracted mind

A further modification of the first main form of insanity under discussion is *distraction*. This consists in a non-awareness of the immediate present. This non-awareness is often the beginning of insanity; but there is also a lofty distractedness far removed from insanity. This can occur when the mind, by profound meditation, withdraws its attention from everything relatively unimportant. Archimedes, for instance, was once so absorbed in a geometrical problem that for several days he seemed to have forgotten everything else and had to be roused by force out of this concentration of his mind on a single point. But distractedness, properly speaking, is an absorption in a quite *abstract self-feeling*, a lapse of the self-possessed objective consciousness into inactivity, into a non-awareness of things of which it should be aware. A person in this state confuses his true situation in a particular case with a false one, apprehends external circumstances in a one-sided manner, not in the totality of their relationships. One of many amusing instances of this psychical state is that of a French count who, when his wig got caught on a chandelier, laughed heartily and looked round to see whose wig had been pulled off and who was showing a bald pate. Another instance of this kind is recorded of Newton. This savant is supposed on one occasion to have taken hold of a lady's finger in order to use it as a tobacco-stopper for his pipe. Such distractedness can be the result of excessive study; it is not uncommon to find it in scholars, especially those of past times. But distractedness is often the outcome, too, of the desire to be universally esteemed, which results in individuals being obsessed with their subjectivity, and in the process forgetting the objective world.

The rambling mind

In contrast to the distracted mind, the rambling mind interests itself in everything. This springs from an inability to *fix* one's attention on anything definite, and consists in the malady of stumbling from one object to another. This malady is mostly incurable. Fools of this kind are the most troublesome. Pinel tells of such a person who was a perfect type of chaos. He says: 'This patient approaches me and swamps me with his chatter. Immediately afterwards he does the same thing to someone else. When this individual comes into a room he turns everything in it upside down, shakes chairs and tables and puts them in the wrong places without betraying any particular aim. You have hardly turned your eyes when he is already out in the neighbouring street, behaving there just as aimlessly as in the room, chattering, throwing stones, pulling up plants, going on further, turning back again, without knowing why.' The rambling mind always stems from a weakening of the power of the rational consciousness to hold together the totality of its mental representations. But rambling minds often suffer from delirium—therefore, not merely from a non-awareness of what is immediately present to them but from unconsciously turning it topsyturvy. So much for the first main form of insanity.

2. The second main form of insanity—madness proper

This occurs when the natural mind which is shut up within itself and whose various modifications we have just considered, acquires a *definite* content and this content becomes a *fixed idea*, the mind which is not as yet fully self-possessed becoming just as much absorbed in it as in *idiocy* it is absorbed in its own self, in the abyss of its *indeterminateness*. It is hard to say exactly where madness proper begins. For example, in small towns one finds people, especially women, who are so absorbed in an extremely limited circle of particular interests and who feel so comfortable in this narrow life of theirs that we rightly call them crazy. But madness in the narrower meaning of the word implies that the mind is fixed in a single, merely subjective idea and accords it objective significance. This psychical state mostly comes about when someone who is dissatisfied with his actual world shuts himself up in his subjectivity. The passion of vanity and pride is the chief cause of this psychical self-imprisonment. Then the mind which is thus nestled in its interior life easily loses its understanding of the actual world and is at home only in its subjective ideas. This behaviour can soon give rise to complete madness. For should there still be any vitality in this solitary consciousness, the latter will readily be led to create some content or other from its own resources and to regard this purely subjective content as objective and to *fix* it as such. For whereas, as we have seen, in idiocy and in the rambling mind the soul does not possess the power to hold on to anything definite, this power *is* possessed in madness proper and by this very fact demonstrates that it is still consciousness, that in madness there is, therefore, still a *differentiation* of the soul from its content, from its *fixed* idea. Therefore, although on the one hand this content forms part of the madman's consciousness yet, on the other hand, the latter's universal nature enables it to transcend the particular content of the insane idea. Therefore madmen, besides their craziness on one point, at the same time possess a proper, rational consciousness, a correct appreciation of things and the ability to act rationally. This, in addition to the suspicious reserve of madmen, makes it possible that sometimes a madman is not at once recognized as such and, in particular, that there can be doubts about his cure and consequent discharge.

The differences between madmen are mainly determined by the multifarious ideas which become fixed in them.

Disgust with life can be reckoned as one of the most indefinite forms of madness when it is not caused by the loss of loved and worthy persons or by a breakdown in the ethical sphere. An indefinite, unfounded disgust with life is not an *indifference* to it, for in the latter case life is endured; rather is it the inability to endure it, a fluctuation between desire for and aversion to everything pertaining to the actual world, an imprisonment in the fixed idea of the loathsomeness of life associated with an effort to overcome this idea. It is mostly the English who succumb to this quite irrational disgust with the actual world, as well as to other forms of madness; perhaps because with them the tenacious clinging to subjective particularity is so prevalent. In the English, this disgust with life is manifested mainly as *melancholy*, the state in which mind constantly broods over its unhappy idea and is unable to rise to spontaneous thought and action. Not infrequently this psychical state develops into an uncontrollable impulse to commit suicide; sometimes this impulse has only been eradicated by the victim being violently taken out of himself. For instance, the story is told of an Englishman who was on the point of drowning himself in the Thames when he was attacked by robbers; he offered the fiercest resistance and suddenly feeling that life was worth while, he lost all thoughts of suicide. Another Englishman who had hanged himself, on being cut down by his servant not only regained the desire to live but also the disease of avarice; for when discharging the servant, he deducted twopence from his wages because the man had acted without instructions in cutting the rope with which his master had hanged himself.

Over against the indeterminate form of mental derangement just delineated in which all spontaneity is extinguished, there is an endless variety of forms of insanity having a *single, isolated* content, in which the patient is vividly, even passionately, interested. In some cases this content depends on the particular passion which occasioned the insanity; but it can also be determined by some other chance circumstance. In the first group we should have to include those lunatics who, for example, take themselves to be God, or Christ, or a king. The second group, on the other hand, comprises lunatics who, for example, imagine themselves to be a grain of barley, or a dog, or to have a carriage in their stomach. But in both cases the *simple* lunatic has no *definite awareness* of the *contradiction* which exists between his fixed idea and the objective world. We alone are aware of this contradiction; the lunatic himself is not tormented by the feeling of his inner disruption.

3. *The third main form of insanity—mania or frenzy*

Only in this third form do we find that the maniac himself is aware of the disruption of his consciousness into two mutually contradictory modes, that the maniac himself has a vivid feeling of the contradiction between his merely subjective idea and the objective world, and yet cannot rid himself of this idea but is fully intent on making it an actuality or on destroying what is actual. It is implied in this notion of mania that it need not spring from an empty conceit, but can be brought about especially by a stroke of great misfortune, by a derangement of a person's individual world, or by the violent upheaval and putting out of joint of the general state of the world if the individual lives with his feelings exclusively in the *past* and is thus unable to find himself in the *present* by which he feels himself alike repelled and bound. In the French revolution, for example, the almost complete collapse of civil society caused many people to become insane. Religious causes can often produce the same effect in the most frightful manner, when the individual is plunged into absolute uncertainty whether God's grace has been granted to him.

But in maniacs, the feeling of their inner disruption can equally well be a *tranquil* pain as it can also develop into a rage of reason against unreason and vice versa, and thus become a *frenzy*. For this unhappy feeling of the maniac very easily joins itself not only to a hypochondriacal mood which torments him with whims and fancies, but also to a suspicious, false, jealous, mischievous, and malicious disposition, to a furious resentment against the restraints imposed on him by his actual environment, against those from whom he suffers a limitation of his will; just as, conversely, in those *spoilt* individuals who are accustomed to getting their own way in everything, their rambling, headstrong nature easily turns to mania when the rational will which desires the universal opposes a dam to their caprice, a dam which their overweening subjectivity is unable to break through. Fits of ill-will occur in everyone; but the ethical, or at least prudent, person knows how to subdue them. But in mania, where one particular idea usurps the authority of the rational mind, the particularity of the subject manifests itself unchecked, and the natural impulses and those developed by reflection belonging to this particularity consequently throw off the yoke of the moral laws rooted in the truly universal will, with the result that the dark, infernal powers of the heart are set free. The madman in his rage often develops a positive mania for injuring others and, though he may have a horror of murder, may even be seized with a sudden irresistible desire to kill those whom otherwise he loves tenderly. But as we have just indicated, the malice of the maniac does not prevent him from having moral and ethical feelings; on the contrary, just because of his distress, just because he is mastered by the *unmediated opposition* present in him, these feelings can have an increased intensity. Pinel expressly states that nowhere has he seen more affectionate spouses and fathers than in lunatic asylums.

As regards the *physical* side of mania, its manifestation is often connected with general changes in Nature, especially with the course of the sun. Very hot and very cold seasons exercise a particular influence in this connection. It has also been noticed that the approach of storms and abrupt changes in the weather produce temporary disturbances and outbursts among lunatics. With regard to age, it has been observed that mania does not usually occur before the age of fifteen. As regards other physical differences, it is known that in strong muscular persons with black hair, fits of rage are usually more violent than in blond individuals. But to what extent insanity is connected with a morbid condition of the nervous system, is a point which does not come within the purview of the physician who considers insanity from the outside, or of the anatomist.

The cure of insanity

The last point we have to discuss in connection with mania and insanity relates to the curative method to be applied to both diseases. This method is partly physical and partly psychological. In some cases the former alone is sufficient; but in most cases it is necessary to supplement this by psychological treatment which, in its turn, can sometimes effect a cure by itself. There is no known remedy universally applicable for the physical side of treatment. The medical remedies employed are, on the contrary, for the most part empirical and are therefore uncertain in their action. But this much is certain, that the worst method of all is the one formerly practised at Bedlam which was limited to a thorough purging of the lunatics four times a year. Sometimes, though, the mentally deranged have been physically cured by the very thing that is liable to cause insanity in those not afflicted, namely, by falling heavily on their heads. The celebrated Montfaucon is said to have been cured of his imbecility in this way in his youth.

But the most effective treatment is always psychological. While this is unable to cure idiocy, it can often be successful in the treatment of insanity proper and mania because in these psychical states consciousness is still spontaneously active, and along with an insanity connected with a *particular* idea, there also exists a consciousness which in its other ideas is rational, and from this a skilful psychiatrist is able to develop sufficient power to overcome the particular fixed idea. (It is the merit of Pinel in particular to have grasped this residue of rationality in lunatics and maniacs as the foundation of treatment and to have conducted his treatment of such persons accordingly. His paper on this subject must be considered the best in this sphere of medicine.)

In the psychological treatment of the insane, it is more important than anything else to win their confidence. This can be won because the insane are still moral beings. But the surest way to win their confidence is to be quite frank with them yet at the same time not to let this frankness degenerate into a direct attack on their insane idea. Pinel relates an example of this method of treatment and of its successful outcome. A hitherto amiable man became insane, and to prevent him from doing injury to others he had to be locked up. This put him in a rage and he had to be bound, which made him even more furious. He was therefore put in a lunatic asylum. Here the warden entered into a quiet conversation with him and gave in to his absurdities which calmed him. He then ordered his bonds to be removed, led him into his new house and by continuing this kind of treatment cured this lunatic in a very short time. After the confidence of the insane has been won, one must try to obtain a proper authority over them and to awaken in them the feeling that there are, in general, things of importance and worth. The insane feel their mental weakness, their dependence on the rational person. This makes it possible for the latter to win their respect. In learning to respect the one who is treating him, the lunatic acquires the ability forcibly to restrain his subjectivity which is in conflict with the objective world. So long as he is unable to do this himself others have forcibly to restrain him. Consequently if, for example, a lunatic refuses to eat, or even destroys things around him, then obviously this cannot be tolerated. It is particularly necessary—and this is often very difficult in the case of persons of rank, such as George III for instance—to humble the conceitedness of the proud maniac by making him feel his dependence. Pinel gives a noteworthy example of this form of mania and of the method of treating it.

An individual who took himself to be Mahomet arrived at the lunatic asylum full of pride and arrogance, demanded homage, issued daily a host of decrees of banishment and death and raved in royal fashion. Now although his delusion was not corrected, he was forbidden to give way to raving as this was unbecoming, and when he did not obey he was locked up and reprimanded for his conduct. He promised to improve his behaviour, was discharged, but began again to give way to fits of rage. This 'Mahomet' was now roughly dealt with, again locked up, and informed that he must expect no more mercy. But the warden's wife by an agreed arrangement, pretended to be touched by his earnest entreaties for liberty and asked him to promise faithfully not to abuse his freedom by giving way to outbursts of rage because this caused her unpleasantness. He gave his promise and was then released. From this moment onwards he behaved well. If he fell into a rage, a glance from the warden's wife was sufficient to send him to his room to hide his rage there. The respect he had for this woman and his determination to conquer his fits of rage restored him to sanity in six months.

As in the case just cited, it is most important always to remember that if at times it is necessary to deal severely with the insane, *in general* they deserve considerate treatment because their rational nature is not yet entirely destroyed. For this reason, the restraint which has to be applied to these unfortunates should always be of such a kind as to have the moral significance of a just punishment. Lunatics still have a feeling of what is right and good; they know, for example, that one should not harm others. Consequently they can be made aware of the wrong they have committed, can be made accountable for it and punished for it, and can be made to see the justice of the punishment meted out to them. Thereby their better self is encouraged and when this happens they gain confidence in their own moral strength. Having reached this point, they become capable by associating with good people of recovering completely. On the other hand, the moral self-feeling of the insane can be so easily wounded by harsh, arrogant, contemptuous treatment that they fly into the most furious rage and frenzy. Also one should not be so imprudent, especially in the case of religious maniacs, as to let anything come in their way which could serve to strengthen their mania. On the contrary, one should strive to get lunatics to think about other things and so make them forget their fancies. A specially effective way of dispelling the fixed idea is to compel the insane to occupy themselves mentally and especially physically; by working, they are forced out of their diseased subjectivity and impelled towards the real world. A case of this kind is that of a Scottish farmer who became noted for curing the insane, although his method was simply and solely to harness them, half a dozen at a time, to a plough and make them work until they were completely tired out. Of the remedies acting primarily on the body, the see-saw especially has proved efficacious, particularly with raving lunatics. The see-saw movement induces giddiness in the patient and loosens his fixed idea. But a great deal can also be achieved for the recovery of the insane by sudden and powerful action on their fixed idea. It is true that the insane are extremely distrustful when they notice that attempts are being made to wean them away from their fixed idea. Yet at the same time they are stupid and are easily taken by surprise. They can therefore not infrequently be cured by someone pretending to enter into their delusion and then suddenly doing something in which the patient catches a glimpse of liberation from his imagined complaint. There is a well-known case of an Englishman who believed he had a hay-cart with four horses in his stomach and who was freed from his delusion by a doctor who, having assured him that he could feel the cart and horses and so gained his confidence, persuaded him that he possessed a remedy for reducing the size of the things supposedly in his stomach. Finally, he gave the lunatic an emetic and made him vomit out of the window just as, with the doctor's connivance, a hay-cart was passing by outside which the lunatic believed he had vomited. Another way of effecting a cure of insanity consists in getting lunatics to perform actions which directly refute the *specific* delusion which plagues them. Thus, for example, someone who imagined he had glass feet was cured by a feigned attack by robbers, when he found his feet extremely useful for running away. Another who held himself to be dead, did not move and would not eat, came to his senses again when someone pretended to share his delusion. The lunatic was put in a coffin and laid in a vault in which was another coffin occupied by a man who at first pretended to be dead but who, soon after he was left alone with the lunatic, sat up, told the latter how pleased he was to have company in death, and finally got up, ate the food that was by him and told the astonished lunatic that he had already been dead a long time and therefore knew how the dead go about things. The lunatic was pacified by the assurance, likewise ate and drank and was cured. Sometimes lunacy can also be cured by a word or by a joke acting direcˌly on the delusion. For instance, a lunatic who believed that he was the Holy Ghost recovered when another lunatic said to him: How can you be the Holy Ghost? *I* am it. An equally interesting instance is that of a watch-maker who imagined he had been guillotined although innocent. The remorseful judge ordered that his head be given back to him, but through an unfortunate mishap a different, much worse, thoroughly useless head had been put back on him. As this lunatic was once defending the legend according to which St. Dionysius had kissed his own severed head, another lunatic retorted: You arrant fool, with what did St. Dionysius kiss his head, with his heel perhaps? This question so shook the lunatic watch-maker that he completely recovered from his delusion. A joke of this kind will, however, completely dispel the delusion only if this malady has already diminished in intensity.

(γ) Habit[1]

§ 409

Self-feeling, immersed in the detail of the feelings (in simple sensations, and also desires, instincts, passions, and their gratification), is undistinguished from them. But in the self there is latent a simple self-relation of ideality, a nominal universality (which is the truth of these details): and as so universal, the self is to be stamped upon, and made appear in, this life of feeling, yet so as to distinguish itself from the particular details, and be a realized universality. But this universality is not the full and sterling truth of the specific feelings and desires; what they specifically

[1] Gewohnheit.

contain is as yet left out of account. And so too the particularity is, as now regarded, equally formal; it counts only as the *particular being* or immediacy of the soul in opposition to its equally formal and abstract realization. This particular being of the soul is the factor of its corporeity; here we have it breaking with this corporeity, distinguishing it from itself—itself a *simple* being—and becoming the 'ideal', subjective substantiality of it—just as in its latent notion (§ 389) it was the substance, and the mere substance, of it.

But this abstract realization of the soul in its corporeal vehicle is not yet the self—not the existence of the univeral which is for the universal. It is the corporeity reduced to its mere *ideality*; and so far only does corporeity belong to the soul as such. That is to say, just as space and time as the abstract one-outside-another, as, therefore, empty space and empty time, are only subjective forms, a pure act of intuition; so is that pure *being* (which, through the supersession in it of the particularity of the corporeity, or of the immediate corporeity as such, has realized itself) mere intuition and no more, lacking consciousness, but the basis of consciousness. And consciousness it becomes, when the corporeity, of which it is the subjective substance, and which still continues to exist, and that as a barrier for it, has been absorbed by it, and it has been invested with the character of self-centred subject.

§ 410

The soul's making itself an abstract universal being, and reducing the particulars of feelings (and of consciousness) to a mere feature of its being is Habit. In this manner the soul has the contents in possession, and contains them in such manner that in these features it is not as sentient, nor does it stand in relationship with them as distinguishing itself from them, nor is absorbed in them, but has them and moves in them, without feeling or consciousness of the fact. The soul is freed from them, so far as it is not interested in or occupied with them: and whilst existing in these forms as its possession, it is at the same time open to be otherwise occupied and engaged—say with feeling and with mental consciousness in general.

This process of building up the particular and corporeal expressions of feeling into the being of the soul appears as a *repetition* of them, and the generation of habit as *practice*. For, this being of the soul, if in respect of the natural particular phase it be called an abstract universality to which the former is transmuted, is a reflexive universality (§ 175); i.e. the one and the same, that recurs in a series of units of sensation, is reduced to unity, and this abstract unity expressly stated.

Habit, like memory, is a difficult point in mental organization: habit is the mechanism of self-feeling, as memory is the mechanism of intelligence. The natural qualities and alterations of age, sleep, and waking are 'immediately' natural: habit, on the contrary, is the mode of feeling (as well as intelligence, will, etc., so far as they belong to self-feeling) made into a natural and mechanical existence. Habit is rightly called a second nature; nature, because it is an immediate being of the soul; a second nature, because it is an immediacy created by the soul, impressing and moulding the corporeality which enters into the modes of feeling as such and into the representations and volitions so far as they have taken corporeal form (§ 401).

In habit the human being's mode of existence is 'natural', and for that reason not free; but still free, so far as the merely natural phase of feeling is by habit reduced to a mere being of *his*, and he is no longer involuntarily attracted or repelled by it, and so no longer interested, occupied, or dependent in regard to it. The want of freedom in habit is partly merely formal, as habit merely attaches to the being of the soul; partly only relative, so far as it strictly speaking arises only in the case of bad habits, or so far as a habit is opposed by another purpose: whereas the habit of right and goodness is an embodiment of liberty. The main point about Habit is that by its means man gets emancipated from the feelings, even in being affected by them. The different forms of this may be described as follows: (α) The *immediate* feeling is negated and treated as indifferent. One who gets inured against external sensations (frost, heat, weariness of the limbs, etc., sweet tastes, etc.), and who hardens the heart against misfortune, acquires a strength which consists in this, that although the frost, etc.—or the misfortune—is felt, the affection is deposed to a mere externality and immediacy; the universal psychical life keeps its own abstract independence in it, and the self-feeling as such, consciousness, reflection, and any other purposes and activity, are no longer bothered with it. (β) There is indifference towards the satisfaction: the desires and impulses are by the *habit* of their satisfaction deadened. This is the rational liberation from them; whereas monastic renunciation and forcible interference do not free from them, nor are they in conception rational. Of course in all this it is assumed that the impulses are kept as the finite modes they naturally are, and that they, like their satisfaction, are subordinated as partial factors to the reasonable will. (γ) In habit regarded as *aptitude*, or skill, not merely has the abstract psychical life to be kept intact *per se*, but it has to be imposed as a subjective aim, to be made a power in the bodily part, which is rendered subject and thoroughly pervious to it. Conceived as having the inward purpose of the subjective soul thus imposed upon it, the body is treated as an immediate externality and a barrier. Thus comes out the more decided rupture between the soul as simple self-concentration, and its earlier naturalness and immediacy; it has lost its original and immediate identity with the bodily nature, and as external has first to be reduced to that position. Specific feelings can only get bodily shape in a perfectly specific way (§ 410); and the immediate portion of body is a particular possibility for a specific aim (a particular aspect of its differentiated structure, a particular organ of its organic system). To mould such an aim in the organic body is to bring out and express the 'ideality' which is implicit in matter always, and especially so in the specific bodily part, and thus to enable the soul, under its volitional and conceptual characters, to exist as substance in its corporeity. In this way an aptitude shows the corporeity rendered completely pervious, made into an instrument, so that when the conception (e.g. a series of musical notes) is in me, then without resistance and with ease the body gives them correct utterance.

The form of habit applies to all kinds and grades of mental action. The most external of them, i.e. the spatial direction of an individual, viz. his upright posture, has been by will made a habit —a position taken without adjustment and without consciousness —which continues to be an affair of his persistent will; for the man stands only because and in so far as he wills to stand, and only so long as he wills it without consciousness. Similarly our eyesight is the concrete habit which, without an express adjustment, combines in a single act the several modifications of sensation, consciousness, intuition, intelligence, etc., which make it up. Thinking, too, however free and active in its own pure element it becomes, no less requires habit and familiarity (this impromptuity or form of immediacy), by which it is the property of my single self where I can freely and in all directions range. It is through this habit that I come to realize my *existence* as a thinking being. Even here, in this spontaneity of self-centred thought, there is a partnership of soul and body (hence, want of habit and too-long-continued thinking cause headache); habit diminishes this feeling, by making the natural function an immediacy of the soul. Habit on an ampler scale, and carried out in the strictly intellectual range, is recollection and memory, whereof we shall speak later.

Habit is often spoken of disparagingly and called lifeless, casual, and particular. And it is true that the form of habit, like any other, is open to anything we chance to put into it; and it is habit of living which brings on death, or, if quite abstract, is death itself: and yet habit is indispensable for the *existence* of all intellectual life in the individual, enabling the subject to be a concrete immediacy, an 'ideality' of soul—enabling the matter of consciousness, religious, moral, etc., to be his as *this* self, *this* soul, and no other, and be neither a mere latent possibility, nor a transient emotion or idea, nor an abstract inwardness, cut off from action and reality, but part and parcel of his being. In scientific studies of the soul and the mind, habit is usually passed over—either as something contemptible—or rather for the further reason that it is one of the most difficult questions of psychology.

Zusatz. We are accustomed to the idea of habit; none the less to determine the Notion of habit is hard. For this reason we wish to give here some further elucidations of this Notion.

First of all, the necessity of the dialectical progress from insanity (considered in § 408) to habit (treated in §§ 409 and 410) must be indicated. To this end we recall that in insanity the soul strives to restore itself to the perfect inner harmony of mind out of the existing contradiction between its objective consciousness and its fixed idea. This restoration can just as well fail as succeed. For the individual soul, therefore, the

attainment of free, inwardly harmonious self-feeling appears as a contingent affair. But in itself, or in principle, the absolute liberation of self-
feeling, the soul's untroubled self-communion in every particularity of
its content, is a necessity; for in itself the soul is absolute ideality, that
which overarches all its determinatenesses; and there is implied in the
Notion of soul that by overcoming all the particularities which have
become fixed in it, it proves itself to be the unlimited power over them,
that it reduces what is still *immediate, merely affirmative* in it to a mere
property, a mere moment, in order to become by this absolute negation
a free, self-existent individuality. Now we have already had to consider
in the relation of the human soul to its genius, a being-for-self of the self.
But there this being-for-self still had the form of externality, of separation
into two individualities, into a dominating and a dominated self; and
between these two sides there was as yet no decided opposition, no contradiction, so that the genius, this determinate inwardness, manifested
itself unhindered in the human individual. But here, on the contrary, at
the stage we have now reached in the development of subjective mind,
we come to a being-for-self of the soul that has been brought into being
by the Notion of soul which has overcome the inner contradiction of mind
present in insanity, has put an end to the complete dividedness of the self.
This being-at-home-with-oneself we call habit. In this, the soul which is
no longer confined to a merely subjective particular idea by which it is
displaced from the centre of its concrete actuality, has so completely
received into its ideality the immediate and particularized content presented to it, has come to feel so at home in it, that it moves about in it in
freedom. In other words, whereas in mere sensation I am contingently
affected now by this object and now by that, and in this sensation the soul
is immersed in its content, lost in it, does not feel its concrete self—
as is also the case in any other activity of mind so long as this is something
to which the subject is not yet accustomed—in habit, on the contrary,
man relates himself not to a contingent single sensation, idea, appetite,
etc., but to himself, to a universal mode of action which constitutes his
individuality, which is posited by himself and has become his own and
for that very reason appears as free. The universal to which the soul relates itself in habit, in distinction from the self-determining, concrete
universal which exists only for pure thinking is, however, only the
abstract universality produced by reflection from the repetition of many
single instances. It is only to this form of the universal that the natural
soul can attain, occupied as it is with an immediate and therefore single
content. But the universal that is related to mutually external singulars
is the *necessary*. Consequently although, on the one hand, habit makes a
man free, yet, on the other hand, it makes him its slave, and though it is
not an immediate, first nature dominated by single sensations but rather
a second nature posited by soul, yet it is all the same a nature, something
posited which takes the shape of immediacy, an ideality of what is simply
given, which is still burdened with the form of [mere] being, and con-

sequently something not correspondent to free mind, something merely anthropological.

The soul, having become a self-relating ideality in the manner just indicated, namely, by overcoming its dividedness and its inner contradiction, has disengaged itself from its corporeity with which it was previously immediately identical, and at the same time exerts the power of its ideality on the corporeity thus released into immediacy. At this stage, therefore, we have to consider not the indeterminate separation of a simply inner world from a world already confronting it, but the process of subjecting this corporeity to the domination of the soul. This seizure of the corporeity forms the condition of the soul's liberation, of its attaining objective consciousness. Of course, the individual soul is *in itself* already physically exclusive; as alive, I have an organic body and this is not something extraneous to me; on the contrary, it belongs to my Idea, is the immediate, outer existence of my Notion, constitutes my individual natural life. Incidentally, therefore, one must pronounce to be completely empty the opinion of those who fancy that, strictly speaking, man should not have an organic body because this compels him to attend to the satisfaction of his physical needs and thus diverts him from his purely spiritual life and prevents him from enjoying true freedom. Even the unsophisticated religious man is far removed from this shallow view, since he holds the satisfaction of his bodily needs worthy of being the object of his prayers to God, to the Eternal Spirit. But philosophy has to recognize that mind is only *for itself* by opposing to itself material being, partly in the shape of its *own* corporeity and partly as an external world, and by leading back what is thus differentiated into unity with itself, a unity mediated by the opposition of material being and the overcoming of it. Between mind and its *own* body there is naturally a more intimate association than between the rest of the external world and mind. Just because of this necessary connection of my body with my soul, the activity exercised by the latter on the former is not a *finite*, not a merely *negative*, activity. In the first place, I have to maintain myself in this immediate harmony of my soul and my body; true, I do not have to make this an end in itself as athletes and tightrope dancers do, but I must give my body its due, must take care of it, keep it healthy and strong, and must not therefore despise it or treat it as an enemy. It is just by neglecting or even ill-treating my body that I would bring myself into subjection to it and to the external necessity of the connection with it; for in this way I would make it into something—despite its identity with me—negative towards me and consequently hostile, and would force it to rise up against me, to avenge itself on my mind. But if, on the other hand, I behave in accordance with the laws of my physical organism, my soul is free in its body.

Yet all the same, the soul cannot remain in this immediate unity with its body. The form of immediacy of this harmony contradicts the Notion of soul, its determination as self-relating ideality. In order to become adequate to this its Notion, the soul must do what at this stage it has not as yet done, namely, it must transform its identity with its body into an identity brought about or mediated by mind, must take possession of its body, must form it into a pliant and skilful instrument of its activity, so transform it that in it soul relates itself to itself and its body becomes an accident brought into harmony with its substance, with freedom. Body is the middle term by which I come together with the external world as such. Consequently, if I want to realize my aims, I must make my body capable of carrying over this subjectivity into the external objective world. My body is not by nature fitted to do this; on the contrary, it immediately performs only what conforms to its animal nature. The purely organic functions are not as yet functions performed at the behest of my mind. For this service my body must first be trained. Whereas in the case of animals the body, in obedience to their instinct, carries out in an immediate manner everything which the Idea of the animal prescribes as necessary to it, man, on the contrary, has first to make himself master of his body by his own exertions. At the beginning, the human soul pervades its body only in a quite indefinitely general manner. In order that this pervasion become determinate, training is required. In the initial stages, the body shows itself intractable, its movements are uncertain and are either too strong or too weak for the purpose in hand. The correct measure of strength can only be achieved when one directs particular attention to all the manifold circumstances of the external environment in which one's aims are to be carried out and adjusts each separate movement of one's body in accordance with these circumstances. Therefore, even a person with a decided talent can only straightway hit on the right solution to a problem if he is technically trained.

With the frequent repetition of bodily activities in the service of mind, they acquire an ever higher degree of adequacy, for the soul gains an ever-increasing familiarity with the circumstances to be considered, hence becomes more and more at home in expressing itself and consequently achieves an ever-growing capacity for immediately embodying its inner intentions and accordingly transforms the body more and more into its property, into its serviceable instrument; there thus arises a *magical* relation, an immediate operation of mind on body.

But since the single activities of man acquire by repeated exercise the character of habit, the form of something received into recollection, into the universality of mental inwardness, the soul brings into its bodily activities a universal mode of action, a *rule*, to be transmitted to other activities. This rule is so concentrated in its simplicity that in it I am no longer conscious of the *particular* differences of my single activities. That this is so we see, for example, in writing. When we are learning to write we must fix our attention on every detail, on a vast number of mediations. If, on the other hand, the activity of writing has become a habit with us, then our self has so completely mastered all the relevant details, has so infected them with its universality, that they are no longer present to us as single details and we keep in view only their universal aspect. We see, therefore, that in habit our consciousness is at the same time *present* in the subject-matter, *interested* in it, yet conversely *absent* from it, *indifferent* to it; that our self just as much *appropriates* the subject-matter as, on the contrary, it *draws away* from it, that the soul, on the one hand, completely *pervades* its bodily activities and, on the other hand, *deserts* them, thus giving them the shape of something *mechanical*, of a merely *natural effect*.

(c) THE ACTUAL SOUL[1]

§ 411

The Soul, when its corporeity has been moulded and made thoroughly its own, finds itself there a *single* subject; and the corporeity is an externality which stands as a predicate, in being related to which, it is related to itself. This externality, in other words, represents not itself, but the soul, of which it is the *sign*. In this identity of interior and exterior, the latter subject to the former, the soul is *actual*: in its corporeity it has its free shape, in which it *feels itself* and makes *itself felt*, and which as the Soul's work of art has *human* pathognomic and physiognomic expression.

Under the head of human expression are included, for example, the upright figure in general, and the formation of the limbs, especially the hand, as the absolute instrument, of the mouth—laughter, weeping, etc., and the note of mentality diffused over the whole, which at once announces the body as the externality of a higher nature. This note is so slight, indefinite, and inexpressible a modification, because the figure in its externality is something immediate and natural, and can therefore only be an indefinite and quite imperfect sign for the mind, unable to represent it in its actual universality. Seen from the animal world, the human figure is the supreme phase in which mind makes an appearance. But for the mind it is only its first appearance, while language is its perfect expression. And the human figure, though the proximate phase of mind's existence, is at the same time in its physiognomic and pathognomic quality something contingent to it. To try to raise physiognomy and above all cranioscopy (phrenology) to the rank of sciences, was therefore one of the vainest fancies, still vainer

[1] Die wirkliche Seele.

than a *signatura rerum*, which supposed the shape of a plant to afford indication of its medicinal virtue.

Zusatz. As we have already asserted in § 390 in anticipation, the *actual* soul forms the third and last main section of Anthropology. We began our consideration of Anthropology with the merely immediate soul as yet unseparated from its natural mode; then, in the second main section, we passed on to the soul which separates from itself its immediate being and in its determinatenesses is *abstractly* a *being-for-self*, that is to say, to the *feeling* soul; and now, in the third main section, we come as already intimated to the soul that has developed out of that separation into a mediated unity with its natural being, that in its corporeity is *concretely* a being-for-self, hence *actual* soul. The transition to this stage of development is made by the Notion of *habit* considered in the previous Paragraph. For, as we have seen, in habit the ideal determinations of the soul receive the form of mere being, of something external to itself, and conversely, corporeity on its side becomes something unresistingly pervaded by soul, something subjected to the liberated power of the soul's ideality. Thus by the separation of the soul from its corporeity and by the cancellation of this separation, there arises the mediated unity of the inner being of the former and the outer being of the latter. This unity which, from being a result becomes an immediate unity, we call the *actuality* of the soul.

From the standpoint we have now reached, the body no longer comes into consideration from the side of its organic process, but only in so far at it is an externality that is transformed into an ideality even in its outer existence and in which the soul, no longer restricted to the involuntary embodiment of its inner sensations, is brought to manifestation with as much freedom as it has so far won by overcoming the obstacles to its ideality.

The involuntary embodiment of inner sensations considered at the close of the first main section of Anthropology (§ 401) is, in part, something which man has in common with the animals. On the other hand, the embodiments which occur *freely* and are now to be discussed, impart to the human body such a characteristic mental or spiritual stamp that it is distinguished by it from the animals far more than by any mere natural quality. On his purely physical side, man is not greatly different from the ape; but the mind- or spirit-pervaded aspect of his body distinguishes him from that animal to such a degree that there exists less difference between the appearance of an ape and that of a bird than between the body of a man and that of an ape.

But the mental or spiritual expression is concentrated mainly in the face, because the head is the true seat of the mental or spiritual. In the rest of the body, which belongs more or less to the natural as such and, therefore, among civilized peoples is clothed for the sake of modesty, the spiritual reveals itself especially in the body's carriage. This, incidentally, received particular attention in the works of artists of the ancient world who gave visible expression to mind or spirit above all in its diffused presence throughout the bodily nature. So far as spiritual expression is conveyed by the facial muscles it is called, as we know, the play of features; gestures in the narrower sense of the word originate with the other parts of the body. Man's absolute gesture is his erect posture; he alone is able to do this, whereas even the orang-outang can stand upright only with the aid of a stick. Man does not hold himself erect naturally but stands upright by the energy of his will; and although his erect posture, after it has become a habit, requires no further effort of will, yet it must always remain pervaded by our will if we are not momentarily to collapse. The human arm and especially the hand are likewise peculiar to man; no animal has such a flexible instrument for external movement. The human hand—this instrument *par excellence*—is adapted for a multitude of willed activities. As a rule we begin to gesticulate with the hand and then go on to use the whole arm and the rest of the body.

Expression by means of facial muscles and gestures provides an interesting topic for consideration. But it is sometimes not altogether easy to discover the ground of the specific symbolic nature of certain facial expressions and gestures, the connection of their *meaning* with what they are *in themselves*. We do not wish to discuss here all the relevant phenomena but only the commonest of them. Nodding—to begin with this—signifies an affirmation, for by this we intimate a kind of submission. Bowing as a sign of respect is always done only with the upper part of the body by us Europeans, since in the act we do not wish to surrender our independence. Orientals, on the other hand, express reverence for their master by prostrating themselves before him; they may not look him in the eye, for by doing so they would be asserting their independence, but the master alone has the right freely to ignore the servant and slave. Shaking the head signifies an answer in the negative; for this action indicates vacillation, denial. Tossing up one's head expresses contempt, superiority over another. Turning up one's nose indicates disgust as if one smelt something nasty. Frowning is a sign of anger, a concentration of oneself in opposition to someone else. Pulling a long face means that we have been disappointed in our expectation; for in such a case we feel, as it were, undone. The most expressive gestures have their seat in the mouth and in its surrounding parts, since it is from the mouth that the utterance of speech proceeds involving many and varied modifications of the lips. As regards the hands, when we express astonishment by clapping them over our head, this is in some measure an attempt to find a support in oneself (*sich über sich selber zusammenzuhalten*). Shaking hands when making a promise indicates, as is easy to see, unanimity. The movement of the lower extremities, *gait*, is also very significant. First and foremost, gait must be under control; in it the soul must betray its mastery over the body. But not only refinement and uncouthness, but also, slackness, affectation, vanity, hypocrisy, etc., on the one hand, and orderliness, modesty, good sense, magnanimity, etc., on the other, express themselves in the peculiar style of walking; so that it is easy to distinguish people from one another by their gait.

Moreover the cultured man is more restrained in his facial expressions and gestures than the uneducated person. Just as the former curbs the inward raging of his passions, so does he also preserve outwardly a calm demeanour and imparts to the voluntary embodiment of his feelings a certain measure of moderation; whereas the uncouth person, lacking control over his inner feelings, believes that he can make himself understood in no other way than by extravagant airs and gestures, by which he is sometimes led into grimacing and in this way giving himself a comical air, because in a grimace the inner feeling at once completely externalizes itself, the person allowing each single feeling to diffuse itself throughout his entire bodily existence with the result that, almost like an animal, he immerses himself exclusively in this specific feeling. The cultured person does not need to indulge in extravagant airs and gestures; he possesses in speech the worthiest and most suitable means of expressing himself; for speech is able immediately to receive and reproduce every modification of our ideational faculty, for which reason the ancients even went to the extreme of making their actors appear with masks on their faces, and so, contenting themselves with this immobile physiognomy of the actor in his part, they dispensed altogether with the lively play of his features.

Now just as the voluntary embodiments of the mental or spiritual here discussed become mechanical through habit, requiring no particular effort of will, so also, conversely, some of the involuntary embodiments of the soul's feelings considered in § 401 can take place consciously and freely. This is true above all of the human voice; when this becomes speech, it ceases to be an involuntary utterance of the soul. Similarly laughing, in the form of mockery, becomes something freely produced. Sighing, too, is not so much something uncontrollable as arbitrary. Herein lies the justification for discussing the above-mentioned utterances of the soul in two different places, namely, when dealing with the purely feeling soul and also with the actual soul. It is also for this reason that we pointed out as far back as § 401 that among the involuntary embodiments of the mental or spiritual there are many 'in the line of the pathognomic and physiognomic' which were treated again in § 411 above. The difference between these two determinations is that the pathognomic expression relates more to transient passions, whereas the physiognomic is related to character, hence to something permanent. However, the pathognomic becomes physiognomic when a man's passions are not merely transient but permanently dominate him. Lasting anger, for example, firmly engrains itself in the face; and similarly, too, a sanctimonious nature gradually impresses itself indelibly in the face and in the whole bearing of the body.

Every man has a physiognomic appearance, appears at first sight as a pleasant or unpleasant, strong or weak, personality. According to this appearance one instinctively forms a first, general impression about others. However, it is easy to be mistaken in this, since this externality characterized mainly by immediacy, does not perfectly correspond to mind or spirit but only in a greater or less degree. Consequently, an unfavourable, like a favourable, exterior can conceal a personality different from what that exterior might at first lead one to expect. The biblical saying: Beware of those whom God hath marked, is, therefore, often misused; and a judgement based on physiognomic expression has accordingly only the value of an immediate judgement, which can just as well be untrue as true. For this reason, the exaggerated regard formerly shown to physiognomy about which Lavater created such a stir and which, it was said, promised to be profitable in the highest degree for the much vaunted knowledge of human nature, has rightly been dropped. Man is known much less by his outward appearance than by his deeds. Language itself is exposed to the fate of serving just as much to conceal as to reveal human thoughts.

§ 412

Implicitly the soul shows the untruth and unreality of matter; for the soul, in its concentrated self, cuts itself off from its immediate being, placing the latter over against it as a corporeity incapable of offering resistance to its moulding influence. The soul, thus setting in opposition its being to its (conscious) self, absorbing it, and making it its own, has lost the meaning of mere soul, or the 'immediacy' of mind. The actual soul with its sensation and its concrete self-feeling turned into habit, has implicitly realised the 'ideality' of its qualities; in this externality it has recollected and inwardized itself, and is infinite self-relation. This free universality thus made explicit shows the soul awaking to the higher stage of the ego, or abstract universality, in so far as it is *for* the abstract universality. In this way it gains the position of thinker and subject—specially a subject of the judgement in which the ego excludes from itself the sum total of its merely natural features as an object, a world external to it—but with such respect to that object that in it it is immediately reflected into itself. Thus soul rises to become *Consciousness*.

Zusatz. The soul's pervasion of its bodily nature dealt with in the two previous Paragraphs is not absolute, does not completely set aside the difference of soul and body. On the contrary, the nature of the logical Idea which develops everything from itself demands that this difference still remain in being. One side of corporeity remains, therefore, purely organic and consequently withdrawn from the power of the soul, so that the soul's pervasion of its body is only one side of the latter. The soul, when it feels this limitation of its power, reflects itself into itself and expels the corporeity from itself as something extraneous to it. By this reflection-into-self, mind consummates its liberation from the form of mere being, gives itself the form of essence and becomes 'I'. It is true that the soul, in so far as it is subjectivity or selfhood, is already *in itself*, or *implicitly*, 'I'. But the *actuality* of the 'I' involves more than the soul's immediate, natural subjectivity; for the 'I' is this universal, simple being that in truth exists only when it has itself for object, when it has become the being-for-self of the simple in the simple, the relation of the universal to the universal. The self-related universal exists nowhere save in the 'I'. In external Nature, as was already stated in the introduction to the doctrine of subjective mind, the universal only attains the highest manifestation of its power by destruction of the individual existence, hence does not attain to an actual being-for-self. The natural soul too is, in the first instance, only the real possibility of this being-for-self. Only in the 'I' does this possibility become an actuality. Therefore, in the 'I' a waking ensues of a higher kind than the natural waking which is confined to the mere sensation of single things; for the 'I' is the lightning which pierces through the natural soul and consumes its natural being. In the 'I', therefore, the ideality of natural being, and so the essence of the soul, becomes *for* the soul.

It is to this goal that the whole anthropological development presses forward. Looking back over it we shall recall how the *human* soul, in contrast to the animal soul which remains sunk in the singleness and limitation of sensation, has raised itself above the limited content of what is felt or sensed, a content which is in contradiction with its inherently infinite nature, has transformed this content into an ideal moment, and particularly in habit has made it into something universal, inwardized, and total, into a being; and also how by this very act it has filled the initially empty space of its inwardness with a content appropriate to its universality, has placed the being of the content within itself, just as, on the other hand, it has transformed its body into the likeness of its ideality, of its freedom, and thus has reached the stage where it exists in the 'I' as the self-related, individually determined universal, a self-existent, abstract totality freed from corporeity. Whereas in the sphere of the merely feeling soul the self is manifested in the shape of the genius, as a power acting only externally and at the same time only internally on the existent individuality, at the stage of the soul's development now reached, the self as already shown has actualized itself in the soul's outer existence, in its bodily nature, and, conversely, has given a being to itself; so that now the self or the 'I' beholds itself in its Other and is this intuiting of itself.

B. PHENOMENOLOGY OF MIND

CONSCIOUSNESS

§ 413

Consciousness constitutes the reflected or correlational grade of mind: the grade of mind as *appearance*. *Ego* is infinite self-relation of mind, but as subjective or as self-certainty. The immediate identity of the natural soul has been raised to this pure 'ideal' self-identity; and what the former *contained* is for this self-subsistent reflection set forth as an *object*. The pure abstract freedom of mind lets go from it its specific qualities—the soul's natural life—to an equal freedom as an independent *object*. It is of this latter, as external to it, that the *ego* is in the first instance aware (conscious), and as such it is Consciousness. Ego, as this absolute negativity, is implicitly the identity in the otherness: the *ego* is itself that other and stretches over the object (as if that object were implicitly cancelled)—it is one side of the relationship and the whole relationship—the light, which manifests itself and something else too.

Zusatz. As we remarked in the *Zusatz* to the previous Paragraph, the 'I' must be grasped as the individually determined universal which, in its determinateness, in its difference, relates itself to itself alone. This already implies that the 'I' is immediately *negative* self-relation, consequently the unmediated opposite of its universality which is abstracted from every determinateness, an individuality which is, therefore, equally abstract and simple. It is not only *we* who reflect on it who thus differentiate the 'I' into its opposed moments, but it is the 'I' itself which, in virtue of its immanently universal, hence self-differentiated, individuality, is this distinguishing of itself from itself; for as self-relating, its exclusive individuality excludes itself from itself, i.e. from individuality, and thereby makes itself into its own opposite, an opposite with which it is immediately united; that is, it makes itself into a universality. But the determination of abstractly universal individuality essentially belonging to the 'I' constitutes its *being*. I and my being are therefore inseparably united; the difference of my being from me is a difference that is none. On the one hand we must, of course, distinguish *being* which is absolutely immediate, indeterminate, undifferentiated, from *thought* which is self-differentiating and—by the reduction of difference to a moment—self-mediating, that is, from the 'I'; yet, on the other hand, being is identical with thought, since the latter returns from every mediation to immediacy, from all its self-differentiation to serene unity with itself. The 'I' is, therefore, being or has being as a moment within it. When I set this being as an Other over against me and at the same time as identical with me, I am Knowing (*Wissen*) and have the absolute certainty (*Gewißheit*) of my being. This certainty must not be regarded—as happens from the standpoint of mere mental representation—as a kind of property of the 'I', as a determination *in* its nature; on the contrary, it is to be grasped as the very nature of the 'I', for this cannot exist without distinguishing itself from itself—which simply means, without being directly aware of itself, without having and being the certainty of itself. For this reason, certainty is related to the 'I' as freedom is to the will. Just as the former constitutes the nature of the 'I', so does the latter constitute the nature of the will. To begin with, however, certainty is to be equated only with subjective freedom, with caprice; it is only objective certainty, truth, that corresponds to the genuine freedom of the will.

Accordingly, the self-certain 'I' is, to begin with, the still quite simple subjectivity, whose freedom is quite abstract, the completely indeterminate ideality or negativity of all limitation. Repelling itself from itself, the 'I' attains, therefore, at first a merely formal, not an actual, difference from itself. But as is demonstrated in Logic, the *implicit* difference must also be made *explicit*, must be developed into an *actual* difference. The manner in which this development proceeds in regard to the 'I' is that the latter—not relapsing into the anthropological sphere, into the unconscious unity of the mental or spiritual and the natural, but remaining self-certain and maintaining itself in its freedom—lets its Other unfold itself into a totality similar to the totality of the 'I', and by this very action lets a corporeal being appertaining to the soul become an independent being confronting it, an object (*Gegenstand*) in the strict sense of this word. Since the 'I' is at first only a wholly abstract subjectivity, the merely formal, empty distinguishing of itself from itself, the *actual* difference, the *determinate* content, exists outside of the 'I', belongs solely to the objects. But since the 'I' already possesses *in itself*, or in principle, difference within itself, or, in other words, since it is *in itself* the unity of itself and its Other, it is necessarily related to the difference existent in the object and immediately reflected out of this its Other into itself. The 'I' overlaps or overarches, therefore, the actual difference from itself, is at home with itself in this its Other, and in every intuition remains self-certain. Only when I come to apprehend myself as 'I', does the Other become objective to me, confronts me, and is at the same time converted into an ideal moment in me, and hence brought back to unity with me. That is why in the above Paragraph the 'I' was compared to light. Just as light is the manifestation of itself and its Other, darkness, and can manifest itself only by manifesting that Other, so too the 'I' is manifest to itself only in so far as its Other is manifest to it in the shape of something independent of it.

From this general exposition of the nature of the 'I' it is sufficiently evident that since the 'I' enters into conflict with external objects, it is superior to the impotent natural soul which is entrapped, so to speak, in a childlike unity with the world, to the soul in which, just because it is impotent, fall the states of mental disease we have previously considered.

§ 414

The self-identity of the mind, thus first made explicit as the Ego, is only its abstract formal ideality. As *soul* it was under the phase of *substantial* universality; now, as subjective reflection in itself, it is referred to this substantiality as to its negative, something dark and beyond it. Hence consciousness, like reciprocal dependence in general, is the contradiction between the independence of the two sides and their identity in which they are merged into one. The mind as ego is *essence*; but since reality, in the sphere of essence, is represented as in immediate being and at the same time as 'ideal', it is as consciousness only the *appearance* (phenomenon) of mind.

Zusatz. The negativity which the wholly *abstract* 'I', or mere consciousness, exercises on its Other is as yet completely indeterminate, superficial, not absolute. Consequently, at this stage there arises the contradiction that the object, on the one hand is in me, and on the other hand, has an independent existence outside of me similar to that of darkness outside of light. To consciousness the object appears not as something posited by the 'I', but as something immediate, merely present, given; for consciousness does not as yet know that the object is in itself identical with mind and is released into a seemingly complete independence only by a self-diremption of mind. That this is so, is known only by *us* who have pressed forward to the *Idea* of mind and therefore have raised ourselves above the abstract, formal identity of the 'I'.

§ 415

As the ego is by itself only a formal identity, the dialectical movement of its intelligible unity, i.e. the successive steps in further specification of consciousness, does not, to it, seem to be its own activity, but is implicit, and to the ego it seems an alteration of the object. Consciousness consequently appears differently modified according to the difference of the given object; and the gradual specification of consciousness appears as a variation in the characteristics of its objects. Ego, the subject of consciousness, is thinking: the logical process of modifying the object is what is identical in subject and object, their absolute interdependence, what makes the object the subject's own.

The Kantian philosophy may be most accurately described as having viewed the mind as consciousness, and as containing the propositions only of a *phenomenology* (not of a *philosophy*) of mind. The Ego Kant regards as reference to something away and beyond (which in its abstract description is termed the thing-in-itself); and it is only from this finite point of view that he treats both intellect and will. Though in the notion of a power of *reflective* judgement he touches upon the *Idea* of mind—a subject-objectivity, an *intuitive intellect*, etc., and even the Idea of Nature, still this Idea is again deposed to an appearance, i.e. to a subjective maxim (§ 58). Reinhold may therefore be said to have correctly appreciated Kantism when he treated it as a theory of consciousness (under the name of 'faculty of ideation'). Fichte kept to the same point of view: his non-ego is only something set over against the ego, only defined as in *consciousness*: it is made no more than an infinite 'shock', i.e. a thing-in-itself. Both systems therefore have clearly not reached the intelligible unity or the mind as it actually and essentially is, but only as it is in reference to something else.

As against Spinozism, again, it is to be noted that the mind in the judgement by which it 'constitutes' itself an ego (a free subject contrasted with its qualitative affection) has emerged from substance, and that the philosophy, which gives this judgement as the absolute characteristic of mind, has emerged from Spinozism.

Zusatz. 1. Although the progressive determination of consciousness proceeds from its *own* inner being and also has a *negative* direction towards the object which, therefore, is *altered* by consciousness, yet this alteration appears to consciousness as one brought about without its subjective activity, and the determinations it places in the object count for it as belonging only to the latter, as immediately given in it.

2. With Fichte there is always the difficulty of how the 'I' is to dispose of the 'non-I'. He does not reach any genuine unity of these two sides; this unity always remains something that only *ought to be*, because at the outset it is falsely presupposed that 'I' and 'non-I' in their separateness, in their finitude, are something absolute.

§ 416

The aim of conscious mind is to make its appearance identical with its essence, to raise its *self-certainty to truth*. The *existence* of mind in the stage of consciousness is finite, because it is merely a nominal self-relation, or mere certainty. The object is only abstractly characterized as *its*; in other words, in the object it is only as an abstract ego that the mind is reflected into itself: hence its existence there has still a content, which is not as its own.

Zusatz. Ordinary thinking does not distinguish between certainty and truth. What it is *certain* of, what it holds to be a subjective thought that agrees with the object, this it calls *true*, no matter how trivial and bad the content of this subjective thought may be. Philosophy, on the contrary, must essentially distinguish the Notion of *truth* from mere *certainty*; for the certainty which mind has of itself at the stage of mere consciousness is something as yet untrue and self-contradictory, since here, along with the abstract certainty of being at home with itself, mind has the directly opposite certainty of being related to something essentially other to it. This contradiction must be resolved; the urge to resolve it lies in the contradiction itself. Subjective certainty must not find itself limited by the object but must acquire true objectivity; and, conversely, the object, on its side, must become *mine* not merely in an abstract manner but with regard to every aspect of its concrete nature. This goal is already anticipated by Reason which *believes* in itself, but is attained only by the Reason that *knows*, by *comprehensive cognition*.

§ 417

The grades of this elevation of certainty to truth are three in number: first (*a*) consciousness in general, with an object set against it; (*b*) self-consciousness, for which *ego* is the object; (*c*) unity of consciousness and self-consciousness, where the mind sees itself embodied in the object and sees itself as implicitly and explicitly determinate, as Reason, the *notion* of mind.

Zusatz. The three stages of the rise of consciousness to Reason indicated in the above Paragraph are determined by the power of the Notion, which is active alike in the subject as in the object. These stages can therefore be considered as three *judgements*. But as we have already remarked, the abstract 'I', mere consciousness, as yet knows nothing of this. Consequently when the 'non-I' which, to begin with, is for consciousness self-subsistent, is deprived of its self-subsistent status by the power of the Notion active in it, when the object is given the form not of immediacy, externality, and individuality but of a universal, of an inwardness, and consciousness has received this inwardness into itself, the 'I's *own* internalization thereby brought about appears to it as an internalization of the object. Only when the object has been internalized into the 'I' and consciousness has in this way developed into self-consciousness, does mind know the power of its own inwardness as a power present and active in the object. Therefore, what in the sphere of consciousness is only for *us* who contemplate it, becomes in the sphere of self-consciousness for mind itself. Self-consciousness has consciousness for its object, hence sets itself over against it. But, at the same time, consciousness is also retained as a *moment* in self-consciousness itself. Self-consciousness progresses, therefore, to the stage where, by the repulsion of itself from itself, it confronts itself with another self-consciousness and in this gives itself an object with which it is identical and yet which is at the same time self-subsistent. This object is, in the first instance, an immediate, single 'I'. But when this is freed from the form of one-sided subjectivity still clinging to it and grasped as a reality pervaded by the subjectivity of the Notion, consequently as Idea, then self-consciousness leaves behind its opposition to consciousness and moves on to a mediated unity with it and thereby becomes the concrete being-for-self of the 'I', the absolutely free Reason which cognizes in the objective world its own self.

It is hardly necessary to remark that Reason, which in our exposition appears as the third and last stage, is not merely a last stage that has resulted from something extraneous to it but is, on the contrary, the foundation of consciousness and self-consciousness, therefore the *prius*, and by the supersession of these two one-sided forms it proves itself to be their original unity and their truth.

(*a*) CONSCIOUSNESS PROPER[1]

(α) *Sensuous consciousness*

§ 418

Consciousness is, first, *immediate* consciousness, and its reference to the object accordingly the simple and underived certainty of it. The object similarly, being immediate, an existent, reflected in itself, is further characterized as immediately singular. This is sense-consciousness.

Consciousness—as a case of correlation—comprises only the categories belonging to the abstract ego or formal thinking; and

---

[1] Das Bewußtsein als solches: (α) Das sinnliche Bewußtsein.

these it treats as features of the object (§ 415). Sense-consciousness therefore is aware of the object as an existent, a something, an existing thing, a singular, and so on. It appears as wealthiest in matter, but as poorest in thought. That wealth of matter is made out of sensations: they are the *material* of consciousness (§ 414), the substantial and qualitative, what the soul in its anthropological sphere *is* and finds *in itself*. This material the ego (the reflection of the soul in itself) separates from itself, and puts it first under the category of being. Spatial and temporal Singularness, *here* and *now* (the terms by which in the Phenomenology of the Mind (*Werke* ii, p. 73), I described the object of sense-consciousness) strictly belongs to *intuition*. At present the object is at first to be viewed only in its correlation to *consciousness*, i.e. a something *external* to it, and not yet as external on its own part, or as being beside and out of itself.

Zusatz. The first of the three developmental stages of mind in its phenomenal aspect named in the above Paragraph, namely, consciousness, itself contains three stages:

(1) sensuous consciousness,
(2) sense-perception, and
(3) intellect.

In this sequence there is revealed a logical progress.

(1) At first, the object is quite immediate, merely given; it is thus that it appears to sensuous consciousness. But this immediacy has no truth; the advance must be made to the *essential* being of the object.

(2) When the essence of things becomes the object of consciousness, this is no longer sensuous consciousness but sense-perception. At this stage, single, individual things are referred to a universal, but only *referred* to it; what we have here is, therefore, not yet a true unity of the individual and the universal, but only a mixture of these two sides. In this lies a contradiction which leads on to the third stage of consciousness, namely,

(3) to intellect, where it finds its solution in the sense that there the object is reduced or raised to the appearance of a self-existent inner being. Such an appearance is the living being. It is in the contemplation of this, that self-consciousness is kindled; for in the living being the object is suddenly changed into something subjective; there consciousness discovers that it is itself the essential being of the object, it reflects itself out of the object into itself, becomes objective to itself.

After this general survey of the three developmental stages of consciousness, we shall now turn first of all to consider more closely *sensuous consciousness*.

This is distinguished from the other modes of consciousness, not by the fact that in it alone the object is given to us by the senses, but rather by the fact that on this stage the object, whether an inner or an outer object, has no other thought-determination than first, that of simply being, and secondly, of being an independent Other over against me, something reflected into itself, an individual confronting me as an individual, an immediate. The particular content of the sensuous, for example, smell, taste, colour, etc., belongs, as we saw in § 401, to sensation. But the form peculiar to the sensuous, namely, externality to self, the diremption into space and time, is the determination of the object apprehended by intuition in such a manner that for sensuous consciousness as such only the said thought-determination remains, in virtue of which the manifold particular content of sensations concentrates itself into a unity that is outside of me, a unity that, at this stage, is known by me in an immediate, isolated manner—enters and leaves my consciousness contingently; in general, a unity whose existence and nature is for me something given, something, therefore, of which I know neither whence it comes nor why it has this specific nature, nor whether it is something true.

It is clear from this brief statement of the nature of immediate or sensuous consciousness that it is an entirely inadequate form for the absolutely universal content of right, of the ethical sphere and of religion, a form which spoils their content, since in this consciousness what is absolutely necessary, eternal, infinite, and inward, is given a finite, isolated, self-external shape. Consequently, the modern view which would concede only an immediate knowledge of God limits one to a knowledge of him which can merely assert that he is, that he exists outside of us, and that he seems to possess such and such properties. Such a consciousness with its arbitrary assertions regarding the nature of the divine, which for it lies in the beyond, is productive of nothing but vain and boastful talk which it holds to be religious.

§ 419

The *sensible* as somewhat becomes an *other*: the reflection in itself of this *somewhat*, the *thing*, has *many* properties; and as a single (thing) in its immediacy has several *predicates*. The muchness of the sense-singular thus becomes a breadth—a variety of relations, reflectional attributes, and universalities. These are logical terms introduced by the thinking principle, i.e. in this case by the Ego, to describe the sensible. But the Ego as itself apparent sees in all this characterization a change in the object; and sensuous consciousness, so construing the object, is sense-perception.

Zusatz. The content of sensuous consciousness is in itself dialectical. It is supposed to be *the* single, isolated individual; but it is just this that makes it not *a* single individual but all individuals, and just by excluding from itself the individual content of another it relates itself to another, proves that it goes out of and beyond itself, that it is dependent on another, is mediated by it and has the other within itself. The proximate truth of what is *immediately* individual is therefore its relatedness to another. The determinations of this relation are those which are called determinations of reflection, and the consciousness which apprehends these determinations is *perception*.

(β) Sense-perception[1]

§ 420

Consciousness, having passed beyond the sensible, wants to take the object in its truth, not as merely immediate, but as mediated, reflected in itself, and universal. Such an object is a combination of sense qualities with attributes of wider range by which thought defines concrete relations and connections. Hence the identity of consciousness with the object passes from the abstract identity of 'I am sure' to the definite identity of 'I know, and am aware'.

The particular grade of consciousness on which Kantism conceives the mind is perception: which is also the general point of view taken by ordinary consciousness, and more or less by the sciences. The sensuous certitudes of single apperceptions or observations form the starting-point: these are supposed to be elevated to truth, by being regarded in their bearings, reflected upon, and on the lines of definite categories turned at the same time into something necessary and universal, viz. *experiences*.

Zusatz. Although perception starts from observation of sensuous materials it does not stop short at these, does not confine itself simply to smelling, tasting, seeing, hearing, and feeling (touching), but necessarily goes on to relate the sensuous to a universal which is not observable in an immediate manner, to cognize each individual thing as an internally coherent whole: in force, for example, to comprehend all its manifestations; and to seek out the connections and mediations that exist between separate individual things. While therefore the merely sensuous consciousness merely *shows* things, that is to say, exhibits them in their immediacy,

[1] Wahrnehmung.

perception, on the other hand, apprehends the connectedness of things, demonstrates that when such and such circumstances are present such and such a thing follows, and thus begins to demonstrate the truth of things. This demonstration is, however, still defective, not final. For that by which something is hereby supposed to be demonstrated is itself *presupposed*, and consequently in need of demonstration; with the result that in this field one goes from one presupposition to another and lapses into the progress to infinity. This is the standpoint occupied by empiricism. Everything must be experienced. But if it is philosophy we are supposed to be discussing, then we must rise above this empirical demonstration which remains tied to presuppositions, to a proof of the absolute necessity of things.

Already in § 415 it was said that the progressive determination of consciousness appears as an alteration of the determinations of its object. With reference to this point, it can be added here that while perception removes from things their singleness, gives them an ideal being and thereby negates the externality of the relation of the object to the 'I', the latter withdraws into itself and itself gains in inwardness, although consciousness regards this withdrawal into itself as falling in the object.

§ 421

This conjunction of individual and universal is admixture—the individual remains at the bottom hard and unaffected by the universal, to which, however, it is related. It is therefore a tissue of contradictions—between the single things of sense apperception, which form the alleged ground of general experience, and the universality which has a higher claim to be the essence and ground —between the individuality of a thing which, taken in its concrete content, constitutes its independence and the various properties which, free from this negative link and from one another, are independent universal *matters* (§ 123). This contradiction of the finite which runs through all forms of the logical spheres turns out most concrete, when the somewhat is defined as *object* (§§ 194 seqq.).

(γ) *The Intellect*[1]

§ 422

The proximate *truth* of perception is that it is the object which is an *appearance*, and that the object's reflection in self is on the

[1] Der Verstand.

contrary a self-subsistent inward and universal. The consciousness of such an object is *intellect*. This inward, as we called it, of the thing is, on one hand, the suppression of the multiplicity of the sensible, and, in that manner, an abstract identity: on the other hand, however, it also for that reason contains the multiplicity, but as an interior 'simple' difference, which remains self-identical in the vicissitudes of appearance. The simple difference is the realm of *the laws* of the phenomena—a copy of the phenomenon, but brought to rest and universality.

Zusatz. The contradiction indicated in the previous Paragraph is resolved in the first instance by the fact that the manifold determinations of the sensible, which are independent both relatively to one another and to the inner unity of each individual thing, are reduced to the *appearance* of a self-existent *inner being*, and the development of the object thus progresses from the contradiction of its reflection-into-self and its reflection-into-other to the essential relation of itself to itself. But when consciousness rises from the observation of immediate individuality and from the mixture of the individual and the universal, to the comprehension of the inwardness of the object, and therefore determines the object in a manner similar to the 'I', then this latter becomes the intellectual consciousness. It is only in this non-sensuous inner being that intellect believes it has the truth. At first, however, this inner being is *abstractly* identical, inwardly undifferentiated; an inner being of this kind is provided by the categories of force and cause. The true inner, on the contrary, must be characterized as concrete, as immanently differentiated. Understood in this way, it is what we call *law*. For the essence of law, whether this relates to external Nature or the ethical world order, consists in an inseparable unity, a necessary inner connection, of distinct determinations. Thus it is that law necessarily links punishment with crime; it is true that the criminal may regard punishment as something extraneous to him, but the Notion of crime essentially involves its opposite—punishment. Similarly, as regards external Nature, for example, the law of planetary motion (according to which, as we know, the squares of the periods of revolution vary as the cubes of the distances) must be grasped as an inner, necessary unity of distinct determinations. This unity is, of course, only comprehended by the speculative thinking of Reason, but it was already discovered by the abstractive, intellectual consciousness in the multiplicity of phenomena. Laws are determinations of the intellectual consciousness inherent in the world itself; therefore, the intellectual consciousness finds in them its own nature and thus becomes objective to itself.

§ 423

The law, at first stating the mutual dependence of universal, permanent terms, has, in so far as its distinction is the inward one, its necessity on its own part; the one of the terms, as not externally different from the other, lies immediately in the other. But in this manner the interior distinction is, what it is in truth, the distinction on its own part, or the distinction which is none. With this new form-characteristic, on the whole, consciousness *implicitly* vanishes: for consciousness as such implies the reciprocal independence of subject and object. The ego in its judgement has an object which is not distinct from it—it has itself. Consciousness has passed into self-consciousness.

Zusatz. What has been said in the above Paragraph about internal differences constituting the essence of law, namely, that this difference is one which is no difference, holds equally true of the difference that exists in the 'I' that is objective to itself. Just as law is something differentiated within itself and not merely relatively to an Other, an identity with itself in its difference, so, too, is the 'I' that has itself for object, that is aware of itself. Consequently, consciousness, as intellect, in being aware of laws relates itself to an object in which the 'I' finds again the counterpart or reflex of its own self and is thus on the point of developing into self-consciousness as such. But since, as was remarked in the *Zusatz* to § 422, the merely abstractive, intellectual consciousness does not as yet attain to a *comprehension* of the unity of the distinct determinations which is present in law, i.e. does not succeed in developing dialectically from one of these determinations its opposite, this unity still remains for this consciousness something dead, something, therefore, not corresponding to the activity of the 'I'. In the living being, on the other hand, consciousness beholds the process itself of positing and annulling the distinct determinations, perceives that the difference is no difference, that is, no absolutely fixed difference. For life is that inner existence which does not remain *abstractly* inner but enters wholly into its manifestation; it is an existence mediated by the negation of what is immediate and external, an existence which itself transforms this mediation into an immediacy, a sensuous, external, and at the same time absolutely internal, existence; a material existence in which the asunderness of the parts appears as overcome and the individual part is reduced to an ideal moment, to a *member* of the whole; in short, life must be grasped as self-end (*Selbstzweck*), as an end which possesses its means within itself, as a totality in which each distinct moment is alike end and means. It is, therefore, in the consciousness of this *dialectical*, this *living* unity of distinct moments that self-consciousness is kindled, the consciousness of the simple, ideal existence that is its own object and therefore differentiated within itself, in other words, the knowledge of the *truth* of natural existence, of the 'I'.

(b) SELF-CONSCIOUSNESS[1]

§ 424

Self-consciousness is the truth of consciousness: the latter is a consequence of the former, all consciousness of an other object being as a matter of fact also self-consciousness. The object is my idea: I am aware of the object as mine; and thus in it I am aware of me. The formula of self-consciousness is I = I:—abstract freedom, pure 'Ideality'; and thus it lacks 'reality': for as it is its own object, there is strictly speaking no object, because there is no distinction between it and the object.

Zusatz. In the formula, I = I, is enunciated the principle of absolute Reason and freedom. Freedom and Reason consist in this, that I raise myself to the form of I = I, that I know everything as mine, as 'I', that I grasp every object as a member in the system of what I myself am, in short, that I have in one and the same consciousness myself and the world, that in the world I find myself again, and, conversely, in my consciousness have what *is*, what possesses *objectivity*. This unity of the 'I' and the object which constitutes the principle of mind is, however, at first only *abstractly* present in *immediate* self-consciousness, and is known only by *us* who reflect on it, not as yet by self-consciousness itself. Immediate self-consciousness has not as yet for its object the I = I, but only the 'I'; therefore, it is free only for us, not for itself, is not as yet aware of its freedom, and contains only the foundation of it, but not as yet freedom that is truly *actual*.

§ 425

Abstract self-consciousness is the first negation of consciousness, and for that reason it is burdened with an external object, or, nominally, with the negation of it. Thus it is at the same time the antecedent stage, consciousness: it is the contradiction of itself as self-consciousness and as consciousness. But the latter aspect and the negation in general is in I = I potentially suppressed; and hence as this certitude of self against the object it is the *impulse*

---

[1] Selbstbewußtsein.

to realize its implicit nature, by giving its abstract self-awareness content and objectivity, and in the other direction to free itself from its sensuousness, to set aside the given objectivity and identify it with itself. The two processes are one and the same, the identification of its consciousness and self-consciousness.

Zusatz. The defect of abstract self-consciousness lies in the fact that it and consciousness are still simply two different things, that they have not yet made themselves equal to each other. In consciousness, we see the tremendous *difference*, on the one side, of the 'I', this wholly *simple* existence, and on the other side, of the infinite variety of the world. It is this opposition of the 'I' and the world which has not yet reached a genuine mediation, that constitutes the finitude of consciousness. Self-consciousness, on the other hand, has its finitude in its still quite abstract self-identity. What is present in the I = I of immediate self-consciousness is a difference that merely *ought* to be, not yet a *posited* or *actual* difference.

This disunion between self-consciousness and consciousness forms an internal contradiction of self-consciousness with itself, because the latter is also its immediately antecedent stage—consciousness—consequently, is the opposite of itself. In other words, since abstract self-consciousness is only the *first*, hence still *conditioned*, negation of the immediacy of consciousness, and not already *absolute* negativity, that is, negation of that negation, infinite affirmation, it has itself still the form of mere being, of an immediate, of a being which in spite of, or rather just on account of, its differenceless internal being is still filled with external being. Therefore, it contains negation not merely within it but also outside of it as an external object, as a 'non-I', and it is just this that makes it consciousness

The contradiction here outlined must be resolved, and the way in which this happens is that self-consciousness which has itself as consciousness, as 'I', for object, goes on to develop the simple ideality of the 'I' into a real difference, and thus by superseding its one-sided subjectivity gives itself objectivity; this process is identical with its converse, by which the object is at the same time given a subjective determination by the 'I', is immersed in the inwardness of the self, and in this way the dependence of the 'I' on an external reality which is a feature of consciousness is destroyed. Self-consciousness thus reaches the stage where it does not have consciousness *alongside* it, is not externally connected with it, but truly pervades it and contains it dissolved within it.

To reach this goal, self-consciousness has to traverse three developmental stages.

1. The first of these stages presents us with the single self-consciousness which is immediate, simply self-identical, and at the same time and contradictorily, is related to an external object. As thus determined, self-consciousness is the certainty of itself as merely being, in face of

which the object has the determination of something only seemingly independent, but is in fact a nullity. This is *appetitive self-consciousness*.

2. On the second stage, the objective 'I' acquires the determination of another 'I', and hence there arises the relation of one self-consciousness to another self-consciousness, and between these two the *process* of *recognition*. Here, self-consciousness is no longer merely a single self-consciousness, but in it there already begins a union of *individuality* and *universality*.

3. Furthermore, since the otherness of the selves confronting each other is overcome and these, though independent are yet identical with each other, there emerges the third stage, *universal self-consciousness*.

(α) *Appetite or Instinctive Desire*[1]

§ 426

Self-consciousness, in its immediacy, is a singular, and a desire (appetite)—the contradiction implied in its abstraction which should yet be objective—or in its immediacy which has the shape of an external object and should be subjective. The certitude of one's self, which issues from the suppression of mere consciousness, pronounces the *object* null: and the outlook of self-consciousness towards the object equally qualifies the abstract ideality of such self-consciousness as null.

Zusatz. As we have already remarked in the *Zusatz* to the previous Paragraph, appetite is that form in which self-consciousness appears on the first stage of its development. Here in the second main part in the doctrine of subjective mind, appetite has as yet no further determination than that of impulse—so far as this is not determined by thought—directed towards an external object in which it seeks to satisfy itself. But the necessity for the appetite so determined to exist in self-consciousness, lies in the fact that self-consciousness (as we likewise brought to notice in the previous Paragraph) is also its immediately antecedent stage, namely, consciousness, and is aware of this internal contradiction. Where a self-identical something bears within it a contradiction and is charged with the feeling of its intrinsic self-identity as well as with the opposite feeling of its internal contradiction, there necessarily emerges the impulse to remove this contradiction. The non-living has no appetite because it is incapable of enduring contradiction, but perishes when the Other of itself forces its way into it. On the other hand, the living being and mind or spirit necessarily possess impulse, since neither soul nor mind can exist without containing contradiction and either

[1] Die Begierde.

feeling or being aware of it. But, as indicated above, in the immediate and therefore natural, individual, exclusive self-consciousness, the shape assumed by the contradiction is that self-consciousness (whose Notion consists in being *self*-related, in being the 'I = I') is, on the contrary, still related to an immediate Other that is not transformed into an ideal moment, is related, that is, to an external object, to a 'non-I' and is external to itself, since although *in itself* it is a totality, a unity of subjectivity and objectivity, it none the less exists to begin with in a one-sided, merely subjective form and only realizes itself as a totality by satisfying its appetite. In spite of this internal contradiction, however, self-consciousness remains absolutely certain of itself because it knows that the immediate, external object has no true reality but is, on the contrary, a nullity over against the subject possessing only a seeming independence, and is, in fact, a being which neither merits nor is capable of an existence of its own, but must succumb to the real power of the subject.

§ 427

Self-consciousness, therefore, knows itself implicit in the object, which in this outlook is conformable to the appetite. In the negation of the two one-sided moments by the ego's own activity, this identity comes to be *for* the ego. To this activity the object, which implicitly and for self-consciousness is self-less, can make no resistance: the dialectic, implicit in it, towards self-suppression exists in this case as that activity of the ego. Thus while the given object is rendered subjective, the subjectivity divests itself of its one-sidedness and becomes objective to itself.

Zusatz. The self-conscious subject knows itself to be *implicitly identical* with the external object, knows that this contains the *possibility* of satisfying its appetite, that the object is, therefore, *conformable* to the appetite and that just for this reason the latter is excited by the object. The relation of the subject to the object is therefore a necessary one. In the object, the subject beholds its own lack, its own one-sidedness, sees in it something which belongs to its own essential nature and yet is lacking in it. Self-consciousness is able to remove this contradiction since it is not [merely] being, but absolute activity; and it removes it by taking possession of the object whose independence is, so to speak, only pretended, satisfies itself by consuming it and, since it is self-end (*Selbstzweck*), maintains itself in this process. In this the object must perish; for here both subject and object are immediate, and the only manner in which they can be in a unity is by the negation of the immediacy, and above all, of the immediacy of the self-less object. By the satisfaction of appetite, the implicit identity of subject and object is made explicit, the one-sidedness of subjectivity and the seeming independence of the object are superseded. But the object in being destroyed by the appetitive self-consciousness may seem to succumb to a completely alien power. This is, however, only apparently so. The immediate object must annul itself in accordance with its own nature, its Notion, since in its individuality it does not correspond to the universality of its Notion. Self-consciousness is the *manifested* Notion of the object itself. In the destruction of the object by self-consciousness, the former perishes, therefore, by the power of its own inner Notion which, just because it is inner, seems to come to it from outside. The object is thus made explicitly subjective. But by this annulment of the object the subject, as we have already remarked, removes its own defect, its diremption into a distinctionless 'I = I' and an 'I' that is related to an external object, and it gives its subjectivity objectivity no less than it makes its object subjective.

§ 428

The product of this process is the fast conjunction of the ego with itself, its satisfaction realized, and itself made actual. On the external side it continues, in this return upon itself, primarily describable as an individual, and maintains itself as such; because its bearing upon the self-less object is purely negative, the latter, therefore, being merely consumed. Thus appetite in its satisfaction is always destructive, and in its content selfish: and as the satisfaction has only happened in the individual (and that is transient) the appetite is again generated in the very act of satisfaction.

Zusatz. The relation of appetite to the object is as yet that of utterly selfish destruction, not a formative relation. In so far as self-consciousness does relate itself as a formative activity to the object, the latter obtains only the *form* of subjectivity, a form which acquires an *existence* in it, but in respect of its *matter* the object is preserved. On the other hand, self-consciousness in satisfying its appetite destroys the self-subsistence of the object, since it does not as yet possess the power to endure the object as an independent being, so that the form of subjectivity does not attain an existence in the object.

Like the object of appetite and appetite itself, the satisfaction of appetite, too, is necessarily a single, transient phenomenon which yields to the incessant renewal of appetite. It is an objectification which is perpetually in contradiction to the universality of the subject, and yet all the same is perpetually stimulated afresh by the lack felt by immediate subjectivity, an objectification which never absolutely attains its goal but only gives rise to the progress *ad infinitum.*

§ 429

But on the inner side, or implicitly, the sense of self which the ego gets in the satisfaction does not remain in abstract self-concentration or in mere individuality; on the contrary—as negation of *immediacy* and individuality the result involves a character of universality and of the identity of self-consciousness with its object. The judgement or diremption of this self-consciousness is the consciousness of a *'free'* object, in which ego is aware of itself as an ego, which however is *also* still outside it.

Zusatz. On its *external* side, as we remarked in the *Zusatz* to the previous Paragraph, immediate self-consciousness is caught up in the monotonous alternation *ad infinitum* of appetite and its satisfaction, in the perpetual relapse into subjectivity from its objectification. On the other hand, on its *inner* side or in accordance with its Notion, self-consciousness by ridding itself of its subjectivity and the external object, has negated its own immediacy, the standpoint of appetite, has given itself the determination of otherness towards itself, and this Other it has filled with the 'I', has made out of something self-less a free, self-like object, another 'I'. It therefore confronts its own self as another, distinct 'I', but in doing so has raised itself above the selfishness of merely destructive appetite.

(β) Self-consciousness Recognitive[1]

§ 430

Here there is a self-consciousness for a self-consciousness, at first *immediately*, as one of two things for another. In that other as ego I behold myself, and yet also an immediately existing object, another ego absolutely independent of me and opposed to me. (The suppression of the singleness of self-consciousness was only a first step in the suppression, and it merely led to the characterization of it as *particular*.) This contradiction gives either self-consciousness the impulse to *show* itself as a free self, and to exist as such for the other:—the process of *recognition*.

Zusatz. The second stage in the development of self-consciousness, indicated in the heading of the above Paragraph has still, to begin with, the determination of *immediacy* in common with the self-consciousness of the first stage which is caught up in appetite. In this determination lies

---

[1] Das anerkennende Selbstbewußtsein.

the tremendous contradiction that, on the one hand, the 'I' is wholly universal, absolutely pervasive, and interrupted by no limit, is the universal essence common to all men, the two mutually related selves therefore constituting one identity, constituting, so to speak, one light; and yet, on the other hand, they are also two selves rigidly and unyieldingly confronting each other, each existing as a reflection-into-self, as absolutely distinct from and impenetrable by the other.

§ 431

The process is a battle. I cannot be aware of me as myself in another individual, so long as I see in that other an other and an immediate existence: and I am consequently bent upon the suppression of this immediacy of his. But in like measure *I* cannot be recognized as immediate, except so far as I overcome the mere immediacy on my own part, and thus give existence to my freedom. But this immediacy is at the same time the corporeity of self-consciousness, in which as in its sign and tool the latter has its own *sense of self*, and its being *for others*, and the means for entering into relation with them.

Zusatz. The more precise form of the contradiction indicated in the *Zusatz* to the previous Paragraph is as follows. The two self-conscious subjects in relation are, since they have an immediate existence, natural and corporeal, existing in the manner of a *thing* which is subjected to an alien power, and they approach each other as such; yet at the same time they are completely free subjects and ought not to be treated as only immediate existences, as merely natural things. To overcome this contradiction, it is necessary that the two opposed selves should make explicit and should recognize in their existence, in their being-for-another, what they essentially are in themselves or according to their Notion, namely, beings who are not merely natural but free. Only in such a manner is true freedom realized; for since this consists in my identity with the other, I am only truly free when the other is also free and is recognized by me as free. This freedom of one in the other unites men in an inward manner, whereas needs and necessity bring them together only externally. Therefore, men must will to find themselves again in one another. But this cannot happen so long as they are imprisoned in their immediacy, in their natural being; for it is just this that excludes them from one another and prevents them from being free in regard to one another. Freedom demands, therefore, that the self-conscious subject should not heed his own natural existence or tolerate the natural existence of others; on the contrary, indifferent to natural existence, he should in his individual, immediate actions stake his own life and the lives of others to win freedom.

Only through struggle, therefore, can freedom be won; the assertion that one is free does not suffice to make one so; at this stage, man demonstrates his capacity for freedom only by risking his own life and that of others.

§ 432

The fight of recognition is a life and death struggle: either self-consciousness imperils the other's life, and incurs a like peril for its own—but only peril, for either is no less bent on maintaining his life, as the existence of his freedom. Thus the death of one, though by the abstract, therefore rude, negation of immediacy, it, from one point of view, solves the contradiction, is yet, from the essential point of view (i.e. the outward and visible recognition), a new contradiction (for that recognition is at the same time undone by the other's death) and a greater than the other.

Zusatz. The *absolute* demonstration of freedom in the fight for recognition is death. The combatants, even by exposing themselves to the risk of death, give to the natural being of both of them a negative character, demonstrate that they regard it as of no account. But by death, the natural being is negated in fact and thereby its contradiction with the mental or spiritual, with the 'I', is at the same time resolved. This resolution is, however, only quite abstract, of a merely negative, not a positive kind. For even if only one of two combatants fighting for mutual recognition succumbs, no recognition is achieved, for the survivor receives just as little recognition as the dead. Consequently, death gives rise to the new and greater contradiction, that those who by fighting have proved their inner freedom, have none the less not attained an existence in which their freedom is recognized.

To prevent any possible misunderstandings with regard to the standpoint just outlined, we must here remark that the fight for recognition pushed to the extreme here indicated can only occur in the natural state, where men exist only as single, separate individuals; but it is absent in civil society and the State because here the recognition for which the combatants fought already exists. For although the State may originate in violence, it does not rest on it; violence, in producing the State, has brought into existence only what is justified in and for itself, namely, laws and a constitution. What dominates in the State is the spirit of the people, custom, and law. There man is recognized and treated as a *rational* being, as free, as a person; and the individual, on his side, makes himself worthy of this recognition by overcoming the natural state of his self-consciousness and obeying a universal, the will that is in essence and actuality will, the *law*; he behaves, therefore, towards others in a manner that is universally valid, recognizing them—as he wishes others to recognize him—as free, as persons. In the State, the citizen derives his honour from the post he fills, from the trade he follows, and from any other kind of working activity. His honour thereby has a content that is substantial, universal, objective, and no longer dependent on an empty subjectivity; honour of this kind is still lacking in the natural state where individuals, whatever they may be and whatever they may do, want to compel others to recognize them.

But it is clear from what has just been said that duelling must definitely not be confused with the fight for recognition which constitutes a necessary moment in the development of the human spirit. Duelling does not belong to the natural state of men, but to a more or less developed form of civil society and the State. Duelling has its strictly world-historical place in the feudal system which was supposed to be a society based on law, but was so only to a very small degree. There the knight, no matter what he might have done, wanted to be esteemed as without stain and without reproach, and the duel was supposed to prove this. Although the right of might (das Faustrecht) was elaborated into certain forms, yet its absolute basis was egotism. Consequently, its practice was not a proof of rational freedom and civic honour, but rather a proof of barbarism and often of the shamelessness of a desire which, in spite of its vileness, was ambitious for outward honour. Duelling is not met with among the peoples of antiquity, for the formalism of empty subjectivity, the desire of the subject to be esteemed in his immediate individuality, was completely alien to them. They had their honour only in their substantial unity with that ethical relationship which is the State. But in our modern States duelling can hardly be said to be anything else but an artificial return to the barbarism of the Middle Ages. At best, the former practice of duelling in the army could have a passably rational meaning, namely, that the individual wished to prove that he had other and higher aims than letting himself be killed for cash.

§ 433

But because life is as requisite as liberty to the solution, the fight ends in the first instance as a one-sided negation with inequality. While the one combatant prefers life, retains his single self-consciousness, but surrenders his claim for recognition, the other holds fast to his self-assertion and is recognized by the former as his superior. Thus arises the status of *master and slave.*

In the battle for recognition and the subjugation under a master, we see, on their phenomenal side, the emergence of man's social life and the commencement of political union. *Force,* which is the basis of this phenomenon, is not on that account a basis of right, but only the necessary and legitimate factor in the passage from

the state of self-consciousness sunk in appetite and selfish isolation into the state of universal self-consciousness. Force, then,
is the external or phenomenal commencement of states, not their
underlying and essential principle.

Zusatz. The relationship of master and slave contains only a *relative*
removal of the contradiction between the particularity, reflected into
itself, of the distinct self-conscious subjects and their mutual identity.
For in this relationship the immediacy of particular self-consciousness
is, to begin with, removed only on the side of the slave, but on the master's
side it is preserved. As long as the natural state of life persists on both
sides, the self-will of the slave surrenders itself to that of his master,
receives for its content the purposes of his master who, on his part, receives into his self-consciousness, not the slave's will, but only care for
the support of the slave's physical life; in such a manner that in this
relationship the *realized* identity of the self-consciousness of the subjects
in relation is achieved only onesidedly.

As regards the historical side of this relationship, it can be remarked
that ancient peoples, the Greeks and Romans, had not yet risen to the
Notion of absolute freedom, since they did not know that man as such,
man as this universal 'I', as rational self-consciousness, is entitled to
freedom. On the contrary, with them a man was held to be free only if
he was born free. With them, therefore, freedom still had the character
of a natural state. That is why slavery existed in their free States and
bloody wars developed in which the slaves tried to free themselves, to
obtain recognition of their eternal human rights.

§ 434

This status, in the first place, implies *common* wants and common
concern for their satisfaction—for the means of mastery, the slave,
must likewise be kept in life. In place of the rude destruction of
the immediate object there ensues acquisition, preservation, and
formation of it, as the instrumentality in which the two extremes
of independence and non-independence are welded together. The
form of universality thus arising in satisfying the want, creates a
permanent means and a provision which takes care for and secures
the future.

§ 435

But secondly, when we look to the distinction of the two, the
master beholds in the slave and his servitude the supremacy of

his *single* self-hood resulting from the suppression of immediate self-hood, a suppression, however, which falls on another. This other, the slave, however, in the service of the master, works off his individualist self-will, overcomes the inner immediacy of appetite, and in this divestment of self and in 'the fear of his lord' makes 'the beginning of wisdom'—the passage to universal self-consciousness.

Zusatz. Since the slave works for the master and therefore not in the exclusive interest of his own individuality, his desire is expanded into being not only the desire of this particular individual but also the desire of another. Accordingly, the slave rises above the selfish individuality of his natural will, and his worth to that extent exceeds that of his master who, imprisoned in his egotism, beholds in the slave only his immediate will and is only formally recognized by an unfree consciousness. This subjugation of the slave's egotism forms the *beginning* of true human freedom. This quaking of the single, isolated will, the feeling of the worthlessness of egotism, the habit of obedience, is a necessary moment in the education of all men. Without having experienced the discipline which breaks self-will, no one becomes free, rational, and capable of command. To become free, to acquire the capacity for self-control, all nations must therefore undergo the severe discipline of subjection to a master. It was necessary, for example, that after Solon had given the Athenians democratic free laws, Pisistratus invested himself with power to compel the Athenians to obey them. Only when this obedience had taken root did the domination of Pisistratus become superfluous. Thus Rome, too, had to live through the strict rule of the kings under which natural egotism was broken down, before it could give birth to that admirable Roman virtue of patriotism which was ready to make any sacrifice. Slavery and tyranny are, therefore, in the history of nations a necessary stage and hence *relatively* justified. Those who remain slaves suffer no absolute injustice; for he who has not the courage to risk his life to win freedom, that man deserves to be a slave; on the other hand, if a nation does not merely imagine that it wants to be free but actually has the energy to will its freedom, then no human power can hold it back in the servitude of a merely passive obedience to authority.

As we have said, this servile obedience forms only the *beginning* of freedom, because that to which the natural individuality of self-consciousness subjects itself is not the truly universal, rational will which is in and for itself, but the single, contingent will of another person. Here, then, only one moment of freedom is manifested, that of the negativity of the egotistic individuality; whereas the positive side of freedom attains actuality only when, on the one hand, the servile self-consciousness, freeing itself both from the individuality of the master and from its own individuality, grasps the absolutely rational in its universality which is independent of the particularity of the subjects; and when, on the other hand, the master's self-consciousness is brought by the *community* of needs and the concern for their satisfaction existing between him and the slave, and also by beholding the suppression of the immediate individual will made objective in the slave, to realize that this suppression is the truth in regard to himself, too, and therefore to subject his own selfish will to the law of the will that is in and for itself.

(γ) *Universal Self-consciousness*

§ 436

Universal self-consciousness is the affirmative awareness of self in an other self: each self as a free individuality has his own 'absolute' independence, yet in virtue of the negation of its immediacy or appetite without distinguishing itself from that other. Each is thus universal self-consciousness and objective; each has 'real' universality in the shape of reciprocity, so far as each knows itself recognized in the other freeman, and is aware of this in so far as it recognizes the other and knows him to be free.

This universal reappearance of self-consciousness—the notion which is aware of itself in its objectivity as a subjectivity identical with itself and for that reason universal—is the form of consciousness which lies at the root of all true mental or spiritual life—in family, fatherland, state, and of all virtues, love, friendship, valour, honour, fame. But this appearance of the underlying essence may also be severed from that essence, and be maintained apart in worthless honour, idle fame, etc.

Zusatz. The result of the struggle for recognition brought about by the Notion of mind or spirit is universal self-consciousness, which forms the third stage in this sphere. It is that free self-consciousness for which the other self-consciousness confronting it is no longer, as in the second stage, unfree but is likewise independent. In this stage, therefore, the mutually related self-conscious subjects, by setting aside their unequal particular individuality, have risen to the consciousness of their real universality, of the freedom belonging to all, and hence to the intuition of their specific identity with each other. The master confronted by his slave was not yet truly free, for he was still far from seeing in the former himself. Consequently, it is only when the slave becomes free that the master, too, becomes completely free. In this state of universal freedom, in being reflected into myself, I am immediately reflected into the other person, and, conversely, in relating myself to the other I am immediately *self-related*. Here, therefore, we have the violent diremption of mind or spirit into different selves which are both in and for themselves and for one another, are independent, absolutely impenetrable, resistant, and yet at the same time identical with one another, hence not independent, not impenetrable, but, as it were, fused with one another. The nature of this relationship is thoroughly *speculative*; and when it is supposed that the speculative is something remote and inconceivable, one has only to consider the content of this relationship to convince oneself of the baselessness of this opinion. The speculative, or the rational and true, consists in the unity of the Notion or subjectivity, and objectivity. This unity is manifestly present in the standpoint in question. It forms the substance of ethical life, namely, of the family, of sexual love (there this unity has the form of particularity), of patriotism, this willing of the general aims and interests of the State, of love towards God, of bravery too, when this is a risking of one's life in a universal cause, and lastly, also of honour, provided that this has for its content not some indifferent, particular interest of the individual but something substantial and truly universal.

§ 437

This unity of consciousness and self-consciousness implies in the first instance the individuals mutually throwing light upon each other. But the difference between those who are thus identified is mere vague diversity—or rather it is a difference which is none. Hence its truth is the fully and really existent universality and objectivity of self-consciousness—which is *Reason*.

Reason, as the *Idea* (§ 213) as it here appears, is to be taken as meaning that the distinction between notion and reality which it unifies has the special aspect of a distinction between the self-concentrated notion or consciousness, and the object subsisting external and opposed to it.

Zusatz. What we have called in the previous Paragraph universal self-consciousness, that is in its truth the Notion of *Reason*, the *Notion* in so far as it exists not merely as the logical Idea, but as the Idea that has developed into self-consciousness. For, as we know from Logic, the Idea consists in the unity of subjectivity or the Notion, and objectivity. But universal self-consciousness has revealed itself to us as this unity, for we have seen that this, in its absolute difference from its Other, is yet at the same time absolutely identical with it. It is precisely this identity of subjectivity and objectivity that constitutes the universality now attained by self-consciousness and which overlaps or overarches these two sides or particularities which are resolved in it. But self-consciousness, in attaining this universality, ceases to be self-consciousness in the proper or narrower sense of the word, since it is just this holding fast to the particularity of the self that is proper to self-consciousness as such. By yielding up this particularity, self-consciousness develops into Reason. In this context the name 'Reason' has the meaning only of the initially still abstract or formal unity of self-consciousness with its object. This unity establishes what must be called, in specific contrast to the true, the merely correct. My idea is correct merely if it agrees with the object, even when the latter only remotely corresponds to its Notion and hence has hardly any truth at all. Only when a true content becomes an object for me does my intelligence acquire the significance of Reason in its concrete sense. Reason in this sense will fall to be considered at the close of the development of theoretical mind or spirit (§ 467) where, issuing from an opposition of subjectivity and objectivity much more developed than hitherto, we shall cognize Reason as the unity, pregnant with content, of this opposition.

(c) REASON[1]

§ 438

The essential and actual truth which reason is, lies in the simple identity of the subjectivity of the notion with its objectivity and universality. The universality of reason, therefore, whilst it signifies that the object, which was only given in consciousness *qua* consciousness, is now itself universal, permeating and encompassing the ego, also signifies that the pure ego is the pure form which overlaps the object and encompasses it.

§ 439

Self-consciousness, thus certified that its determinations are no less objective, or determinations of the very being of things, than they are its own thoughts, is Reason, which as such an identity is not only the absolute *substance*, but the *truth* that knows it. For truth here has, as its peculiar mode and immanent form, the self-centred pure notion, ego, the certitude of self as infinite universality. Truth, aware of what it is, is mind (spirit).

[1] Die Vernunft.

C. PSYCHOLOGY

MIND[1]

§ 440

Mind has defined itself as the truth of soul and consciousness—
the former a simple immediate totality, the latter now an infinite
form which is not, like consciousness, restricted by that content,
and does not stand in mere correlation to it as to its object, but is
an awareness of this substantial totality, neither subjective nor
objective. Mind, therefore, starts only from its own being and is in
correlation only with its own features.

Psychology accordingly studies the faculties or general modes of
mental activity *qua* mental—mental vision, ideation, remembering,
etc., desires, etc.—apart both from the content, which on the
phenomenal side is found in empirical ideation, in thinking also
and in desire and will, and from the two forms in which these
modes exist, viz. in the soul as a physical mode, and in consciousness itself as a separately existent object of that consciousness.
This, however, is not an arbitrary abstraction by the psychologist.
Mind is just this elevation above nature and physical modes, and
above the complication with an external object—in one word,
above the material, as its concept has just shown. All it has now to
do is to realize this notion of its freedom, and get rid of the *form*
of immediacy with which it once more begins. The content which
is elevated to intuitions is *its* sensations: it is *its* intuitions also
which are transmuted into representations, and its representations
which are transmuted again into thoughts, etc.

Zusatz. Free mind or spirit, or mind as such, is Reason which sunders itself,
on the one hand, into pure infinite form, into a limitless Knowing, and, on
the other hand, into the object that is identical with that Knowing. Here,
this Knowing has as yet no other content but itself, but it is determined as
embracing within itself all objectivity, so that the object is not anything
externally related to mind or anything mind cannot grasp. Mind or spirit
is thus the absolutely universal certainty of itself, free from any opposition
whatever. Therefore, it is confident that in the world it will find its own
self, that the world must be reconciled with it, that, just as Adam said

[1] Der Geist.

of Eve that she was flesh of his flesh, so mind has to seek in the world Reason that is its own Reason. We have found Reason to be the unity of subjectivity and objectivity, of the Notion that exists for itself, and of reality. Since, therefore, mind is the absolute certainty of itself, a knowing of Reason, it is knowledge of the unity of subjectivity and objectivity, knowledge that its object is the Notion and that the Notion is objective. Free mind or spirit thereby shows itself to be the unity of the two universal stages of development considered in the first and second main parts of the doctrine of subjective mind, namely, of the soul, this simple spiritual substance, or of mind in its immediacy, and of consciousness or manifested mind, the self-diremption of this substance. For the determinations of free mind have, in common with those of the soul, the subjective element, and in common with those of consciousness, the objective element. The principle of free mind is to make the merely given element (*das Seiende*) in consciousness into something mental (*Seelenhaftes*), and conversely to make what is mental into an objectivity. Free mind stands, like consciousness, as one side over against the object, and is at the same time both sides and therefore, like the soul, a totality. Accordingly, whereas soul was truth only as an immediate unconscious totality, and whereas in consciousness, on the contrary, this totality was divided into the 'I' and the object external to it, *free* mind or spirit, is to be cognized as *self-knowing truth.**

However, the Knowing of truth does not itself, to begin with, have the form of truth; for at the stage of development now reached, it is still *abstract*, the formal identity of subjectivity and objectivity. Only when

---

* Therefore, when people assert that man cannot know the truth, they are uttering the worst form of blasphemy. They are not aware of what they are saying. Were they aware of it they would deserve that the truth should be taken away from them. The modern despair of truth being knowable is alien to all speculative philosophy as it is to all genuine religiosity. A poet who was no less religious than he was a thinker—Dante, expressed in such a pregnant fashion his belief that truth can be known, that we permit ourselves to quote his words here. He says in the Fourth Canto of the *Paradiso*, verses 124–30:

> Io veggio ben, che giammai non si sazia
>   Nostro intelletto, se'l *Ver* no lo illustra
>   Di fuor dal qual nessun vero si spazia.
> Posasi in esso, come fera in lustra,
>   Tosto che *giunto* l'ha; e giunger *puollo*; —
>   Se non, ciascun desio sarebbe frustra.

> (I see that nought can fill the mind's vast space,
>   Unless *Truth's* light dwell there as denizen,
>   Beyond which nothing true can find a place.
> In that it rests, like wild beast in its den,
>   When it *attains* it; and it *can* attain,
>   Else frustrate would be all desires of men.

> *Dean Plumptre's translation*)

this identity has developed into an actual difference and has made itself into the identity of itself and its difference, therefore, only when mind or spirit steps forth as an immanently developed totality, not till then has that certainty *established* itself as truth.

§ 441

The soul is finite, so far as its features are immediate or connatural. Consciousness is finite, in so far as it has an object. Mind is finite, in so far as, though it no longer has an object, it has a mode in its knowledge; i.e. it is finite by means of its immediacy, or, what is the same thing, by being subjective or only a notion. And it is a matter of no consequence, which is defined as its notion, and which as the reality of that notion. Say that its notion is the utterly infinite objective reason, then its reality is knowledge or *intelligence*: say that knowledge is its notion, then its reality is that reason, and the realization of knowledge consists in appropriating reason. Hence the finitude of mind is to be placed in the (temporary) failure of knowledge to get hold of the full reality of its reason, or, equally, in the (temporary) failure of reason to attain full manifestation in knowledge. Reason at the same time is only infinite so far as it is 'absolute' freedom; so far, that is, as presupposing itself for its knowledge to work upon, it thereby reduces itself to finitude, and appears as everlasting movement of superseding this immediacy, of comprehending itself, and being a rational knowledge.

Zusatz. Free mind or spirit is, as we have seen, in conformity with its Notion perfect unity of subjectivity and objectivity, of form and content, consequently, absolute totality and therefore infinite, eternal. We have cognized it as a Knowing of Reason. Because it is this, because it has Reason for its object, it must be designated the infinite being-for-self of subjectivity. Therefore the Notion of mind requires that in it the absolute unity of subjectivity and objectivity shall be not merely *in itself* or *implicit*, but *for itself* or *explicit*, and therefore object of our Knowing. On account of this conscious harmony prevailing between Knowing and its object, between form and content, a harmony which excludes all division and so all alteration, mind in its *truth* may be called the Eternal, as also the perfectly blessed and holy. For only that may be called holy which is imbued with Reason and knows the world of Reason. Therefore, neither external Nature nor mere feeling has a right to that name. Immediate feeling which has not been purified by rational knowing is burdened with the quality of the natural, the contingent, of self-externality and asunderness. Consequently, in the content of feeling and of natural things infinity is present only formally, abstractly. Mind, on the contrary, in conformity with its Notion or its truth, is infinite or eternal in this concrete and real sense: that it remains absolutely self-identical in its difference. For this reason we must declare mind to be the likeness of God, the divinity of man.

But in its immediacy—for even mind as such gives itself to begin with the form of immediacy—mind is not yet truly mind; on the contrary, in this form its existence is not in absolute conformity with its Notion, with the divine likeness, the divine is present in it only as the *essence* which has yet to develop into perfect manifestation. Mind in its immediacy has therefore not yet grasped its Notion, only *is* a rational Knowing, but does not yet *know* itself as such. Thus mind, in the first instance, as was already said in the *Zusatz* to the previous Paragraph, is only the indeterminate certainty of Reason, of the unity of subjectivity and objectivity. That is why here it still lacks the *determinate* knowledge of the rationality of the object. To attain this, mind must liberate the intrinsically rational object from the form of contingency, singleness, and externality which at first clings to it, and thereby free *itself* from the connection with something which is for it an Other. It is on the path of this liberation that mind continues to be finite. For so long as it has not yet reached its goal, it does not yet know itself as absolutely identical with its object, but finds itself limited by it.

The finitude of mind must not, however, be taken for something absolutely fixed, but must be recognized as a mode of the manifestation of mind which is none the less infinite according to its essence. This implies that finite mind is immediately a contradiction, an untruth, and at the same time is the process of ridding itself of this untruth. This struggling with the finite, the overcoming of limitation, constitutes the stamp of the divine in the human mind and forms a necessary stage of the eternal mind. Therefore, to talk of the limitations of Reason is worse than it would be to talk about wooden iron. It is infinite mind itself that presupposes itself as soul and as consciousness, thereby making itself finite; and it is infinite mind that equally transforms into a moment of itself this self-made presupposition, this finitude, the opposition—already in principle resolved —between consciousness and soul, on the one hand, and consciousness and an external object, on the other hand. This overcoming of finitude has a different form in free mind from what it has in consciousness. Whereas for the latter, the progressive determination of the 'I' assumes the appearance of an alteration of the object independently of the activity of the 'I', so that at the level of consciousness the logical consideration of this alteration fell only in us: for free mind, the self-developing and altering determinations of the object are explicitly the product of free mind itself, the subjectifying of objectivity and the objectifying of subjectivity are its own work. The determinations of which it is aware are, of course, inherent in the object, but at the same time they are posited by mind. In free mind there is nothing merely immediate. Therefore, when the 'facts of consciousness' are spoken of as if for mind they were something primary and unmediated and must remain for it something merely given, it must be remarked that though at the stage of consciousness a great deal of such given material presents itself, free mind must not leave these facts as given, independent *things*, but must demonstrate and so explain them to be *acts* of mind, to be a content which *it* has posited.

§ 442

The progress of mind is *development*, in so far as its existent phase, viz. knowledge, involves as its intrinsic purpose and burden that utter and complete autonomy which is rationality; in which case the action of translating this purpose into reality is strictly only a nominal passage over into manifestation, and is even there a return into itself. So far as knowledge which has not shaken off its original quality of *mere* knowledge is only abstract or formal, the goal of mind is to give it objective fulfilment, and thus at the same time produce its freedom.

The development here meant is not that of the individual (which has a certain *anthropological* character), where faculties and forces are regarded as successively emerging and presenting themselves in external existence—a series of steps, on the ascertainment of which there was for a long time great stress laid (by the system of Condillac), as if a conjectural natural emergence could exhibit the origin of these faculties and *explain* them. In Condillac's method there is an unmistakable intention to show how the *several* modes of mental activity could be made intelligible without losing sight of mental unity, and to exhibit their necessary interconnection. But the categories employed in doing so are of a wretched sort. Their ruling principle is that the sensible is taken (and with justice) as the *prius* or the initial basis, but that the latter phases that follow this starting-point present themselves as emerging in a solely *affirmative* manner, and the negative aspect of mental activity, by which this material is transmuted into mind and destroyed *as* a sensible, is misconceived and overlooked. As the theory of Condillac states it, the sensible is not merely the empirical first, but is left as if it were the true and essential foundation.

Similarly, if the activities of mind are treated as mere manifestations, forces, perhaps in terms stating their utility or suitability for some other interest of head or heart, there is no indication of the true final aim of the whole business. That can only be the intelligible unity of mind, and its activity can only have itself as aim; i.e. its aim can only be to get rid of the form of immediacy or subjectivity, to reach and get hold of itself, and to liberate itself to itself. In this way the so-called faculties of mind as thus distinguished are only to be treated as steps of this liberation. And this is the only *rational* mode of studying the mind and its various activities.

Zusatz. The existence of mind, or *Knowing* (*das Wissen*), is the absolute form, that is, the form that itself contains the content, or the Notion that exists as Notion and gives itself its own reality. Consequently, the fact that the content or object is for our Knowing something *given*, something coming to it *from outside*, is only an illusory appearance and mind, by removing this appearance, proves itself to be what it is in itself, namely, absolutely self-determining, the infinite negativity of what is external to mind and to itself, the ideal existence that produces all reality *from itself*. The progress of mind has, therefore, only this meaning, that this illusory appearance is removed, that Knowing proves itself to be the form that develops all content from itself. Consequently, the activity of mind, far from being restricted to a mere acceptance of a given material must, on the contrary, be called a creative activity even though the products of mind, in so far as mind is only subjective, do not as yet receive the form of immediate actuality but retain a more or less ideal existence.

§ 443

As consciousness has for its object the stage which preceded it, viz. the natural soul (§ 413), so mind has or rather makes consciousness its object: i.e. whereas consciousness is only the virtual identity of the ego with its other (§ 415), the mind realizes that identity as the concrete unity which it and it only knows. Its productions are governed by the principle of all reason that the contents are at once potentially existent, and are the mind's own, in freedom. Thus, if we consider the initial aspect of mind, that aspect is twofold—as *being* and as *its own*: by the one, the mind finds in itself something which *is*, by the other it affirms it to be only *its own*. The way of mind is therefore (*a*) to be theoretical: it has to do with the rational as its immediate affection which it must render its own: or it has to free knowledge from its pre-supposedness and therefore from its abstractness, and make the affection subjective. When the affection has been rendered its own, and the knowledge consequently characterized as free intelligence, i.e. as having its full and free characterization in itself, it is

(*b*) Will: *practical* mind, which in the first place is likewise formal—i.e. its content is at first *only* its own, and is immediately willed; and it proceeds next to liberate its volition from its subjectivity, which is the one-sided form of its contents, so that it

(*c*) confronts itself as free mind and thus gets rid of both its defects of one-sidedness.

Zusatz. Whereas one cannot very well say of consciousness that it possesses impulse (*Trieb*) since it possesses the object *immediately*, mind, on the other hand, must be grasped as impulse because it is essentially activity. This is, in the first place,

(*a*) the activity by which the seemingly *alien* object receives, instead of the shape of something given, isolated and contingent, the form of something inwardized, subjective, universal, necessary, and rational. Mind, by undertaking this alteration of the object, reacts against the one-sidedness of consciousness which relates itself to objects as to things immediately given and does not know them in a subjective form. As such it is theoretical mind. In this, the urge to know is dominant, the craving for knowledge [of external things]. Of the content of this knowledge I know that it *is*, that it has objectivity, and at the same time that it is in me and therefore subjective. Here, therefore, the object no longer has, as at the stage of consciousness, the determination of being negative towards the 'I'.

(*b*) Practical mind pursues the opposite course. Unlike theoretical mind, it does not start from the seemingly alien object, but from its own aims and interests, that is, from subjective determinations, and *then* proceeds to make these into an objectivity. In doing this it reacts against the one-sided subjectivity of self-consciousness that is shut up within itself, just as theoretical mind reacts against the consciousness that is dependent on a given object.

Theoretical and practical mind reciprocally integrate themselves precisely because they are distinguished in the manner indicated. This distinction is, however, not absolute; for theoretical mind, too, has to deal with its own determinations, with thoughts, and, conversely, the aims of the rational will do not appertain to the *particular* subject but exist in their own right. Both modes of mind are forms of Reason; for both in theoretical and in practical mind what is produced—though in different ways—is that which constitutes Reason, a unity of subjectivity and objectivity. At the same time, however, these dual forms of subjective mind have this defect in common, that in both of them the starting-point is the apparent separateness of subjectivity and objectivity, the unity of these opposed determinations having first to be produced. This is a defect lying in the nature of mind, since this is not something that merely is or is immediately complete but, on the contrary, is an existence that is self-produced, a pure activity which removes its own self-made, implicit presupposition of the opposition of subjectivity and objectivity.

§ 444

The theoretical as well as the practical mind still fall under the general range of Mind Subjective. They are not to be distinguished as active and passive. Subjective mind is productive: but it is a merely nominal productivity. Inwards, the theoretical mind produces only its 'ideal' world, and gains abstract autonomy within; while the practical, while it has to do with autonomous products, with a material which is its own, has a material which is only nominally such, and therefore a restricted content, for which it gains the form of universality. Outwards, the subjective mind (which as a unity of soul and consciousness, is thus also a reality— a reality at once anthropological and conformable to consciousness) has for its products, in the theoretical range, the *word*, and in the practical (not yet deed and action, but) *enjoyment*.

Psychology, like logic, is one of those sciences which in modern times have yet derived least profit from the more general mental culture and the deeper conception of reason. It is still extremely ill off. The turn which the Kantian philosophy has taken has given it greater importance: it has, and that in its empirical condition, been claimed as the basis of metaphysics, which is to consist of nothing but the empirical apprehension and the analysis of the facts of human consciousness, merely as facts, just as they are given. This position of psychology, mixing it up with forms belonging to the range of consciousness and with anthropology, has led to no improvement in its own condition: but it has had the further effect that, both for the mind as such, and for metaphysics and philosophy generally, all attempts have been abandoned to ascertain the necessity of essential and actual reality, to get at the notion and the truth.

Zusatz. Only soul is passive, but free mind is essentially active, productive. It is therefore a mistake when theoretical mind is sometimes distinguished from practical mind by characterizing the forme · a⁻ passive and the latter as active. This distinction does, indeed, appear to be correct. Theoretical mind seems only to accept what is already there, whereas practical mind has to produce something that is not yet externally to hand. In truth, however, as we already indicated in the *Zusatz* to § 442, theoretical mind is not a merely passive acceptance of an Other, of a given object, but reveals itself as active by raising the inherently rational content of the object out of the form of externality and singleness into the form of Reason. But, conversely, practical mind too has a passive side, since, to begin with, its content is for it, though not outwardly, yet inwardly, *given*, hence is an immediate content, one not posited by the activity of the rational will and which first has to be made such a posited content by means of a cognitive Knowing, and therefore by means of theoretical mind.

A distinction which is no less false than the one just discussed between theoretical and practical mind, is that which would make intelligence limited and will unlimited. The truth is quite the reverse; it is will that can be said to be the more limited of the two, since it is engaged in a struggle with external matter which offers resistance, with the exclusive singleness of the actual, and at the same time is confronted by other human wills; whereas intelligence as such in its manifestation, its utterance, only goes as far as the *word*, this fleeting, vanishing, completely *ideal* realization which proceeds in an unresisting element, so that in its utterance intelligence remains at home with itself, satisfies itself internally, demonstrates that it is its own end (*Selbstzweck*), is divine and, in the form of comprehensive cognition, brings into being the unlimited freedom and reconciliation of mind with itself.

Both modes of subjective mind, both intelligence and will have, however, in the first instance, only *formal* truth. For in both the content does not immediately correspond to the infinite form of Knowing, hence this form, too, is still not *truly filled*.

In theoretical mind the object is, on the one hand, certainly subjective but, on the other hand, there still remains a content of the object outside of the unity with subjectivity. This is why subjectivity here constitutes a form which does not absolutely pervade the object and the latter is, therefore, not an object posited absolutely by mind. In the practical sphere, on the contrary, subjectivity does not as yet possess immediately any true objectivity, since in its immediacy it is not anything absolutely universal that has a being in and for itself, but something appertaining to the singularity of the individual.

When mind has overcome this defect, that is, when its content no longer conflicts with its form, but, on the contrary, the certainty of Reason, of the unity of subjectivity and objectivity, is no longer *formal* but *fulfilled*, when, therefore, the Idea forms the sole content of mind, then subjective mind has reached its goal and passes over into objective mind. This latter knows its freedom, knows that its subjectivity, in its truth, constitutes absolute objectivity itself, and it apprehends itself not merely inwardly as Idea but brings itself forth as an outwardly existent world of freedom.

(a) THEORETICAL MIND

§ 445

Intelligence[1] *finds* itself determined: this is its apparent aspect from which in its immediacy it starts. But as knowledge, intelligence consists in treating what is found as its own. Its activity has to do with the empty form—the pretence of *finding* reason: and its aim is to realize its concept or to be reason actual, along with which the content is realized as rational. This activity is *cognition*. The nominal knowledge, which is only certitude, elevates itself, as reason is concrete, to definite and conceptual knowledge. The course of this elevation is itself rational, and consists in a necessary passage (governed by the concept) of one grade or term of intelligent activity (a so-called faculty of mind) into another. The refutation which such cognition gives of the semblance that the rational is *found*, starts from the certitude or the faith of intelligence in its capability of rational knowledge, and in the possibility of being able to appropriate the reason, which it and the content virtually is.

The distinction of Intelligence from Will is often incorrectly taken to mean that each has a fixed and separate existence of its own, as if volition could be without intelligence, or the activity of intelligence could be without will. The possibility of a culture of the intellect which leaves the heart untouched, as it is said, and of the heart without the intellect—of hearts which in one-sided way want intellect, and heartless intellects—only proves at most that bad and radically untrue existences occur. But it is not philosophy which should take such untruths of existence and of mere

---

[1] Die Intelligenz.

imagining for truth—take the worthless for the essential nature. A host of other phrases used of intelligence, e.g. that it receives and accepts impressions from outside, that ideas arise through the causal operations of external things upon it, etc., belong to a point of view utterly alien to the mental level or to the position of philosophic study.

A favourite reflectional form is that of powers and faculties of soul, intelligence, or mind. Faculty, like power or force, is the fixed quality of any object of thought, conceived as reflected into self. Force (§ 136) is no doubt the infinity of form—of the inward and the outward: but its essential finitude involves the indifference of content to form (ib. note). In this lies the want of organic unity which by this reflectional form, treating mind as a 'lot' of forces, is brought into mind, as it is by the same method brought into nature. Any aspect which can be distinguished in mental action is stereotyped as an independent entity, and the mind thus made a skeleton-like mechanical collection. It makes absolutely no difference if we substitute the expression 'activities' for powers and faculties. Isolate the activities and you similarly make the mind a mere aggregate, and treat their essential correlation as an external incident.

The action of intelligence as theoretical mind has been called *cognition* (knowledge). Yet this does not mean intelligence *inter alia* knows—besides which it also intuits, conceives, remembers, imagines, etc. To take up such a position is in the first instance part and parcel of that isolating of mental activity just censured; but it is also in addition connected with the great question of modern times, as to whether true knowledge or the knowledge of truth is possible—which, if answered in the negative, must lead to abandoning the effort. The numerous aspects and reasons and modes of phrase with which external reflection swells the bulk of this question are cleared up in their place: the more external the attitude of understanding in the question, the more diffuse it makes its simple object. At the present place the simple concept of cognition is what confronts the quite general assumption taken up by the question, viz. the assumption that the possibility of true knowledge in general is in dispute, and the assumption that it is possible for us at our will either to prosecute or to abandon cognition. The concept or possibility of cognition has come out as intelligence itself, as the certitude of reason: the act of cognition itself is therefore the actuality of intelligence. It follows from this that it is absurd to speak of intelligence and yet at the same time of the possibility or choice of knowing or not. But cognition is genuine, just so far as it realizes itself, or makes the concept its own. This nominal description has its concrete meaning exactly where cognition has it. The stages of its realizing activity are intuition, conception, memory, etc.: these activities have no other immanent meaning: their aim is solely the concept of cognition (§ 445 note). If they are isolated, however, then an impression is implied that they are useful for something else than cognition, or that they severally procure a cognitive satisfaction of their own; and that leads to a glorification of the delights of intuition, remembrance, imagination. It is true that even as isolated (i.e. as non-intelligent), intuition, imagination, etc. can afford a certain satisfaction: what physical nature succeeds in doing by its fundamental quality—its out-of-selfness—exhibiting the elements or factors of immanent reason external to each other—that the intelligence can do by voluntary act, but the same result may happen where the intelligence is itself only natural and untrained. But the *true satisfaction*, it is admitted, is only afforded by an intuition permeated by intellect and mind, by rational conception, by products of imagination which are permeated by reason and exhibit ideas—in a word, by *cognitive* intuition, cognitive conception, etc. The truth ascribed to such satisfaction lies in this, that intuition, conception, etc. are not isolated, and exist only as 'moments' in the totality of cognition itself.

Zusatz. As we have remarked in the *Zusatz* to § 441, mind that is mediated by the negation of soul and of consciousness has itself, in the first instance, still the form of immediacy and consequently the illusory appearance of being external to itself, of relating itself, like consciousness, to the rational as to something outside of it, something merely *found*, not *mediated* by mind. But by the supersession of these two antecedent main stages of development, of these presuppositions made by itself, mind has already exhibited itself to us as *self-mediating*, as withdrawing itself from its Other into itself, as the unity of subjectivity and objectivity. Consequently, the activity of mind that has come to itself, that has already implicitly overcome the externality of the object, necessarily proceeds also to remove this *illusory appearance* of its own immediacy and that of its object, the pretence of merely *finding* the object. Accordingly, to begin with, intelligence's activity appears indeed as a formal, unfilled activity, as *unknowing* mind; and the very first thing to be done is to remove this 'unknowingness'. To this end intelligence fills itself with the immediately given object which, on account of its immediacy, is burdened with all the contingency, worthlessness and untruth of outer existence. But intelligence, far from confining itself to merely accepting this immediately presented content of the object, purges the latter of its purely external, contingent, and worthless elements. Therefore, while it seems to *consciousness* that its development starts from the spontaneously altering determinations of its object, intelligence, on the contrary, is expressly that form of mind in which mind itself alters its object, and by developing it also develops itself into truth. Intelligence, in altering the external object into an internal one, inwardizes itself. These two, the internalizing of the object and the inwardizing (*Erinnerung*) of mind, are one and the same thing. What mind rationally knows, just because it is rationally known, becomes a rational content. Thus intelligence strips the object of the form of contingency, grasps its rational nature and posits it as subjective; and, conversely, it at the same time develops the subjectivity into the form of objective rationality. Thus our Knowing, which was at first abstract and formal, becomes a Knowing that is filled with a true content and is therefore objective. When intelligence attains this goal set for it by its Notion, it is in truth what, to begin with, it only *ought* to be, namely, cognition (*Erkennen*). The latter must be clearly distinguished from simple Knowing or awareness (*Wissen*). For consciousness is already a Knowing. But free mind does not content itself with a simple Knowing; it wants to *cognize*, in other words, it wants to know not merely *that* an object *is*, and what it is *in general* and with respect to its contingent, external determinations, but it wants to know in what the object's *specific, substantial nature* consists. This distinction between simple knowing or awareness (*Wissen*) and cognition (*Erkennen*) is familiar to educated thought. Thus it is said, for example, that though we know or are aware that God is, we are incapable of comprehending him. The meaning of this assertion is that while we can indeed have an indefinite idea of the *abstract* being of God, we are supposed to be incapable of comprehending his determinate, concrete nature. Those who talk in this way may, as regards themselves, be perfectly right. For although even those theologians who declare God to be unknowable go to a great deal of trouble exegetical, critical, and historical about him and in this way expand theology into a complex detailed science, yet in their hands the science gets no further than a knowledge of externals, for they throw out the substantial content of their subject-matter as indigestible by their weak minds and accordingly renounce all claim to a *cognition* of God, since, as we have said, a knowledge of externals does not suffice for cognition, which requires a grasp of the substantial, specific nature of the subject-matter. Such a science as the one just named occupies the standpoint of consciousness, not of true intelligence which has also been rightly called the faculty of cognition, although the term faculty wrongly suggests a mere possibility.

To facilitate a general survey, we shall now indicate in anticipation and assertorically the formal course of the development of intelligence to cognition. This is as follows. Intelligence has first, an *immediate* object; secondly, an inwardized material reflected into itself; thirdly, an object that is no less subjective than objective.

This gives rise to three stages:

(α) a Knowing that is related to an immediately *single* object, a *material* Knowing, or *intuition*;

(β) intelligence that withdraws into itself from the relationship in which it is related to the *singleness* of the object and relates the object to a universal—mental representation;

(γ) intelligence that *comprehends* the concrete universal nature of objects, or *thought* in the specific sense that what we *think* also *is*, also has objectivity.

(α) The stage of intuition, of *immediate* cognition, or of consciousness posited with the determination of rationality and pervaded by mind's self-certainty, again falls into three subdivisions:

1. Intelligence here starts from *sensation* of the immediate material;

2. then it develops into *attention* which fixes the object but no less separates itself from it; and

3. becomes in this way *intuition* proper, which posits the object as something *self-external*.

(β) The second main stage of intelligence, *representation*, comprises three stages:

(αα) Recollection,

(ββ) Imagination,

(γγ) Memory

(γ) Lastly, the third main stage in this sphere, *thought*, has for content:

1. Understanding,

2. Judgement, and

3. Reason.

(α) Intuition (Intelligent Perception)[1]

§ 446

The mind which as soul is physically conditioned—which as consciousness stands to this condition on the same terms as to an outward object—but which as intelligence *finds itself* so characterized

[1] Anschauung.

—is (1) an inarticulate embryonic life, in which it is to itself as it were palpable and has the whole *material* of its knowledge. In consequence of the immediacy in which it is thus originally, it is in this stage only as an individual and possesses a vulgar subjectivity. It thus appears as mind in the guise of *feeling*.

If feeling formerly turned up (§ 399) as a mode of the *soul's* existence, the finding of it or its immediacy was in that case essentially to be conceived as a congenital or corporeal condition; whereas at present it is only to be taken abstractly in the general sense of immediacy.

Zusatz. We have already had on two occasions to speak of *feeling*, but on each occasion in a different connection. First, we had to consider it in connection with soul, and more precisely at the point where soul, awaking from its self-confined natural life, finds within itself the determinations of the content of its sleeping nature: it is just this that makes it a feeling soul. But by overcoming the restrictedness of sensation it attains to the feeling of its Self, of its totality, and lastly, apprehending itself as 'I', awakes to consciousness. At the stage of consciousness, we again spoke of feeling. But there, the determinations of feeling were the manifested material of consciousness separated from soul in the shape of an independent object. Now, thirdly and lastly, feeling signifies the form which mind as such, which is the unity and truth of soul and consciousness, gives itself in the first instance. In this form of mind, the content of feeling is liberated from the double one-sidedness which attached to it, on the one hand, at the stage of soul, and, on the other hand, at the stage of consciousness. For that content is now characterized as being in itself both objective and subjective; and mind's activity is now directed only towards making itself *explicitly* the unity of subjectivity and objectivity.

§ 447

The characteristic form of feeling is that though it is a mode of some 'affection', this mode is simple. Hence feeling, even should its import be most sterling and true, has the form of casual particularity—not to mention that its import may also be the most scanty and most untrue.

It is commonly enough assumed that mind has in its feeling the material of its ideas, but the statement is more usually understood in a sense the opposite of that which it has here. In contrast with the simplicity of feeling it is usual rather to assume that the primary mental phase is judgement generally, or the distinction of consciousness into subject and object; and the special quality of sensation is derived from an independent *object*, external or internal. With us, in the truth of mind, the mere consciousness point of view, as opposed to true mental 'idealism', is swallowed up, and the matter of feeling has rather been supposed already as *immanent* in the mind.—It is commonly taken for granted that as regards content there is more in feeling than in thought: this being specially affirmed of moral and religious feelings. Now the material, which the mind as it feels is to itself, is *here* the result and the mature result of a fully organized reason: hence under the head of feeling is comprised all rational and indeed all spiritual content whatever. But the form of selfish singleness to which feeling reduces the mind is the lowest and worst vehicle it can have—one in which it is not found as a free and infinitely universal principle, but rather as subjective and private, in content and value entirely contingent. Trained and sterling feeling is the feeling of an educated mind which has acquired the consciousness of the true differences of things, of their essential relationships and real characters; and it is with such a mind that this rectified material enters into its feeling and receives this form. Feeling is the immediate, as it were the closest, contact in which the thinking subject can stand to a given content. Against that content the subject reacts first of all with its particular self-feeling, which though it *may* be of more sterling value and of wider range than a one-sided intellectual standpoint, may just as likely be narrow and poor; and in any case is the form of the particular and subjective. If a man on any topic appeals not to the nature and notion of the thing, or at least to reasons—to the generalities of common sense—but to his feeling, the only thing to do is to let him alone, because by his behaviour he refuses to have any lot or part in common rationality, and shuts himself up in his own isolated subjectivity—his private and particular self.

Zusatz. In feeling, there is present the whole of Reason, the entire content of mind. All our representations, thoughts, and notions of the external world, of right, of morality, and of the content of religion develop from our feeling intelligence; just as, conversely, they are concentrated into the simple form of feeling after they have been fully explicated. It was, therefore, rightly said by an ancient philosopher that men have formed their gods out of their feelings and passions. But the way in which this development of mind from feeling is usually understood, implies that intelligence is originally completely empty and therefore receives all its content from outside as something entirely extraneous to it. This is an error. For what intelligence appears to receive from outside is, in truth, none other than the rational and is consequently identical with mind and immanent in it. The activity of mind has, therefore, no other aim than, by the removal of the apparent self-externality of the intrinsically rational object, to refute even the appearance of the object's externality to mind.

§ 448

(2) As this immediate finding is broken up into elements, we have the one factor in *Attention*—the abstract *identical* direction of mind (in feeling, as also in all other more advanced developments of it)—an active self-collection—the factor of fixing it as our own, but with an as yet only nominal autonomy of intelligence. Apart from such attention there is nothing for the mind. The other factor is to invest the special quality of feeling, as contrasted with this inwardness of mind, with the character of something existent, but as a *negative* or as the abstract otherness of itself. Intelligence thus defines the content of sensation as something that is out of itself, projects it into time and space, which are the forms in which it is intuitive. To the view of consciousness the material is only an object of consciousness, a relative other: from mind it receives the rational characteristic of being *its very other* (§§ 247, 254).

Zusatz. The unity of mind with the object, which in sensation and feeling is immediate and therefore undeveloped, is still mindless. Therefore, intelligence puts an end to the simplicity of sensation, determines the sensed object as negative towards it, and thus separates itself from the object, yet at the same time posits it in its separatedness as its own. Only by this dual activity of removing and restoring the unity between myself and the object do I come to apprehend the content of sensation. This takes place, to begin with, in attention. Without this, therefore, no apprehension of the object is possible; only by attention does mind become present in the subject-matter and obtain *knowledge* of it, even though this is as yet only superficial, not systematic, knowledge (for the latter requires a further development of mind). Attention constitutes, therefore, the beginning of education. But it must be understood more exactly as the filling of oneself with a content that is both objective and subjective, or, in other words, that is not only for me, but also possesses a being of its own. Therefore, in attention there necessarily occurs a division and a unity of subjectivity and objectivity, a spontaneous reflection of free mind into itself and at the same time an identical turning of mind towards the object. This already implies that attention depends on my caprice, therefore, that I am only attentive when I want to be. But it does not follow that attention is an easy matter. On the contrary, it demands an effort since a man, if he wants to apprehend one particular object, must make abstraction from everything else, from all the thousand and one things going round in his head, from his other interests, even from his own person; he must suppress his own conceit which would rashly judge the subject-matter before it had a chance to speak for itself, must stubbornly absorb himself in the subject-matter, must fix his attention on it and let it have *its* say without obtruding his own reflections. Attention contains, therefore, the negation of one's self-assertion and also the surrender of oneself to the matter in hand; two moments just as necessary to mental aptitude and capability as they are usually held to be superfluous for so-called higher culture, since this is supposed to imply that one is already finished and done with everything and regards everything with indifference. This state of indifference is, to a certain extent, a relapse into a state of barbarism. The savage attends to practically nothing; he lets everything pass him by without fixing his attention on it. Only by training the mind does attention acquire strength and fulfil its function. The botanist, for example, observes incomparably more in a plant than one ignorant of botany does in the same time. The same thing is naturally true in regard to all other objects of knowledge. A man of great intelligence and education has at once a complete intuition of the matter in hand; with him sensation bears throughout the character of recollection.

As we have seen in the foregoing, there takes place in attention a division and a unity of subjectivity and objectivity. But in so far as attention in the first instance makes its appearance in *feeling*, the unity is preponderant, and accordingly the difference between these two sides is as yet indeterminate. But intelligence necessarily goes on to develop this difference, to distinguish the object from the subject in a determinate manner. The first form in which it does this is intuition. In this the *difference* between subjectivity and objectivity is no less preponderant than is the *unity* of these opposed determinations in formal attention.

We have now to examine here more closely the objectification in intuition of what is sensed. In this connection we have to discuss both the internal and external sensations.

As regards the former, it is especially true of them that in them man is subject to the power of his feelings, but that he withdraws himself from that power if he is able to visualize them. Thus we know, for example, that if anyone is able to form a clear picture to himself, say in a poem, of the feelings of joy or sorrow that are overwhelming him he rids himself of the thing that was oppressing his mind and thereby procures for himself relief or complete freedom. For although by contemplating the many aspects of his feelings he seems to increase their power over him, yet he does in fact diminish this power by making his feelings into something confronting him, something that becomes external to him. Goethe, for instance, particularly in his *Werther*, brought himself relief while subjecting the readers of this romance to the power of feeling. The educated man, because he contemplates what is felt in all its various aspects, feels more deeply than the uneducated, but is at the same time superior in his mastery over feeling because he moves especially in the element of rational thought which is raised above the narrowness of feeling.

The internal sensations are, therefore, as just indicated, more or less separable from us according to the degree of intensity of our reflective and rational thinking.

In the case of the external sensations, on the other hand, the extent to which they are separable depends on whether the object to which they are related is one that persists or vanishes. It is in accordance with this determination that the five senses range themselves in such a manner that on the one side stand smell and taste, and on the other side, sight and touch, with hearing coming in the middle. Smell is connected with the volatilization or evaporation of the object, taste with its consumption. Thus the object presents itself to these two senses in its complete lack of self-subsistence, only in its material vanishing. Here, therefore, intuition falls into time, and the transposition of what is sensed, from the subject into the object, is not so easy as with the sense of touch which is related mainly to the resistant aspect of the object, and also with the sense proper to intuition, namely, sight, which is concerned with the object as predominantly self-subsistent, as persisting ideally and materially and which has only an ideal relation to it, senses only its ideal aspect, colour, by means of light, but leaves the material side of the object untouched. Lastly, for hearing, the object is one that subsists materially but vanishes ideally; in sound, the ear perceives the vibration, that is, the merely ideal, not real, negation of the object's self-subsistence. Therefore, in hearing, the separability of sensation is slighter than in sight, but greater than in taste and smell. We cannot help hearing sound because, separating itself from the object, it forces itself on us and we readily connect it with a particular object because the latter preserves its self-subsistence in its vibration.

Accordingly, the activity of intuition produces to begin with simply a shifting of sensation away from us, a transformation of what is sensed into an object existing outside of us. The content of sensation is not altered by this attention; on the contrary, it is here still one and the same thing in mind and in the external object, so that mind here has not as yet a content peculiar to itself which it could compare with the content of intuition. Consequently, what intuition brings about is merely the transformation of the form of internality into that of externality. This forms the first manner, one which is still formal, in which intelligence becomes a determining activity. About the significance of this externality two remarks must be made: first, that the sensed object in becoming external to the inwardness of mind, receives the form of self-externality, since the mental or the rational constitutes the object's own nature. Secondly, we must remark that since this transformation of the sensed object originates in mind as such, the former thereby acquires a *mental*, i.e. an *abstract* externality and by this acquires that universality which can *immediately* belong to an external thing, namely, a universality that is still quite formal, without content. But the form of the Notion itself falls apart in this abstract externality. Accordingly, the latter has the dual form of space and of time (cf. §§ 254–9). Sensations are therefore made spatial and temporal by intuition. The spatial aspect presents itself as the form of indifferent juxtaposition and quiescent subsistence; the temporal aspect, on the other hand, presents itself as the form of unrest, of the immanently negative, of successiveness, of arising and vanishing, so that the temporal *is*, in that it *is not*, and *is not*, in that it *is*. But both forms of abstract externality are identical with one another in the sense that each is in its own self utterly discrete and at the same time utterly continuous. Their continuity, which includes within itself absolute discreteness, consists precisely in the abstract *universality* of the externality, a universality which derives from mind and has not yet developed any *actual* separation into parts.

But when we said that what is sensed receives from the intuiting mind the form of the spatial and temporal, this statement must not be understood to mean that space and time are only subjective forms. This is what Kant wanted to make them. But things are in truth themselves spatial and temporal; this double form of asunderness is not one-sidedly given to them by our intuition, but has been originally imparted to them by the intrinsically infinite mind, by the creative eternal Idea. Since, therefore, our intuitive mind honours the determinations of sensation by giving them the abstract form of space and time, thereby making them into real objects as well as assimilating them to itself, the supposition of subjective idealism that we receive only the *subjective* results of our determining activity and not the object's own determinations is completely refuted. However, the answer to those who stupidly attach quite extraordinary importance to the question as to the *reality* of space and time, is that space and time are extremely meagre and superficial determinations, consequently, that things obtain very little from these forms and the loss of them, were this in some way possible, would therefore amount to very little. Cognitive thinking does not halt at these forms; it apprehends things in their Notion in which space and time are contained as ideal moments. Just as in external Nature space and time, by the dialectic of the Notion immanent in them, raise themselves into matter (§ 261) as their truth, so free intelligence is the self-existent dialectic of these forms of immediate asunderness.

§ 449

(3) When intelligence reaches a concrete unity of the two factors, that is to say, when it is at once self-collected in this externally existing material, and yet in this self-collectedness sunk in the out-of-selfness, it is *Intuition* or Mental Vision.

Zusatz. Intuition must not be confused either with representation proper, to be dealt with later, or with the merely phenomenological consciousness already discussed.

First of all, as regards the relation of intuition to representation, the former has only this in common with the latter, that in both forms of mind the object is separate from me and at the same time also my own. But the object's character of being mine is only implicitly present in intuition and first becomes explicit in representation. In intuition, the objectivity of the content predominates. Not until I reflect that it is I who have the intuition, not until then do I occupy the standpoint of representation.

But with reference to the relation of intuition to consciousness, the following remark must be made. In the broadest sense of the word, one could of course give the name of intuition to the immediate or sensuous consciousness considered in § 418. But if this name is to be taken in its proper significance, as rationally it must, then between that consciousness and intuition the essential distinction must be made that the former, in the *unmediated*, quite abstract certainty of itself, relates itself to the *immediate* individuality of the object, an individuality sundered into a multiplicity of aspects; whereas intuition is consciousness *filled* with the certainty of Reason, whose object is *rationally* determined and consequently not an individual torn asunder into its various aspects but a totality, a unified fullness of determinations. It was in this sense that Schelling formerly spoke of intuition. Mindless intuition is merely sensuous consciousness which remains external to the object. Mindful, true intuition, on the contrary, apprehends the genuine substance of the object. A talented historian, for example, has before him a vivid intuition of the circumstances and events he is to describe; on the other hand, one who has no talent for writing history confines himself to details and overlooks what is essential. It is, therefore, rightly insisted on that in all branches of science, and particularly also in philosophy, one should speak from an intuitive grasp of the subject-matter. This demands that a man should have his heart and soul, in short, his whole mind or spirit, in the subject-matter, should place himself in the centre of it and give it free play. Only thinking that is firmly based on an intuitive grasp of the substance of the subject-matter can, without deserting the truth, go on to treat of the details which, though rooted in that substance, become valueless when separated from it. On the other hand, if a substantial intuition of the subject-matter is lacking at the outset or later vanishes, reflective thought loses itself in the contemplation of the manifold, separate determinations and relations it encounters in the subject-matter, and the abstractive understanding tears the subject-matter apart, even when this is a living thing, a plant or an animal, by its one-sided finite categories of cause and effect, external end and means, and so on, and in this manner, despite all its cleverness fails to grasp the concrete nature of the subject-matter, to apprehend the spiritual bond unifying all the details.

But the necessity for going beyond mere intuition, lies in the fact that intelligence, according to its Notion, is *cognition*, whereas intuition is not as yet a *cognitive* awareness of the subject-matter since as such it does not attain to the *immanent development* of the substance of the subject-matter but confines itself rather to seizing the *unexplicated* substance still wrapped up in the inessentials of the external and contingent. Intuition is, therefore, only the *beginning* of cognition and it is to this its status that Aristotle's saying refers, that all knowledge starts from wonder. For since subjective Reason, as intuition, has the certainty, though only the indeterminate certainty, of finding itself again in the object, which to begin with is burdened with an irrational form, the object inspires it with wonder and awe. But philosophical thinking must rise above the standpoint of wonder. It is quite erroneous to imagine that one truly knows the object when one has an immediate intuition of it. Perfect cognition belongs only to the pure thinking of Reason which comprehends its object, and only he who has risen to this thinking possesses a perfectly determinate, true intuition. With him intuition forms only the substantial form into which his completely developed cognition concentrates itself again. In immediate intuition, it is true that I have the entire object before me; but not until my cognition of the object developed in all its aspects has returned into the form of simple intuition does it confront my intelligence as an articulated, systematic totality. In general, it is the educated man who has an intuition free from a mass of contingent detail and equipped with a wealth of rational insights. An intelligent, educated man, even though he does not philosophize, can grasp the essentials, the core, of the subject-matter in its simple qualitative nature. Reflection is, however, always necessary to achieve this. People often imagine that the poet, like the artist in general, must go to work purely intuitively. This is absolutely not the case. On the contrary, a genuine poet, before and during the execution of his work, must meditate and reflect; only in this way can he hope to bring out the heart, or the soul, of the subject-matter, freeing it from all the externalities in which it is shrouded and by so doing, *organically* develop his intuition.

§ 450

At and towards this its own out-of-selfness, intelligence no less essentially directs its attention. In this its immediacy it is an awaking to itself, a recollection of itself. Thus intuition becomes a concretion of the material with the intelligence, which makes it its own, so that it no longer needs this immediacy, no longer needs to find the content.

Zusatz. At the standpoint of mere intuition we are outside of ourselves, in the elements of space and time, these two forms of asunderness. Here intelligence is immersed in the external material, is one with it, and has no other content than that of the intuited object. Therefore, in intuition we can become unfree in the highest degree. But, as we already remarked in the *Zusatz* to § 448, intelligence is the *self-existent dialectic* of this immediate asunderness. Accordingly, mind posits intuition as its own, pervades it, makes it into something inward, recollects (inwardizes) itself in it, becomes present to itself in it, and hence free. By this withdrawal into itself, intelligence raises itself to the stage of mental representation. In representation, mind *has* intuition; the latter is *ideally present* in mind, it has not *vanished* or merely *passed away*. Therefore, when speaking of an intuition that has been raised to a representation, language is quite correct in saying: I *have* seen this. By this is expressed no mere past, but also in fact *presence*; here the past is purely *relative* and exists only in the *comparison* of *immediate* intuition with what we now have in representation. But the word 'have', employed in the perfect tense, has quite peculiarly the meaning of presence; what I have seen is something not merely that I *had*, but still *have*, something, therefore, that is present in me. In this use of the word 'have' can be seen a general sign of the inwardness of the modern mind, which makes the reflection, not merely that the past in its immediacy has passed away, but also that in mind the past is still preserved.

(β) *Representation (or Mental Idea)*[1]

§ 451

Representation is this recollected or inwardized intuition, and as such is the middle between that stage of intelligence where it finds itself immediately subject to modification and that where intelligence is in its freedom, or, as thought. The representation is the property of intelligence; with a preponderating subjectivity, however, as its right of property is still conditioned by contrast with the immediacy, and the representation cannot as it stands be said to *be*. The path of intelligence in representations is to render the immediacy inward, to invest itself with intuitive action in

[1] Vorstellung.

itself, and at the same time to get rid of the subjectivity of the inwardness, and inwardly divest itself of it; so as to be in itself in an externality of its own. But as representation begins from intuition and the ready-found material of intuition, the intuitional contrast still continues to affect its activity, and makes its concrete products still 'syntheses', which do not grow to the concrete immanence of the notion till they reach the stage of thought.

Zusatz. The various forms of mind coming under the standpoint of representation are usually regarded, even more than is the case with the antecedent stage of intelligence, as isolated, mutually independent powers or faculties. Along with the faculty of representation in general, one speaks of the faculties of imagination and memory, treating the mutual independence of these forms of mind as something completely fixed and settled. But the truly philosophical grasp of these forms just consists in comprehending the rational connection existing between them, in recognizing them as stages in the organic development of intelligence.

To facilitate a survey of the stages of this development, we shall now in a general way indicate them in advance.

(αα) The first of these stages we call recollection (inwardization) in the peculiar meaning of the word according to which it consists in the involuntary calling up of a content which is already ours. Recollection forms the most abstract stage of intelligence operating with representations. Here the represented content is still the same as in intuition; in the latter it receives its verification, just as, conversely, the content of intuition verifies itself in my representation. We have, therefore, at this stage a content which is not only intuitively perceived in its immediacy, but is at the same time recollected, inwardized, posited as *mine*. As thus determined, the content is what we call *image*.

(ββ) The second stage in this sphere is imagination. Here there enters the opposition between my subjective or represented content, and the intuitively perceived content, of the object. Imagination fashions for itself a content peculiar to it by *thinking* the object, by bringing out what is universal in it, and giving it determinations which belong to the ego. In this way imagination ceases to be a merely formal recollection (inwardization) and becomes a recollection which affects the *content*, *generalizes* it, thus creating *general* representations or ideas. Since at this stage the opposition of subjectivity and objectivity is dominant, the unity here of these determinations cannot be an *immediate* unity as at the stage of mere recollection, but only a *restored* unity. The manner in which this restoration takes place is that the intuitively perceived external content is subjugated to the mentally represented content which has been raised to universality, is reduced to a *sign* of the latter content which is, however, thereby made objective, external, is imaged.

(γγ) Memory is the third stage of representation. Here, on the one hand, the sign is inwardized, taken up into intelligence; on the other hand, the latter is thereby given the form of something external and mechanical, and in this way a unity of subjectivity and objectivity is produced which forms the transition to thought as such.

(αα) *Recollection*[1]

§ 452

Intelligence, as it at first recollects the intuition, places the content of feeling in its own inwardness—in a space and a time of its own. In this way that content is (1) an *image* or picture, liberated from its original immediacy and abstract singleness amongst other things, and received into the universality of the ego. The image loses the full complement of features proper to intuition, and is arbitrary or contingent, isolated, we may say, from the external place, time, and immediate context in which the intuition stood.

Zusatz. Since intelligence is, according to its Notion, self-existent, infinite ideality, or universality, its space and time is *universal* space and *universal* time. Consequently, in placing the content of feeling in the inwardness of intelligence and thereby making it a mental representation, I lift it out of the *particularity* of space and time to which, in its immediacy, it is tied and on which I, too, am dependent in feeling and intuition. From this it follows, first, that whereas the immediate presence of the thing is necessary for feeling and intuition, I can form a mental image of something wherever I am, even of what is remotest from me in external space and time. Secondly, it follows from the foregoing that all that happens possesses duration for us only when it is taken up by ideating intelligence, whereas happenings deemed unworthy of being so taken up become things wholly of the past. However, what is imaged gains this imperishableness only at the expense of the clarity and freshness of the immediate individuality of what is intuitively perceived in all its firmly determined aspects; the intuition, in becoming an image, is obscured and obliterated.

As regards time, the further remark can be made concerning the subjective character it acquires in mental representation, that in *intuition* time becomes short for us when we have plenty to perceive, but long when the lack of given material drives us to the contemplation of our empty subjectivity; but that, conversely, in mental representation those times in which we were occupied in various different ways appear long to us,

[1] Die Erinnerung.

whereas those times in which we were not very busy seem to be short. Here, in recollection, we attend to our inner subjectivity, our inwardness, and measure time according to the interest which this has had for us. In the case of intuition, we are immersed in the contemplation of the *object*, and time seems short to us when it is filled with an ever-changing content, but long when nothing interrupts its monotony.

§ 453

(2) The image is of itself transient, and intelligence itself is as attention its time and also its place, its when and where. But intelligence is not only consciousness and actual existence, but *qua* intelligence is the subject and the potentiality of its own specializations. The image when thus kept in mind is no longer existent, but stored up out of consciousness.

To grasp intelligence as this night-like mine or pit in which is stored a world of infinitely many images and representations, yet without being in consciousness, is from the one point of view the universal postulate which bids us treat the notion as concrete, in the way we treat, for example, the germ as affirmatively containing, in virtual possibility, all the qualities that come into existence in the subsequent development of the tree. Inability to grasp a universal like this, which, though intrinsically concrete, still continues *simple*, is what has led people to talk about special fibres and areas as receptacles of particular ideas. It was felt that what was diverse should in the nature of things have a local habitation peculiar to itself. But whereas the reversion of the germ from its existing specializations to its simplicity in a purely potential existence takes place only in another germ—the germ of the fruit; intelligence *qua* intelligence shows the potential coming to free existence in its development, and yet at the same time collecting itself in its inwardness. Hence from the other point of view intelligence is to be conceived as this subconscious mine, i.e. as the *existent* universal in which the different has not yet been realized in its separations. And it is indeed this potentiality which is the first form of universality offered in mental representation.

Zusatz. The image is mine, it belongs to me; but, to begin with, it has no further homogeneity with me, for it is still not *thought*, still not raised into the form of Reason. On the contrary, between it and myself there exists a relationship which is not truly free, which still stems from the standpoint of intuition and according to which I am only the inner side, and the image is for me something external. Therefore, to begin with, I do not as yet have full command over the images slumbering in the mine or pit of my inwardness, am not as yet able to recall them at will. No one knows what an infinite host of images of the past slumbers in him; now and then they do indeed accidentally awake, but one cannot, as it is said, call them to mind. Thus the images are *ours* only in a *formal* manner.

§ 454

(3) An image thus abstractly treasured up needs, if it is to exist, an actual intuition: and what is strictly called Remembrance is the reference of the image to an intuition—and that as a sub-sumption of the immediate single intuition (impression) under what is in point of form universal, under the representation (idea) with the same content. Thus intelligence recognizes the specific sensation and the intuition of it as what is already its own—in them it is still within itself: at the same time it is aware that what is only its (primarily) internal image is also an immediate object of intuition, by which it is authenticated. The image, which in the mine of intelligence was only its *property*, now that it has been endued with externality, comes actually into its *possession*. And so the image is at once rendered distinguishable from the intuition and separable from the blank night in which it was originally submerged. Intelligence is thus the force which can give forth its property, and dispense with external intuition for its existence in it. This 'synthesis' of the internal image with the recollected existence is *representation* proper: by this synthesis the internal now has the qualification of being able to be presented before intelligence and to have its existence in it.

Zusatz. The manner in which the images of the past lying hidden in the dark depths of our inner being become our actual possession, is that they present themselves to our intelligence in the luminous, plastic shape of an *existent* intuition of *similar* content, and that with the help of this *present* intuition we recognize them as intuitions we have already had. Thus it happens, for example, that we recognize out of hundreds of thousands a man whose image was already quite dim in our mind, as soon as we catch sight of him again. If, therefore, I am to *retain* something in my memory, I must have repeated intuitions of it. At first, the image will,

of course, be recalled not so much by myself as by the corresponding·
immediate intuition; but the image, by being frequently recalled in this
way, acquires such intense vividness and is so present to me that I no
longer need the external intuition to remind me of it. It is in this way that
children pass from intuition to recollection. The more educated a man is,
the less he lives in immediate intuition, but, in all his intuitions, at the
same time lives in recollections; so that for him there is little that is
altogether new but, on the contrary, the substantial import of most new
things is something already familiar to him. Similarly, an educated man
contents himself for the most part with his images and seldom feels the
need of immediate intuition. The curious multitude, on the other hand,
are always hurrying to where there is something to gape at.

($\beta\beta$) *Imagination*[1]

§ 455

(1) The intelligence which is active in this possession is the
reproductive imagination, where the images issue from the inward
world belonging to the ego, which is now the power over them.
The images are in the first instance referred to this external,
immediate time and space which is treasured up along with them.
But it is solely in the conscious subject, where it is treasured up,
that the image has the individuality in which the features composing it are conjoined: whereas their original concretion, i.e. at first
only in space and time, as a *unit* of intuition, has been broken up.
The content reproduced, belonging as it does to the self-identical
unity of intelligence, and an out-put from its universal mine, has a
general idea (representation) to supply the link of association for
the images which according to circumstances are more abstract or
more concrete ideas.

The so-called *laws of the association of ideas* were objects of
great interest, especially during that outburst of empirical psychology which was contemporaneous with the decline of philosophy. In the first place, it is not *Ideas* (properly so called) which
are associated. Secondly, these modes of relation are not *laws*, just
for the reason that there are so many laws about the same thing,
as to suggest a caprice and a contingency opposed to the very
nature of law. It is a matter of chance whether the link of associa-

[1] Die Einbildungskraft.

tion is something pictorial, or an intellectual category, such as likeness and contrast, reason and consequence. The train of images and representations suggested by association is the sport of vacant-minded ideation, where, though intelligence shows itself by a certain formal universality, the matter is entirely pictorial. —Image and Idea, if we leave out of account the more precise definition of those forms given above, present also a distinction in content. The former is the more sensuously concrete idea, whereas the idea (representation), whatever be its content (from image, notion, or idea), has always the peculiarity, though belonging to intelligence, of being in respect of its content given and immediate. It is still true of this idea or representation, as of all intelligence, that it finds its material, as a matter of fact, to *be* so and so; and the universality which the aforesaid material receives by ideation is still abstract. Mental representation is the mean in the syllogism of the elevation of intelligence, the link between the two significations of self-relatedness—viz. *being* and *universality*, which in consciousness receive the title of object and subject. Intelligence complements what is merely found by the attribution of universality, and the internal and its own by the attribution of being, but a being of its own institution. (On the distinction of representations and thoughts, see Introduction to the Logic, § 20 note.)

Abstraction, which occurs in the ideational activity by which general ideas are produced (and ideas *qua* ideas virtually have the form of generality), is frequently explained as the incidence of many similar images one upon another and is supposed to be thus made intelligible. If this superimposing is to be no mere accident and without principle, a force of attraction in like images must be assumed; or something of the sort, which at the same time would have the negative power of rubbing off the dissimilar elements against each other. This force is really intelligence itself— the self-identical ego which by its internalizing recollection gives the images *ipso facto* generality, and subsumes the single intuition under the already internalized image (§ 453).

Zusatz. The second stage of development of representation is, as we have already indicated in the *Zusatz* to § 451, imagination. The manner in which the first form of mental representation, recollection, has raised itself to this stage is that intelligence, emerging from its abstract inward being into determinateness, disperses the night-like darkness enveloping the wealth of its images and banishes it by the luminous clarity of a present image.

But imagination, in its turn, contains three forms into which it unfolds itself. It is, in general, the determinant of the images.

At first, however, it does no more than determine the images as entering into existence. As such, it is merely reproductive imagination. This has the character of a merely formal activity.

But, secondly, imagination not merely recalls the images existent in it but connects them with one another and in this way raises them to *general* ideas or representations. Accordingly, at this stage, imagination appears as the activity of *associating* images.

The third stage in this sphere is that in which intelligence posits its *general* ideas or representations as identical with the *particular* aspect of the image and so gives the former a pictorial existence. This sensuous existence has the double form of symbol and sign, so that this third stage comprises creative imagination (*Phantasie*), which produces symbols and signs, the latter forming the transition to memory.

Reproductive Imagination

The first activity is the formal one of reproducing images. It is true that pure thoughts can also be reproduced, but imagination has to do not with them but only with images. But the production of images by imagination occurs *voluntarily* and without the help of an immediate intuition. It is this that distinguishes this form of ideating intelligence from mere recollection, which does not operate spontaneously but requires a present intuition and *involuntarily* causes the images to appear.

Associative Imagination

A higher activity than the simple reproduction of images is the connecting of them with one another. The content of the images has, on account of its immediacy or sensuousness, the form of finitude, of relation to an Other. Now since here it is I in general who determine or posit, I, too, posit this connection. By this, intelligence gives the images a subjective bond in place of their objective one. But the former still has in part the shape of externality relatively to what is thereby connected. I have, for example, the image of an object before me; to this image is linked quite externally the image of persons with whom I have talked about this object, or who own it, etc. Often the images are linked together only by space and time. Ordinary social conversation mostly rambles on from one idea to another in a very external and contingent manner. It is only when the conversation has a definite aim that it acquires a firmer coherence. The various moods of feeling impart a characteristic touch to every representation—a gay mood, a touch of gaiety, a sad mood, a touch of sadness. Even more is this true of the passions. The degree of intelligence also produces a difference in the way images are connected; clever, witty persons are therefore distinguished from ordinary folk in this respect, too; a clever person seeks out images that contain something substantial and profound. Wittiness connects ideas which, although remote from one another, none the less have in fact in inner connection. Punning, too, must be included in this sphere; the deepest passion can give itself up to this pastime; for a great mind, even in the most unfortunate circumstances, knows how to bring everything it encounters into relation with its passion.

§ 456

Thus even the association of ideas is to be treated as a subsumption of the individual under the universal, which forms their connecting link. But here intelligence is more than merely a general form: its inwardness is an internally definite, concrete subjectivity with a substance and value of its own, derived from some interest, some latent concept or Ideal principle, so far as we may by anticipation speak of such. Intelligence is the power which wields the stores of images and ideas belonging to it, and which thus (2) freely combines and subsumes these stores in obedience to its peculiar tenor. Such is creative imagination[1]—symbolic, allegoric, or poetical imagination—where the intelligence gets a definite embodiment in this store of ideas and informs them with its general tone. These more or less concrete, individualized creations are still 'syntheses': for the material, in which the subjective principles and ideas get a mentally pictorial existence, is derived from the data of intuition.

Zusatz. Images are already more universal than intuitions; they still have, however, a sensuously concrete content whose connection with another such content is myself. Now it is in turning my attention to this connection that I arrive at *general* ideas, or to ideas (representations) in the strict sense of this word. For that which connects the single images to one another consists precisely in what is common to them. This common element is either any one *particular* side of the object raised to the form of *universality*, such as, for example, in the rose, the red colour; or the *concrete universal*, the genus, for example, in the rose, the plant; but in each case it is an idea (representation) which comes into being through the dissolution by intelligence of the empirical connection of the manifold

[1] Phantasie.

determinations of the object. In generating general ideas, intelligence is spontaneously active; it is, therefore, a stupid mistake to assume that general ideas arise, without any help from the mind, by a number of similar images coming into contact with one another, that, for example, the red colour of the rose seeks the red of other images in my head, and thus conveys to me, a mere spectator, the general idea of red. Of course, the *particular* element belonging to the image is something given; but the analysis of the concrete individuality of the image and the resultant form of universality come, as remarked, from myself.

Abstract ideas, to mention this in passing, are often called Notions. The philosophy of Fries consists essentially of such ideas. When it is asserted that they lead one to a knowledge of truth, the rejoinder must be that they do just the opposite, and that the man of good sense, holding on to the concrete element of images, rightly rejects such empty wisdom of the schools. But there is no need here to labour this point. Just as little are we concerned here with the precise nature of the content, whether this comes from the external world or from the sphere of reason, of law, ethics, and religion. What we are concerned with here is simply and solely the *generality* of the idea. From this point of view we remark as follows.

In the subjective sphere where we now find ourselves, the *general* idea is the inward side; the image, on the other hand, is the external side. These two mutually opposed determinations, to begin with, still fall apart, but in their dividedness are one-sided. The former lacks externality, figuration, and the latter, elevation to the expression of a determinate universal. The truth of these two sides is, therefore, their unity. More exactly, this unity, the imaging of the universal and the generalization of the image, comes about not by the general idea uniting with the image to form a *neutral*, so to speak, *chemical* product, but by the idea actively proving itself to be the *substantial* power over the image, subjugating it as an *accident*, making itself into the image's soul, and becoming in the image *for itself*, inwardizing itself, manifesting its own self. Intelligence, having brought about this unity of the universal and the particular, of the inward and the outward, of idea (representation) and intuition, and in this way restoring the totality present in intuition as now authenticated, the ideating activity is completed within itself in so far as it is productive imagination. This forms the formal aspect of art; for art represents the true universal, or the Idea in the form of sensuous existence, of the image.

§ 457

In creative imagination intelligence has been so far perfected as to need no aids for intuition. Its self-sprung ideas have pictorial existence. This pictorial creation of its intuitive spontaneity is subjective—still lacks the side of existence. But as the creation unites the internal idea with the vehicle of materialization, intelligence has therein *implicitly* returned both to identical self-relation and to immediacy. As reason, its first start was to appropriate the immediate datum in itself (§§ 445, 435), i.e. to universalize it; and now its action as reason (§ 438) is from the present point directed towards giving the character of an existent to what in it has been perfected to concrete auto-intuition. In other words, it aims at making itself *be* and be a fact. Acting on this view, it is self-uttering, intuition-producing: the imagination which creates signs.

Productive imagination is the centre in which the universal and being, one's own and what is picked up, internal and external, are completely welded into one. The preceding 'syntheses' of intuition, recollection, etc., are unifications of the same factors, but they are 'syntheses'; it is not till creative imagination that intelligence ceases to be the vague mine and the universal, and becomes an individuality, a concrete subjectivity, in which the self-reference is defined both to being and to universality. The creations of imagination are on all hands recognized as such combinations of the mind's own and inward with the matter of intuition; what further and more definite aspects they have is a matter for other departments. For the present this internal studio of intelligence is only to be looked at in these abstract aspects. —Imagination, when regarded as the agency of this unification, is reason, but only a nominal reason, because the matter or theme it embodies is to imagination *qua* imagination a matter of indifference; whilst reason *qua* reason also insists upon the *truth* of its content.

Another point calling for special notice is that, when imagination elevates the internal meaning to an image and intuition, and this is expressed by saying that it gives the former the character of an *existent*, the phrase must not seem surprising that intelligence makes itself *be* as a *thing*; for its ideal import is itself, and so is the aspect which it imposes upon it. The image produced by imagination of an object is a bare mental or subjective intuition: in the sign or symbol it adds intuitability proper; and in mechanical memory it completes, so far as it is concerned, this form of *being*.

Zusatz. As we have seen in the *Zusatz* to the previous Paragraph, in creative imagination the general idea or representation constitutes the subjective element which gives itself objectivity in the image and thereby authenticates itself. This authentication is, however, itself immediately still a subjective one, since intelligence in the first instance still has regard to the given content of the images, is guided by it in symbolizing its general ideas. This conditioned, only relatively free, activity of intelligence we call *symbolic* imagination. This selects for the expression of its general ideas only that sensuous material whose independent signification corresponds to the specific content of the universal to be symbolized. Thus, for example, the strength of Jupiter is represented by the eagle because this is looked upon as strong. *Allegory* expresses the subjective element more by an *ensemble* of separate details. Lastly, *poetic* imagination, though it is freer than the plastic arts in its use of materials, may only select such sensuous material as is adequate to the content of the idea to be represented.

But intelligence necessarily progresses from subjective authentication of the general idea mediated by the image, to its objective, absolute authentication. For since the content of the general idea to be authenticated unites only with itself in the content of the image serving as symbol, this mediated form of the authentication, of this unity of subjectivity and objectivity, straightway changes into the form of immediacy. By this dialectical movement, the general idea reaches the point where it no longer needs the image's content for its authentication, but is authenticated in and for itself alone, is, therefore, immediately valid. Now the general idea, liberated from the image's content, in making its freely selected external material into something that can be intuitively perceived, produces what has to be called a sign—in specific distinction from symbol. The sign must be regarded as a great advance on the symbol. Intelligence, in indicating something by a sign, has finished with the content of intuition, and the sensuous material receives for its soul a signification foreign to it. Thus, for example, a cockade, or a flag, or a tomb-stone, signifies something totally different from what it immediately indicates. The arbitrary nature of the connection between the sensuous material and a general idea occurring here, has the necessary consequence that the significance of the sign must first be learned. This is especially true of language signs.

§ 458

In this unity (initiated by intelligence) of an independent representation with an intuition, the matter of the latter is, in the first instance, something accepted, somewhat immediate or given (for example, the colour of the cockade, etc.). But in the fusion of the two elements, the intuition does not count positively or as representing itself, but as representative of something else. It is an image, which has received as its soul and meaning an independent mental representation. This intuition is the *Sign*.

The sign is some immediate intuition, representing a totally different import from what naturally belongs to it; it is the pyramid into which a foreign soul has been conveyed, and where it is conserved. The *sign* is different from the *symbol*: for in the symbol the original characters (in essence and conception) of the visible object are more or less identical with the import which it bears as symbol; whereas in the sign, strictly so-called, the natural attributes of the intuition, and the connotation of which it is a sign, have nothing to do with each other. Intelligence therefore gives proof of wider choice and ampler authority in the use of intuitions when it treats them as designatory (significative) rather than as symbolical.

In logic and psychology, signs and language are usually foisted in somewhere as an appendix, without any trouble being taken to display their necessity and systematic place in the economy of intelligence. The right place for the sign is that just given: where intelligence—which as intuiting generates the form of time and space, but appears as recipient of sensible matter, out of which it forms ideas—now gives its own original ideas a definite existence from itself, treating the intuition (or time and space as filled full) as its own property, deleting the connotation which properly and naturally belongs to it, and conferring on it an other connotation as its soul and import. This sign-creating activity may be distinctively named 'productive' Memory (the primarily abstract 'Mnemosyne'); since memory, which in ordinary life is often used as interchangeable and synonymous with remembrance (recollection), and even with conception and imagination, has always to do with signs only.

§ 459

The intuition—in its natural phase a something given and given in space—acquires, when employed as a sign, the peculiar characteristic of existing only as superseded and sublimated. Such is the negativity of intelligence; and thus the truer phase of the intuition used as a sign is existence in *time* (but its existence vanishes in the moment of being), and if we consider the rest of its external psychical quality, its *institution* by intelligence, but an institution growing out of its (anthropological) own naturalness. This institution of the natural is the vocal note, where the inward idea manifests itself in adequate utterance. The vocal note which receives further articulation to express specific ideas—speech and, its system, language—gives to sensations, intuitions, conceptions, a second and higher existence than they naturally possess—invests them with the right of existence in the ideational realm.

Language here comes under discussion only in the special aspect of a product of intelligence for manifesting its ideas in an external medium. If language had to be treated in its concrete nature, it would be necessary for its vocabulary or material part to recall the anthropological or psychophysiological point of view (§ 401), and for the grammar or formal portion to anticipate the standpoint of analytic understanding. With regard to the elementary *material* of language, while on one hand the theory of mere accident has disappeared, on the other the principle of imitation has been restricted to the slight range it actually covers—that of vocal objects. Yet one may still hear the German language praised for its wealth—that wealth consisting in its special expression for special sounds—*Rauschen, Sausen, Knarren*, etc.;—there have been collected more than a hundred such words, perhaps: the humour of the moment creates fresh ones when it pleases. Such superabundance in the realm of sense and of triviality contributes nothing to form the real wealth of a cultivated language. The strictly raw material of language itself depends more upon an inward symbolism than a symbolism referring to external objects; it depends, i.e. on anthropological articulation, as it were the posture in the corporeal act of oral utterance. For each vowel and consonant accordingly, as well as for their more abstract elements (the posture of lips, palate, tongue in each) and for their combinations, people have tried to find the appropriate signification. But these dull subconscious beginnings are deprived of their original importance and prominence by new influences, it may be by external agencies or by the needs of civilization. Having been originally sensuous intuitions, they are reduced to signs, and thus have only traces left of their original meaning, if it be not altogether extinguished. As to the *formal* element, again, it is the work of analytic intellect which informs language with its categories: it is this logical instinct which gives rise to grammar. The study of languages still in their original state, which we have first really begun to make acquaintance with in modern times, has shown on this point that they contain a very elaborate grammar and express distinctions which are lost or have been largely obliterated in the languages of more civilized nations. It seems as if the language of the most civilized nations has the most imperfect grammar, and that the same language has a more perfect grammar when the nation is in a more uncivilized state than when it reaches a higher civilization. (Cf. W. von Humboldt's *Essay on the Dual.*)

In speaking of vocal (which is the original) language, we may touch, only in passing, upon written language—a further development in the particular sphere of language which borrows the help of an externally practical activity. It is from the province of immediate spatial intuition to which written language proceeds that it takes and produces the signs (§ 454). In particular, hieroglyphics uses spatial figures to designate *ideas*; alphabetical writing, on the other hand, uses them to designate vocal notes which are already signs. Alphabetical writing thus consists of signs of signs—the words or concrete signs of vocal language being analysed into their simple elements, which severally receive designation.—Leibniz's practical mind misled him to exaggerate the advantages which a complete written language, formed on the hieroglyphic method (and hieroglyphics are used even where there is alphabetic writing, as in our signs for the numbers, the planets, the chemical elements, etc.), would have as a universal language for the intercourse of nations and especially of scholars. But we may be sure that it was rather the intercourse of nations (as was probably the case in Phoenicia, and still takes place in Canton—see *Macartney's Travels* by Staunton) which occasioned the need of alphabetical writing and led to its formation. At any rate a comprehensive hieroglyphic language for ever completed is impracticable. Sensible objects no doubt admit of permanent signs; but, as regards signs for mental objects, the progress of thought and the continual development of logic lead to changes in the views of their internal relations and thus also of their nature; and this would involve the rise of a new hieroglyphical denotation. Even in the case of sense-objects it happens that their names, i.e. their signs in vocal language, are frequently changed, as, for example, in chemistry and mineralogy. Now that it has been forgotten what names properly are, viz. externalities which of themselves have no sense, and only get signification as signs, and now that, instead of names proper, people ask for terms expressing a sort of definition, which is frequently changed capriciously and fortuitously, the denomination, i.e. the composite name formed of signs of their generic characters or other supposed characteristic properties, is altered in accordance with the differences of view with regard to the genus or other supposed specific property. It is only a stationary civilization, like the Chinese, which admits of the hieroglyphic language of that nation; and its method of writing moreover can only be the lot of that small part of a nation which is in exclusive possession of mental culture.—The progress of the vocal language depends most closely on the habit of alphabetical writing; by means of which only does vocal language acquire the precision and purity of its articulation. The imperfection of the Chinese vocal language is notorious: numbers of its words possess several utterly different meanings, as many as ten and twenty, so that, in speaking, the distinction is made perceptible merely by accent and intensity, by speaking low and soft or crying out. The European, learning to speak Chinese, falls into the most ridiculous blunders before he has mastered these absurd refinements of accentuation. Perfection here consists in the opposite of that *parler sans accent* which in Europe is justly required of an educated speaker. The hieroglyphic mode of writing keeps the Chinese vocal language from reaching that objective precision which is gained in articulation by alphabetic writing.

Alphabetic writing is on all accounts the more intelligent: in it the *word*—the mode, peculiar to the intellect, of uttering its ideas most worthily—is brought to consciousness and made an object of reflection. Engaging the attention of intelligence, as it does, it is analysed; the work of sign-making is reduced to its few simple elements (the primary postures of articulation) in which the sense-factor in speech is brought to the form of universality, at the same time that in this elementary phase it acquires complete precision and purity. Thus alphabetic writing retains at the same time the advantage of vocal language, that the ideas have names strictly so called: the name is the simple sign for the exact idea, i.e. the simple plain idea, not decomposed into its features and compounded out of them. Hieroglyphics, instead of springing from the direct analysis of sensible signs, like alphabetic writing, arise from an antecedent analysis of ideas. Thus a theory readily arises that all ideas may be reduced to their elements, or simple logical terms, so that from the elementary signs chosen to express these (as, in the case of the Chinese *Koua*, the simple straight stroke, and the stroke broken into two parts) a hieroglyphic system would be generated by their composition. This feature of hieroglyphic—the analytical designations of ideas—which misled Leibniz to regard it as preferable to alphabetic writing is rather in antagonism with the fundamental desideratum of language— the name. To want a name means that for the immediate idea (which, however ample a connotation it may include, is still for the mind simple in the name), we require a simple immediate sign which for its own sake does not suggest anything, and has for its sole function to signify and represent sensibly the simple idea as such. It is not merely the image-loving and image-limited intelligence that lingers over the simplicity of ideas and redinte-grates them from the more abstract factors into which they have been analysed: thought too reduces to the form of a simple thought the concrete connotation which it 'resumes' and reunites from the mere aggregate of attributes to which analysis has reduced it. Both alike require such signs, simple in respect of their meaning: signs, which though consisting of several letters or syllables and even decomposed into such, yet do not exhibit a combination of several ideas.—What has been stated is the principle for settling the value of these written languages. It also follows that in hieroglyphics the relations of concrete mental ideas to one another must neces-sarily be tangled and perplexed, and that the analysis of these (and the proximate results of such analysis must again be analysed) appears to be possible in the most various and divergent ways. Every divergence in analysis would give rise to another forma-tion of the written name; just as in modern times (as already noted, even in the region of sense) muriatic acid has undergone several changes of name. A hieroglyphic written language would require a philosophy as stationary as is the civilization of the Chinese.

What has been said shows the inestimable and not sufficiently appreciated educational value of learning to read and write an alphabetic character. It leads the mind from the sensibly concrete image to attend to the more formal structure of the vocal word and its abstract elements, and contributes much to give stability and independence to the inward realm of mental life. Acquired habit subsequently effaces the peculiarity by which alphabetic writing appears, in the interest of vision, as a roundabout way to ideas by means of audibility; it makes them a sort of hieroglyphic to us, so that in using them we need not consciously realize them by means of tones, whereas people unpractised in reading utter aloud what they read in order to catch its meaning in the sound. Thus, while (with the faculty which transformed alphabetic writing into hieroglyphics) the capacity of abstraction gained by the first practice remains, hieroglyphic reading is of itself a deaf reading and a dumb writing. It is true that the audible (which is in time) and the visible (which is in space), each have their own basis, one no less authoritative than the other. But in the case of alphabetic writing there is only a *single* basis: the two aspects occupy their rightful relation to each other: the visible language is related to the vocal only as a sign, and intelligence expresses itself immediately and unconditionally by speaking.—The instrumental function of the comparatively non-sensuous element of tone for all ideational work shows itself further as peculiarly important in memory which forms the passage from representation to thought.

§ 460

The name, combining the intuition (an intellectual production) with its signification, is primarily a single transient product; and conjunction of the idea (which is inward) with the intuition (which is outward) is itself outward. The reduction of this outwardness to inwardness is (verbal) Memory.

(γγ) *Memory*[1]

§ 461

Under the shape of memory the course of intelligence passes through the same inwardizing (recollecting) functions, as regards the intuition of the *word*, as representation in general does in dealing with the first immediate intuition (§ 451). (1) Making its own the synthesis achieved in the sign, intelligence, by this inwardizing (memorizing) elevates the *single* synthesis to a univerversal, i.e. permanent, synthesis, in which name and meaning are for it objectively united, and renders the intuition (which the name originally is) a representation. Thus the import (connotation) and sign, being identified, form one representation: the representation in its inwardness is rendered concrete and gets existence for its import: all this being the work of memory which retains names (retentive Memory).

Zusatz. We shall consider memory under the three forms of:

1. the memory which retains names (retentive memory);
2. reproductive memory;
3. mechanical memory.

Of primary importance here, therefore, is the retention of the meaning of names, of our ability to remember the ideas objectively linked to language-signs. Thus when we hear or see a word from a foreign language, its meaning becomes present to our mind; but it does not follow that the converse is true, that we can produce for our ideas the corresponding word-signs in that language. We learn to speak and write a language later than we understand it.

§ 462

The name is thus the thing so far as it exists and counts in the ideational realm. (2) In the name, *Reproductive* memory has and recognizes the thing, and with the thing it has the name, apart from intuition and image. The name, as giving an *existence* to the content in intelligence, is the externality of intelligence to itself; and the inwardizing or recollection of the name, i.e. of an intuition of intellectual origin, is at the same time a self-externalization to

[1] Gedächtnis.

which intelligence reduces itself on its own ground. The association of the particular names lies in the meaning of the features sensitive, representative, or cogitant—series of which the intelligence traverses as it feels, represents, or thinks.

Given the name lion, we need neither the actual vision of the animal, nor its image even: the name alone, if we *understand* it, is the unimaged simple representation. We *think* in names.

The recent attempts—already, as they deserved, forgotten—to rehabilitate the Mnemonic of the ancients, consist in transforming names into images, and thus again deposing memory to the level of imagination. The place of the power of memory is taken by a permanent tableau of a series of images, fixed in the imagination, to which is then attached the series of ideas forming the composition to be learned by rote. Considering the heterogeneity between the import of these ideas and those permanent images, and the speed with which the attachment has to be made, the attachment cannot be made otherwise than by shallow, silly, and utterly accidental links. Not merely is the mind put to the torture of being worried by idiotic stuff, but what is thus learnt by rote is just as quickly forgotten, seeing that the same tableau is used for getting by rote every other series of ideas, and so those previously attached to it are effaced. What is mnemonically impressed is not like what is retained in memory really got by heart, i.e. strictly produced from within outwards, from the deep pit of the ego, and thus recited, but is, so to speak, read off the tableau of fancy.—Mnemonic is connected with the common prepossession about memory, in comparison with fancy and imagination; as if the latter were a higher and more intellectual activity than memory. On the contrary, memory has ceased to deal with an image derived from intuition—the immediate and incomplete mode of intelligence; it has rather to do with an object which is the product of intelligence itself—such a *without-book*[1] as remains locked up in the *within-book*[2] of intelligence, and is, within intelligence, only its outward and existing side.

Zusatz. The word as *sounded* vanishes in *time*; the latter thus demonstrates itself in the former to be an *abstract*, that is to say, merely *destructive,*

---

[1] Auswendiges.   [2] Inwendiges.

negativity. The true, concrete negativity of the language-sign is *intelligence*, since by this the sign is changed from something outward to something inward and as thus transformed is preserved. Words thus attain an existence animated by thought. This existence is absolutely necessary to our thoughts. We only know our thoughts, only have definite, actual thoughts, when we give them the form of objectivity, of a being distinct from our inwardness, and therefore the shape of externality, and of an externality, too, that at the same time bears the stamp of the highest inwardness. The articulated sound, the *word*, is alone such an inward externality. To want to think without words as Mesmer once attempted is, therefore, a manifestly irrational procedure which, as Mesmer himself admitted, almost drove him insane. But it is also ridiculous to regard as a defect of thought and a misfortune, the fact that it is tied to a word; for although the common opinion is that it is just the *ineffable* that is the most excellent, yet this opinion, cherished by conceit, is unfounded, since what is ineffable is, in truth, only something obscure, fermenting, something which gains clarity only when it is able to put itself into words. Accordingly, the word gives to thoughts their highest and truest existence. Of course, one can also indulge in a mass of verbiage, yet fail to grasp the matter in hand. But then what is at fault is not the word, but a defective, vague, superficial thinking. Just as the true *thought* is the very thing itself, so too is the *word* when it is employed by genuine thinking. Intelligence, therefore, in filling itself with the word, receives into itself the nature of the thing. But this reception has, at the same time, the meaning that intelligence thereby takes on the nature of a *thing* and to such a degree that subjectivity, in its distinction from the thing, becomes quite empty, a mindless container of words, that is, a mechanical memory. In this way the profusion of remembered words can, so to speak, switch round to become the extreme alienation of intelligence. The more familiar I become with the meaning of the word, the more, therefore, that this becomes united with my inwardness, the more can the objectivity, and hence the definiteness, of meaning, vanish and consequently the more can memory itself, and with it also the words, become something bereft of mind.

§ 463

(3) As the interconnection of the names lies in the meaning, the conjunction of their meaning with the reality as names is still an (external) synthesis; and intelligence in this its externality has not made a complete and simple return into self. But intelligence is the universal—the single plain truth of its particular self-divestments; and its consummated appropriation of them abolishes that distinction between meaning and name. This supreme inwardizing of representation is the supreme self-divestment of intelligence,

in which it renders itself the mere *being*, the universal space of names as such, i.e. of meaningless words. The ego, which is this abstract being, is, because subjectivity, at the same time the power over the different names—the link which, having nothing in itself, fixes in itself series of them and keeps them in stable order. So far as they merely *are*, and intelligence is here itself this *being* of theirs, its power is a merely abstract subjectivity—memory; which, on account of the complete externality in which the members of such series stand to one another, and because it is itself this externality (subjective though that be), is called mechanical (§ 195).

A composition is, as we know, not thoroughly conned by rote, until one attaches no meaning to the words. The recitation of what has been thus got by heart is therefore of course accentless. The correct accent, if it is introduced, suggests the meaning: but this introduction of the signification of an idea disturbs the mechanical nexus and therefore easily throws out the reciter. The faculty of conning by rote series of words, with no principle governing their succession, or which are separately meaningless, for example, a series of proper names, is so supremely marvellous, because it is the very essence of mind to have its wits about it; whereas in this case the mind is estranged in itself, and its action is like machinery. But it is only as uniting subjectivity with objectivity that the mind has its wits about it. Whereas in the case before us, after it has in intuition been at first so external as to pick up its facts ready made, and in representation inwardizes or recollects this datum and makes it its own—it proceeds as memory to make itself external in itself, so that what is its own assumes the guise of something found. Thus one of the two dynamic factors of thought, viz. objectivity, is here put in intelligence itself as a quality of it.—It is only a step further to treat memory as mechanical—the act implying no intelligence—in which case it is only justified by its uses, its indispensability perhaps for other purposes and functions of mind. But by so doing we overlook the proper signification it has in the mind.

§ 464

If it is to be the fact and true objectivity, the mere name as an existent requires something else—to be interpreted by the representing intellect. Now in the shape of mechanical memory, intelligence is at once that external objectivity and the meaning. In this way intelligence is explicitly made an *existence* of this identity, i.e. it is explicitly active as such an identity which as reason it is implicitly. Memory is in this manner the passage into the function of *thought*, which no longer has a *meaning*, i.e. its objectivity is no longer severed from the subjective, and its inwardness does not need to go outside for its existence.

The German language has etymologically assigned memory (*Gedächtnis*), of which it has become a foregone conclusion to speak contemptuously, the high position of direct kindred with thought (*Gedanke*).—It is not matter of chance that the young have a better memory than the old, nor is their memory solely exercised for the sake of utility. The young have a good memory because they have not yet reached the stage of reflection; their memory is exercised with or without design so as to level the ground of their inner life to pure being or to pure space in which the fact, the implicit content, may reign and unfold itself with no antithesis to a subjective inwardness. Genuine ability is in youth generally combined with a good memory. But empirical statements of this sort help little towards a knowledge of what memory intrinsically is. To comprehend the position and meaning of memory and to understand its organic interconnection with thought is one of the hardest points, and hitherto one quite unregarded in the theory of mind. Memory *qua* memory is itself the merely *external* mode, or merely *existential* aspect of thought, and thus needs a complementary element. The passage from it to thought is to our view or implicitly the identity of reason with this existential mode: an identity from which it follows that reason only exists in a subject, and as the function of that subject. Thus active reason is *Thinking*.

(γ) *Thinking*[1]

§ 465

Intelligence is recognitive: it cognizes an intuition, but only because that intuition is already its own (§ 454); and in the name it rediscovers the fact (§ 462): but now it finds *its* universal in the double signification of the universal as such, and of the universal as immediate or as being—finds that is the genuine universal which is its own unity overlapping and including its other, viz. being. Thus intelligence is explicitly, and on its own part cognitive: *virtually* it is the universal—its product (the thought) is the thing: it is a plain identity of subjective and objective. It knows that what is *thought*, *is*, and that what *is*, only *is* in so far as it is a thought (§§ 5, 21); the thinking of intelligence is to *have thoughts*: these are as its content and object.

Zusatz. Thinking is the third and last main stage in the development of intelligence; for in it the *immediate, implicit* unity of subjectivity and objectivity present in intuition is restored out of the opposition of these two sides in representation as a unity enriched by this opposition, hence as a unity both in essence and in actuality. The end is accordingly bent back into the beginning. Whereas, then, at the stage of representation the unity of subjectivity and objectivity effected partly by imagination and partly by mechanical memory—though in the latter I do violence to my subjectivity—still retains a subjective character, in thinking, on the other hand, this unity receives the form of a unity that is both subjective and objective, since it knows itself to be the *nature of the thing*. Those who have no comprehension of philosophy become speechless, it is true, when they hear the proposition that *Thought* is *Being*. None the less, underlying all our actions is the presupposition of the unity of Thought and Being. It is as rational, thinking beings that we make this presupposition. But it is well to distinguish between only *being* thinkers, and *knowing* ourselves as thinkers. The former we always are in all circumstances; but the latter, on the contrary, is perfectly true only when we have risen to *pure* thinking. Pure thinking knows that it alone, and not feeling or representation, is capable of grasping the truth of things, and that the assertion of Epicurus that the true is what is sensed, must be pronounced a complete perversion of the nature of mind. Of course, thinking must not stop at abstract, formal thinking, for this breaks up the content of truth, but must always develop into concrete thinking, to a cognition that *comprehends* its object.

[1] Das Denken.

§ 466

But cognition by thought is still in the first instance formal: the universality and its being is the plain subjectivity of intelligence. The thoughts therefore are not yet fully and freely determinate, and the representations which have been inwardized to thoughts are so far still the given content.

Zusatz. In the first instance, thinking knows the unity of subjectivity and objectivity as a quite abstract, indeterminate unity, only a *certain* unity, not one that is *filled* or *authenticated*. The determinateness of the rational content is, therefore, still external to this unity, consequently a *given* determinateness, and cognition is hence a *formal* affair. But since this determinateness is *implicitly* contained in thinking cognition, the said formalism contradicts it and is, therefore, removed by thought.

§ 467

As dealing with this given content, thought is (α) *understanding* with its formal identity, working up the representations, that have been memorized, into species, genera, laws, forces, etc., in short into categories—thus indicating that the raw material does not get the truth of its being save in these thought-forms. As intrinsically infinite negativity, thought is (β) essentially an act of partition—*judgement*, which, however, does not break up the concept again into the old antithesis of universality and being, but distinguishes on the lines supplied by the interconnections peculiar to the concept. Thirdly (γ), thought supersedes the formal distinction and institutes at the same time an identity of the differences—thus being nominal *reason* or inferential understanding. Intelligence, as the act of thought, cognizes. And (α) understanding out of its generalities (the categories) *explains* the individual, and is then said to comprehend or understand itself: (β) in the judgement it explains the individual to be a universal (species, genus). In these forms the *content* appears as given: (γ) but in inference (syllogism) it characterizes a content from itself, by superseding that form-difference. With the perception of the necessity, the last immediacy still attaching to formal thought has vanished.

In *Logic* there was thought, but in its implicitness, and as reason develops itself in this distinction-lacking medium. So in *consciousness* thought occurs as a stage (§ 437 note). Here reason is as the truth of the antithetical distinction, as it had taken shape within the mind's own limits. Thought thus recurs again and again in these different parts of philosophy, because these parts are different only through the medium they are in and the antitheses they imply; while thought is this one and the same centre, to which as to their truth the antitheses return.

Zusatz. Prior to Kant, no distinction had been made between Understanding and Reason. But unless one wants to sink to the level of the vulgar consciousness which crudely obliterates the distinct forms of pure thought, the following distinction must be firmly established between Understanding and Reason: that for the latter, the object is determined in and for itself, is the identity of content and form, of universal and particular, whereas for the former it falls apart into form and content, into universal and particular, and into an empty 'in-itself' to which the determinateness is added from outside; that, therefore, in the thinking of the Understanding, the content is indifferent to its form, while in the comprehensive thinking of Reason the content produces its form from itself.

But though Understanding has this inherent defect just indicated, it is none the less a necessary moment of rational thinking. Its activity consists, in general, in making abstraction. When it separates the contingent from the essential it is quite in its right and appears as what in truth it ought to be. Therefore, one who pursues a substantial aim is called a man of understanding. Without Understanding, no firm character is possible, for this requires a man to hold firmly to his individual, essential nature. But also, conversely, Understanding can give to a one-sided determination the form of universality and thereby become the opposite of sound common sense, which is endowed with a sense for what is essential.

The second moment of pure thinking is judging. Intelligence which, as Understanding, forcibly separates from one another and from the object the various *abstract determinations* immediately united in the concrete individuality of the object, necessarily proceeds, in the first place, to *connect* the object with these *general determinations* of thought, hence to consider the object as *relation*, as an objective togetherness, as a totality. This activity of intelligence is often, but incorrectly, called comprehension; for from this standpoint the object is still grasped as something given, as dependent on something else by which it is conditioned. The circumstances which condition an object still have the value here of self-subsistent existences. Hence the identity of the inter-related phenomena is still only internal, and just for that reason merely external. Here, therefore, the Notion does not as yet reveal itself in its own shape, but in the form of an irrational necessity.

Only on the third stage of pure thinking is the Notion as such known. Therefore, this stage represents comprehension in the strict sense of the word. Here the universal is known as self-particularizing, and from the particularization gathering itself together into individuality; or, what is the same thing, the particular loses its self-subsistence to become a moment of the Notion. Accordingly, the universal is here no longer a form external to the content, but the true form which produces the content from itself, the self-developing Notion of the thing. Consequently, on this stage, thinking has no other content than itself, than its own determinations which constitute the immanent content of the form; in the object, it seeks and finds only itself. Here, therefore, the object is distinguished from thought only by having the form of being, of subsisting on its own account. Thus thinking stands here in a completely free relation to the object.

In this thinking, which is identical with its object, intelligence reaches its consummation, its goal; for now it is *in fact* that which in its immediacy it was only *supposed* to be, self-knowing truth, self-cognizing Reason. *Knowing* now constitutes the *subjectivity* of Reason, and *objective* Reason is posited as a *Knowing*. This reciprocal interpenetration of thinking subjectivity and objective Reason is the final result of the development of theoretical mind through the stages, antecedent to pure thinking, of intuition and mental representation.

§ 468

Intelligence which as theoretical appropriates an immediate mode of being, is, now that it has completed *taking possession*, in its own *property*: the last negation of immediacy has implicitly required that the intelligence shall itself determine its content. Thus thought, as free notion, is now also free in point of *content*. But when intelligence is aware that it is determinative of the content, which is *its* mode no less than it is a mode of being, it is Will.

Zusatz. Pure thinking is, to begin with, a disinterested (*unbefangenes*) activity in which it is absorbed in the object. But this action necessarily also becomes *objective to itself*. Since objective cognition is absolutely at home with itself in the object, it must recognize that *its* determinations are determinations of the *object*, and that, conversely, the *objectively* valid determinations *immediately present* in the object are *its* determinations. By this recollection (*Erinnerung*), this *withdrawal into itself* of intelligence, the latter becomes *will*. For the ordinary consciousness this transition does not, of course, exist; on the contrary, for ordinary thinking,

thought and will fall outside of each other. But in truth, as we have just
seen, thought determines itself into will and remains the substance of the
latter; so that without thought there can be no will, and even the uneducated person wills only in so far as he has thought; the animal, on the
other hand, because it does not think is also incapable of possessing a
will.

(b) MIND PRACTICAL[1]

§ 469

As will, the mind is aware that it is the author of its own con-
clusions, the origin of its self-fulfilment. Thus fulfilled, this
independency or individuality forms the side of existence or of
reality for the Idea of mind. As will, the mind steps into actuality;
whereas as cognition it is on the soil of notional generality. Supply-
ing its own content, the will is self-possessed, and in the widest
sense free: this is its characteristic trait. Its finitude lies in the
formalism that the spontaneity of its self-fulfilment means no
more than a general and abstract ownness, not yet identified with
matured reason. It is the function of the essential will to bring
liberty to exist in the formal will, and it is therefore the aim of that
formal will to fill itself with its essential nature, i.e. to make liberty
its pervading character, content, and aim, as well as its sphere of
existence. The essential freedom of will is, and must always be,
a thought: hence the way by which will can make itself objective
mind is to rise to be a thinking will—to give itself the content which
it can only have as it thinks itself.

True liberty, in the shape of moral life, consists in the will
finding its purpose in a universal content, not in subjective or
selfish interests. But such a content is only possible in thought and
through thought: it is nothing short of absurd to seek to banish
thought from the moral, religious, and law-abiding life.

Zusatz. Intelligence has demonstrated itself to be mind that withdraws
into itself from the object, that recollects itself in it and recognizes its
inwardness as *objectivity*. Conversely, will at the start of its self-objecti-
fication is still burdened with the form of subjectivity. But here, in the
sphere of *subjective* mind, we have only to pursue this externalization to
the point where volitional intelligence becomes objective mind, that is,

[1] Der praktische Geist.

to the point where the product of will ceases to be merely enjoyment and starts to become deed and action.

Now, in general, the course of development of practical mind is as follows.

At first, will appears in the form of immediacy; it has not yet *posited* itself as intelligence freely and objectively determining itself, but only *finds* itself as such objective determining. As such, it is (1) *practical feeling*, has a *single* content and is itself an *immediately individual, subjective* will which, as we have just said, feels itself as objectively determining, but still lacks a content that is liberated from the form of subjectivity, a content that is truly objective and universal in and for itself. For this reason, will is, to begin with, only *implicitly* or *notionally*, free. But it belongs to the Idea of freedom that the will should make its Notion, which is *freedom itself*, its content or aim. When it does this it becomes *objective* mind, constructs for itself a world of its freedom, and thus gives to its true content a self-subsistent existence. But will achieves this aim only by ridding itself of its [abstract] individuality, by developing its initially only implicit universality into a content that is universal in and for itself.

The next step on this path is made by will when (2), as impulse, it goes on to make the agreement of its inward determinateness with objectivity, which in feeling is only *given*, into an agreement that *ought* first to be *posited* by will.

The further step consists (3) in the subordination of *particular* impulses to a *universal* one—*happiness*. But since this universal is only a universality of reflection, it remains external to the particular aspect of the impulses, and is connected with this particular aspect only by the wholly abstract individual will, that is, by *caprice*.

Both the indeterminate universal of happiness as well as the immediate particularity of impulses and the abstract individuality of caprice are, in their mutual externality, untrue, and that is why they come together in the will that wills the *concrete* universal, the Notion of freedom which, as already remarked, forms the goal of practical mind.

§ 470

Practical mind, considered at first as formal or immediate will, contains a double ought—(1) in the contrast which the new mode of being projected outward by the will offers to the immediate positivity of its old existence and condition—an antagonism which in consciousness grows to correlation with external objects. (2) That first self-determination, being itself immediate, is not at once elevated into a thinking universality: the latter, therefore, virtually constitutes an obligation on the former in point of form, as it may also constitute it in point of matter;—a distinction which only exists for the observer.

(α) *Practical Sense or Feeling*[1]

§ 471

The autonomy of the practical mind at first is immediate and therefore formal, i.e. it *finds* itself as an *individuality* determined in *its* inward *nature*. It is thus 'practical feeling', or instinct of action. In this phase, as it is at bottom a subjectivity simply identical with reason, it has no doubt a rational content, but a content which as it stands is individual, and for that reason also natural, contingent and subjective—a content which may be determined quite as much by mere personalities of want and opinion, etc., and by the subjectivity which selfishly sets itself against the universal, as it may be virtually in conformity with reason.

An appeal is sometimes made to the sense (feeling) of right and morality, as well as of religion, which man is alleged to possess— to his benevolent dispositions—and even to his heart generally —i.e. to the subject so far as the various practical feelings are in it all combined. So far as this appeal implies (1) that these ideas are immanent in his own self, and (2) that when feeling is opposed to the logical understanding, it, and not the partial abstractions of the latter, *may* be the *totality*—the appeal has a legitimate meaning. But on the other hand, feeling too *may* be one-sided, unessential, and bad. The rational, which exists in the shape of rationality when it is apprehended by thought, is the same content as the *good* practical feeling has, but presented in its universality and necessity, in its objectivity and truth.

Thus it is, on the one hand, *silly* to suppose that in the passage from feeling to law and duty there is any loss of import and excellence; it is this passage which lets feeling first reach its truth. It is equally silly to consider intellect as superfluous or even harmful to feeling, heart, and will; the truth and, what is the same thing, the actual rationality of the heart and will can only be at home in

---

[1] Das praktische Gefühl.

the universality of intellect, and not in the singleness of feeling as feeling. If feelings are of the right sort, it is because of their quality or content—which is right only so far as it is intrinsically universal or has its source in the thinking mind. The difficulty for the logical intellect consists in throwing off the separation it has arbitrarily imposed between the several faculties of feeling and thinking mind, and coming to see that in the human being there is only *one* reason, in feeling, volition, and thought. Another difficulty connected with this is found in the fact that the Ideas which are the special property of the thinking mind, namely God, law and morality, can also be *felt*. But feeling is only the form of the immediate and peculiar individuality of the subject, in which these facts, like any other objective facts (which consciousness also sets over against itself), may be placed.

On the other hand, it is *suspicious* or even worse to cling to feeling and heart in place of the intelligent rationality of law, right, and duty; because all that the former holds more than the latter is only the particular subjectivity with its vanity and caprice. For the same reason it is out of place in a scientific treatment of the feelings to deal with anything beyond their form, and to discuss their content; for the latter, when thought, is precisely what constitutes, in their universality and necessity, the rights and duties which are the true works of mental autonomy. So long as we study practical feelings and dispositions specially, we have only to deal with the selfish, bad, and evil; it is these alone which belong to the individuality which retains its opposition to the universal: their content is the reverse of rights and duties, and precisely in that way do they—but only in antithesis to the latter— retain a speciality of their own.

§ 472

The 'Ought' of practical feeling is the claim of its essential autonomy to control some existing mode of fact—which is assumed to be worth nothing save as adapted to that claim. But as both, in their immediacy, lack objective determination, this relation of the *requirement* to existent fact is the utterly subjective and superficial feeling of pleasant or unpleasant.

Delight, joy, grief, etc., shame, repentance, contentment, etc., are partly only modifications of the formal 'practical feeling' in *general*, but are partly different in the features that give the special tone and character mode to their 'Ought'.

The celebrated question as to the origin of evil in the world, so far at least as evil is understood to mean what is disagreeable and painful merely, arises on this stage of the formal practical feeling. Evil is nothing but the incompatibility between what is and what ought to be. 'Ought' is an ambiguous term—indeed infinitely so, considering that casual aims may also come under the form of Ought. But where the objects sought are thus casual, evil only executes what is rightfully due to the vanity and nullity of their planning: for they themselves were radically evil. The finitude of life and mind is seen in their judgement: the contrary which is separated from them they also have as a negative in them, and thus they are the contradiction called evil. In the lifeless there is neither evil nor pain: for in inorganic nature the intelligible unity (concept) does not confront its existence and does not in the difference at the same time remain its permanent subject. Whereas in life, and still more in mind, we have this immanent distinction present: hence arises the Ought: and this negativity, subjectivity, ego, freedom are the principles of evil and pain. Jacob Böhme viewed egoity (selfhood) as pain and torment, and as the fountain of nature and of spirit.

Zusatz. Although in practical feeling, will has the form of simple self-identity, none the less, in this identity there is also difference; for though practical feeling knows its self-determining to be, on the one hand, objectively valid, to be determined in and for itself, yet, on the other hand, it also knows itself to be determined immediately or from outside, to be subjected to the *alien* determinateness of external influences (*Affectionen*). The *feeling* will is, therefore, the comparing of the immediate determinateness coming to it from outside, with the determinateness posited in it by its own nature. Since the latter has the significance of what *ought* to be, will demands that the affection shall agree with it. This agreement is the pleasant or agreeable, disagreement is the unpleasant or disagreeable.

But since this inward determinateness to which the affection is related is still an immediate one belonging to my natural individuality, is still subjective, only *felt*, the judgement resulting from this relation can be only quite superficial and contingent. Therefore, where important things are concerned, the circumstance that something is agreeable or disagreeable to me is a matter of complete indifference.

Practical feeling receives, however, still further determinations than the superficial ones just discussed.

There are, namely, in the second place, feelings which, since their content originates in intuition or representation, are more determinate than the feeling merely of agreeableness or disagreeableness. To this class of feelings belong, for example, pleasure, joy, hope, fear, anguish, pain, etc. Joy consists in the feeling of accordance of my whole being with a single event, thing, or person. Contentment, on the other hand, is more a lasting, peaceful harmony without intensity. In gaiety, however, a more lively harmony is manifested. Fear is the feeling of my Self, and at the same time of an evil that threatens to destroy my self-feeling. In terror, I feel the *sudden* discordance between something external to me and my positive self-feeling.

All these feelings have no content *immanent* in them, belonging to their own peculiar nature; the content enters into them from outside.

Lastly, there is a third kind of feelings arising when the substantial content of right, morality, ethics, and religion, which originates in *thought*, is received into the feeling will. When this happens, we have to do with feelings which are distinguished from one another by their own peculiar content which gives them their justification. To this class also belong shame and remorse, for both have, as a rule, an ethical basis. Remorse is the feeling of the discordance between my deed and my duty, or even only my advantage; in each case, therefore, between my deed and something that is determined in and for itself.

But when we said that the feelings just discussed possess their own peculiar content, this must not be understood to mean that the content of right, ethics, and religion is *necessarily* felt. That this content is not indivisibly part and parcel of the feeling is empirically evident in the fact that even a good deed can give rise to a feeling of remorse. It is, too, very far from being absolutely necessary that in relating my action to my duty, I should experience the agitation and warmth of feeling; on the contrary, I can also settle the relation in my ideational consciousness and content myself with a detached consideration of the matter.

Just as little need the content enter into feeling in the second kind of feelings discussed above. A thoughtful person, one of great character, can find something in harmony with his will without giving way to feelings of joy, and, conversely, can suffer misfortune without giving way to feelings of pain. He who gives way to such feelings is more or less caught up in the conceit of attaching special importance to the fact that just he—this particular ego—is experiencing either a piece of good fortune or the reverse.

(β) The Impulses and Choice[1]

§ 473

The practical ought is a 'real' judgement. Will, which is essentially
self-determination, finds in the conformity—as immediate and
merely *found* to hand—of the existing mode to its requirement a
negation, and something inappropriate to it. If the will is to
satisfy itself, if the implicit unity of the universality and the special
mode is to be realized, the conformity of its inner requirement and
of the existent thing ought to be its act and institution. The will,
as regards the form of its content, is at first still a natural will,
directly identical with its specific mode:—natural *impulse* and
inclination. Should, however, the totality of the practical spirit
throw itself into a single one of the many restricted forms of
impulse, each being always in conflict to another, it is *passion*.

Zusatz. In practical feeling, it is a matter of contingency whether the
immediate affection is in harmony with the inward determinateness of the
will or not. This contingency, this dependence on an external objectivity,
is in contradiction with the will that knows itself to be determined in and
for itself, that knows objectivity to be contained in its subjectivity. This
will cannot, therefore, halt at *comparing* its immanent determinateness
with an external one and merely *finding* that these two sides are in agreement, but must go on to *posit* the objectivity as a *moment* of its self-determination, and therefore to produce this agreement, its satisfaction, itself.
Volitional intelligence thereby develops into *impulse*. This is a subjective
determination of the will which is itself the source of its objectivity.
Impulse must be distinguished from mere appetite. The latter belongs,
as we saw in § 426, to *self-consciousness* and occupies, therefore, the standpoint where the opposition between subjectivity and objectivity is not as
yet overcome. It is something *single*, and seeks only what is single for a
single, momentary satisfaction. Impulse, on the other hand, since it is a
form of volitional intelligence, starts from the surmounted opposition
of subjectivity and objectivity, and embraces a series of satisfactions, hence
is a whole, a universal. At the same time, however, impulse coming as it
does from the singleness of practical feeling and forming only the first
negation of it, is still something particular. That is why the man who is
controlled by impulses is manifestly unfree.

[1] Die Triebe und die Willkühr.

§ 474

Inclinations and passions embody the same constituent features as the practical feeling. Thus, while, on one hand, they are based on the rational nature of the mind; they, on the other, as part and parcel of the still subjective and single will, are infected with contingency, and appear as particular to stand to the individual and to each other in an external relation and with a necessity which creates bondage.

The special note in *passion* is its restriction to one special mode of volition, in which the whole subjectivity of the individual is merged, be the value of that mode what it may. In consequence of this formalism, passion is neither good nor bad; the title only states that a subject has thrown his whole soul—his interests of intellect, talent, character, enjoyment—on one aim and object. Nothing great has been and nothing great can be accomplished without passion. It is only a dead, too often, indeed, a hypocritical moralizing which inveighs against the form of passion as such.

But with regard to the inclinations, the question is directly raised, Which are good and bad?—Up to what degree the good continue good;—and (as there are many, each with its private range) In what way have they, being all in one subject and hardly all, as experience shows, admitting of gratification, to suffer at least reciprocal restriction? And, first of all, as regards the numbers of these impulses and propensities, the case is much the same as with the psychical powers, whose aggregate is to form the mind theoretical—an aggregate which is now increased by the host of impulses. The nominal rationality of impulse and propensity lies merely in their general impulse not to be subjective merely, but to get realized, overcoming the subjectivity by the subject's own agency. Their genuine rationality cannot reveal its secret to a method of outer reflection which pre-supposes a number of *independent* innate tendencies and immediate instincts, and therefore is wanting in a single principle and final purpose for them. But the immanent 'reflection' of mind itself carries it beyond their particularity and their natural immediacy, and gives their contents a rationality and objectivity, in which they exist as necessary ties of social relation, as rights and duties. It is this objectification which evinces their real value, their mutual connections, and their truth. And thus it was a true perception when Plato (especially including as he did the mind's whole nature under its right) showed that the full reality of justice could be exhibited only in the *objective* phase of justice, namely in the construction of the State as the ethical life.

The answer to the question, therefore, What are the good and rational propensities, and how they are to be co-ordinated with each other? resolves itself into an exposition of the laws and forms of common life produced by the mind when developing itself as *objective* mind—a development in which the *content* of autonomous action loses its contingency and optionality. The discussion of the true intrinsic worth of the impulses, inclinations, and passions is thus essentially the theory of legal, moral, and social *duties*.

§ 475

The subject is the act of satisfying impulses, an act of (at least) formal rationality, as it translates them from the subjectivity of content (which so far is *purpose*) into objectivity, where the subject is made to close with itself. If the content of the impulse is distinguished as the thing or business from this act of carrying it out, and we regard the thing which has been brought to pass as containing the element of subjective individuality and its action, this is what is called the *interest*. Nothing therefore is brought about without interest.

An action is an aim of the subject, and it is his agency too which executes this aim: unless the subject were in this way even in the most disinterested action, i.e. unless he had an interest in it, there would be no action at all.—The impulses and inclinations are sometimes depreciated by being contrasted with the baseless chimera of a happiness, the free gift of nature, where wants are supposed to find their satisfaction without the agent doing anything to produce a conformity between immediate existence and his own inner requirements. They are sometimes contrasted, on the whole to their disadvantage, with the morality of duty for duty's sake. But impulse and passion are the very life-blood of all action: they are needed if the agent is really to be in his aim and the execution thereof. The morality concerns the content of the aim, which as such is the universal, an inactive thing, that finds its actualizing in the agent; and finds it only when the aim is immanent in the agent, is his interest and—should it claim to engross his whole efficient subjectivity—his passion.

Zusatz. Even in the purest righteous, ethical, and religious will whose sole content is its Notion, that is, *freedom*, there is also involved the separation into a particular, natural individual. This moment of individuality must be satisfied even in the pursuit of the most objective aims; I, as this individual, do not wish, nor ought I, to perish in the pursuit of the aim. This is my *interest*, and this must not be confused with *selfishness*, for this *prefers* its particular content to the objective content.

§ 476

The will, as thinking and implicitly free, distinguishes itself from the particularity of the impulses, and places itself as simple subjectivity of thought above their diversified content. It is thus 'reflecting' will.

§ 477

Such a particularity of impulse has thus ceased to be a mere datum: the reflective will now sees it as its own, because it closes with it and thus gives itself specific individuality and actuality. It is now on the standpoint of *choosing* between inclinations, and is option or *choice*.

§ 478

Will as choice claims to be free, reflected into itself as the negativity of its merely immediate autonomy. However, as the content, in which its former universality concludes itself to actuality, is nothing but the content of the impulses and appetites, it is actual only as a subjective and contingent will. It realizes itself in a particularity, which it regards at the same time as a nullity, and finds a satisfaction in what it has at the same time emerged from. As thus contradictory, it is the process of distraction and of suspending one desire or enjoyment by another—and one satisfaction, which is just as much no satisfaction, by another, without end.

But the truth of the particular satisfactions is the universal, which under the name of *happiness* the thinking will makes its aim.

(γ) *Happiness*[1]

§ 479

In this idea, which reflection and comparison have educed, of a universal satisfaction, the impulses, so far as their particularity goes, are reduced to a mere negative; and it is held that partly they are to be sacrificed to each other for the behoof of that aim, partly sacrificed to that aim directly, either altogether or in part. Their mutual limitation, on one hand, proceeds from a mixture of qualitative and quantitative considerations: on the other hand, as happiness has its sole *affirmative* contents in the springs of action, it is on them that the decision turns, and it is the subjective feeling and good pleasure which must have the casting vote as to where happiness is to be placed.

§ 480

Happiness is the mere abstract and merely imagined universality of things desired—a universality which only ought to be. But the particularity of the satisfaction which just as much *is* as it is abolished, and the abstract singleness, the option which gives or does not give itself (as it pleases) an aim in happiness, find their truth in the intrinsic *universality* of the will, i.e. its very autonomy or freedom. In this way choice is will only as pure subjectivity, which is pure and concrete at once, by having for its contents and aim only that infinite mode of being—freedom itself. In this truth of its autonomy where concept and object are one, the will is an *actually free will*.

Free Mind[2]

§ 481

Actual free will is the unity of theoretical and practical mind: a free will, which realizes its own freedom of will, now that the

---

[1] Die Glückseligkeit.   [2] Der freie Geist.

formalism, fortuitousness, and contractedness of the practical
content up to this point have been superseded. By superseding the
adjustments of means therein contained, the will is the *immediate
individuality* self-instituted—an individuality, however, also purified of all that interferes with its universalism, i.e. with freedom
itself. This universalism the will has as its object and aim, only
so far as it thinks itself, knows this its concept, and is *will* as free
intelligence.

§ 482

The mind which knows itself as free and wills itself as this its
object, i.e. which has its true being for characteristic and aim,
is in the first instance the rational will in general, or *implicit* Idea,
and because implicit only the *notion* of absolute mind. As *abstract*
Idea again, it is existent only in the *immediate* will—it is the
existential side of reason—the *single* will as aware of this its universality constituting its contents and aim, and of which it is only the
formal activity. If the will, therefore, in which the Idea thus appears
is only finite, that will is also the act of developing the Idea, and
of investing its self-unfolding content with an existence which,
as realizing the idea, is *actuality*. It is thus 'Objective' Mind.

No Idea is so generally recognized as indefinite, ambiguous,
and open to the greatest misconceptions (to which therefore it
actually falls a victim) as the idea of Liberty: none in common
currency with so little appreciation of its meaning. Remembering
that free mind is *actual* mind, we can see how misconceptions
about it are of tremendous consequence in practice. When individuals and nations have once got in their heads the abstract
concept of full-blown liberty, there is nothing like it in its uncontrollable strength, just because it is the very essence of mind,
and that as its very actuality. Whole continents, Africa and the
East, have never had this Idea, and are without it still. The
Greeks and Romans, Plato and Aristotle, even the Stoics, did not
have it. On the contrary, they saw that it is only by birth (as, for
example, an Athenian or Spartan citizen), or by strength of character, education, or philosophy (—the sage is free even as a slave
and in chains) that the human being is actually free. It was through
Christianity that this Idea came into the world. According to

Christianity, the individual *as such* has an infinite value as the object and aim of divine love, destined as mind to live in absolute relationship with God himself, and have God's mind dwelling in him: i.e. man is implicitly destined to supreme freedom. If, in religion as such, man is aware of this relationship to the absolute mind as his true being, he has also, even when he steps into the sphere of secular existence, the divine mind present with him, as the substance of the state, of the family, etc. These institutions are due to the guidance of that spirit, and are constituted after its measure; whilst by their existence the moral temper comes to be indwelling in the individual, so that in this sphere of particular existence, of present sensation and volition, he is *actually* free.

If to be aware of the Idea—to be aware, that is, that men are aware of freedom as their essence, aim, and object—is matter of *speculation*, still this very Idea itself is the actuality of men—not something which they *have*, as men, but which they *are*. Christianity in its adherents has realized an ever-present sense that they are not and cannot be slaves; if they are made slaves, if the decision as regards their property rests with an arbitrary will, not with laws or courts of justice, they would find the very substance of their life outraged. This will to liberty is no longer an *impulse* which demands its satisfaction, but the permanent character—the spiritual consciousness grown into a non-impulsive nature. But this freedom, which the content and aim of freedom has, is itself only a notion—a principle of the mind and heart, intended to develop into an objective phase, into legal, moral, religious, and not less into scientific actuality.

SECTION TWO ✦ MIND OBJECTIVE

§ 483

The objective Mind is the absolute Idea, but only existing *in posse*: and as it is thus on the territory of finitude, its actual rationality retains the aspect of external apparency. The free will finds itself immediately confronted by differences which arise from the circumstance that freedom is its *inward* function and aim, and is in relation to an external and already subsisting objectivity, which splits up into different heads: viz. anthropological data (i.e. private and personal needs), external things of nature which exist for consciousness, and the ties of relation between individual wills which are conscious of their own diversity and particularity. These aspects constitute the external material for the embodiment of the will.

§ 484

But the purposive action of this will is to realize its concept, Liberty, in these externally objective aspects, making the latter a world moulded by the former, which in it is thus at home with itself, locked together with it: the concept accordingly perfected to the Idea. Liberty, shaped into the actuality of a world, receives the *form of Necessity*, the deeper substantial nexus of which is the system or organization of the principles of liberty, whilst its phenomenal nexus is power or authority, and the sentiment of obedience awakened in consciousness.

§ 485

This unity of the rational will with the single will (this being the peculiar and immediate medium in which the former is actualized) constitutes the simple actuality of liberty. As it (and its content) belongs to thought, and is the virtual *universal*, the content has its right and true character only in the form of universality. When invested with this character for the intelligent consciousness, or instituted as an authoritative power, it is a *Law*.[1] When, on the

[1] Gesetz

other hand, the content is freed from the mixedness and fortuitousness, attaching to it in the practical feeling and in impulse, and is
set and grafted in the individual will, not in the form of impulse,
but in its universality, so as to become its habit, temper, and
character, it exists as manner and custom, or *Usage*.[1]

§ 486

This 'reality', in general, where free will has *existence*, is the *Law*
(Right)—the term being taken in a comprehensive sense not
merely as the limited juristic law, but as the actual body of all the
conditions of freedom. These conditions, in relation to the *subjective*
will, where they, being universal, ought to have and can only have
their existence, are its *Duties*; whereas as its temper and habit they
are *Manners*. What is a right is also a duty, and what is a duty, is
also a right. For a mode of existence is a right, only as a consequence of the free substantial will: and the same content of fact,
when referred to the will distinguished as subjective and individual,
is a duty. It is the same content which the subjective consciousness
recognizes as a duty, and brings into existence in these several
wills. The finitude of the objective will thus creates the semblance
of a distinction between rights and duties.

In the phenomenal range right and duty are *correlata*, at least in
the sense that to a right on my part corresponds a duty in some one
else. But, in the light of the concept, my right to a thing is not
merely possession, but as possession by a *person* it is *property*, or
legal possession, and it is a *duty* to possess things as *property*, i.e. to
be as a person. Translated into the phenomenal relationship, viz.
relation to another person—this grows into the duty of some one
else to respect *my* right. In the morality of the conscience, duty in
general is in me—a free subject—at the same time a right of my
subjective will or disposition. But in this individualist moral sphere,
there arises the division between what is only inward purpose (disposition or intention), which only has its being in me and is merely
subjective duty, and the actualization of that purpose: and with
this division a contingency and imperfection which makes the
inadequacy of mere individualistic morality. In social ethics these
two parts have reached their truth, their absolute unity; although

[1] Sitte

even right and duty return to one another and combine by means of certain adjustments and under the guise of necessity. The rights of the father of the family over its members are equally duties towards them; just as the children's duty of obedience is their right to be educated to the liberty of manhood. The penal judicature of a government, its rights of administration, etc., are no less its duties to punish, to administer, etc.; as the services of the members of the State in dues, military service, etc., are duties and yet their right to the protection of their private property and of the general substantial life in which they have their root. All the aims of society and the State are the private aims of the individuals. But the set of adjustments, by which their duties come back to them as the exercise and enjoyment of right, produces an appearance of diversity: and this diversity is increased by the variety of shapes which value assumes in the course of exchange, though it remains intrinsically the same. Still it holds fundamentally good that he who has no rights has no duties and vice versa.

Subdivision
§ 487

The free will is:

(A) Itself at first immediate, and hence as a single being—the *person*: the existence which the person gives to its liberty is *property*. The *Right as Right* (law) is *formal, abstract right*.

(B) When the will is reflected into self, so as to have its existence inside it, and to be thus at the same time characterized as a *particular*, it is the right of the *subjective* will, *morality* of the individual conscience.

(C) When the free will is the substantial will, made actual in the subject and conformable to its concept and rendered a totality of necessity—it is the ethics of actual life in family, civil society, and State.

A. LAW[1]

(a) PROPERTY

§ 488

Mind, in the immediacy of its self-secured liberty, is an individual, but one that knows its individuality as an absolutely free will: it is a *person*, in whom the inward sense of this freedom, as in itself still abstract and empty, has its particularity and fulfilment not yet on its own part, but on an external *thing*. This thing, as something devoid of will, has no rights against the subjectivity of intelligence and volition, and is by that subjectivity made adjectival to it, the external sphere of its liberty—*possession*.

§ 489

By the judgement of possession, at first in the outward appropriation, the thing acquires the predicate of 'mine'. But this predicate, on its own account merely 'practical', has here the signification that I import my personal will into the thing. As so characterized, possession is *property*, which as possession is a *means*, but as existence of the personality is an *end*.

§ 490

In his property the person is brought into union with himself. But the thing is an abstractly external thing, and the I in it is abstractly external. The concrete return of me into me in the externality is that I, the infinite self-relation, am as a person the repulsion of me from myself, and have the existence of my personality in the *being of other persons*, in my relation to them and in my recognition by them, which is thus mutual.

§ 491

The thing is the *mean* by which the extremes meet in one. These extremes are the persons who, in the knowledge of their identity as free, are simultaneously mutually independent. For them my will has its *definite recognizable existence* in the thing by the immediate bodily act of taking possession, or by the formation of the thing or, it may be, by mere designation of it.

[1] Das Recht.

§ 492

The casual aspect of property is that I place my will in *this* thing: so far my will is *arbitrary*, I can just as well put it in it as not—just as well withdraw it as not. But so far as my will lies in a thing, it is only I who can withdraw it: it is only with my will that the thing can pass to another, whose property it similarly becomes only with his will:—*Contract*.

(*b*) CONTRACT

§ 493

The two wills and their agreement in the contract are as an *internal* state of mind different from its realization in the *performance*. The comparatively 'ideal' utterance (of contract) in the *stipulation* contains the actual surrender of a property by the one, its changing hands, and its acceptance by the other will. The contract is thus thoroughly binding: it does not need the performance of the one or the other to become so—otherwise we should have an infinite regress or infinite division of thing, labour, and time. The utterance in the stipulation is complete and exhaustive. The inwardness of the will which surrenders and the will which accepts the property is in the realm of ideation, and in that realm the word is deed and thing (§ 462)—the full and complete deed, since here the conscientiousness of the will does not come under consideration (as to whether the thing is meant in earnest or is a deception), and the will refers only to the external thing.

§ 494

Thus in the stipulation we have the *substantial* being of the contract standing out in distinction from its real utterance in the performance, which is brought down to a mere sequel. In this way there is put into the thing or performance a distinction between its immediate specific *quality* and its substantial being or *value*, meaning by value the quantitative terms into which that qualitative feature has been translated. One piece of property is thus made comparable with another, and may be made equivalent to a thing which is (in quality) wholly heterogeneous. It is thus treated in general as an abstract, universal thing or commodity.

§ 495

The contract, as an agreement which has a voluntary origin and deals with a casual commodity, involves at the same time the giving to this 'accidental' will a positive fixity. This will may just as well not be conformable to law (right), and, in that case, produces a *wrong*: by which, however, the absolute law (right) is not superseded, but only a relationship originated of right to wrong.

(c) RIGHT *versus* WRONG

§ 496

Law (right) considered as the realization of liberty in externals, breaks up into a multiplicity of relations to this external sphere and to other persons (§§ 491, 493 seqq.). In this way there are (1) several titles or grounds at law, of which (seeing that property both on the personal and the real side is exclusively individual) only one is the right, but which, because they face each other, each and all are invested with a *show* of right, against which the former is defined as the intrinsically right.

§ 497

Now so long as (compared against this show) the one intrinsically right, still presumed identical with the several titles, is affirmed, willed, and recognized, the only diversity lies in this, that the special thing is subsumed under the one law or right by the *particular* will of *these* several persons. This is naïve, non-malicious wrong. Such wrong in the several claimants is a simple *negative judgement*, expressing the *civil suit*. To settle it there is required a third judgement, which, as the judgement of the intrinsically right, is disinterested, and a power of giving the one right existence as against that semblance.

§ 498

But (2) if the semblance of right as such is willed *against* the right intrinsically by the particular will, which thus becomes *wicked*, then the external *recognition* of right is separated from the right's true value; and while the former only is respected, the latter is violated. This gives the wrong of *fraud*—the infinite judgement as identical

(§ 173)—where the nominal relation is retained, but the sterling value is let slip.

§ 499

(3) Finally, the particular will sets itself in opposition to the intrinsic right by negating that right itself as well as its recognition or semblance. (Here there is a negatively infinite judgement (§ 173) in which there is denied the class as a whole, and not merely the particular mode—in this case the apparent recognition.) Thus the will is violently wicked, and commits a *crime*.

§ 500

As an outrage on right, such an action is essentially and actually null. In it the agent, as a volitional and intelligent being, sets up a law—a law, however, which is nominal and recognized by him only—a universal which holds good *for him*, and under which he has at the same time subsumed himself by his action. To display the nullity of such an act, to carry out simultaneously this nominal law and the intrinsic right, in the first instance by means of a subjective individual will, is the work of *Revenge*. But revenge, starting from the interest of an immediate particular personality, is at the same time only a new outrage; and so on without end. This progression, like the last, abolishes itself in a third judgement, which is disinterested—*punishment*.

§ 501

The instrumentality by which authority is given to intrinsic right is (α) that a particular will, that of the judge, being conformable to the right, has an interest to turn against the crime (which in the first instance, in revenge, is a matter of chance), and (β) that an executive power (also in the first instance casual) negates the negation of right that was created by the criminal. This negation of right has its existence in the will of the criminal; and consequently revenge or punishment directs itself against the person or property of the criminal and exercises *coercion* upon him. It is in this legal sphere that coercion in general has possible scope—compulsion against the thing, in seizing and maintaining it against another's seizure: for in this sphere the will has its existence immediately in externals as such, or in corporeity, and can be seized only in this quarter. But more than *possible* compulsion is not, so long as I can withdraw myself as free from every mode of existence, even from the range of all existence, i.e. from life. It is legal only as abolishing a first and original compulsion.

§ 502

A distinction has thus emerged between the law (right) and the subjective will. The 'reality' of right, which the personal will in the first instance gives itself in immediate wise, is seen to be due to the instrumentality of the subjective will—whose influence as on one hand it gives existence to the essential right, so may on the other cut itself off from and oppose itself to it. Conversely, the claim of the subjective will to be in this abstraction a power over the law of right is null and empty of itself: it gets truth and reality essentially only so far as that will in itself realises the reasonable will. As such it is *morality*[1] proper.

The phrase 'Law of Nature', or Natural Right,[2] in use for the philosophy of law involves the ambiguity that it may mean either right as something existing ready-formed in nature, or right as governed by the nature of things, i.e. by the notion. The former used to be the common meaning, accompanied with the fiction of a *state of nature*, in which the law of nature should hold sway; whereas the social and political state rather required and implied a restriction of liberty and a sacrifice of natural rights. The real fact is that the whole law and its every article are based on free person-ality alone—on self-determination or autonomy, which is the very contrary of determination by nature. The law of nature—strictly so called—is for that reason the predominance of the strong and the reign of force, and a state of nature a state of violence and wrong, of which nothing truer can be said than that one ought to depart from it. The social state, on the other hand, is the condition in which alone right has its actuality: what is to be restricted and sacrificed is just the wilfulness and violence of the state of nature.

[1] Moralität.   [2] Naturrecht.

B. THE MORALITY OF CONSCIENCE[1]

§ 503

The free individual, who, in mere law, counts only as a *person*, is now characterized as a *subject*—a will reflected into itself so that, be its affection what it may, it is distinguished (as existing in it) as *its own* from the existence of freedom in an external thing. Because the affection of the will is thus inwardized, the will is at the same time made a particular, and there arise further particularizations of it and relations of these to one another. This affection is partly the essential and implicit will, the reason of the will, the essential basis of law and moral life: partly it is the existent volition, which is before us and throws itself into actual deeds, and thus comes into relationship with the former. The subjective will is *morally* free, so far as these features are its inward institution, its own, and willed by it. Its utterance in deed with this freedom is an *action*, in the externality of which it only admits as its own, and allows to be imputed to it, so much as it has consciously willed.

This subjective or 'moral' freedom is what a European especially calls freedom. In virtue of the right thereto a man must possess a personal knowledge of the distinction between good and evil in general: ethical and religious principles shall not merely lay their claim on him as external laws and precepts of authority to be obeyed, but have their assent, recognition, or even justification in his heart, sentiment, conscience, intelligence, etc. The subjectivity of the will in itself is its supreme aim and absolutely essential to it.

The 'moral' must be taken in the wider sense in which it does not signify the morally good merely. In French *le moral* is opposed to *le physique*, and means the mental or intellectual in general. But here the moral signifies volitional mode, so far as it is in the interior of the will in general; it thus includes purpose and intention—and also moral wickedness.

(a) PURPOSE[2]

§ 504

So far as the action comes into immediate touch with *existence, my part* in it is to this extent formal, that external existence is also *independent* of the agent. This externally can pervert his action and bring to light something else than lay in it. Now, though any alteration as such, which is set on foot by the subjects' action, is its *deed*,[1] still the subject does not for that reason recognize it as its *action*,[2] but only admits as its own that existence in the deed which lay in its knowledge and will, which was its *purpose*. Only for that does it hold itself *responsible*.

(*b*) INTENTION AND WELFARE[3]

§ 505

As regards its empirically concrete *content* (1) the action has a variety of particular aspects and connections. In point of *form*, the agent must have known and willed the action in its essential feature, embracing these individual points. This is the right of *intention*. While *purpose* affects only the immediate fact of existence, *intention* regards the underlying essence and aim thereof. (2) The agent has no less the right to see that the particularity of content in the action, in point of its matter, is not something external to him, but is a particularity of his own—that it contains his needs, interests, and aims. These aims, when similarly comprehended in a single aim, as in happiness (§ 479), constitute his *well-being*. This is the right to well-being. Happiness (good fortune) is distinguished from well-being only in this, that happiness implies no more than some sort of immediate existence, whereas well-being is regarded as having a moral justification.

§ 506

But the essentiality of the intention is in the first instance the abstract form of generality. Reflection can put in this form this and that particular aspect in the empirically concrete action, thus making it essential to the intention or restricting the intention to it. In this way the supposed essentiality of the intention and the real essentiality of the action may be brought into the greatest contradiction—e.g. a good intention in case of a crime. Similarly well-being is abstract and may be placed in this or that: as appertaining to this single agent, it is always something particular.

---

[1] That. [2] Handlung. [3] Die Absicht und das Wohl.

(c) GOODNESS AND WICKEDNESS[1]

§ 507

The truth of these particularities and the concrete unity of their formalism is the content of the universal, essential and actual, will—the law and underlying essence of c very phase of volition, the essential and actual good. It is thus the absolute final aim of the world, and *duty* for the agent who *ought* to have *insight* into the *good*, make it his *intention* and bring it about by his activity.

§ 508

But though the good is the universal of will—a universal determined in itself—and thus including in it particularity—still so far as this particularity is in the first instance still abstract, there is no principle at hand to determine it. Such determination therefore starts up also outside that universal; and as heteronomy or determinance of a will which is free and has rights of its own, there awakes here the deepest contradiction. (α) In consequence of the indeterminate determinism of the good, there are always *several sorts* of good and *many kinds of duties*, the variety of which is a dialectic of one against another and brings them into *collision*. At the same time because good is one, they *ought* to stand in harmony; and yet each of them, though it is a particular duty, is as good and as duty absolute. It falls upon the agent to be the dialectic which, superseding this absolute claim of each, concludes such a combination of them as excludes the rest.

§ 509

(β) To the agent, who in his existent sphere of liberty is essentially as a *particular*, his *interest and welfare* must, on account of that existent sphere of liberty, be essentially an aim and therefore a duty. But at the same time in aiming at the good, which is the not-particular but only universal of the will, the particular interest *ought not* to be a constituent motive. On account of this independency of the two principles of action, it is likewise an accident whether they harmonize. And yet they *ought* to harmonize, because the agent, as individual and universal, is always fundamentally one identity.

[1] Das Gute und das Böse.

(γ) But the agent is not only a mere particular in his existence; it is also a form of his existence to be an abstract self-certainty, an abstract reflection of freedom into himself. He is thus distinct from the reason in the will, and capable of making the universal itself a particular and in that way a semblance. The good is thus reduced to the level of a mere 'may happen' for the agent, who can therefore decide on something opposite to the good, can be wicked.

§ 510

(δ) The external objectivity, following the distinction which has arisen in the subjective will (§ 503), constitutes a peculiar world of its own—another extreme which stands in no rapport with the internal will-determination. It is thus a matter of chance whether it harmonizes with the subjective aims, whether the good is realized, and the wicked, an aim essentially and actually null, nullified in it: it is no less matter of chance whether the agent finds in it his well-being, and more precisely whether in the world the good agent is happy and the wicked unhappy. But at the same time the world *ought* to allow the good action, the essential thing, to be carried out in it; it *ought* to grant the good agent the satisfaction of his particular interest, and refuse it to the wicked; just as it *ought* also to make the wicked itself null and void.

§ 511

The all-round contradiction, expressed by this repeated *ought*, with its absoluteness which yet at the same time is *not*—contains the most abstract 'analysis' of the mind in itself, its deepest descent into itself. The only relation the self-contradictory principles have to one another is in the abstract certainty of self; and for this infinitude of subjectivity the universal will, good, right, and duty, no more exist than not. The subjectivity alone is aware of itself as choosing and deciding. This pure self-certitude, rising to its pitch, appears in the two directly inter-changing forms—of *Conscience* and *Wickedness*. The former is the will of goodness; but a goodness which to this pure subjectivity is the *non-objective*, non-universal, the unutterable; and over which the agent is conscious that *he* in his *individuality* has the decision. Wickedness is the same awareness that the single self possesses the decision, so far as the single self does not merely remain in this abstraction, but takes up the content of a subjective interest contrary to the good.

§ 512

This supreme pitch of the '*phenomenon*' of will—sublimating itself to this absolute vanity—to a goodness, which has no objectivity, but is only sure of itself, and a self-assurance which involves the nullification of the universal—collapses by its own force. Wickedness, as the most intimate reflection of subjectivity itself, in opposition to the objective and universal (which it treats as mere sham) is the same as the good sentiment of abstract goodness, which reserves to the subjectivity the determination thereof:—the utterly abstract semblance, the bare perversion and annihilation of itself. The result, the truth of this semblance, is, on its negative side, the absolute nullity of this volition which would fain hold its own against the good, and of the good, which would only be abstract. On the affirmative side, in the notion, this semblance thus collapsing is the same simple universality of the will, which is the good. The subjectivity, in this its *identity* with the good, is only the infinite form, which actualizes and develops it. In this way the standpoint of bare reciprocity between two independent sides— the standpoint of the *ought*, is abandoned, and we have passed into the field of ethical life.

C. THE MORAL LIFE, OR SOCIAL ETHICS[1]

§ 513

The moral life is the perfection of spirit objective—the truth of the subjective and objective spirit itself. The failure of the latter consists—partly in having its freedom *immediately* in reality, in something external therefore, in a thing—partly in the abstract universality of its goodness. The failure of spirit subjective similarly consists in this, that it is, as against the universal, abstractly self-determinant in its inward individuality. When these two imperfections are suppressed, subjective *freedom* exists as the covertly and

[1] Die Sittlichkeit.

overtly *universal* rational will, which is sensible of itself and actively disposed in the consciousness of the individual subject, whilst its practical operation and immediate universal *actuality* at the same time exist as moral usage, manner and custom—where self-conscious *liberty* has become *nature*.

§ 514

The consciously free substance, in which the absolute 'ought' is no less an 'is', has actuality as the spirit of a nation. The abstract disruption of this spirit singles it out into *persons*, whose independence it, however, controls and entirely dominates from within. But the person, as an intelligent being, feels that underlying essence to be his own very being—ceases when so minded to be a mere accident of it—looks upon it as his absolute final aim. In its actuality he sees not less an achieved present, than somewhat he brings about by his action—yet somewhat which without all question *is*. Thus, without any selective reflection, the person performs his duty as *his own* and as something which *is*; and in this necessity *he* has himself and his actual freedom.

§ 515

Because the substance is the absolute unity of individuality and universality of freedom, it follows that the actuality and action of each individual to keep and to take care of his own being, while it is on one hand conditioned by the pre-supposed total in whose complex alone he exists, is on the other a transition into a universal product.—The social disposition of the individuals is their sense of the substance, and of the identity of all their interests with the total; and that the other individuals mutually know each other and are actual only in this identity, is confidence (trust)—the genuine ethical temper.

§ 516

The relations between individuals in the several situations to which the substance is particularized form their *ethical duties* The ethical personality, i.e. the subjectivity which is permeated by the substantial life, is *virtue*. In relation to the bare facts of external being, to *destiny*, virtue does not treat them as a mere negation, and is thus a quiet repose in itself: in relation to substantial objectivity, to the total of ethical actuality, it exists as confidence, as deliberate work for the community, and the capacity of sacrificing self thereto; whilst in relation to the incidental relations of social circumstance, it is in the first instance justice and then benevolence. In the latter sphere, and in its attitude to its own visible being and corporeity, the individuality expresses its special character, temperament, etc. as personal *virtues*.

§ 517

The ethical substance is:

(*a*) as 'immediate' or *natural* mind—the *Family*.

(*b*) The 'relative' totality of the 'relative' relations of the individuals as independent persons to one another in a formal universality—*Civil Society*.

(*c*) The self-conscious substance, as the mind developed to an organic actuality—the *Political Constitution*.

(*a*). THE FAMILY
§ 518

The ethical spirit, in its *immediacy*, contains the *natural* factor that the individual has its substantial existence in its natural universal, i.e. in its kind. This is the sexual tie, elevated, however, to a spiritual significance,—the unanimity of love and the temper of trust. In the shape of the family, mind appears as feeling.

§ 519

(1) The physical difference of sex thus appears at the same time as a difference of intellectual and moral type. With their exclusive individualities these personalities combine to form a *single person*: the subjective union of hearts, becoming a 'substantial' unity, makes this union an ethical tie—*Marriage*. The 'substantial' union of hearts makes marriage an indivisible personal bond—monogamic marriage: the bodily conjunction is a sequel to the moral attachment. A further sequel is community of personal and private interests.

§ 520

(2) By the community in which the various members constituting the family stand in reference to property, that property of the one person (representing the family) acquires an ethical interest, as do also its industry, labour, and care for the future.

§ 521

The ethical principle which is conjoined with the natural generation of the children, and which was assumed to have primary importance in first forming the marriage union, is actually realized in the second or spiritual birth of the children—in educating them to independent personality.

§ 522

(3) The children, thus invested with independence, leave the concrete life and action of the family to which they primarily belong, acquire an existence of their own, destined, however, to found anew such an actual family. Marriage is of course broken up by the *natural* element contained in it, the death of husband and wife: but even their union of hearts, as it is a mere 'substantiality' of feeling, contains the germ of liability to chance and decay. In virtue of such fortuitousness, the members of the family take up to each other the status of persons; and it is thus that the family finds introduced into it for the first time the element, originally foreign to it, of *legal* regulation.

(b) CIVIL SOCIETY[1]

§ 523

As the substance, being an intelligent substance, particularizes itself abstractly into many persons (the family is only a single person), into families or individuals, who exist independent and free, as private persons, it loses its ethical character: for these persons as such have in their consciousness and as their aim not the absolute unity, but their own petty selves and particular interests. Thus

---

[1] Die bürgerliche Gesellschaft.

arises the system of *atomistic*: by which the substance is reduced to a general system of adjustments to connect self-subsisting extremes and their particular interests. The developed totality of this connective system is the state as civil society, or *state external*.

(α) *The System of Wants*[1]

§ 524

(α) The particularity of the persons includes in the first instance their wants. The possibility of satisfying these wants is here laid on the social fabric, the general stock from which all derive their satisfaction. In the condition of things in which this method of satisfaction by indirect adjustment is realized, immediate seizure (§ 488) of external objects as means thereto exists barely or not at all: the objects are already property. To acquire them is only possible by the intervention, on one hand, of the possessor's will, which as particular has in view the satisfaction of their variously defined interests; while, on the other hand, it is conditioned by the ever-continued production of fresh means of exchange by the exchangers' *own labour*. This instrument, by which the labour of all facilitates satisfaction of wants, constitutes the general stock.

§ 525

(β) The glimmer of universal principle in this particularity of wants is found in the way intellect creates differences in them, and thus causes an indefinite multiplication both of wants and of means for their different phases. Both are thus rendered more and more abstract. This 'morcellement' of their content by abstraction gives rise to the *division of labour*. The habit of this abstraction in enjoyment, information, learning, and demeanour constitutes training in this sphere, or nominal culture in general.

§ 526

The labour which thus becomes more abstract tends on one hand by its uniformity to make labour easier and to increase production— on another to limit each person to a single kind of technical skill,

[1] Das System der Bedürfnisse.

and thus produce more unconditional dependence on the social system. The skill itself becomes in this way mechanical, and gets the capability of letting the machine take the place of human labour.

§ 527

(γ) But the concrete division of the general stock—which is also a general business (of the whole society)—into particular masses determined by the factors of the notion—masses each of which possesses its own basis of subsistence, and a corresponding mode of labour, of needs, and of means for satisfying them, also of aims and interests, as well as of mental culture and habit—constitutes the difference of Estates (orders or ranks). Individuals apportion themselves to these according to natural talent, skill, option, and accident. As belonging to such a definite and stable sphere, they have their actual existence, which as existence is essentially a particular; and in it they have their social morality, which is *honesty*, their recognition and their *honour*.

Where civil society, and with it the State, exists, there arise the several estates in their difference: for the universal substance, as vital, *exists* only so far as it organically *particularizes* itself. The history of constitutions is the history of the growth of these estates, of the legal relationships of individuals to them, and of these estates to one another and to their centre.

§ 528

To the 'substantial', natural estate the fruitful soil and ground supply a natural and stable capital; its action gets direction and content through natural features, and its moral life is founded on faith and trust. The second, the 'reflected' estate has as its allotment the social capital, the medium created by the action of middlemen, of mere agents, and an ensemble of contingencies, where the individual has to depend on his subjective skill, talent, intelligence, and industry. The third, 'thinking' estate has for its business the general interests; like the second it has a subsistence procured by means of its own skill, and like the first a certain subsistence, certain, however, because guaranteed through the whole society.

(β) *Administration of Justice*[1]

§ 529

When matured through the operation of natural need and free option into a system of universal relationships and a regular course of external necessity, the principle of casual particularity gets that stable articulation which liberty requires in the shape of *formal right*. (1) The actualization which right gets in this sphere of mere practical intelligence is that it be brought to consciousness as the stable universal, that it be known and stated in its specificality with the voice of authority—the *Law*.[2]

The *positive* element in laws concerns only their form of *publicity* and *authority*—which makes it possible for them to be known by all in a customary and external way. Their content *per se* may be reasonable—or it may be unreasonable and so wrong. But when right, in the course of definite manifestation, is developed in detail, and its content analyses itself to gain definiteness, this analysis, because of the finitude of its materials, falls into the falsely infinite progress: the *final* definiteness, which is absolutely essential and causes a break in this progress of unreality, can in this sphere of finitude be attained only in a way that savours of contingency and arbitrariness. Thus whetherthree years, ten thalers, or only $2\frac{1}{2}$, $2\frac{3}{4}$, $2\frac{4}{5}$ years, and so on *ad infinitum*, be the right and just thing, can by no means be decided on intelligible principles—and yet it should be decided. Hence, though of course only at the final points of deciding, on the side of external existence, the 'positive' principle naturally enters law as contingency and arbitrariness. This happens and has from of old happened in all legislations: the only thing wanted is clearly to be aware of it, and not be misled by the talk and the pretence as if the ideal of law were, or could be, to be, at *every* point, determined through reason or legal intelligence, on purely reasonable and intelligent grounds. It is a futile perfectionism to have such expectations and to make such requirements in the sphere of the finite.

There are some who look upon laws as an evil and a profanity, and who regard governing and being governed from natural love, hereditary divinity or nobility, by faith and trust, as the genuine

---

[1] Die Rechtspflege.   [2] Gesetz.

order of life, while the reign of law is held an order of corruption and injustice. These people forget that the stars—and the cattle too—are governed and well governed too by laws;—laws, however, which are only internally in these objects, not *for them*, not as laws *set to* them:—whereas it is man's privilege to *know* his law. They forget therefore that he can truly obey only such known law—even as his law can only be a just law, as it is a *known* law;—though in other respects it must be in its essential content contingency and caprice, or at least be mixed and polluted with such elements.

The same empty requirement of perfection is employed for an opposite thesis—viz. to support the opinion that a code is impossible or impracticable. In this case there comes in the additional absurdity of putting essential and universal provisions in one class with the particular detail. The finite material is definable on and on to the false infinite: but this advance is not, as in the mental images of space, a generation of new spatial characteristics of the same quality as those preceding them, but an advance into greater and ever greater speciality by the acumen of the analytic intellect, which discovers new distinctions, which again make new decisions necessary. To provisions of this sort one may give the name of *new* decisions or *new* laws; but in proportion to the gradual advance in specialization the interest and value of these provisions declines. They fall within the already subsisting 'substantial', general laws, like improvements on a floor or a door, within the house—which though something *new*, are not a new *house*. But there is a contrary case. If the legislation of a rude age began with single provisos, which go on by their very nature always increasing their number, there arises, with the advance in multitude, the need of a simpler code—the need, i.e. of embracing that lot of singulars in their general features. To find and be able to express these principles well beseems an intelligent and civilized nation. Such a gathering up of single rules into general forms, first really deserving the name of laws, has lately been begun in some directions by the English Minister Peel, who has by so doing gained the gratitude, even the admiration, of his countrymen.

§ 530

(2) The positive form of Laws—to be *promulgated and made known* as laws—is a condition of the *external obligation* to obey them;

inasmuch as, being laws of strict right, they touch only the abstract will—itself at bottom external—not the moral or ethical will. The subjectivity to which the will has in this direction a right is here only that the laws be known. This subjective existence, is as existence of the absolute truth in this sphere of Right, at the same time an externally *objective* existence, as universal authority and necessity.

The legality of property and of private transactions concerned therewith—in consideration of the principle that all law must be promulgated, recognized, and thus become authoritative—gets its universal guarantee through *formalities*.

§ 531

(3) Legal forms get the necessity, to which objective existence determines itself, in the *judicial system*. Abstract right has to exhibit itself to the *court*—to the individualized right—as *proven*:—a process in which there may be a difference between what is abstractly right and what is provably right. The court takes cognisance and action in the interest of right as such, deprives the existence of right of its contingency, and in particular transforms this existence—as this exists as revenge—into *punishment* (§ 500).

The comparison of the two species, or rather two elements in the judicial conviction, bearing on the actual state of the case in relation to the accused—(1) according as that conviction is based on mere circumstances and other people's witness alone—or (2) in addition requires the confession of the accused, constitutes the main point in the question of the so-called jury-courts. It is an essential point that the two ingredients of a judicial cognisance, the judgement as to the state of the fact, and the judgement as application of the law to it, should, as at bottom different sides, be exercised as *different functions*. By the said institution they are allotted even to bodies differently qualified—from the one of which individuals belonging to the official judiciary are expressly excluded. To carry this separation of functions up to this separation in the courts rests rather on extra-essential considerations: the main point remains only the separate performance of these essentially different functions.—It is a more important point whether the confession of the accused is or is not to be made a condition of penal judgement. The institution of the jury-court loses sight of this condition. The point is that on this ground certainty is completely inseparable from truth: but the confession is to be regarded as the very acme of certainty-giving which in its nature is subjective. The final decision therefore lies with the confession. To this therefore the accused has an absolute right, if the proof is to be made final and the judges to be convinced. No doubt this factor is incomplete, because it is only one factor; but still more incomplete is the other when no less abstractly taken—viz. mere circumstantial evidence. The jurors are essentially judges and pronounce a judgement. In so far, then, as all they have to go on are such objective proofs, whilst at the same time their defect of certainty (incomplete in so far as it is only *in them*) is admitted, the jury-court shows traces of its barbaric origin in a confusion and admixture between objective proofs and subjective or so-called 'moral' conviction.—It is easy to call *extraordinary* punishments an absurdity; but the fault lies rather with the shallowness which takes offence at a mere name. Materially the principle involves the difference of objective probation according as it goes with or without the factor of absolute certification which lies in confession.

§ 532

The function of judicial administration is only to actualize to necessity the abstract side of personal liberty in civil society. But this actualization rests at first on the particular subjectivity of the judge, since here as yet there is not found the necessary unity of it with right in the abstract. Conversely, the blind necessity of the system of wants is not lifted up into the consciousness of the universal, and worked from that point of view.

(γ) *Police and Corporation*[1]

§ 533

Judicial administration naturally has no concern with such part of actions and interests as belongs only to particularity, and leaves to chance not only the occurrence of crimes but also the care for public weal. In civil society the sole end is to satisfy want—and

---

[1] Die Polizei und die Corporation.

that, because it is man's want, in a uniform general way, so as to *secure* this satisfaction. But the machinery of social necessity leaves in many ways a casualness about this satisfaction. This is due to the variability of the wants themselves, in which opinion and subjective good-pleasure play a great part. It results also from circumstances of locality, from the connections between nation and nation, from errors and deceptions which can be foisted upon single members of the social circulation and are capable of creating disorder in it—as also and especially from the unequal capacity of individuals to take advantage of that general stock. The onward march of this necessity also sacrifices the very particularities by which it is brought about, and does not itself contain the affirmative aim of securing the satisfaction of individuals. So far as concerns them, it *may* be far from beneficial: yet here the individuals are the morally justifiable end.

§ 534

To keep in view this general end, to ascertain the way in which the powers composing that social necessity act, and their variable ingredients, and to maintain that end in them and against them, is the work of an institution which assumes on *one* hand, to the concrete of civil society, the position of an external universality. Such an order acts with the power of an external state, which, in so far as it is rooted in the higher or substantial state, appears as state-'police'. On the *other* hand, in this sphere of particularity the only recognition of the aim of substantial universality and the only carrying of it out is restricted to the business of particular branches and interests. Thus we have the *corporation*, in which the particular citizen in his private capacity finds the securing of his stock, whilst at the same time he in it emerges from his single private interest, and has a conscious activity for a comparatively universal end, just as in his legal and professional duties he has his social morality.

(c) THE STATE

§ 535

The State is the *self-conscious* ethical substance, the unification of the family principle with that of civil society. The same unity, which is in the family as a feeling of love, is its essence, receiving, however, at the same time through the second principle of conscious and spontaneously active volition the *form* of conscious universality. This universal principle, with all its evolution in detail, is the absolute aim and content of the knowing subject, which thus identifies itself in its volition with the system of reasonableness.

§ 536

The state is (α) its inward structure as a self-relating development—constitutional (inner-state) law: (β) a particular individual, and therefore in connection with other particular individuals—international (outer-state) law; (γ) but these particular minds are only stages in the general development of mind in its actuality: universal history.

(α) *Constitutional Law*[1]

§ 537

The essence of the state is the universal, self-originated, and self-developed—the reasonable spirit of will; but, as self-knowing and self-actualizing, sheer subjectivity, and—as an actuality—one individual. Its *work* generally—in relation to the extreme of individuality as the multitude of individuals—consists in a double function. First it maintains them as persons, thus making right a necessary actuality, then it promotes their welfare, which each originally takes care of for himself, but which has a thoroughly general side; it protects the family and guides civil society. Secondly, it carries back both, and the whole disposition and action of the individual—whose tendency is to become a centre of his own—into the life of the universal substance; and, in this direction, as a free power it interferes with those subordinate spheres and maintains them in substantial immanence.

§ 538

The laws express the special provisions for objective freedom. First, to the immediate agent, his independent self-will and particular interest, they are restrictions. But, secondly, they are an absolute final end and the universal work: hence they are a product

[1] Inneres Staatsrecht.

of the 'functions' of the various orders which parcel themselves more and more out of the general particularizing, and are a fruit of all the acts and private concerns of individuals. Thirdly, they are the substance of the volition of individuals—which volition is thereby free—and of their disposition: being as such exhibited as current usage.

§ 539

As a living mind, the state only is as an organized whole, differentiated into particular agencies, which, proceeding from the one notion (though not known as notion) of the reasonable will, continually produce it as their result. The *constitution* is this articulation or organization of state-power. It provides for the reasonable will—in so far as it is in the individuals only *implicitly* the universal will—coming to a consciousness and an understanding of itself and being *found*; also for that will being put in actuality, through the action of the government and its several branches, and not left to perish, but protected both against *their* casual subjectivity and against that of the individuals. The constitution is existent *justice*—the actuality of liberty in the development of all its reasonable provisions.

Liberty and Equality are the simple rubrics into which is frequently concentrated what should form the fundamental principle, the final aim and result of the constitution. However true this is, the defect of these terms is their utter abstractness: if stuck to in this abstract form, they are principles which either prevent the rise of the concreteness of the state, i.e. its articulation into a constitution and a government in general, or destroy them. With the state there arises inequality, the difference of governing powers and of governed, magistracies, authorities, directories, etc. The principle of equality, logically carried out, rejects all differences, and thus allows no sort of political condition to exist. Liberty and equality are indeed the foundation of the state, but as the most abstract also the most superficial, and for that very reason naturally the most familiar. It is important therefore to study them closer.

As regards, first, Equality, the familiar proposition, All men are by nature equal, blunders by confusing the 'natural' with the 'notion'. It ought rather to read: *By nature* men are only unequal. But the *notion* of liberty, as it exists as such, without further specification and development, is abstract subjectivity, as a person capable of property (§ 488). This single abstract feature of personality constitutes the actual *equality* of human beings. But that this freedom should exist, that it should be *man* (and not as in Greece, Rome, etc. *some* men) that is recognized and legally regarded as a person, is so little *by nature*, that it is rather only a result and product of the consciousness of the deepest principle of mind, and of the universality and expansion of this consciousness. That the citizens are equal before the law contains a great truth, but which so expressed is a tautology: it only states that the legal status in general exists, that the laws rule. But, as regards the concrete, the citizens—besides their personality—are equal before the law only in these points when they are otherwise equal *outside the law*. Only that equality which (in whatever way it be) they, as it happens, otherwise have in property, age, physical strength, talent, skill, etc.—or even in crime, can and ought to make them deserve equal treatment before the law:—only it can make them—as regards taxation, military service, eligibility to office, etc.—punishment, etc.—equal in the concrete. The laws themselves, except in so far as they concern that narrow circle of personality, presuppose unequal conditions, and provide for the unequal legal duties and appurtenances resulting therefrom.

As regards Liberty, it is originally taken partly in a negative sense against arbitrary intolerance and lawless treatment, partly in the affirmative sense of subjective freedom; but this freedom is allowed great latitude both as regards the agent's self-will and action for his particular ends, and as regards his claim to have a personal intelligence and a personal share in general affairs. Formerly the legally defined rights, private as well as public rights of a nation, town, etc. were called its 'liberties'. Really, every genuine law is a liberty: it contains a reasonable principle of objective mind; in other words, it embodies a liberty. Nothing has become, on the contrary, more familiar than the idea that each must *restrict* his liberty in relation to the liberty of others: that the state is a condition of such reciprocal restriction, and that the laws are restrictions. To such habits of mind liberty is viewed as only casual good-pleasure and self-will. Hence it has also been said that 'modern' nations are only susceptible of equality, or of equality more than liberty: and that for no other reason than that, with an assumed definition of liberty (chiefly the participation of all in political affairs and actions), it was impossible to make ends meet in actuality—which is at once more reasonable and more powerful than abstract presuppositions. On the contrary, it should be said that it is just the great development and maturity of form in modern states which produces the supreme concrete inequality of individuals in actuality: while, through the deeper reasonableness of laws and the greater stability of the legal state, it gives rise to greater and more stable liberty, which it can without incompatibility allow. Even the superficial distinction of the words liberty and equality points to the fact that the former tends to inequality: whereas, on the contrary, the current notions of liberty only carry us back to equality. But the more we fortify liberty,—as security of property, as possibility for each to develop and make the best of his talents and good qualities, the more it gets taken for granted: and then the sense and appreciation of liberty especially turns in a *subjective* direction. By this is meant the liberty to attempt action on every side, and to throw oneself at pleasure in action for particular and for general intellectual interests, the removal of all checks on the individual particularity, as well as the inward liberty in which the subject has principles, has an insight and conviction of his own, and thus gains moral independence. But this liberty itself on one hand implies that supreme differentiation in which men are unequal and make themselves more unequal by education; and on another it only grows up under conditions of that objective liberty, and is and could grow to such height only in modern states. If, with this development of particularity, there be simultaneous and endless increase of the number of wants, and of the difficulty of satisfying them, of the lust of argument and the fancy of detecting faults, with its insatiate vanity, it is all but part of that indiscriminating relaxation of individuality in this sphere which generates all possible complications, and must deal with them as it can. Such a sphere is of course also the field of restrictions, because liberty is there under the taint of natural self-will and self-pleasing, and has therefore to restrict itself: and that, not merely with regard to the naturalness, self-will and self-conceit, of others, but especially and essentially with regard to reasonable liberty.

The term political liberty, however, is often used to mean formal participation in the public affairs of state by the will and action even of those individuals who otherwise find their chief function in the particular aims and business of civil society. And it has in part become usual to give the title constitution only to the side of the state which concerns such participation of these individuals in general affairs, and to regard a state, in which this is not formally done, as a state without a constitution. On this use of the term the only thing to remark is that by constitution must be understood the determination of rights, i.e. of liberties in general, and the organization of the actualization of them; and that political freedom in the above sense can in any case only constitute a part of it. Of it the following paragraphs will speak.

§ 540

The guarantee of a constitution (i.e. the necessity that the laws be reasonable, and their actualization secured) lies in the collective spirit of the nation—especially in the specific way in which it is itself conscious of its reason. (Religion is that consciousness in its absolute substantiality.) But the guarantee lies also at the same time in the actual organization or development of that principle in suitable institutions. The constitution presupposes that consciousness of the collective spirit, and conversely that spirit presupposes the constitution: for the actual spirit only has a definite consciousness of its principles, in so far as it has them actually existent before it.

The question—To whom (to what authority and how organized) belongs the power to make a constitution? is the same as the question, Who has to make the spirit of a nation? Separate our idea of a constitution from that of the collective spirit, as if the latter exists or has existed without a constitution, and your fancy only proves how superficially you have apprehended the nexus between the spirit in its self-consciousness and in its actuality. What is thus called 'making' a 'constitution', is—just because of this inseparability—a thing that has never happened in history, just as little as the making of a code of laws. A constitution only develops from the national spirit identically with that spirit's own development, and runs through at the same time with it the grades of formation and the alterations required by its concept. It is the indwelling spirit and the history of the nation (and, be it added, the history is only that spirit's history) by which constitutions have been and are made.

§ 541

The really living totality—that which preserves, in other words continually produces the state in general and its constitution, is the *government*. The organization which natural necessity gives is seen in the rise of the family and of the 'estates' of civil society. The government is the *universal* part of the constitution, i.e. the part which intentionally aims at preserving those parts, but at the same time gets hold of and carries out those general aims of the whole which rise above the function of the family and of civil society. The organization of the government is likewise its differentiation into powers, as their peculiarities have a basis in principle; yet without that difference losing touch with the *actual unity* they have in the notion's subjectivity.

As the most obvious categories of the notion are those of *universality* and *individuality*, and their relationship that of *subsumption* of individual under universal, it has come about that in the state the legislative and executive power have been so distinguished as to make the former *exist* apart as the absolute superior, and to subdivide the latter again into administrative (government) power and judicial power, according as the laws are applied to public or private affairs. The *division* of these powers has been treated as *the* condition of political equilibrium, meaning by division their *independence* one of another in existence—subject always, however, to the abovementioned subsumption of the powers of the individual under the power of the general. The theory of such 'division' unmistakably implies the elements of the notion, but so combined by 'understanding' as to result in an absurd collocation, instead of the self-redintegration of the living spirit. The one essential canon to make liberty deep and real is to give every business belonging to the general interests of the state a separate organization wherever they are essentially distinct. Such real division must be: for liberty is only deep when it is differentiated in all its fullness and these differences manifested in existence. But to make the business of legislation an independent power—to make it the first power, with the further proviso that all

citizens shall have part therein, and the government be merely
executive and dependent, presupposes ignorance that the true idea,
and therefore the living and spiritual actuality, is the self-redinte-
grating notion, in other words, the subjectivity which contains in it
universality as only one of its moments. (A mistake still greater, if
it goes with the fancy that the constitution and the fundamental
laws were still one day to make—in a state of society, which includes
an already existing development of differences.) Individuality is
the first and supreme principle which makes itself felt through the
state's organization. Only through the government, and by its
embracing in itself the particular businesses (including the abstract
legislative business, which taken apart is also particular), is the
state *one*. These, as always, are the terms on which the different
elements essentially and alone truly stand towards each other in the
logic of 'reason', as opposed to the external footing they stand on in
'understanding', which never gets beyond subsuming the individual and particular under the universal. What disorganizes the
unity of logical reason, equally disorganizes actuality.

§ 542

In the government—regarded as organic totality—the sovereign
power (principate) is (*a*) *subjectivity* as the *infinite* self-unity of the
notion in its development;—the all-sustaining, all-decreeing will of
the state, its highest peak and all-pervasive unity. In the perfect
form of the state, in which each and every element of the notion has
reached free existence, this subjectivity is not a so-called 'moral
person', or a decree issuing from a majority (forms in which the
unity of the decreeing will has not an *actual* existence), but an
actual individual—the will of a decreeing individual,—*monarchy*.
The monarchical constitution is therefore the constitution of
developed reason: all other constitutions belong to lower grades of
the development and realization of reason.

The unification of all concrete state-powers into one existence,
as in the patriarchal society—or, as in a democratic constitution,
the participation of all in all affairs—impugns the principle of the
division of powers, i.e. the developed liberty of the constituent
factors of the Idea. But no whit less must the division (the working
out of these factors each to a free totality) be reduced to 'ideal'

unity, i.e. to *subjectivity*. The mature differentiation or realization of the Idea means, essentially, that this subjectivity should grow to be a *real* 'moment', an *actual* existence; and this actuality is not otherwise than as the individuality of the monarch—the subjectivity of abstract and final decision existent in *one* person. All those forms of collective decreeing and willing—a common will which shall be the sum and the resultant (on aristocratic or democratic principles) of the atomistic of single wills, have on them the mark of the unreality of an abstraction. Two points only are all-important, first to see the necessity of each of the notional factors, and secondly the form in which it is actualized. It is only the nature of the speculative notion which can really give light on the matter. That subjectivity—being the 'moment' which emphasizes the need of abstract deciding in general—partly leads on to the proviso that the name of the monarch appear as the bond and sanction under which everything is done in the government;—partly, being simple self-relation, has attached to it the characteristic of *immediacy*, and then of *nature*—whereby the destination of individuals for the dignity of the princely power is fixed by inheritance.

§ 543

(b) In the *particular* government-power there emerges, first, the division of state-business into its branches (otherwise defined), legislative power, administration of justice or judicial power, administration and police, and its consequent distribution between particular boards or offices, which having their business appointed by law, to that end and for that reason, possess independence of action, without at the same time ceasing to stand under higher supervision. Secondly, too, there arises the participation of *several* in state-business, who together constitute the 'general order' (§ 528) in so far as they take on themselves the charge of universal ends as the essential function of their particular life;—the further condition for being able to take individually part in this business being a certain training, aptitude, and skill for such ends.

§ 544

The estates-collegium or provincial council is an institution by which all such as belong to civil society in general, and are to that degree private persons, participate in the governmental power, especially in legislation—viz. such legislation as concerns the universal scope of those interests which do not, like peace and war, involve the, as it were, personal interference and action of the State as one man, and therefore do not belong specially to the province of the sovereign power. By virtue of this participation subjective liberty and conceit, with their general opinion, can show themselves palpably efficacious and enjoy the satisfaction of feeling themselves to count for something.

The division of constitutions into democracy, aristocracy and monarchy, is still the most definite statement of their difference in relation to sovereignty. They must at the same time be regarded as necessary structures in the path of development—in short, in the history of the State. Hence it is superficial and absurd to represent them as an object of *choice*. The pure forms—necessary to the process of evolution—are, in so far as they are finite and in course of change, conjoined both with forms of their degeneration—such as ochlocracy, etc., and with earlier transition-forms. These two forms are not to be confused with those legitimate structures. Thus, it may be—if we look only to the fact that the will of one individual stands at the head of the state—oriental despotism is included under the vague name monarchy—as also feudal monarchy, to which indeed even the favourite name of 'constitutional monarchy' cannot be refused. The true difference of these forms from genuine monarchy depends on the true value of those principles of right which are in vogue and have their actuality and guarantee in the state-power. These principles are those expounded earlier, liberty of property, and above all personal liberty, civil society, with its industry and its communities, and the regulated efficiency of the particular bureaux in subordination to the laws.

The question which is most discussed is in what sense we are to understand the participation of private persons in state affairs. For it is as private persons that the members of bodies of estates are primarily to be taken, be they treated as mere individuals, or as representatives of a number of people or of the nation. The aggregate of private persons is often spoken of as the *nation*: but as such an aggregate it is *vulgus*, not *populus*: and in this direction it is the one sole aim of the state that a nation should *not* come to existence,

to power and action, *as such an aggregate.* Such a condition of a
nation is a condition of lawlessness, demoralization, brutishness: in
it the nation would only be a shapeless, wild, blind force, like that
of the stormy, elemental sea, which, however, is not self-destructive, as the nation—a spiritual element—would be. Yet such a
condition may be often heard described as that of true freedom. If
there is to be any sense in embarking upon the question of the
participation of private persons in public affairs, it is not a brutish
mass, but an already organized nation—one in which a governmental power exists—which should be presupposed. The desirability
of such participation, however, is not to be put in the superiority
of particular intelligence, which private persons are supposed
to have over state officials—the contrary must be the case—nor in
the superiority of their goodwill for the general best. The members
of civil society as such are rather people who find their nearest duty
in their private interest and (as especially in the feudal society) in
the interest of their privileged corporation. Take the case of *England*
which, because private persons have a predominant share in public
affairs, has been regarded as having the freest of all constitutions.
Experience shows that that country—as compared with the other
civilized states of Europe—is the most backward in civil and
criminal legislation, in the law and liberty of property, in arrangements for art and science, and that objective freedom or rational
right is rather *sacrificed* to formal right and particular private
interest; and that this happens even in the institutions and posses-
sions supposed to be dedicated to religion. The desirability of
private persons taking part in public affairs is partly to be put in
their concrete, and therefore more urgent, sense of general wants.
But the true motive is the right of the collective spirit to appear as
an *externally universal* will, acting with orderly and express efficacy
for the public concerns. By this satisfaction of this right it gets its
own life quickened, and at the same time breathes fresh life in the
administrative officials; who thus have it brought home to them
that not merely have they to enforce duties but also to have regard
to rights. Private citizens are in the state the incomparably greater
number, and form the multitude of such as are recognized as persons. Hence the will-reason exhibits its existence in them as a preponderating majority of freemen, or in its 'reflectional' universality,

which has its actuality vouchsafed it as a participation in the sovereignty. But it has already been noted as a 'moment' of civil society (§§ 527, 534) that the individuals rise from external into substantial universality, and form a *particular* kind—the Estates: and it is not in the inorganic form of mere individuals as such (after the *democratic* fashion of election), but as organic factors, as estates, that they enter upon that participation. In the state a power or agency must never appear and act as a formless, inorganic shape, i.e. basing itself on the principle of multeity and mere numbers.

Assemblies of Estates have been wrongly designated as the *legislative power*, so far as they form only one branch of that power—a branch in which the special government-officials have an *ex officio* share, while the sovereign power has the privilege of final decision. In a civilized state, moreover, legislation can only be a further modification of existing laws, and so-called new laws can only deal with minutiae of detail and particularities (cf. § 529 note), the main drift of which has been already prepared or preliminarily settled by the practice of the law-courts. The so-called *financial law*, in so far as it requires the assent of the estates, is really a government affair: it is only improperly called a law, in the general sense of embracing a wide, indeed the whole, range of the external means of government. The finances deal with what in their nature are only particular needs, ever newly recurring, even if they touch on the sum total of such needs. If the main part of the requirement were—as it very likely is—regarded as permanent, the provision for it would have more the nature of a law: but to be a law it would have to be made once for all, and not to be made yearly, or every few years, afresh. The part which varies according to time and circumstances concerns in reality the smallest part of the amount, and the provisions with regard to it have even less the character of a law: and yet it is and may be only this slight variable part which is matter of dispute, and can be subjected to a varying yearly esti- mate. It is this last then which falsely bears the high-sounding names of the '*Grant*' of the *Budget*, i.e. of the whole of the finances. A law for one year and made each year has even to the plain man something palpably absurd: for he distinguishes the essential and developed universal, as content of a true law, from the reflectional universality which only externally embraces what in its nature is many. To give the name of a law to the annual fixing of financial requirements only serves—with the presupposed separation of legislative from executive—to keep up the illusion of that separation having real existence, and to conceal the fact that the legislative power, when it makes a decree about finance, is really engaged with strict executive business. But the importance attached to the power of from time to time granting 'supply', on the ground that the assembly of estates possesses in it a *check* on the government, and thus a guarantee against injustice and violence—this importance is in one way rather plausible than real. The financial measures necessary for the state's subsistence cannot be made conditional on any other circumstances, nor can the state's subsistence be put yearly in doubt. It would be a parallel absurdity if the government were, e.g., to grant and arrange the judicial institutions always for a limited time merely; and thus, by the threat of suspending the activity of such an institution and the fear of a consequent state of brigandage, reserve for itself a means of coercing private individuals. Then again, the pictures of a condition of affairs, in which it might be useful and necessary to have in hand means of compulsion, are partly based on the false conception of a contract between rulers and ruled, and partly presuppose the possibility of such a divergence in spirit between these two parties as would make constitution and government quite out of the question. If we suppose the empty possibility of getting *help* by such compulsive means brought into existence, such help would rather be the derangement and dissolution of the state, in which there would no longer be a government, but only parties, and the violence and oppression of one party would only be helped away by the other. To fit together the several parts of the state into a constitution after the fashion of mere understanding—i.e. to adjust within it the machinery of a balance of powers external to each other—is to contravene the fundamental idea of what a state is.

§ 545

The final aspect of the state is to appear in immediate actuality as a single nation marked by physical conditions. As a single individual it is exclusive against other like individuals. In their mutual relations, waywardness and chance have a place; for each person in the aggregate is autonomous: the universal of law is only postulated between them, and not actually existent. This independence of a central authority reduces disputes between them to terms of mutual violence, a *state of war*, to meet which the general estate in the community assumes the particular function of maintaining the state's independence against other states, and becomes the estate of dravery.

§ 546

This state of war shows the omnipotence of the state in its individuality—an individuality that goes even to abstract negativity. Country and fatherland then appear as the power by which the particular independence of individuals and their absorption in the external existence of possession and in natural life is convicted of its own nullity—as the power which procures the maintenance of the general substance by the patriotic sacrifice on the part of these individuals of this natural and particular existence—so making nugatory the nugatoriness that confronts it.

(β) *External Public Law*[1]

§ 547

In the state of war the independence of States is at stake. In one case the result may be the mutual recognition of free national individualities (§ 430): and by peace-conventions supposed to be for ever, both this general recognition, and the special claims of nations on one another, are settled and fixed. External state-rights rest partly on these positive treaties, but to that extent contain only rights falling short of true actuality (§ 545): partly so-called *international* law, the general principle of which is its presupposed recognition by the several States. It thus restricts their otherwise unchecked action against one another in such a way that the possibility of peace is left; and distinguishes individuals as private persons (non-belligerents) from the state. In general, international law rests on social usage.

---

[1] Das äussere Staatsrecht.

(γ) *Universal History*[1]
§ 548

As the mind of a special nation is actual and its liberty is under natural conditions, it admits on this nature-side the influence of geographical and climatic qualities. It is in time; and as regards its range and scope, has essentially a *particular* principle on the lines of which it must run through a development of its consciousness and its actuality. It has, in short, a history of its own. But as a restricted mind its independence is something secondary; it passes into universal world-history, the events of which exhibit the dialectic of the several national minds—the judgement of the world.

§ 549

This movement is the path of liberation for the spiritual substance, the deed by which the absolute final aim of the world is realized in it, and the merely implicit mind achieves consciousness and self-consciousness. It is thus the revelation and actuality of its essential and completed essence, whereby it becomes to the outward eye a universal spirit—a world-mind. As this development is in time and in real existence, as it is a history, its several stages and steps are the national minds, each of which, as single and endued by nature with a specific character, is appointed to occupy only one grade, and accomplish one task in the whole deed.

The presupposition that history has an essential and actual end, from the principles of which certain characteristic results logically flow, is called an *a priori* view of it, and philosophy is reproached with *a priori* history-writing. On this point, and on history-writing in general, this note must go into further detail. That history, and above all universal history, is founded on an essential and actual aim, which actually is and will be realized in it—the plan of Providence; that, in short, there is Reason in history, must be decided on strictly philosophical ground, and thus shown to be essentially and in fact necessary. To presuppose such aim is blameworthy only when the assumed conceptions or thoughts are arbitrarily adopted, and when a determined attempt is made to force events and actions into conformity with such conceptions. For such *a priori* methods

[1] Die Weltgeschichte.

of treatment at the present day, however, those are chiefly to blame who profess to be purely historical, and who at the same time take opportunity expressly to raise their voice against the habit of philosophizing, first in general, and then in history. Philosophy is to them a troublesome neighbour: for it is an enemy of all arbitrariness and hasty suggestions. Such *a priori* history-writing has sometimes burst out in quarters where one would least have expected it, especially on the philological side, and in Germany more than in France and England, where the art of historical writing has gone through a process of purification to a firmer and maturer character. Fictions, like that of a primitive age and its primitive people, possessed from the first of the true knowledge of God and all the sciences—of sacerdotal races—and, when we come to minutiae, of a Roman epic, supposed to be the source of the legends which pass current for the history of ancient Rome, etc., have taken the place of the pragmatizing which detected psychological motives and associations. There is a wide circle of persons who seem to consider it incumbent on a *learned* and *ingenious* historian drawing from the original sources to concoct such baseless fancies, and form bold combinations of them from a learned rubbish-heap of out-of-the-way and trivial facts, in defiance of the best-accredited history.

Setting aside this subjective treatment of history, we find what is properly the opposite view forbidding us to import into history an *objective purpose*. This is after all synonymous with what *seems* to be the still more legitimate demand that the historian should proceed with *impartiality*. This is a requirement often and especially made on the *history of philosophy*: where it is insisted there should be no prepossession in favour of an idea or opinion, just as a judge should have no special sympathy for one of the contending parties. In the case of the judge it is at the same time assumed that he would administer his office ill and foolishly, if he had not an interest, and an exclusive interest in justice, if he had not that for his aim and one sole aim, or if he declined to judge at all. This requirement which we may make upon the judge may be called *partiality* for justice; and there is no difficulty here in distinguishing it from *subjective* partiality. But in speaking of the impartiality required from the historian, this self-satisfied insipid chatter lets the distinction disappear, and rejects both kinds of interest. It demands that the historian shall bring with him no definite aim and view by which he may sort out, state, and criticize events, but shall narrate them exactly in the casual mode he finds them, in their incoherent and unintelligent particularity. Now it is at least admitted that a history must have an object, e.g. Rome and its fortunes, or the Decline of the grandeur of the Roman empire. But little reflection is needed to discover that this is the presupposed end which lies at the basis of the events themselves, as of the critical examination into their comparative importance, i.e. their nearer or more remote relation to it. A history without such aim and such criticism would be only an imbecile mental divagation, not as good as a fairy tale, for even children expect a *motif* in their stories, a purpose at least dimly surmiseable with which events and actions are put in relation.

In the existence of a *nation* the substantial aim is to be a state and preserve itself as such. A nation with no state formation (a *mere nation*), has, strictly speaking, no history—like the nations which existed before the rise of states and others which still exist in a condition of savagery. What happens to a nation, and takes place within it, has its essential significance in relation to the state: whereas the mere particularities of individuals are at the greatest distance from the true object of history. It is true that the general spirit of an age leaves its imprint in the character of its celebrated individuals, and even their particularities are but the very distant and the dim media through which the collective light still plays in fainter colours. Ay, even such singularities as a petty occurrence, a word, express not a subjective particularity, but an age, a nation, a civilization, in striking portraiture and brevity; and to select such trifles shows the hand of a historian of genius. But, on the other hand, the main mass of singularities is a futile and useless mass, by the painstaking accumulation of which the objects of real historical value are overwhelmed and obscured. The essential characteristic of the spirit and its age is always contained in the great events. It was a correct instinct which sought to banish such portraiture of the particular and the gleaning of insignificant traits, into the *Novel* (as in the celebrated romances of Walter Scott, etc.). Where the picture presents an unessential aspect of life it is certainly in good taste to conjoin it with an unessential material, such as the romance tales from private events and subjective passions. But to take the individual pettinesses of an age and of the persons in it, and, in the interest of so-called truth, weave them into the picture of general interests, is not only against taste and judgement, but violates the principles of objective truth. The only truth for mind is the substantial and underlying essence, and not the trivialities of external existence and contingency. It is therefore completely indifferent whether such insignificances are duly vouched for by documents, or, as in the romance, invented to suit the character and ascribed to this or that name and circumstances.

The point of interest of *Biography*—to say a word on that here—appears to run directly counter to any universal scope and aim. But biography too has for its background the historical world, with which the individual is intimately bound up: even purely personal originality, the freak of humour, etc. suggests by allusion that central reality and has its interest heightened by the suggestion. The mere play of sentiment, on the contary, has another ground and interest than history.

The requirement of impartiality addressed to the history of philosophy (and also, we may add, to the history of religion, first in general, and secondly, to church history) generally implies an even more decided bar against presupposition of any objective aim. As the State was already called the point to which in political history criticism had to refer all events, so here the '*Truth*' must be the object to which the several deeds and events of the spirit would have to be referred. What is actually done is rather to make the contrary presupposition. Histories with such an object as religion or philosophy are understood to have only subjective aims for their theme, i.e. only opinions and mere ideas, not an essential and realized object like the truth. And that with the mere excuse that there is no truth. On this assumption the sympathy with truth appears as only a partiality of the usual sort, a partiality for opinion and mere ideas, which all alike have no stuff in them. and are all treated as indifferent. In that way historical truth means but correctness—an accurate report of externals, without critical treatment save as regards this correctness—admitting, in this case, only qualitative and quantitative judgements, no judgements of necessity or notion (cf. notes to §§ 172 and 175). But, really, if Rome or

the German empire, etc. are an actual and genuine object of
political history, and the aim to which the phenomena are to be
related and by which they are to be judged; then in universal
history the genuine spirit, the consciousness of it, and of its essence,
is even in a higher degree a true and actual object and theme, and
an aim to which all other phenomena are essentially and actually
subservient. Only therefore through their relationship to it, i.e.
through the judgement in which they are subsumed under it,
while it inheres in them, have they their value and even their
existence. It is the spirit which not merely broods *over* history as
over the waters but lives in it and is alone its principle of movement: and in the path of that spirit, liberty, i.e. a development
determined by the notion of spirit, is the guiding principle and
only its notion its final aim, i.e. truth. For Spirit is consciousness.
Such a doctrine—or in other words that Reason is in history—will be
partly at least a plausible faith, partly it is a cognition of philosophy.

§ 550

This liberation of mind, in which it proceeds to come to itself and
to realize its truth, and the business of so doing, is the supreme
right, the absolute Law. The self-consciousness of a particular
nation is a vehicle for the contemporary development of the collective spirit in its actual existence: it is the objective actuality in
which that spirit for the time invests its will. Against this absolute
will the other particular natural minds have no rights: *that* nation
dominates the world: but yet the universal will steps onward over
its property for the time being, as over a special grade, and then
delivers it over to its chance and doom.

§ 551

To such extent as this business of actuality appears as an action,
and therefore as a work of *individuals*, these individuals, as regards
the substantial issue of their labour, are *instruments*, and their
subjectivity, which is what is peculiar to them, is the empty form of
activity. What they personally have gained therefore through the
individual share they took in the substantial business (prepared
and appointed independently of them) is a formal universality or
subjective mental idea—*Fame*, which is their reward.

§ 552

The national spirit contains nature-necessity, and stands in external existence (§ 483): the ethical substance, potentially infinite, is
actually a particular and limited substance (§§ 549, 550); on its
subjective side it labours under contingency, in the shape of its
unreflective natural usages, and its content is presented to it as
something *existing* in time and tied to an external nature and
external world. The spirit, however (which *thinks* in this moral
organism) overrides and absorbs within itself the finitude attaching
to it as national spirit in its state and the state's temporal interests,
in the system of laws and usages. It rises to apprehend itself in its
essentiality. Such apprehension, however, still has the immanent
limitedness of the national spirit. But the spirit which thinks in
universal history, stripping off at the same time those limitations of
the several national minds and its own temporal restrictions, lays
hold of its concrete universality, and rises to apprehend the absolute mind, as the eternally actual truth in which the contemplative
reason enjoys freedom, while the necessity of nature and the
necessity of history are only ministrant to its revelation and the
vessels of its honour.

The strictly technical aspects of the Mind's elevation to God
have been spoken of in the Introduction to the Logic (cf. especially
§ 51, note). As regards the starting-point of that elevation, Kant has
on the whole adopted the most correct, when he treats belief in
God as proceeding from the practical Reason. For that starting-
point contains the material or content which constitutes the content
of the notion of God. But the true concrete material is neither
Being (as in the cosmological) nor mere action by design (as in the
physico-theological proof) but the Mind, the absolute characteristic and function of which is effective reason, i.e. the self-determining and self-realizing notion itself—Liberty. That the elevation of
subjective mind to God which these considerations give is by Kant
again deposed to a *postulate*—a mere 'ought'—is the peculiar per-
versity, formerly noticed, of calmly and simply reinstating as true
and valid that very antithesis of finitude, the supersession of which
into truth is the essence of that elevation.

As regards the 'mediation' which, as it has been already shown
(§ 192, cf. § 204 note), that elevation to God really involves, the

point specially calling for note is the 'moment' of negation through which the essential content of the starting-point is purged of its finitude so as to come forth free. This factor, abstract in the formal treatment of logic, now gets its most concrete interpretation. The finite, from which the start is now made, is the real ethical self-consciousness. The negation through which that consciousness raises its spirit to its truth, is the purification, *actually* accomplished in the ethical world, whereby its conscience is purged of subjective opinion and its will freed from the selfishness of desire. Genuine religion and genuine religiosity only issue from the moral life: religion is that life rising to think, i.e. becoming aware of the free universality of its concrete essence. Only from the moral life and by the moral life is the Idea of God seen to be free spirit: outside the ethical spirit therefore it is vain to seek for true religion and religiosity.

But—as is the case with all speculative process—this development of one thing out of another means that what appears as sequel and derivative is rather the absolute *prius* of what it appears to be mediated by, and here in mind is also known as its truth.

Here then is the place to go more deeply into the reciprocal relations between the state and religion, and in doing so to elucidate the terminology which is familiar and current on the topic. It is evident and apparent from what has preceded that moral life is the state retracted into its inner heart and substance, while the state is the organization and actualization of moral life; and that religion is the very substance of the moral life itself and of the state. At this rate, the state rests on the ethical sentiment, and that on the religious. If religion then is the consciousness of '*absolute*' *truth*, then whatever is to rank as right and justice, as law and duty, i.e. as *true* in the world of free will, can be so esteemed only as it is participant in that truth, as it is subsumed under it and is its sequel. But if the truly moral life is to be a sequel of religion, then perforce religion must have the *genuine* content; i.e. the idea of God it knows must be the true and real. The ethical life is the divine spirit as indwelling in self-consciousness, as it is actually present in a nation and its individual members. This self-consciousness retiring upon itself out of its empirical actuality and bringing its truth to consciousness has, in its *faith* and in its *conscience*, only what it has consciously secured in its spiritual actuality. The two are inseparable: there cannot be two kinds of conscience, one religious and another ethical, differing from the former in body and value of truth. But in point of form, i.e. for thought and knowledge—(and religion and ethical life belong to intelligence and are a thinking and knowing)—the body of religious truth, as the pure self-subsisting and therefore supreme truth, exercises a sanction over the moral life which lies in empirical actuality. Thus for self-consciousness religion is the 'basis' of moral life and of the state. It has been the monstrous blunder of our times to try to look upon these inseparables as separable from one another, and even as mutually indifferent. The view taken of the relationship of religion and the state has been that, whereas the state had an independent existence of its own, springing from some force and power, religion was a later addition, something desirable perhaps for strengthening the political bulwarks, but purely subjective in individuals:—or it may be, religion is treated as something without effect on the moral life of the state, i.e. its reasonable law and constitution which are based on a ground of their own.

As the inseparability of the two sides has been indicated, it may be worth while to note the separation as it appears on the side of religion. It is primarily a point of form: the attitude which self-consciousness takes to the body of truth. So long as this body of truth is the very substance or indwelling spirit of self-consciousness in its actuality, then self-consciousness in this content has the certainty of itself and is free. But if this present self-consciousness is lacking, then there may be created, in point of form, a condition of spiritual slavery, even though the *implicit* content of religion is absolute spirit. This great difference (to cite a specific case) comes out within the Christian religion itself, even though here it is not the nature-element in which the idea of God is embodied, and though nothing of the sort even enters as a factor into its central dogma and sole theme of a God who is known in spirit and in truth. And yet in Catholicism this spirit of all truth is in actuality set in rigid opposition to the self-conscious spirit. And, first of all, God is in the 'host' presented to religious adoration as an *external thing*. (In the Lutheran Church, on the contrary, the host as such is not at first consecrated, but in the moment of enjoyment, i.e. in the annihilation of its externality, and in the act of faith, i.e. in the free self-certain spirit: only then is it consecrated and exalted to be present God.) From that first and supreme status of externalization flows every other phase of externality—of bondage, non-spirituality, and superstition. It leads to a laity, receiving its knowledge of divine truth, as well as the direction of its will and conscience from without and from another order—which order again does not get possession of that knowledge in a spiritual way only, but to that end essentially requires an external consecration. It leads to the non-spiritual style of praying—partly as mere moving of the lips, partly in the way that the subject foregoes his right of directly addressing God, and prays others to pray—addressing his devotion to miracle-working images, even to bones, and expecting miracles from them. It leads, generally, to justification by external works, a merit which is supposed to be gained by acts, and even to be capable of being transferred to others. All this binds the spirit under an externalism by which the very meaning of spirit is perverted and misconceived at its source, and law and justice, morality and conscience, responsibility and duty are corrupted at their root.

Along with this principle of spiritual bondage, and these applications of it in the religious life, there can only go in the legislative and constitutional system a legal and moral bondage, and a state of lawlessness and immorality in political life. Catholicism has been loudly praised and is still often praised—logically enough—as the one religion which secures the stability of governments. But in reality this applies only to governments which are bound up with institutions founded on the bondage of the spirit (of that spirit which should have legal and moral liberty), i.e. with institutions that embody injustice and with a morally corrupt and barbaric state of society. But these governments are not aware that in fanaticism they have a terrible power, which does not rise in hostility against them, only so long as and only on condition that they remain sunk in the thraldom of injustice and immorality. But in mind there is a very different power available against that externalism and dismemberment induced by a false religion. Mind collects itself into its inward free actuality. Philosophy awakes in the spirit of governments and nations the wisdom to discern what is essentially and actually right and reasonable in the real world. It was well to call these products of thought, and in a special sense Philosophy, the wisdom of the world;[1] for thought makes the spirit's truth an actual present, leads it into the real world, and thus liberates it in its actuality and in its own self.

Thus set free, the content of religion assumes quite another shape. So long as the form, i.e. our consciousness and subjectivity, lacked liberty, it followed necessarily that self-consciousness was conceived as not immanent in the ethical principles which religion embodies, and these principles were set at such a distance as to seem to have true being only as negative to actual self-consciousness. In this unreality ethical content gets the name of *Holiness*. But once the divine spirit introduces itself into actuality, and actuality emancipates itself to spirit, then what in the world was a postulate of holiness is supplanted by the actuality of *marql* life. Instead of the vow of chastity, *marriage* now ranks as the ethical relation; and, therefore, as the highest on this side of humanity stands the family. Instead of the vow of poverty (muddled up into a contradiction of assigning merit to whosoever gives away goods to the poor, i.e. whosoever enriches them) is the precept of action to acquire goods through one's own intelligence and industry,—of honesty in commercial dealing, and in the use of property—in short moral life in the socio-economic sphere. And instead of the vow of obedience, true religion sanctions obedience to the law and the legal arrangements of the state—an obedience which is itself the true freedom, because the state is a self-possessed, self-realizing reason—in short, moral life in the state. Thus, and thus only, can law and morality exist. The precept of religion, 'Give to Caesar what is Caesar's and to God what is God's' is not enough: the question is to settle what is Caesar's, what belongs to the secular authority: and it is sufficiently notorious that the secular no less than the ecclesiastical authority have claimed almost everything as their own. The divine spirit must interpenetrate the entire secular life: whereby wisdom is concrete within it, and it carries the terms of its own justification. But that concrete indwelling is only the aforesaid ethical organizations. It is the morality of marriage as against the sanctity of a celibate order;—the morality of economic and industrial action against the sanctity of poverty and its indol-

[1] Weltweisheit.

ence;—the morality of an obedience dedicated to the law of the state as against the sanctity of an obedience from which law and duty are absent and where conscience is enslaved. With the growing need for law and morality and the sense of the spirit's essential liberty, there sets in a conflict of spirit with the religion of unfreedom. It is no use to organize political laws and arrangements on principles of equity and reason, so long as in religion the principle of unfreedom is not abandoned. A free state and a slavish religion are incompatible. It is silly to suppose that we may try to allot them separate spheres, under the impression that their diverse natures will maintain an attitude of tranquillity one to another and not break out in contradiction and battle. Principles of civil freedom can be but abstract and superficial, and political institutions deduced from them must be, if taken alone, untenable, so long as those principles in their wisdom mistake religion so much as not to know that the maxims of the reason in actuality have their last and supreme sanction in the religious conscience in subsumption under the consciousness of 'absolute' truth. Let us suppose even that, no matter how, a code of law should arise, so to speak *a priori*, founded on principles of reason, but in contradiction with an established religion based on principles of spiritual unfreedom; still, as the duty of carrying out the laws lies in the hands of individual members of the government, and of the various classes of the administrative *personnel*, it is vain to delude ourselves with the abstract and empty assumption that the individuals will act only according to the letter or meaning of the law, and not in the spirit of their religion where their inmost conscience and supreme obligation lies. Opposed to what religion pronounces holy, the laws appear something made by human hands: even though backed by penalties and externally introduced, they could offer no lasting resistance to the contradictions and attacks of the religious spirit. Such laws, however sound their provisions may be, thus founder on the conscience, whose spirit is different from the spirit of the laws and refuses to sanction them. It is nothing but a modern folly to try to alter a corrupt moral organization by altering its political constitution and code of laws without changing the religion,—to make a revolution without having made a reformation, to suppose that a political constitution opposed to the old religion could live in peace and

harmony with it and its sanctities, and that stability could be procured for the laws by external guarantees, e.g., so-called 'chambers',
and the power given them to fix the budget, etc. (cf. § 544 note).
At best it is only a temporary expedient—when it is obviously too
great a task to descend into the depths of the religious spirit and to
raise that same spirit to its truth—to seek to separate law and
justice from religion. Those guarantees are but rotten bulwarks
against the consciences of the persons charged with administering
the laws—among which laws these guarantees are included. It is
indeed the height and profanity of contradiction to seek to bind and
subject to the secular code the religious conscience to which mere
human law is a thing profane.

The perception had dawned upon Plato with great clearness of
the gulf which in his day had commenced to divide the established
religion and the political constitution, on one hand, from those
deeper requirements which, on the other hand, were made upon
religion and politics by liberty which had learnt to recognize its
inner life. Plato gets hold of the thought that a genuine constitution
and a sound political life have their deeper foundation on the Idea—
on the essentially and actually universal and genuine principles of
eternal righteousness. Now to see and ascertain what these are is
certainly the function and the business of *philosophy*. It is from this
point of view that Plato breaks out into the celebrated or notorious
passage where he makes Socrates emphatically state that philosophy and political power must coincide, that the Idea must be
regent, if the distress of nations is to see its end. What Plato thus
definitely set before his mind was that the Idea—which implicitly
indeed is the free self-determining thought—could not get into
consciousness save only in the form of a thought; that the substance
of the thought could only be true when set forth as a universal, and
as such brought to consciousness under its most abstract form.

To compare the Platonic standpoint in all its definiteness with
the point of view from which the relationship of state and religion
is here regarded, the notional differences on which everything turns
must be recalled to mind. The first of these is that in natural things
their substance or genus is different from their existence in which
that substance is as subject: further that this subjective existence of
the genus is distinct from that which it gets, when specially set in

relief as genus, or, to put it simply, as the universal in a mental concept or idea. This additional 'individuality'—the soil on which the universal and underlying principle *freely* and expressly exists—is the intellectual and thinking *self*. In the case of *natural* things their truth and reality does not get the form of universality and essentiality through themselves, and their 'individuality' is not itself the form: the form is only found in subjective thinking, which in philosophy gives that universal truth and reality an existence of its own. In man's case it is otherwise: his truth and reality is the free mind itself, and it comes to existence in his self-consciousness. This absolute nucleus of man—mind intrinsically concrete—is just this—to have the form (to have thinking) itself for a content. To the height of the thinking consciousness of this principle Aristotle ascended in his notion of the entelechy of thought (which is νόησις τῆς νοήσεως), thus surmounting the Platonic Idea (the genus, or essential being). But thought always—and that on account of this very principle—contains the immediate self-subsistence of subjectivity no less than it contains universality; the genuine Idea of the intrinsically concrete mind is just as essentially under the one of its terms (subjective consciousness) as under the other (universality): and in the one as in the other it is the same substantial content. Under the subjective form, however, fall feeling, intuition, pictorial representation; and it is in fact necessary that in point of time the consciousness of the absolute Idea should be first reached and apprehended in this form: in other words, it must exist in its immediate reality as religion, earlier than it does as philosophy. Philosophy is a later development from this basis (just as Greek philosophy itself is later than Greek religion), and in fact reaches its completion by catching and comprehending in all its definite essentiality that principle of spirit which first manifests itself in religion. But Greek philosophy could set itself up only in opposition to Greek religion: the unity of thought and the substantiality of the Idea could take up none but a hostile attitude to an imaginative polytheism, and to the gladsome and frivolous humours of its poetic creations. The *form* in its infinite truth, the *subjectivity* of mind, broke forth at first only as a subjective free *thinking*, which was not yet identical with the *substantiality* itself—and thus this underlying principle was not yet apprehended as *absolute mind*.

Thus religion might appear as first purified only through philosophy
—through pure self-existent thought: but the form pervading
this underlying principle—the form which philosophy attacked
—was that creative imagination.

Political power, which is developed similarly, but earlier than
philosophy, from religion, exhibits the onesidedness, which in the
actual world may infect its *implicitly* true Idea, as demoralization.
Plato, in common with all his thinking contemporaries, perceived
this demoralization of democracy and the defectiveness even of its
principle; he set in relief accordingly the underlying principle of
the state, but could not work into his idea of it the infinite form of
subjectivity, which still escaped his intelligence. His state is therefore, on its own showing, wanting in subjective liberty (§ 503 note,
§ 513, etc.). The truth which should be immanent in the state, should
knit it together and control it, he, for these reasons, got hold of
only in the form of thought-out truth, of philosophy; and hence he
makes that utterance that 'so long as philosophers do not rule in the
states, or those who are now called kings and rulers do not soundly
and comprehensively philosophize, so long neither the state nor the
race of men can be liberated from evils—so long will the idea of the
political constitution fall short of possibility and not see the light of
the sun'. It was not vouchsafed to Plato to go on so far as to say
that so long as true religion did not spring up in the world and hold
sway in political life, so long the genuine principle of the state had
not come into actuality. But so long too this principle could not
emerge even in thought, nor could thought lay hold of the genuine
idea of the state—the idea of the substantial moral life, with which
is identical the liberty of an independent self-consciousness. Only
in the principle of mind, which is aware of its own essence, is
implicitly in absolute liberty, and has its actuality in the act of
self-liberation, does the absolute possibility and necessity exist for
political power, religion, and the principles of philosophy coincid-
ing in one, and for accomplishing the reconciliation of actuality in
general with the mind, of the state with the religious conscience as
well as with the philosophical consciousness. Self-realizing subjectivity is in this case absolutely identical with substantial universality. Hence religion as such, and the state as such—both as forms
in which the principle exists—each contain the absolute truth: so

that the truth, in its philosophic phase, is after all only in one of its forms. But even religion, as it grows and expands, lets other aspects of the Idea of humanity grow and expand also (§ § 566 seqq.). As it left therefore behind, in its first immediate, and so also one-sided phase, Religion may, or rather *must*, appear in its existence degraded to sensuous externality, and thus in the sequel become an influence to oppress liberty of spirit and to deprave political life. Still the principle has in it the infinite 'elasticity' of the 'absolute' form, so as to overcome this depraving of the form-determination (and of the content by these means), and to bring about the reconciliation of the spirit in itself. Thus ultimately, in the Protestant conscience the principles of the religious and of the ethical conscience come to be one and the same: the free spirit learning to see itself in its reasonableness and truth. In the Protestant state, the constitution and the code, as well as their several applications, embody the principle and the development of the moral life, which proceeds and can only proceed from the truth of religion, when reinstated in its original principle and in that way as such first become actual. The moral life of the state and the religious spirituality of the state are thus reciprocal guarantees of strength.

SECTION THREE ✦ ABSOLUTE MIND[1]

§ 553

The *notion* of mind has its *reality* in the mind. If this reality n identity with that notion is to exist as the consciousness of the absolute Idea, then the necessary aspect is that the *implicitly* free intelligence be in its actuality liberated to its notion, if that actuality is to be a vehicle worthy of it. The subjective and the objective spirit are to be looked on as the road on which this aspect of *reality* or existence rises to maturity.

§ 554

The absolute mind, while it is self-centred *identity*, is always also identity returning and ever returned into itself: if it is the one and universal *substance* it is so as a spirit, discerning itself into a self and a consciousness, for which it is as substance. *Religion*, as this supreme sphere may be in general designated, if it has on one hand to be studied as issuing from the subject and having its home in the subject, must no less be regarded as objectively issuing from the absolute spirit which as spirit is in its community,

That here, as always, belief or faith is not opposite to consciousness or knowledge, but rather to a sort of knowledge, and that belief is only a particular form of the latter, has been remarked already (§ 63 note). If nowadays there is so little consciousness of God, and his objective essence is so little dwelt upon, while people speak so much more of the subjective side of religion, i.e. of God's indwelling in us, and if that and not the truth as such is called for—in this there is at least the correct principle that God must be apprehended as spirit in his community.

§ 555

The subjective consciousness of the absolute spirit is essentially and intrinsically a process, the immediate and substantial unity of which is the *Belief* in the witness of the spirit as the *certainty* of

[1] Der absolute Geist.

objective truth. Belief, at once this immediate unity and containing it as a reciprocal dependence of these different terms, has in *devotion*—the implicit or more explicit act of worship (*cultus*)—passed over into the process of superseding the contrast till it becomes spiritual liberation, the process of authenticating that first certainty by this intermediation, and of gaining its concrete determination, viz. reconciliation, the actuality of the spirit.

A. ART

§ 556

As this consciousness of the Absolute first takes shape, its immediacy produces the factor of finitude in Art. On one hand, that is, it breaks up into a work of external common existence, into the subject which produces that work, and the subject which contemplates and worships it. But, on the other hand, it is the concrete *contemplation* and mental picture of implicitly absolute spirit as the *Ideal*. In this ideal, or the concrete shape born of the subjective spirit, its natural immediacy, which is only a *sign* of the Idea, is so transfigured by the informing spirit in order to express the Idea, that the figure shows it and it alone:—the shape or form of *Beauty*.

§ 557

The sensuous externality attaching to the beautiful,—the *form of immediacy* as such—at the same time *qualifies* what it *embodies*: and the God (of art) has with his spirituality at the same time the stamp upon him of a natural medium or natural phase of existence—He contains the so-called *unity* of nature and spirit—i.e. the immediate unity in sensuously intuitional form—hence not the spiritual unity, in which the natural would be put only as 'ideal', as superseded in spirit, and the spiritual content would be only in self-relation. It is not the absolute spirit which enters this consciousness. On the subjective side the community has of course an ethical life, aware, as it is, of the spirituality of its esssence: and its self-consciousness and actuality are in it elevated to substantial liberty. But with the stigma of immediacy upon it, the subject's liberty is only a *manner of life*, without the infinite self-reflection and the subjective inwardness of *conscience*. These considerations govern in their further developments the devotion and the worship in the religion of fine art.

§ 558

For the objects of contemplation it has to produce, Art requires not only an external given material—(under which are also included subjective images and ideas), but—for the expression of spiritual truth—must use the given forms of nature with a significance which art must divine and possess (cf. § 411). Of all such forms the human is the highest and the true, because only in it can the spirit have its corporeity and thus its visible expression.

This disposes of the principle of the *imitation of nature* in art: a point on which it is impossible to come to an understanding while a distinction is left thus abstract—in other words, so long as the natural is only taken in its externality, not as the 'characteristic' meaningful nature-form which is significant of spirit.

§ 559

In such single shapes the 'absolute' mind cannot be made explicit: in and to art therefore the spirit is a limited natural spirit whose implicit universality, when steps are taken to specify its fullness in detail, breaks up into an indeterminate polytheism. With the essential restrictedness of its content, Beauty in general goes no further than a penetration of the vision or image by the spiritual principle— something formal, so that the thought embodied, or the idea, can, like the material which it uses to work in, be of the most diverse and unessential kind, and still the work be something beautiful and a work of art.

§ 560

The one-sidedness of *immediacy* on the part of the Ideal involves the opposite one-sidedness (§ 556) that it is something *made* by the artist. The subject or agent is the mere technical activity: and the work of art is only then an expression of the God, when there is no sign of subjective particularity in it, and the net power of the in- dwelling spirit is conceived and born into the world, without ad- mixture and unspotted from its contingency. But as liberty only goes as far as there is thought, the action inspired with the fullness of this indwelling power, the artist's *enthusiasm*, is like a foreign force under which he is bound and passive; the artistic *production* has on its part the form of natural immediacy, it belongs to the *genius* or particular endowment of the artist—and is at the same time a labour concerned with technical cleverness and mechanical externalities. The work of art therefore is just as much a work due to free option, and the artist is the master of the God.

§ 561

In work so inspired the reconciliation appears so obvious in its initial stage that it is without more ado accomplished in the subjective self-consciousness, which is thus self-confident and of good cheer, without the depth and without the sense of its antithesis to the absolute essence. On the further side of the perfection (which is reached in such reconciliation, in the beauty of *classical art*) lies the art of sublimity—*symbolic art*, in which the figuration suitable to the Idea is not yet found, and the thought as going forth and wrestling with the figure is exhibited as a negative attitude to it, and yet all the while toiling to work itself into it. The meaning or theme thus shows it has not yet reached the infinite form, is not yet known, not yet conscious of itself, as free spirit. The artist's theme only is as the abstract God of pure thought, or an effort towards him—a restless and unappeased effort which throws itself into shape after shape as it vainly tries to find its goal.

§ 562

In another way the Idea and the sensuous figure it appears in are incompatible; and that is where the infinite form, subjectivity, is not as in the first extreme a mere superficial personality, but its inmost depth, and God is known not as only seeking his form or satisfying himself in an external form, but as only finding himself in himself, and thus giving himself his adequate figure in the spiritual world alone. *Romantic art* gives up the task of showing him as such in external form and by means of beauty: it presents him as only condescending to appearance, and the divine as the heart of hearts in an externality from which it always disengages itself. Thus the external can here appear as contingent towards its significance.

The Philosophy of Religion has to discover the logical necessity in the progress by which the Being, known as the Absolute, assumes fuller and firmer features; it has to note to what particular feature the kind of cultus corresponds—and then to see how the secular self-consciousness, the consciousness of what is the supreme vocation of man—in short how the nature of a nation's moral life, the principle of its law, of its actual liberty, and of its constitution, as well as of its art and science, corresponds to the principle which constitutes the substance of a religion. That all these elements of a nation's actuality constitute one systematic totality, that one spirit creates and informs them, is a truth on which follows the further truth that the history of religions coincides with the world-history.

As regards the close connection of art with the various religions it may be specially noted that *beautiful* art can only belong to those religions in which the spiritual principle, though concrete and intrinsically free, is not yet absolute. In religions where the Idea has not yet been revealed and known in its free character, though the craving for art is felt in order to bring in imaginative visibility to consciousness the idea of the supreme being, and though art is the sole organ in which the abstract and radically indistinct content—a mixture from natural and spiritual sources—can try to bring itself to consciousness;—still this art is defective; its form is defective because its subject-matter and theme is so—for the defect in subject-matter comes from the form not being immanent in it. The representations of this symbolic art keep a certain tastelessness and stolidity—for the principle it embodies is itself stolid and dull, and hence has not the power freely to transmute the external to significance and shape. Beautiful art, on the contrary, has for its condition the self-consciousness of the free spirit—the consciousness that compared with it the natural and sensuous has no standing of its own: it makes the natural wholly into the mere expression of spirit, which is thus the inner form that gives utterance to itself alone.

But with a further and deeper study, we see that the advent of art, in a religion still in the bonds of sensuous externality, shows that such religion is on the decline. At the very time it seems to give religion the supreme glorification, expression, and brilliancy, it has lifted the religion away over its limitation. In the sublime

divinity to which the work of art succeeds in giving expression the
artistic genius and the spectator find themselves at home, with
their personal sense and feeling, satisfied and liberated: to them
the vision and the consciousness of free spirit has been vouchsafed
and attained. Beautiful art, from its side, has thus performed the
same service as philosophy: it has purified the spirit from its thraldom. The older religion in which the need of fine art, and just for
that reason, is first generated, looks up in its principle to an other-
world which is sensuous and unmeaning: the images adored by its
devotees are hideous idols regarded as wonder-working talismans,
which point to the unspiritual objectivity of that other world—and
bones perform a similar or even a better service than such images.
But even fine art is only a grade of liberation, not the supreme
liberation itself.—The genuine objectivity, which is only in the
medium of thought—the medium in which alone the pure spirit is
for the spirit, and where the liberation is accompanied with reverence—is still absent in the sensuous beauty of the work of art, still
more in that external, unbeautiful sensuousness.

§ 563

Beautiful Art, like the religion peculiar to it, has its future in true
religion. The restricted value of the Idea passes utterly and naturally into the universality identical with the infinite form;—the
vision in which consciousness has to depend upon the senses passes
into a self-mediating knowledge, into an existence which is itself
knowledge—into *revelation*. Thus the principle which gives the
Idea its content is that it embody free intelligence, and as 'absolute'
spirit it is for the spirit.

B. REVEALED RELIGION[1]

§ 564

It lies essentially in the notion of religion,—the religion i.e. whose
content is absolute mind—that it be *revealed*, and, what is more,
revealed *by God*. Knowledge (the principle by which the substance
is mind) is a self-determining principle, as infinite self-realizing

[1] Die geoffenbarte Religion.

form—it therefore is manifestation out and out. The spirit is only spirit in so far as it is for the spirit, and in the absolute religion it is the absolute spirit which manifests no longer abstract elements of its being but itself.

The old conception—due to a one-sided survey of human life— of Nemesis, which made the divinity and its action in the world only a levelling power, dashing to pieces everything high and great —was confronted by Plato and Aristotle with the doctrine that God is not *envious*. The same answer may be given to the modern assertions that man cannot ascertain God. These assertions (and more than assertions they are not) are the more illogical, because made within a religion which is expressly called the revealed; for according to them it would rather be the religion in which nothing of God was revealed, in which he had not revealed himself, and those belonging to it would be the heathen 'who know not God'. If the word 'God' is taken in earnest in religion at all, it is from Him, the theme and centre of religion, that the method of divine knowledge may and must begin: and if self-revelation is refused Him, then the only thing left to constitute His nature would be to ascribe envy to Him. But clearly if the word 'Mind' is to have a meaning, it implies the revelation of Him.

If we recollect how intricate is the knowledge of the divine Mind for those who are not content with the homely pictures of faith but proceed to thought—at first only 'rationalizing' reflection, but afterwards, as in duty bound, to speculative comprehension, it may almost create surprise that so many, and especially theologians whose vocation it is to deal with these Ideas, have tried to get off their task by gladly accepting anything offered them for this behoof. And nothing serves better to shirk it than to adopt the con- clusion that man knows nothing of God. To know what God as spirit is—to apprehend this accurately and distinctly in thoughts— requires careful and thorough speculation. It includes, in its fore- front, the propositions: God is God only so far as he knows him- self: his self-knowledge is, further, a self-consciousness in man and man's knowledge *of* God, which proceeds to man's self- knowledge *in* God.—See the profound elucidation of these propo- sitions in the work from which they are taken: *Aphorisms on Knowing and Not-knowing*, &c., by C. F. G—l.: Berlin 1829.

§ 565

When the immediacy and sensuousness of shape and knowledge is superseded, God is, in point of content, the essential and actual spirit of nature and spirit, while in point of form he is, first of all, presented to consciousness as a mental representation. This quasi-pictorial representation gives to the elements of his content, on one hand, a separate being, making them presuppositions towards each other, and phenomena which succeed each other; their relationship it makes a series of events according to finite reflective categories. But, on the other hand, such a form of finite representationalism is also overcome and superseded in the faith which realizes one spirit and in the devotion of worship.

§ 566

In this separating, the form parts from the content: and in the form the different functions of the notion part off into special spheres or media, in each of which the absolute spirit exhibits itself; (α) as eternal content, abiding self-centred, even in its manifestation; (β) as distinction of the eternal essence from its manifestation, which by this difference becomes the phenomenal world into which the content enters; (γ) as infinite return, and reconciliation with the eternal being, of the world it gave away—the withdrawal of the eternal from the phenomenal into the unity of its fullness.

§ 567

(α) Under the 'moment' of *Universality*—the sphere of pure thought or the abstract medium of essence—it is therefore the absolute spirit, which is at first the presupposed principle, not, however, staying aloof and inert, but (as underlying and essential power under the reflective category of causality) creator of heaven and earth: but yet in this eternal sphere rather only begetting himself as his *son*, with whom, though different, he still remains in original identity—just as, again, this differentiation of him from the universal essence eternally supersedes itself, and, through this mediating of a self-superseding mediation, the first substance is essentially as *concrete individuality* and subjectivity—is the *Spirit*.

§ 568

(β) Under the 'moment' of *particularity*, or of judgement, it is this concrete eternal being which is presupposed: its movement is the creation of the phenomenal world. The eternal 'moment' of mediation—of the only Son—divides itself to become the antithesis of two separate worlds. On one hand is heaven and earth, the elemental and the concrete nature—on the other hand, standing in action and reaction with such nature, the spirit, which therefore is finite. That spirit, as the extreme of inherent negativity, completes its independence till it becomes wickedness, and is that extreme through its connection with a confronting nature and through its own naturalness thereby investing it. Yet, amid that naturalness, it is, when it thinks, directed towards the Eternal, though, for that reason, only standing to it in an external connection.

§ 569

(γ) Under the 'moment' of *individuality* as such—of subjectivity and the notion itself, in which the contrast of universal and particular has sunk to its identical ground, the place of presupposition (1) is taken by the *universal* substance, as actualized out of its abstraction into an *individual* self-consciousness. This individual, who as such is identified with the essence—(in the Eternal sphere he is called the Son)—is transplanted into the world of time, and in him wickedness is implicitly overcome. Further, this immediate, and thus sensuous, existence of the absolutely concrete is represented as putting himself in judgement and expiring in the pain of *negativity*, in which he, as infinite subjectivity, keeps himself unchanged, and thus, as absolute return from that negativity and as universal unity of universal and individual essentiality, has realized his being as the Idea of the spirit, eternal, but alive and present in the world.

§ 570

(2) This objective totality of the divine man who is the Idea of the spirit is the implicit presupposition for the *finite* immediacy of the single subject. For such subject therefore it is at first an Other, an object of contemplating vision—but the vision of implicit truth, through which witness of the spirit in him, he, on account of his

immediate nature, at first characterized himself as nought and wicked. But, secondly, after the example of his truth, by means of the faith on the unity (in that example implicitly accomplished) of universal and individual essence, he is also the movement to throw off his immediacy, his natural man and self-will, to close himself in unity with that example (who is his implicit life) in the pain of negativity, and thus to know himself made one with the essential Being. Thus the Being of Beings (3) through this mediation brings about its own indwelling in self-consciousness, and is the actual presence of the essential and self-subsisting spirit who is all in all.

<h2 style="text-align:center">§ 571</h2>

These three syllogisms, constituting the one syllogism of the absolute self-mediàtion of spirit, are the revelation of that spirit whose life is set out as a cycle of concrete shapes in pictorial thought. From this its separation into parts, with a temporal and external sequence, the unfolding of the mediation contracts itself in the result—where the spirit closes in unity with itself—not merely to the simplicity of faith and devotional feeling, but even to thought. In the immanent simplicity of thought the unfolding still has its expansion, yet is all the while known as an indivisible coherence of the universal, simple, and eternal spirit in itself. In this form of truth, truth is the object of *philosophy*.

If the result—the realized Spirit in which all mediation has superseded itself—is taken in a merely formal, contentless sense, so that the spirit is not also at the same time known as *implicitly* existent and objectively self-unfolding;—then that infinite subjectivity is the merely formal self-consciousness, knowing itself in itself as absolute—Irony. Irony, which can make every objective reality nought and vain, is itself the emptiness and vanity, which from itself, and therefore by chance and its own good pleasure, gives itself direction and content, remains master over it, is not bound by it—and, with the assertion that it stands on the very summit of religion and philosophy, falls back rather into the vanity of wilfulness. It is only in proportion as the pure infinite form, the self-centred manifestation, throws off the one-sidedness of subjectivity in which it is the vanity of thought, that it is the free thought which has its infinite characteristic at the same time as essential and actual content, and has that content as an object in which it is also free. Thinking, so far, is only the formal aspect of the absolute content.

C. PHILOSOPHY

§ 572

This science is the unity of Art and Religion. Whereas the vision-method of Art, external in point of form, is but subjective production and shivers the substantial content into many separate shapes, and whereas Religion, with its separation into parts, opens it out in mental picture, and mediates what is thus opened out; Philosophy not merely keeps them together to make a totality, but even unifies them into the simple spiritual vision, and then in that raises them to self-conscious thought. Such consciousness is thus the intelligible unity (cognized by thought) of art and religion, in which the diverse elements in the content are cognized as necessary, and this necessary as free.

§ 573

Philosophy thus characterizes itself as a cognition of the necessity in the content of the absolute picture-idea, as also of the necessity in the two forms—on one hand, immediate vision and its poetry, and the objective and external revelation presupposed by representation—on the other hand, first the subjective retreat inwards, then the subjective movement of faith and its final identification with the presupposed object. This cognition is thus the *recognition* of this content and its form; it is the liberation from the one-sidedness of the forms, elevation of them into the absolute form, which determines itself to content, remains identical with it, and is in that the cognition of that essential and actual necessity. This movement, which philosophy is, finds itself already accomplished, when at the close it seizes its own notion—i.e. only *looks back* on its knowledge.

Here might seem to be the place to treat in a definite exposition of the reciprocal relations of philosophy and religion. The whole question turns entirely on the difference of the forms of speculative thought from the forms of mental representation and 'reflecting' intellect. But it is the whole cycle of philosophy, and of logic in particular, which has not merely taught and made known this difference, but also criticized it, or rather has let its nature develop and judge itself by these very categories. It is only by an insight into the value of these forms that the true and needful conviction can be gained, that the content of religion and philosophy is the same—leaving out, of course, the further details of external nature and finite mind which fall outside the range of religion. But religion is the truth *for all men*: faith rests on the witness of the spirit, which as witnessing is the spirit in man. This witness—the under-lying essence in all humanity—takes, when driven to expound itself, its first definite form under those acquired habits of thought which his secular consciousness and intellect otherwise employs. In this way the truth becomes liable to the terms and conditions of finitude in general. This does not prevent the spirit, even in em-ploying sensuous ideas and finite categories of thought, from retain-ing its content (which as religion is essentially speculative) with a tenacity which does violence to them, and acts *inconsistently* to-wards them. By this inconsistency it corrects their defects. Nothing easier therefore for the 'Rationalist' than to point out contradictions in the exposition of the faith, and then to prepare triumphs for its principle of formal identity. If the spirit yields to this finite reflection, which has usurped the title of reason and philosophy—('Rationalism')—it strips religious truth of its infinity and makes it in reality nought. Religion in that case is completely in the right in guarding herself against such reason and philosophy and treating them as enemies. But it is another thing when religion sets herself against comprehending reason, and against philosophy in general, and specially against a philosophy of which the doctrine is specula-tive, and so religious. Such an opposition proceeds from failure to appreciate the difference indicated and the value of spiritual form in general, and particularly of the logical form; or, to be more precise still, from failure to note the distinction of the content—which may be in both the same—from these forms. It is on the ground of form that philosophy has been reproached and accused by the religious party; just as conversely its speculative content has brought the same changes upon it from a self-styled philosophy—

and from a pithless orthodoxy. It had too little of God in it for the former; too much for the latter.

The charge of *Atheism*, which used often to be brought against philosophy (that it has *too little* of God), has grown rare: the more wide-spread grows the charge of Pantheism, that it has *too much* of him:—so much so, that it is treated not so much as an imputation, but as a proved fact, or a sheer fact which needs no proof. Piety, in particular, which with its pious airs of superiority fancies itself free to dispense with proof, goes hand in hand with empty rationalism— (which means to be so much opposed to it, though both repose really on the same habit of mind)—in the wanton assertion, almost as if it merely mentioned a notorious fact, that Philosophy is the All-one doctrine, or Pantheism. It must be said that it was more to the credit of piety and theology when they accused a philosophical system (e.g. Spinozism) of Atheism than of Pantheism, though the former imputation at the first glance looks more cruel and invidious (cf. § 71 note). The imputation of Atheism presupposes a definite idea of a full and real God, and arises because the popular idea does not detect in the philosophical notion the peculiar form to which it is attached. Philosophy indeed can recognize its own forms in the categories of religious consciousness, and even its own teaching in the doctrine of religion—which therefore it does not disparage. But the converse is not true: the religious consciousness does not apply the criticism of thought to itself, does not comprehend itself, and is therefore, as it stands, exclusive. To impute Pantheism instead of Atheism to Philosophy is part of the modern habit of mind—of the new piety and new theology. For them philosophy has too much of God:—so much so, that, if we believe them, it asserts that God is everything and everything is God. This new theology, which makes religion only a subjective feeling and denies the knowledge of the divine nature, thus retains nothing more than a God in general without objective characteristics. Without interest of its own for the concrete, fulfilled notion of God, it treats it only as an interest which *others* once had, and hence treats what belongs to the doctrine of God's concrete nature as something merely historical. The indeterminate God is to be found in all religions; every kind of piety (§ 72)—that of the Hindu to asses, cows—or to dalai-lamas—that of the Egyptians to the ox—is always adoration of an object which, with all its absurdities, also contains the generic abstract, God in General. If this theory needs no more than such a God, so as to find God in everything called religion, it must at least find such a God recognized even in philosophy, and can no longer accuse it of Atheism. The mitigation of the reproach of Atheism into that of Pantheism has its ground therefore in the superficial idea to which this mildness has attenuated and emptied God. As that popular idea clings to its abstract universality, from which all definite quality is excluded, all such definiteness is only the non-divine, the secularity of things, thus left standing in fixed undisturbed substantiality. On such a presupposition, even after philosophy has maintained God's absolute universality, and the consequent untruth of the being of external things, the hearer clings as he did before to his belief that secular things still keep their being, and form all that is definite in the divine universality. He thus changes that universality into what he calls the pantheistic:—*Everything is*—(empirical things, without distinction, whether higher or lower in the scale, *are*)—all possess substantiality; and so—thus he understands philosophy—each and every secular thing is God. It is only his own stupidity, and the falsifications due to such misconception, which generate the imagination and the allegation of such pantheism.

But if those who give out that a certain philosophy is Pantheism, are unable and unwilling to see this—for it is just to see the notion that they refuse—they should before everything have verified the alleged fact that *any one philosopher, or any one man,* had really ascribed substantial or objective and inherent reality to *all* things and regarded them as God:—that such an idea had ever come into the head of anybody but themselves. This allegation I will further elucidate in this exoteric discussion: and the only way to do so is to set down the evidence. If we want to take so-called Pantheism in its most poetical, most sublime, or if you will, its grossest shape, we must, as is well known, consult the oriental poets: and the most copious delineations of it are found in Hindu literature. Amongst the abundant resources open to our disposal on this topic, I select— as the most authentic statement accessible—the Bhagavat-Gita, and amongst its effusions, prolix and reiterative *ad nauseam*, some of the most telling passages. In the 10th Lesson (in Schlegel, p. 162)

Krishna says of himself:[1]—'1 am the self, seated in the hearts of all beings. I am the beginning and the middle and the end also of all beings . . . I am the beaming sun amongst the shining ones, and the moon among the lunar mansions. . . . Amongst the Vedas I am the Sâma-Veda: I am mind amongst the senses: I am consciousness in living beings. And I am Sankara (Siva) among the Rudras, . . . Meru among the high-topped mountains, . . . the Himalaya among the firmly-fixed (mountains). . . . Among beasts I am the lord of beasts. . . . Among letters I am the letter A. . . . I am the spring among the seasons. . . . I am also that which is the seed of all things: there is nothing moveable or immoveable which can exist without me.'

Even in these totally sensuous delineations, Krishna (and we must not suppose there is, besides Krishna, still God, or a God besides; as he said before he was Siva, or Indra, so it is afterwards said that Brahma too is in him) makes himself out to be—not everything, but only—the most excellent of everything. Everywhere there is a distinction drawn between external, unessential existences, and one essential amongst them, which he is. Even when, at the beginning of the passage, he is said to be the beginning, middle, and end of living things, this totality is distinguished from the living things themselves as single existences. Even such a picture which extends deity far and wide in its existence cannot be called pantheism: we must rather say that in the infinitely multiple empirical world, everything is reduced to a limited number of essential existences, to a polytheism. But even what has been quoted shows that these very substantialities of the externally existent do not retain the independence entitling them to be named Gods; even Siva, Indra, etc. melt into the one Krishna.

This reduction is more expressly made in the following scene (7th Lesson, pp. 7 seqq.). Krishna says: 'I am the producer and the destroyer of the whole universe. There is nothing else higher than myself; all this is woven upon me, like numbers of pearls upon a thread. I am the taste in water; . . . I am the light of the sun and the moon; I am "Om" in all the Vedas. . . . I am life in all beings. . . . I

[1] [The citation given by Hegel from Schlegel's translation is here replaced by the version (in one or two points different) in the *Sacred Books of the East*, vol. viii.]

am the discernment of the discerning ones. . . . I am also the strength of the strong.' Then he adds: 'The whole universe deluded by these three states of mind developed from the qualities [sc. goodness, passion, darkness] does not know me who am beyond them and inexhaustible: for this delusion of mine [even the Maya is *his*, nothing independent], developed from the qualities is divine and difficult to transcend. Those cross beyond this delusion who resort to me alone.' Then the picture gathers itself up in a simple expression: 'At the end of many lives, the man possessed of knowledge approaches me, (believing) that Vasudeva is everything. Such a high-souled mind is very hard to find. Those who are deprived of knowledge by various desires approach other divinities . . . Whichever form of deity one worships with faith, from it he obtains the beneficial things he desires really given by me. But the fruit thus obtained by those of little judgement is perishable. . . . The undiscerning ones, not knowing my transcendent and inexhaustible essence, than which there is nothing higher, think me who am unperceived to have become perceptible.'

This 'All', which Krishna calls himself, is not, any more than the Eleatic One, and the Spinozan Substance, the Everything. This everything, rather, the infinitely manifold sensuous manifold of the finite is in all these pictures, but defined as the 'accidental', without essential being of its very own, but having its truth in the substance, the One which, as different from that accidental, is alone the divine and God. Hinduism, however, has the higher conception of Brahma, the pure unity of thought in itself, where the empirical everything of the world, as also those proximate substantialities, called Gods, vanish. On that account Colebrooke and many others have described the Hindu religion as at bottom a Monotheism. That this description is not incorrect is clear from these short citations. But so little concrete is this divine unity—spiritual as its idea of God is—so powerless its grip, so to speak—that Hinduism, with a monstrous inconsistency, is also the maddest of polytheisms. But the idolatry of the wretched Hindu, when he adores the ape, or other creature, is still a long way from that wretched fancy of a Pantheism, to which everything is God, and God everything. Hindu monotheism, moreover, is itself an example how little comes of mere monotheism, if the Idea of God is not deeply determinate in itself. For that unity, if it be intrinsically abstract and therefore empty, tends of itself to let whatever is concrete, outside it—be it as a lot of Gods or as secular, empirical individuals—keep its independence. That pantheism indeed—on the shallow conception of it—might with a show of logic as well be called a monotheism: for if God, as it says, is identical with the world, then as there is only one world there would be in that pantheism only one God. Perhaps the empty numerical unity must be predicated of the world: but such abstract predication of it has no further special interest; on the contrary, a mere numerical unity just means that its *content* is an infinite multeity and variety of finitudes. But it is that delusion with the empty unity, which alone makes possible and induces the wrong idea of pantheism. It is only the picture—floating in the indefinite blue—of the world as *one thing, the all*, that could ever be considered capable of combining with God: only on that assumption could philosophy be supposed to teach that God is the world: for if the world were taken as it is, as everything, as the endless lot of empirical existence, then it would hardly have been even held possible to suppose a pantheism which asserted of such stuff that it is God.

But to go back again to the question of fact. If we want to see the consciousness of the One—not as with the Hindus split between the featureless unity of abstract thought, on one hand, and on the other, the long-winded weary story of its particular detail, but—in its finest purity and sublimity, we must consult the Mohammedans. If, e.g., in the excellent Jelaleddin-Rumi in particular, we find the unity of the soul with the One set forth, and that unity described as love, this spiritual unity is an exaltation above the finite and vulgar, a transfiguration of the natural and the spiritual, in which the externalism and transitoriness of immediate nature, and of empirical secular spirit, is discarded and absorbed.[1]

[1] In order to give a clearer impression of it, I cannot refrain from quoting a few passages, which may at the same time give some indication of the marvellous skill of Rückert, from whom they are taken, as a translator. [For Rückert's verses a version is here substituted in which I have been kindly helped by Miss May Kendall.]

III
I saw but One through all heaven's starry spaces gleaming:
I saw but One in all sea billows wildly streaming.

I refrain from accumulating further examples of the religious
and poetic conceptions which it is customary to call pantheistic.
Of the philosophies to which that name is given, the Eleatic, or
Spinozist, it has been remarked earlier (§ 50, note) that so far are

I looked into the heart, a waste of worlds, a sea,—
    I saw a thousand dreams,—yet One amid all dreaming.
And earth, air, water, fire, when thy decree is given,
    Are molten into One: against thee none hath striven.
There is no living heart but beats unfailingly
    In the one song of praise to thee, from earth and heaven.

v

As one ray of thy light appears the noonday sun,
But yet thy light and mine eternally are one.
As dust beneath thy feet the heaven that rolls on high:
Yet only one, and one for ever, thou and I.
The dust may turn to heaven, and heaven to dust decay;
Yet art thou one with me, and shalt be one for aye.
How may the words of life that fill heaven's utmost part
Rest in the narrow casket of one poor human heart?
How can the sun's own rays, a fairer gleam to fling,
Hide in a lowly husk, the jewel's covering?
How may the rose-grove all its glorious bloom unfold,
Drinking in mire and slime, and feeding on the mould?
How can the darksome shell that sips the salt sea stream
Fashion a shining pearl, the sunlight's joyous beam?
Oh, heart! should warm winds fan thee, should'st thou floods endure,
One element are wind and flood; but be thou pure.

IX

I'll tell thee how from out the dust God moulded man,—
Because the breath of Love He breathed into his clay:
I'll tell thee why the spheres their whirling paths began,—
They mirror to God's throne Love's glory day by day:
I'll tell thee why the morning winds blow o'er the grove,—
It is to bid Love's roses bloom abundantly:
I'll tell thee why the night broods deep the earth above,—
Love's bridal tent to deck with sacred canopy:
 All riddles of the earth dost thou desire to prove?—
To every earthly riddle is Love alone the key.

xv

Life shrinks from Death in woe and fear,
    Though Death ends well Life's bitter need:
So shrinks the heart when Love draws near,
    As though 'twere Death in very deed:
For wheresoever Love finds room,

[footnote cont. on p. 310]

they from identifying God with the world and making him finite, that in these systems this 'everything' has no truth, and that we should rather call them monotheistic, or, in relation to the popular idea of the world, acosmical. They are most accurately called systems which apprehend the Absolute only as substance. Of the oriental, especially the Mohammedan, modes of envisaging God, we may rather say that they represent the Absolute as the utterly universal genus which dwells in the species or existences, but dwells so potently that these existences have no actual reality. The fault of all these modes of thought and systems is that they stop short of defining substance as subject and as mind.

These systems and modes of pictorial conception originate from the one need common to all philosophies and all religions of getting an idea of God, and, secondly, of the relationship of God and the world. (In philosophy it is specially made out that the determination of God's nature determines his relations with the world.) The 'reflective' understanding begins by rejecting all systems and modes of conception, which, whether they spring from heart, imagination or speculation, express the interconnection of God and the world: and in order to have God pure in faith or consciousness, he is as essence parted from appearance, as infinite

> There Self, the sullen tyrant, dies.
> So let him perish in the gloom,—
> Thou to the dawn of freedom rise.

In this poetry, which soars over all that is external and sensuous, who would recognize the prosaic ideas current about so-called pantheism—ideas which let the divine sink to the external and the sensuous? The copious extracts which Tholuck, in his work *Anthology from the Eastern Mystics*, gives us from the poems of Jelaleddin and others, are made from the very point of view now under discussion. In his Introduction, Herr Tholuck proves how profoundly his soul has caught the note of mysticism, and there, too, he points out the characteristic traits of its oriental phase, in distinction from that of the West and Christendom. With all their divergence, however, they have in common the mystical character. The conjunction of Mysticism with so-called Pantheism, as he says (p. 33), implies that inward quickening of soul and spirit which inevitably tends to annihilate that external *Everything*, which Pantheism is usually held to adore. But beyond that, Herr Tholuck leaves matters standing at the usual indistinct conception of Pantheism; a profounder discussion of it would have had, for the author's emotional Christianity, no direct interest; but we see that personally he is carried away by remarkable enthusiasm for a mysticism which, in the ordinary phrase, entirely deserves the epithet Pantheistic. Where, however, he tries philosophising (p. 12), he does not get beyond the standpoint of the 'rationalist' metaphysic with its uncritical categories.

from the finite. But, after this partition, the conviction arises also
that the appearance has a relation to the essence, the finite to the
infinite, and so on: and thus arises the question of reflection as to
the nature of this relation. It is in the reflective form that the whole
difficulty of the affair lies, and that causes this relation to be called
incomprehensible by the agnostic. The close of philosophy is not
the place, even in a general exoteric discussion, to waste a word on
what a 'notion' means. But as the view taken of this relation is
closely connected with the view taken of philosophy generally and
with all imputations against it, we may still add the remark that
though philosophy certainly has to do with unity in general, it is
not, however, with abstract unity, mere identity, and the empty
absolute, but with concrete unity (the notion), and that in its whole
course it has to do with nothing else;—that each step in its advance
is a peculiar term or phase of this concrete unity, and that the
deepest and last expression of unity is the unity of absolute mind
itself. Would-be judges and critics of philosophy might be recommended to familiarize themselves with these phases of unity and to
take the trouble to get acquainted with them, at least to know so
much that of these terms there are a great many, and that amongst
them there is great variety. But they show so little acquaintance
with them—and still less take trouble about it—that, when they
hear of unity—and relation *ipso facto* implies unity—they rather
stick fast at quite abstract indeterminate unity, and lose sight of the
chief point of interest—the special mode in which the unity is
qualified. Hence all they can say about philosophy is that dry
identity is its principle and result, and that it is the system of
identity. Sticking fast to the undigested thought of identity, they
have laid hands on, not the concrete unity, the notion and content
of philosophy, but rather its reverse. In the philosophical field they
proceed, as in the physical field the physicist; who also is well
aware that he has before him a variety of sensuous properties and
matters—or usually matters alone (for the properties get transformed into matters also for the physicist)—and that these matters
(elements) *also* stand in *relation* to one another. But the question is,
Of what kind is this relation? Every peculiarity and the whole
difference of natural things, inorganic and living, depend solely on
the different modes of this unity. But instead of ascertaining these

different modes, the ordinary physicist (chemist included) takes up only one, the most external and the worst, viz. *composition*, applies only it in the whole range of natural structures, which he thus renders for ever inexplicable.

The aforesaid shallow pantheism is an equally obvious inference from this shallow identity. All that those who employ this invention of their own to accuse philosophy gather from the study of God's *relation* to the world is that the one, but only the one factor of this category of relation—and that the factor of indeterminateness—is identity. Thereupon they stick fast in this half-perception, and assert—falsely as a fact—that philosophy teaches the identity of God and the world. And as in their judgement either of the two— the world as much as God—has the same solid substantiality as the other, they infer that in the philosophic Idea God is *composed* of God and the world. Such then is the idea they form of pantheism, and which they ascribe to philosophy. Unaccustomed in their own thinking and apprehending of thoughts to go beyond such cate- gories, they import them into philosophy, where they are utterly unknown; they thus infect it with the disease against which they sub- sequently raise an outcry. If any difficulty emerge in comprehend- ing God's relation to the world, they at once and very easily escape it by admitting that this relation contains for them an inexplicable contradiction; and that hence, they must stop at the vague concep- tion of such relation, perhaps under the more familiar names of e.g. omnipresence, providence, etc. Faith in their use of the term means no more than a refusal to define the conception, or to enter on a closer discussion of the problem. That men and classes of untrained intellect are satisfied with such indefiniteness, is what one expects; but when a trained intellect and an interest for reflec- tive study is satisfied, in matters admitted to be of superior, if not even of supreme interest, with indefinite ideas, it is hard to decide whether the thinker is really in earnest with the subject. But if those who cling to this crude 'rationalism' were in earnest, e.g. with God's omnipresence, so far as to realize their faith thereon in a definite mental idea, in what difficulties would they be involved by their belief in the true reality of the things of sense! They would hardly like, as Epicurus does, to let God dwell in the interspaces of things, i.e. in the pores of the physicists—said pores being the

negative, something supposed to exist *beside* the material reality.
This very 'Beside' would give their pantheism its spatiality—their
everything, conceived as the mutual exclusion of parts in space.
But in ascribing to God, in his relation to the world, an action on
and in the space thus filled on the world and in it, they would
endlessly split up the divine actuality into infinite materiality.
They would really thus have the misconception they call pantheism or all-one-doctrine, only as the necessary sequel of their
misconceptions of God and the world. But to put that sort of
thing, this stale gossip of oneness or identity, on the shoulders of
philosophy, shows such recklessness about justice and truth that it
can only be explained through the difficulty of getting into the
head thoughts and notions, i.e. not abstract unity, but the many-
shaped modes specified. If statements as to facts are put forward,
and the facts in question are thoughts and notions, it is indispensable to get hold of their meaning. But even the fulfilment of this
requirement has been rendered superfluous, now that it has long
been a foregone conclusion that philosophy is pantheism, a system
of identity, an All-one doctrine, and that the person therefore who
might be unaware of this fact is treated either as merely unaware of
a matter of common notoriety, or as prevaricating for a purpose.
On account of this chorus of assertions, then, I have believed myself obliged to speak at more length and exoterically on the outward and inward untruth of this alleged fact: for exoteric discussion
is the only method available in dealing with the external apprehension of notions as mere facts—by which notions are perverted into
their opposite. The esoteric study of God and identity, as of cogni-
tions, and notions, is philosophy itself.

§ 574

This notion of philosophy is the self-thinking Idea, the truth
aware of itself (§ 236)—the logical system, but with the signification
that it is universality approved and certified in concrete content as
in its actuality. In this way the science has gone back to its beginning: its result is the logical system but as a spiritual principle: out
of the presupposing judgement, in which the notion was only
implicit and the beginning an immediate—and thus out of the

appearance which it had there—it has risen into its pure principle and thus also into its proper medium.

§ 575

It is this appearing which originally gives the motive of the further development. The first appearance is formed by the syllogism, which is based on the Logical system as starting-point, with Nature for the middle term which couples the Mind with it. The Logical principle turns to Nature and Nature to Mind. Nature, standing between the Mind and its essence, sunders itself, not indeed to extremes of finite abstraction, nor itself to something away from them and independent—which, as other than they, only serves as a link between them: for the syllogism is *in the Idea* and Nature is essentially defined as a transition-point and negative factor, and as implicitly the Idea. Still the mediation of the notion has the external form of *transition*, and the science of Nature presents itself as the course of necessity, so that it is only in the one extreme that the liberty of the notion is explicit as a self-amalgamation.

§ 576

In the second syllogism this appearance is so far superseded, that that syllogism is the standpoint of the Mind itself, which—as the mediating agent in the process—presupposes Nature and couples it with the Logical principle. It is the syllogism where Mind reflects on itself in the Idea: philosophy appears as a subjective cognition, of which liberty is the aim, and which is itself the way to produce it.

§ 577

The third syllogism is the Idea of philosophy, which has self-knowing reason, the absolutely universal, for its middle term: a middle, which divides itself into Mind and Nature, making the former its presupposition, as process of the Idea's subjective activity, and the latter its universal extreme, as process of the objectively and implicitly existing Idea. The self-judging of the Idea into its two appearances (§§ 575, 576) characterizes both as its (the self-knowing reason's) manifestations: and in it there is a unification of the two aspects:—it is the nature of the fact, the

notion, which causes the movement and development, yet this
same movement is equally the action of cognition. The eternal
Idea, in full fruition of its essence, eternally sets itself to work,
engenders and enjoys itself as absolute Mind.

Ἡ δὲ νόησις ἡ καθ' αὑτὴν τοῦ καθ' αὑτὸ ἀρίστου, καὶ ἡ μάλιστα
τοῦ μάλιστα. Αὑτὸν δὲ νοεῖ ὁ νοῦς κατὰ. μετάληψιν τοῦ νοητοῦ·
νοητὸς γὰρ γίγνεται θιγγάνων καὶ νοῶν, ὥστε ταὐτὸν νοῦς καὶ νοητόν.
Τὸ γὰρ δεκτικὸν τοῦ νοητοῦ καὶ τῆς οὐσίας νοῦς. Ἐνεργεῖ δὲ ἔχων.
Ὥστ' ἐκεῖνο μᾶλλον τούτου ὃ δοκεῖ ὁ νοῦς θεῖον ἔχειν, καὶ ἡ θεωρία
τὸ ἥδιστον καὶ ἄριστον. Εἰ οὖν οὕτως εὖ ἔχει, ὡς ἡμεῖς ποτέ, ὁ θεὸς
ἀεί, θαυμαστόν· εἰ δὲ μᾶλλον, ἔτι θαυμασιώτερον. Ἔχει δὲ ὡδί.
Καὶ ζωὴ δέ γε ὑπάρχει· ἡ γὰρ νοῦ ἐνέργεια ζωή, ἐκεῖνος δὲ ἡ ἐνέργεια·
ἐνέργεια δὲ ἡ καθ' αὑτὴν ἐκείνου ζωὴ ἀρίστη καὶ ἀΐδιος. Φαμὲν δὲ
τὸν θεὸν εἶναι ζῷον ἀΐδιον ἄριστον, ὥστε ζωὴ καὶ αἰὼν συνεχὴς καὶ
ἀΐδιος ὑπάρχει τῷ θεῷ· τοῦτο γὰρ ὁ θεός.

(Arist. *Met.* xi. 7.)

INDEX

Made in the USA
Lexington, KY
24 May 2013